D1642179

A RIGHT TO HEALTH

HEALTH, MEDICINE, AND SOCIETY:
A WILEY-INTERSCIENCE SERIES
DAVID MECHANIC, Editor

A RIGHT TO HEALTH

THE PROBLEM OF ACCESS
TO PRIMARY MEDICAL CARE

Charles E. Lewis
Rashi Fein
David Mechanic

A WILEY-INTERSCIENCE PUBLICATION

JOHN WILEY & SONS, New York • London • Sydney • Toronto

Preparation of this volume was assisted by a grant from The Robert Wood Johnson Foundation, Princeton, New Jersey. The opinions, conclusions, and proposals in the text are those of the authors and do not necessarily reflect the view of The Robert Wood Johnson Foundation.

Library of Congress Cataloging in Publication Data:

Lewis, Charles Edwin, 1928–
  A right to health.

  (Health, medicine, and society)
  "A Wiley-Interscience publication."
  Includes bibliographical references and index.
  1. Medical care—United States. 2. Medical policy—United States. I. Fein, Rashi, joint author.
II. Mechanic, David, 1936– joint author. III. Title

RA395.A3L49   362.1′0973   76-18129
ISBN 0-471-01494-X

Printed in the United States of America

10 9 8 7 6 5 4 3

Foreword

The central paradox of American medical care is that we have developed extraordinary capacities in high-technology medicine for meeting the needs of the acutely ill, but have been much less successful in providing satisfactorily for the health care needs of people in their work-a-day lives.

Acute-care medicine lends itself readily to functional organization. Based in the hospital, it can assemble the specialized knowledge, personnel, equipment, and techniques needed to treat life-threatening illness.

However, general medical care, or primary care, poses very different problems. It is directed toward the non-hospitalized patient, and is provided in a variety of private and public settings, widely though unevenly, dispersed throughout the country. To name but a few, these include solo physicians' offices, private physician group practices, prepaid groups, hospital and outpatient departments, emergency rooms, and community health centers.

Such diversity in our primary care services has preserved the American tradition of pluralism and has offered both physicians and patients alike a wide degree of individual choice in the medical care transaction. But at the same time, satisfactory primary care health services have been beyond the reach of many Americans, and the situation has worsened as our new medical graduates choose specialty practice over primary care careers and locate in the suburbs rather than rural communities and inner-city neighborhoods.

Because of this shortfall, the ways in which we might improve the delivery of general front-line kinds of medical care to Americans is receiving serious study from multiple groups. To aid in these efforts, the authors of this volume—Drs. Charles Lewis, Rashi Fein, and David Mechanic—have undertaken a comprehensive examination of the paradoxes and dilemmas of primary care within the structure of the American health system and the society it serves. They have analyzed the nature of the problem, studied past attempts to deal with it, and identified policy options for the future.

Their collaboration has resulted in a volume that should be of value, not only to policy analysts in health, but to professional and graduate students in a number of fields—and, most importantly, to concerned citizens who must ultimately set the future course of American medical care.

The Robert Wood Johnson Foundation is pleased to have contributed funds to allow these three distinguished authors to combine their talents and insights in developing this volume.

DAVID E. ROGERS, President
The Robert Wood Johnson Foundation

Preface

This study on access to medical care is a joint project by the three of us, initiated through a grant from The Robert Wood Johnson Foundation. Although there are many problems in the delivery of health services, accessibility is the most influential factor shaping public perceptions of a health crisis. It is now commonly recognized that access to primary medical care is a *serious* problem, and various governmental and foundation efforts have been undertaken to improve the availability of health-care services.

In embarking on programs to increase accessibility to health care, there is value in looking at the past, examining the efforts made, and assessing what attempts are likely to be most productive in the future. Much of what has been written about primary medical care is vacuous and contradictory. A major difficulty is the lack of a clear perspective for identifying the functions of primary medical care and its role within the larger system of human services. Many programs have dealt with access, but few have been seriously evaluated, and most available data are defective. Although major efforts in the past decade have not been definitively evaluated here because of the insufficiency of data, it has been possible to examine the evolution and contribution of a variety of programs and to come to some conclusions about how effective they were. We appreciate that these are ongoing programs, many still in an evolutionary stage, and we also realize that efforts to orient new programs must take cognizance of the lessons of the past.

With these intentions in mind, the three of us developed a definition of the problem and an approach to it. Although we all participated in the formulation of each part of the project, we delegated responsibility: David Mechanic took over the task of developing a conceptual approach to the problem of access to care; Charles Lewis supervised the effort to examine the history of major programs, their achievements, and their unanticipated consequences; and Rashi Fein agreed to write the part on options. Each approach was discussed by the group, and each of us had some input into all aspects of the project; however, primary responsibility for each part always resides with the one who wrote it.

We appreciate the encouragement of The Robert Wood Johnson Foundation, and particularly Robert Blendon, who participated in our discussions. We are indebted to Allison Avery who compiled much of the data reviewed in Part II. As we examined the programs already in process, we became aware of their complexity and administrative confusion, and we hope that, in reviewing our efforts, the reader may come away with a sense of the causes of confusion without feeling that we have also contributed to it.

CHARLES E. LEWIS
RASHI FEIN
DAVID MECHANIC

University of California, Los Angeles
Harvard University
University of Wisconsin
April 1976

Contents

Part III: Options
RASHI FEIN

Appendixes

Notes and References, 328

Index, 351

A RIGHT TO HEALTH

PART ONE

A CONCEPTUAL APPROACH

DAVID MECHANIC

ONE

The Problem of Access to Medical Care

A large majority of the people of the United States believe that there is a "crisis" in health care in their country. As much as three-fifths of the population believe that this crisis will require basic changes in the way medical services are made available to the public.[1] Whatever the underlying causes of such thinking, those responsible for social policy must respond to it meaningfully. An accurate diagnosis of the basic underlying issues is a prerequisite for an effective response.

The public's perception of a "crisis" in medical care is derived, we believe, from two major concerns: (1) difficulty in gaining access to a physician when in need of medical services and (2) the high and uncertain costs of medical care. Although there are many other problems in the delivery of health services, anxiety results mainly from inadequacies and discontinuities in the provision and delivery of primary medical-care services. It has often been thought that the solution lies in educating more doctors, but as this book shows, such efforts by themselves have not, and cannot, resolve the difficulties the public experiences in obtaining basic medical-care services.

We organize our discussion around certain basic points essential for understanding the problem of access to care. First, the medical-care sector deviates so

3

markedly from the competitive marketplace as to make reliance on market mechanisms ineffective in achieving needed interventions. As Herbert Klarman, the medical economist, has noted: ". . . for any single characteristic of health services that is presumably distinctive it may be possible to find an analogue in the behavior of some other good or service. What is rare or unlikely, however, is another good that shares all of these characteristics or so many."[2] Second, because of the factors restraining natural adjustments in the medical-care marketplace and the complexity of private, professional, and public interests affecting decision-making, it is extraordinarily difficult to distribute services more equitably and efficiently without a more forceful public policy than prevails at present. Despite vast and increased public and private expenditures, and a large and well-trained manpower pool, we have not been willing or able to organize our resources to meet the needs and expectations of the American public. Third, in conceptualizing the problems of improving access to care we must appreciate that the range of problems brought to physicians is very large and that these problems reflect not only obvious physical disease but also the cumulation of life's stresses, failures in coping with life's problems, and a need for social support. Medical care has a broad function in society and contributes to the alleviation of social tensions.[3] Any social policy on access to medical care must, in some fashion, come to terms with these aspects of the demand for medical care and must devise some approach to deal with them appropriately and effectively. The response to such needs must, moreover, realistically fit the problems. Medical interventions, when used inappropriately, may be dangerous to health. Excessive and unnecessary use of surgery, drugs, and other diagnostic and treatment procedures not only may be wasteful but also may contribute to additional illness and disability. Hence, policies for increasing access to medical care require not only appropriate identification of problems and their management but also provision of checks and balances to ensure that medical personnel do not take an excessively technical approach to patients' problems and concerns. Frequently, patients require an opportunity to discuss a problem with health professionals more than they need any particular treatment. Fourth, the solution to the crisis in medical care requires a coherent and coordinated national health strategy. Attempts to correct problems piecemeal— without consideration of the implications of each part of the system for the whole—are doomed to failure from the start.

These issues are developed in some detail in this book: first by describing the forces contributing to difficulties in access; second by examining efforts in the past decade to cope with these problems, and the consequences of these efforts; and finally, by suggesting various policy options for the future. The right of sick persons to receive care in relation to their needs is supported by a large public consensus reflecting diverse groups on the social and political spectrum. As the President of the United States noted in his health message of 1971:

"Just as our National Government has moved to provide equal opportunity in areas such as education, employment and voting, so we must now work to expand the opportunity for all citizens to obtain a decent standard of medical care. We must do all we can to remove any racial, economic, social or geographic barriers which now prevent any of our citizens from obtaining adequate health protection. For without good health, no man can fully utilize his other opportunities."[4]

THE MEDICAL MARKETPLACE

Medical markets depart markedly from traditional models of supply and demand. As Kenneth Arrow has noted, ". . . the failure of the market to insure against uncertainties has created many social institutions in which the usual assumptions of the market are to some extent contradicted. The medical profession is only one example, though in many respects an extreme one."[5] The resulting marketplace is a complex mix of private and public investment, professional dominance, and social regulation. Since the need for medical care tends to be irregular and unpredictable in each case, and peoples' specific needs vary from one occasion to another, they develop little experience or expertness in purchasing medical services. The production of medical activity is complex, and the consumer in need has little information about the specific services he requires or their relative value. Trust in the provider is, therefore, more central in the acquisition of medical services than it is in the acquisition of almost any other commodity or service. The value of the service is uncertain, and it is generally left to the physician to determine the problem, make the necessary appraisal, perform the required diagnostic procedures and tests, and assess the need for hospital or surgical treatment. Much medical activity is, however, highly discretionary and is influenced not only by the needs of the patient but also by the physician's concept of the value of varying services, his specialty or the organization of his practice, the demand of his work load, and the unused medical resources available.[6] Thus physicians' decision-making may depart markedly from independent evaluations of the costs and benefits of various treatments. Physicians tend to be active and take the view "that treatment is dictated by the objective needs of the case and not limited by financial considerations."[7]

The consumer of medical services cannot easily ascertain the price of the care he requires. Professional medical ethics forbid open price competition and advertising, and most medical-care prices do not necessarily decrease with lowered demand. Perhaps most evident is the high cost of general surgery, despite an excess of general surgeons operating well below their potential capacities in many areas. Although the special character of the doctor–patient encounter often makes the prediction of price uncertain, the lack of adequate information on discrete services and commodities, such as drugs or surgical fees, makes it especially difficult for consumers to come to informed choices. This applies particularly to insurance for medical care, where existing policies are so complex and lacking in uniformity as to leave a strong suspicion that the complexity is designed to minimize comparisons.

The medical marketplace further departs from a competitive model because of the medical monopoly prevailing in many parts of the system. Given the expense and specialization of many medical services and facilities, some form of monopoly is required. Most communities of the United States cannot support more than a single hospital or a limited number of specialty and subspecialty services. Duplication and competition often result in a higher total cost for the community, the encouragement of unnecessary services, and inefficient use of manpower and facilities. But one consequence of existing monopolies and of the absence of incentives for improved practice is considerable waste and inefficiency in the use of scarce resources. Moreover, medical dominance over hospital policies and the other health professions makes it difficult to allocate functions among varying health personnel more rationally and efficiently. It has been extremely difficult, for example, both politically and legally, to transfer certain aspects of medical work to physician substitutes.

In sum, recognition of the professional dominance in the provision and character of medical work is important in understanding the difficulty of achieving greater access to medical care, in increasing informed consumer behavior, and in obtaining a more effective distribution of physicians and facilities relative to the population. Because physicians have such great control over the production of medical work, the input of additional physicians has only a marginal effect on location patterns. This problem and the difficulties in remedying distributional problems are described in specific instances in Part II of this volume.

THE FUNCTIONS OF MEDICAL CARE

The goals of medical activity are to support and sustain those suffering pain, distress, and incapacity and to restore them to their maximal potential as functioning members of society. Sickness, the failure of man's adaptive capacities to meet the demands of his environment, finds expression in discomfort, disability, and incapacitation. The maintenance of health reduces suffering and increases the capacity of men to assume their roles and responsibilities in society.

There are substantial indications of dissatisfaction with the availability and responsiveness of medical care in America.[8] Some are puzzled by these indications, pointing to our magnificent technological and scientific accomplishments, the vast funds we allocate to develop medical resources and provide medical services, and the impressive care available to many. The perceived crisis stems, however, not from our lack of technical capacity, but from our failure to ensure that all citizens have equal access to the promise that medical science has made possible and to humane and responsive care. The perceived crisis is a constellation of attitudes. To many with lower incomes, the barriers are economic and relate to the hardships of purchasing necessary care. For middle-class persons, a frequent concern is the possibility of a catastrophic illness and its consequences for the economic viability of the family. For the aged, increasing inflation and gaps in the Medicare program, requiring personal expenditures from their meager resources, are a source of worry. And people in general express concern about impersonal medical care and inadequate interest in the patient as a person.

These are not new problems, but they have been brought to the forefront by developments in medical care and in the larger community. Concurrently with advances in medical technology and science, society has undergone significant transformations in its values and organization. Stimulated by rapid social change, increasing opportunities, and improvements in education and mass communication, social aspirations and expectations have accelerated but have also become more homogeneous. A generation exposed to national television has come to share more than ever before a concept of the American dream and an explicit definition of its rights.

Our social system is dynamic, but rapid social change and progress are always accompanied by various dislocations. As American families become more geographically and socially mobile, neighborhood and kinship supports are disrupted. As mass communications expose persons to new concepts and aspirations, and as a higher standard of living allows persons to be more mobile, neighborhoods and communities are more transitory. And the American dream itself leaves those whose aspirations are unfulfilled with greater dissatisfaction and disappointment.[9]

Social activities and relationships have become more segmented in modern society, and Americans change schools, jobs, and community residence with considerable frequency. Thus the roots of community are increasingly more shallow, and persons experience greater estrangement and isolation. Because of the greater transience of community life, many of the traditional, informal sources of help have broken down, and when illness or other difficulty strikes, the resources of family or long-term friends are less available for assistance. Increasingly, therefore, persons turn to formal sources of help. But our social institutions, including medical care, are responding to similar social forces, and they, too, are increasingly bureaucratized, impersonal, and inaccessible and frequently unresponsive to the needs of people with personal troubles.

Social stress and failures in adaptive capacities are closely linked with symptoms of distress and the occurrence of disease.[10] Illness is a major cause of incapacity and discontinuity in the performance of social obligations; persons who are under strain and feel inadequate experience many physical symptoms: a lack of energy, fatigue, and difficulties in performing ordinary social and physical functions. The demand made on medical facilities is thus in part a reflection of general malaise and often indicates the failure of other institutions in society. Hence, medicine is a major support system in society in alleviating distress and providing hope, in offering support and furthering capacities to cope, and in protecting the social system from more explosive disruptions. Although the technical achievements of curing and alleviating particular illnesses overshadow·the larger functions of medicine in society, the more intangible caring function constitutes an essential aspect of primary medical care.

PUBLIC PERCEPTIONS AND THE CRISIS IN MEDICAL CARE

As medicine has demonstrated greater efficacy, all segments of the population have gained greater appreciation of the high standard of medical care possible in the United States. With heightened expectations the failure to find accessible and responsive services has become a bitter pill to swallow, especially among more deprived groups who see their difficulties as one more manifestation of their exclusion from the mainstream of American society. Innumerable studies support these perceptions by demonstrating that the poor have a greater prevalence of illness, disability, chronicity, and restriction of activity because of health problems than those of higher status and that they have less accessibility to many health services and receive lower quality care.[11] It is well known that the environmental resources influencing the maintenance of health, the prevention of illness, and the amelioration of disease and disability are distributed in society in relation to the abilities of various groups to command them economically.

The crisis in medical care is very tangible for the poor, but it exists for other groups as well. With the growth and development of the technical and scientific aspects of medical care in recent decades, medical organization has undergone an enormous transformation. Increasing specialization and subspecialization have accompanied the growth of medical knowledge, and as medical activity has been organized around specialized technical functions, some of the important psychosocial needs of patients have been neglected. Despite tremendous increases in medical resources and costs, many Americans have found it difficult to obtain a personalized source of care to which they can relate when worried about illness or other life problems. Notwithstanding the fact that most illnesses and life problems require general medical services, the proportion of physicians in primary medical care has decreased for decades,[12] leaving a large corps of physicians untrained to meet (or uninterested in meeting) more basic medical needs. This problem has been exacerbated by the uneven distribution of physicians, who are differentially accessible, depending on the social and geographic characteristics of varying areas of the nation. With increased specialization, even middle-class families in communities with ample facilities often find it difficult to locate a personalized source of care for general medical problems. For the typical consumer, the physician's concern for and interest in him as an individual are as important as his competence, but it has become more difficult to find physicians who direct their attention to the total life constellation of the patient rather than to the particular disease states or parts of the body.

Although a great deal of lip service is given to the personal and supportive aspects of medical care, this care is only rarely evaluated on the basis of these important dimensions. None of the indicators used to measure health status, for example, take into account the essential contribution medical care makes toward relieving worry and uncertainty, alleviating pain and discomfort, providing support and reassurance, and facilitating the ability of individuals to make a better adjustment to their environment. Although attention to the impact of medical care on illness and death is crucial to an overall evaluation of how best to allocate resources, this perspective should not detract from the caring function of medical service.[13] We must begin to focus more accurately on the extent to which medicine aids a person in using his capacities and fulfilling his aspirations within the limits of physical and psychological handicaps. We must try to ascertain how varying modes of delivering medical services differentially affect the patient who is worried and distressed and to learn the extent to which different models provide support and hope. In short, if medicine exists to enhance the quality of life and to lengthen it, we must examine how successfully its technology and mode of organization fulfill these purposes.

Some feel that, given the technical achievements of medicine in the United States, it is misguided to focus on the perceived crisis and the problems of access to medical services. They believe that increased access encourages abuse of medical service for trivial problems and interferes with the proper care of the critically ill. This viewpoint, held by some laymen and physicians, is based on a conception of medicine as primarily a technical function and one with limited scope and responsibility. The statement of this view sharply brings into focus a growing conflict between the conceptions of patients and those who control the bureaucracies that serve them. Access to medical care is thus an important example of a basic and growing dilemma of living in a democratic society that involves the relative roles of consumers and experts in establishing priorities. The adequacy of the mechanisms we develop for accommodating citizens' expectations with the optimal use of expert knowledge and sophisticated technology will be an important indicator of our ability to deal with many other future problems.

Emphasis on access to medical care as an example of the problem of effective accommodation of varying interest groups in society is important for a variety of other reasons. Although persons of varying persuasions may have dissimilar views on the distribution of most resources and services in society, there is general acceptance that persons in need ought to receive adequate medical care regardless of their location or station in life. Further, medical care is a central concern to the average citizen and is important in sustaining persons in the performance of their usual responsibilities. We have ample evidence, moreover, that the existing allocation of services—and the medical-care market within which it is embedded—is incapable by itself of eliminating blatant inequalities and maldistribution of resources. Hence, the distribution of medical resources is not only important in its own right but also indicates other areas of social policy where existing mechanisms are unresponsive to impending problems.

SOME DEFINITIONS

Although we seek to define the typical needs of the medical consumer, we must keep in mind the tremendous variability among persons in their tastes, their reliance on medical care, the types of problems they confront in their daily lives, and the resources and skills they have to deal with adversities. Although many patients give high priority to a continuing relationship with a physician and personalized care, others put a higher premium on immediate access when they are worried and feel a need for medical care. Such persons might value a facility available at all times more than an opportunity to see the same physician each time. Some patients desire a maximum of information from the physician and a reasonable opportunity to participate in decisions affecting their own care. Others wish not to be burdened by choices and detail, and prefer greater dependence on the physician. In short, different models of care must be available, within the limits of reasonable quality and efficiency, to be responsive to the varying tastes and inclinations of patients.

The needs of various subgroups of the population and geographic areas also differ, and medical facilities require varying types of organizational patterns under different circumstances. Population needs and patterns of morbidity vary by culture, socioeconomic status, and geographic location. The priorities in an urban ghetto, a rural county, a middle-class suburb, and an Indian reservation require different types of organization, depending on illness patterns, the motivations and attitudes of the population group involved, the availability of manpower and supporting resources, and many other considerations.

In this discussion we focus on access to primary medical care. Access has several dimensions. First, services must be made available to the community and must be obtainable by any and all subgroups in the population. When persons are worried or feel a need for help, there must be a source of first-contact care available to them that has the capacity to assess the problem. Second, in assessing the problem, the source of first-contact care must have the ability to deal with it promptly within reasonable limits, or if this capacity is insufficient, the source must be adequately linked with other services so as to ensure that appropriate management can begin. Thus *access is measured by the availability of services in the community, the obtainability of services by any and all subgroups of the population, and the comprehensiveness of services offered by the source of first-contact care or facilities linked with it.* (Although financial access to care is a major aspect of the large problem, this volume emphasizes other dimensions of ensuring access to adequate health care.) Barriers to care must thus be seen from the perspectives of both consumers and providers.

The complexity of defining access to medical care becomes more apparent when we appreciate that the concept is specific to time of the day and week, to varying illnesses, and to different groups in the community. Care can be available in the community but unobtainable on nights and weekends. Or it may be easily obtainable by the more affluent and better educated, but sociocultural barriers may make it difficult for certain disadvantaged people to reach necessary services. Moreover, the necessity for immediate care varies by the type of service involved; adequate access to care must be defined differently for chest pain, a chronic complaint, a general health examination, or eye refractions. Furthermore, some adequate basis must be established for deciding which services are reasonably provided by sources of first-contact care and which ones by referral. This, too, varies by type of community and the medical resources available to it.

There are different barriers to medical care. First, there are those that affect the desire or willingness of a person who defines a need for care to seek it—such as economic barriers, the feeling that seeking care will stigmatize or humiliate him, ignorance of what kind of care to seek or where to obtain it, sociocultural attitudes or values that discourage the use of care, or barriers of distance or inconvenience.[14] The second barrier involves the inability of a source of care to initiate appropriate management of the problem. This may result from the way treatment personnel define their functions, from inadequacies of staff and facilities, and from an inadequate network of services. Hence, barriers to access exist not only in reaching a physician or other source of care but also in the inability of health personnel to initiate the necessary response once the problem has been defined. Furthermore, to the extent that the initial source of care is inadequate, barriers to appropriate care may result from misdiagnosis or the failure to assess the patient's problem correctly. In considering what the appropriate source of first-contact care should be, we must consider not only its availability but also its capacity to make the judgments necessary to fit the problems to the services available.

The first barrier to access logically occurs before the patient seeks care, and it is usually assumed that the medical-care system—in contrast to the larger social system—can do little to alleviate the problem. But on closer examination it is clear that the medical-care system can do much either to enlarge or to minimize such barriers by the manner in which it is organized and the way it treats consumers. When services are made reasonably available and are provided in a sympathetic way that acknowledges the individuality and varying needs of patients, there has been no difficulty in reaching all segments of the population. Moreover, medical care planned on the basis of sufficient information can do much to ensure that the population is adequately protected. We know that in many areas the people are inadequately immunized against preventable disease. An effective source of primary care can define the population at risk and develop programs that ensure higher rates of protection.

Barriers to the initiation of appropriate management of a variety of problems may result from the inadequacy of the existing network of services. A service of first contact, whether a solo practitioner or an organized clinic, must be part of a larger pattern of care capable of dealing with a wide variety of morbidity conditions, levels of disability, and life problems. A solo practitioner without access to hospital beds or specialized services, for example, is incapable of providing necessary care that makes full use of existing medical knowledge and technology. Similarly, a highly specialized outpatient department, emphasizing a particular set of diseases, may be so focused on categorical problems that it fails to assess the person's total illness situation and to deal appropriately with it. The existing network may be inadequate because of unplanned and fragmented services, as in many urban communities, or because supporting facilities are just not available, as in some rural areas. Other problems in developing more nearly comprehensive networks include the sponsorship of varying services under different auspices—both public and private—that have little incentive to work together, the categorical emphasis on the financing and organization of services, and the lack of balance among varying levels of service in relation to patient need.

Although it is essential to separate for conceptual purposes the definitions of access and quality, these two concepts are closely interlinked. To the extent that the source of first-contact care is too narrow in orientation or poorly developed in skills and judgmental capacities, the probability is lower that the problem will be properly assessed and adequately managed. When the margin of error is large relative to the level of performance feasible, we can rightfully say that access has been diminished, although some risk of error is inherent in all human activity.

A key element in developing adequate access to primary medical care is the clear determination of who is responsible for organizing ambulatory medical care within a specific geographic area and of how coverage of every person in the defined population can be ensured.[15] Without definitions of the population and its needs it is impossible to develop a comprehensive network of services that ensures access to needed medical care. Coverage of a defined population involves both assurance of financial entitlement to necessary services and an available source of care that is held responsible for providing comprehensive basic services. Entitlement alone, in the absence of other public interventions, will not achieve at tolerable cost the organizational and manpower arrangements necessary for an accessible, efficient, and effective organization of community ambulatory services. Barring the enactment of a comprehensive national health service, it is likely that a variety of auspices of primary medical care will remain. Hence, consideration of the incentives necessary to organize these elements into a coherent system in which leadership and allocation of responsibility are clear is of high priority.

TWO

Relationships Between Medical
Need and Responsiveness of Care

A FRAMEWORK FOR DEVELOPING POLICY OPTIONS

We have now outlined in global terms the issues that define the problem of access to medical care. In this chapter we consider more specific areas that must be taken into account in formulating policy options to increase this access. The discussion develops by first considering the occurrence of health problems in the population and then noting the factors that motivate persons to seek medical care. This is followed by brief treatments of the role of primary care in health maintenance, and existing inequities and inefficiencies in the organization of care. We then bring these two parts together by considering the responsiveness of medical care to patterns of morbidity. To explain some of the discrepancies we have found between the needs and expectations of patients and existing patterns of care, we consider how the physician's perspective is shaped by medical education. Finally, we conclude this part of the discussion by considering how primary care can be more responsive to patients' needs and expectations.

OCCURRENCE OF HEALTH PROBLEMS
AND ILLNESS IN THE POPULATION

There is no simple or definite way of establishing how much medical care is necessary or worthwhile. In reality, limits on economic resources and available manpower and facilities result in services being rationed in some fashion. The issue is not whether services should be rationed, but rather what rationing plan is likely to result in the most responsive and effective use of the resources available. A population perspective is essential for assessing this issue, since it is impossible to construct a view of the quantity and quality of need by examining only those who seek medical care.

Need for medical services depends on population characteristics. When the birth rate decreases, the future requirement for obstetricians and pediatricians is likely to decline unless work patterns are modified. Similarly, as the proportion of elderly persons in the population increases, it is likely that demand will elevate for a variety of services for chronic patients, for nursing-home care, and for rehabilitation facilities. Indeed, with the aging of our population it is inevitable that more medical resources and more supportive services will continue to be devoted to the health problems of the elderly.

In any given month approximately three-fourths of the population have an acute or chronic illness that leads to some action, such as the restriction of activity or the taking of medication.[1] Of these persons who report an illness during the month, approximately one-third seek medical consultation. Although, in general, illnesses that occur more dramatically or that cause greater discomfort or restriction of activity are more likely to lead to medical care, there is substantial overlap between the illnesses of treated and untreated persons.

In community populations, acute respiratory conditions and mild and moderate psychiatric and psychosocial problems constitute the majority of daily morbidity.[2] Whereas patients seek care readily for acute respiratory infections, psychiatric distress is more frequently untreated or presented to the physician in terms of vague or minor somatic complaints.[3] Acute upper respiratory conditions dominate the physician's practice, but he also tends to see many traumas, skin problems, allergies, and infections. Although psychiatric and psychosocial conditions overshadow all other chronic problems, problems that also occur with considerable frequency include chronic dermatitis and eczema, hypertension, ulcers, asthma, malignancies, arthritis, and diabetes mellitus.

The problems seen by a doctor of first contact depend, of course, on the age and sex composition of his patients, the context in which he works (emergency room versus an office), the specialty organization of his practice, and the sociocultural characteristics of his patients. An emergency-room doctor obviously sees more trauma and a pediatrician sees more otitis media. But all doctors of first contact see many of the same problems, and almost half of their patients may present such vague symptoms and problems that they cannot be given a diagnosis that fits the more specific designations of the International Classification of Disease.[4]

It is essential to consider the role of first-contact care in relation to the typical constellation of problems in the community. A functional and appropriate allocation of tasks can be made only by considering typical problems and developing a realistic role structure to deal with them. The failure to adopt such a perspective has perpetuated the reliance on a single model of care that is exceedingly expensive and in many ways ill fitted to cope appropriately with more common types of complaints.

MOTIVATIONS IN SEEKING MEDICAL-CARE SERVICES

The inclination of a person to bring a problem to a medical facility depends on the character of the problem, his background, his social status and attitudes, various characteristics of the health-delivery system, and a variety of precipitating factors.

Problems are more likely to be brought to a medical facility when they cause pain and discomfort, when they disrupt usual functioning or the performance of expected activities, and when they appear unfamiliar and frightening. The symptoms of many serious illnesses do not, however, cause excessive pain or disrupt functioning, and they may—at least in earlier stages—seem relatively trivial. It is particularly in such cases where delay in seeking care may be pronounced, or care may not be sought at all, that public education is most necessary. Symptoms such as strep throat may appear as a common problem and be ignored. Cancer in its early stages may be innocuous, causing neither discomfort nor disruption in activities. Chest pain owing to a myocardial infarction may be perceived as indigestion. The more ordinary the complaint, the more likely it is that seeking help is influenced by social, cultural, and precipitating factors.

Furthermore, the extent to which a symptom is embarrassing or stigmatizing affects the willingness of persons to seek care. Particularly when there are psychiatric conditions, but also when conditions affect the more private regions of the body and behavior, one finds in some segments of the population a considerable resistance to the seeking of care. These barriers can be overcome by responsive and sensitive handling of the complaints, but a lack of sensitivity to these patients may result in a great unwillingness to accept necessary care.

In the psychiatric area, which has received a great deal of study, there are substantial sociocultural differences in the willingness to identify oneself as having a psychological problem and to seek appropriate treatment. Whereas higher status persons are more likely to use a psychological language to describe their problems and to seek specialized assistance, persons from lower socioeconomic groups are more likely to come to a physician complaining of vague and undefined symptoms. Lower status persons are also more likely to enter care late and frequently after symptoms have become extremely severe and disruptive.[5]

The willingness of a person to seek care for a psychiatric condition has been found to be related to the social groups to which he or she belongs and to the perceived acceptability of seeking such care. Persons, for example, who consult psychiatrists tend to know others who have sought such care and, in part, share attitudes and experiences with them.[6] It seems reasonable to infer from these studies that belonging to such a social circle insulates a person from the stigma of seeking care and makes individuals more receptive to psychiatric assistance. Although there has been considerable advancement in recent decades in making care for psychiatric conditions more acceptable, educational programs designed to reduce the isolation and stigma of the person needing care for psychiatric problems will make it easier for him to accept it.

Because of prior upbringing and cultural inclinations people differ in their propensity to seek medical services. Whereas some are highly reliant on medical services and have great faith in physicians, others are more independent and skeptical. Although a variety of social and ethnic differences in responding to symptoms has been noted, education has been the most consistently observed factor influencing medical utilization. Persons with more education use more preventive services, have higher average use of medical facilities, and are more likely to take advantage of new medical programs. Women tend to use more ambulatory services than men, and services are provided more frequently to the very young and the elderly.

Whether services are used by persons with particular symptoms depends on varying precipitating factors that may trigger concern. Persons frequently ignore or neglect symptoms for some time but become worried when some event focuses their attention on their symptoms and possible consequences. Such triggering may occur as a result of exposure to information or social influence, or it may be a consequence of stressful life events and difficulty in coping in general. Pediatricians have noted that the tendency of mothers to bring their children to doctors is frequently stimulated by the mother's anxiety and distress as much as by the particular symptoms of the child. The motivation for seeking care may result as much from failures in functioning as from the specific character of the symptoms that are the focus of the consultation.

Various investigators have attempted to develop models explaining the factors contributing to preventive-health behavior and the use of ambulatory medical care. Common to these social and psychological models is the idea that people respond to symptoms in terms of past learning and experience. The decision to seek or not to seek medical care involves a cost–benefit calculation in which the person assesses the gains and disadvantages of seeking care. To the extent that the condition is painful or incapacitating or arouses fear, and to the extent that the person believes that medical care could be helpful, he or she is more likely to seek care. Barriers to seeking care include financial cost, time and distance, possible embarrassment and stigma, waiting time, and anticipation of unresponsiveness of health personnel. Factors such as education are important because they affect how people come to weigh the various costs and benefits. Similarly, sex is probably related to medical-care use, in part, because women suffer less embarrassment in expressing pain and asking for help, and many are probably less likely to be inconvenienced by seeking care during usual working hours.

The influence of one or another barrier depends on the social situation of the patient. Although income affects ability to overcome economic barriers, the importance of time, skill in surmounting bureaucratic resistance, and fear of embarrassment affect varying clients differently. Access to care is increased when more manpower is available, when facilities are nearby and accessible to available transportation, when facilities maintain hours that allow working people to come without income loss and other penalties, and when persons are made to feel that their problems merit concern.

PRIMARY CARE AND HEALTH MAINTENANCE

In emphasizing problems patients bring to doctors, we must not lose sight of the important functions of first-contact care in preventive medicine, health maintenance, and patient education. Nor can we neglect the responsibility for the support and management of chronic patients and for the performance of various administrative functions expected by society, such as employment and school examinations and disability certification. An adequate preventive program for first-contact care requires, at a minimum, ensuring necessary immunization, providing prenatal and child care, and monitoring overall health needs. Who actually performs such care is less important than the continuing assessment of needs and the provision of responsive services. The adequacy of the informational system available for monitoring needs is crucial, since only through such a mechanism is it possible to ensure that necessary preventive measures are actually taken. To ensure a high level of preventive care, efforts should also be made to educate and motivate recipient populations. A targeted approach to those requiring preventive services requires the maintenance of up-to-date preventive-care histories.

Various preventive health services are believed to be of value, but there is some division of opinion concerning their cost-effectiveness.[7] Services such as an annual medical examination, multiphasic health testing, and genetic counseling have utility but under some circumstances compete with alternative expenditures of resources. It is not our purpose to arrive at judgments where medical opinion is divided, but certainly screening and counseling, when selectively performed, are valuable and cost-effective. Particularly when effective medical treatment is available—as in hypertension—screening can significantly limit morbidity and mortality. Targeted screening that takes into account the vulnerabilities of individual populations, the adequacy and costs of medical interventions, and the prevalence of conditions in the population establishes a reasonable base from which effective intervention can proceed.

The availability of automated, multiphasic technology makes it possible to screen large populations without excessive use of scarce and expensive medical manpower. To be effective, however, such screening must be tied to a health-delivery system, and correctable defects and disorders must receive care once they are identified. It is essential, moreover, that such screening programs be carefully planned, that quality controls be enforced relevant to both personnel and instrumentation, and that persons screened be dealt with respectfully. Screening makes sense only when it results in the correction or prevention of illness, defects, or disabilities. To detect conditions that cannot be corrected or alleviated may only increase anxiety and distress in the population. Screening programs must also try to ensure that diagnoses remain privileged information, to protect against the possible stigmatic effects of unnecessary labeling.

It is apparent that new preventive possibilities are on the horizon of medical practice. Sensitive use of prenatal diagnosis, for example, opens possibilities for preventing the birth of defective fetuses destined to incapacity and discomfort. These new techniques raise serious ethical and moral choices and involve decisions on which all persons are not agreed. As these new techniques are implemented, they must never be used in a coercive and authoritarian manner; these diagnostic techniques can and should be used to widen personal choices and to free persons who make such choices from perceived oppressive consequences.

As the nature of disease in the population continues to change, first-contact care must take greater responsibility for health education and promotion of better health status. Since the population turns to sources of medical care for general guidance in dealing with life problems, health facilities have an enormous opportunity to assist people in improving health practices in nutrition, child care, sexual adjustment, and the like. The medical-care system can, moreover, do much to assist families to aid loved ones who are sick and disabled. As we move farther away from reliance on institutional care for the sick and the disabled, the medical-care system must do more to aid such persons and those with whom they live so as to maximize their comfort and functioning within the limits of their disabilities.

Preventive services are presently highly fragmented and inadequate. Because of the uncoordinated nature of medical practice it is difficult to identify needy persons or to ensure the successful penetration of the population in respect to preventive practices. When the informational system for monitoring preventive needs is inadequate, successful preventive care depends considerably on a motivated consumer. In anticipation that some fragmentation of health services will continue, various devices will be necessary to ensure successful preventive practice. Birth registration and the school census are excellent mechanisms for monitoring the preventive needs of children. School health services could be vastly improved to ensure the adequate health assessments of children. Parents could seek services where they like, but the school health program should be prepared to provide some essential services to those who have not received them. Prenatal and postnatal care provide excellent opportunities for monitoring the health needs of mothers and their children and for providing health-education programs responsive to their needs. Health facilities can become the sponsors of groups dealing with special problems such as alcoholism, sexual difficulties, and management of disabled children. We have hardly begun to exploit the excellent possibilities and technologies available to make help more salient and to assist persons in dealing with the consequences of health problems.

INEQUITIES AND INEFFICIENCIES IN
THE ORGANIZATION OF AMBULATORY
MEDICAL CARE

In 1932 the Committee on the Costs of Medical Care issued its final report *Medical Care for the American People*.[8] It noted the maldistribution of physicians and other medical facilities by geographic area and emphasized the growing imbalance between primary medical care and more specialized practice. Among their conclusions were that "There is a need for geographic distribution and agencies which more closely approximates the medical requirements of the people," and "There should be effective control over the number and types of practitioners trained, and their training should be adjusted so that it will prepare them to serve the true needs of the people." Several decades— and many programs later—we find ourselves facing the very same issues.

We have already noted the concern about access to physician services. The basis of this concern has been the concentration of doctors in urban and suburban areas and the diminishing number of doctors providing primary care. As Part II of this book shows, a typical response to this perceived need has been to attempt to increase the total output of physicians, but such action by itself has not changed, and will not change, substantially the distribution of physicians or the tasks they perform. Unless the output of new physicians is enormous, doctors can continue to work comfortably and profitably without changing their location of practice.[9]

Although lawmakers have intended to force a redistribution in the tasks of physicians and the location of their practices by increasing the number of providers—in the hope of making them thus more competitive—the medical marketplace, for the reasons discussed earlier, is not very responsive to such manipulations. Much medical demand is controlled by decisions of the physician and, thus, physicians are able to adjust to an increased number of competitors by generating additional demand or maintaining high prices for each unit of service. In considering various attempts to influence the distribution of physicians and the content of their work, we must direct our attention as much to how they practice and the forces affecting their decisions as we do to the motivations of the medical consumer.

One consequence of the existing pattern of physician distribution is that, while it is difficult to gain access to basic medical care in some areas, in others physicians must compete for patients. Although it is impossible to specify at what point an area is overserviced, the consequences are clearly definable. Medical care is a highly discretionary activity, and physicians can generate considerable work that they would not be inclined to do if there were more demand for their services. Existing data suggest that the medical resources provided are excellent predictors of the magnitude of services consumed; the more hospital beds or surgeons in a community, the higher the rates of admission to hospitals and of discretionary surgery.[10] It is, of course, difficult to specify precisely an ideal level of services. But general subsidy of medical resources of the nation without specific attention to the nature of unmet need and the factors influencing the motivation and performance of physicians may further contribute to the overall imbalance and maldistribution of resources. A prudent social policy tries to minimize, by its incentives, those aspects of care that introduce needless risks. The appropriate balance of medical activities is central to good medical care, and the proliferation of unneeded specialists or hospital facilities is apt to increase the probability of unnecessary and even dangerous procedures.

THE RESPONSIVENESS OF MEDICAL CARE
TO THE PATTERN OF MORBIDITY

An important issue in discussions of ambulatory medical care is whether the physician should be responsible for the broad range of problems brought by patients and whether it is necessary to manage problems such as alcoholism, unhappiness, obesity, and anxiety within the context of ordinary medical care.

The typical physician—trained to exercise complex technical skills with emphasis on acute care—is frequently frustrated by problems that he feels are technically trivial or that lack a clear and efficacious approach in treatment. Of the consultations with physicians reported in the National Health Interview Survey, almost a third were respiratory conditions and injuries.[11] But physicians commonly perceive such patients as boring and trivial, and this in part explains their reluctance to do primary medical care.

Medicine is one of the few social institutions that can insulate people from stress and excuse their failure to perform usual responsibilities. Unhappy persons or those in confining social situations sometimes take refuge in sickness, whereas those with more pleasurable life activities often ignore even severe and painful symptoms. Discontented people may focus on symptoms widely prevalent in the population, but usually ignored by others, as a way of managing stressful life events. Some persons may even develop a career organized around these responses, managing their lives and others through a vocabulary of illness. Recent research suggests that such patients may be chronic users of medical facilities, but when services responsive to their troubles are offered, their use of medical resources decreases.[12] Of course, life situations are enormously difficult to modify, even with the greatest of commitment, and serious attention must be given to how to incorporate such concerns within new practice models.

The fact is medicine is a role defined by the community, and problems troubling patients cannot be reasonably ignored by physicians simply because they find them uninteresting or because no clear intervention is available. Much ambulatory care involves problems that require only technically simple care or support and reassurance. Patients are frequently reluctant to recognize explicitly what is troubling them and are unwilling to seek assistance from other helping agencies. They accept the physician as an appropriate source of assistance, and there is no effective or desirable mode of keeping such patients out of the medical-care system. The only responsible course is to develop the capacity of ambulatory facilities to provide a broad range of services responsive to the entire spectrum of problems characteristic of persons seeking medical care.

One of the remarkable aspects of primary medical care in the United States is that a significant number of practitioners do not do simple procedures related to common complaints. For example, almost 6 percent of all medical consultations are for sprains and strains and open wounds and lacerations.[13] Almost all general practitioners will tape sprains and suture lacerations; but approximately half the office-based internists and one-fourth of office-based pediatricians never tape sprains, and approximately two-thirds of internists and a fifth of pediatricians never suture lacerations.[14] This is equally true for other procedures, such as excising simple cysts and opening abscesses, which are commonly done by general practitioners. Half of the office-based internists never open abscesses, and the vast majority of internists and pediatricians never excise simple cysts.

Patients frequently complain about the unwillingness of physicians to make home calls, but physicians usually characterize home calls as an antiquated and uneconomic mode of providing medical care. There has been a continuing decline in home visits by physicians, which further declined between the periods 1966 to 1967 and 1969 from 3.3 to 2.3 percent of all consultations, involving nonhospitalized patients.[15] Home visits are most frequently made to elderly persons and those with considerable activity limitation. Although approximately half of all nongroup general practitioners in the United States still make a home visit or two each day, home visiting has virtually disappeared among internists, pediatricians, and obstetricians. The extent of this trend can be appreciated by comparing the work of American and British primary-care physicians. Whereas only 15 percent of British general practitioners report spending less than two hours a day on home calls, 92 percent of nongroup and 99 percent of group physicians in the United States give a comparable response.[16]

It would be desirable to encourage primary-care physicians to enlarge the scope of their practices to manage routine problems better. It is apparent that one way of achieving this is to use trained assistants and technicians who can expertly carry out certain procedures that the doctor is uninterested in doing himself. These procedures might include handling simple trauma, dealing with problems of behavior and child care, doing simple surgery, and providing health education. The vast majority of primary-care physicians approve of the use of physicians' assistants working under the doctor's supervision, ranging from 78 percent of nongroup general practitioners to 93 percent of group pediatricians.[17] But there is no evidence as yet that such assistants are being widely or effectively used.

Nurse practitioners and others could be very helpful in reviving the institution of home visiting, which, if well coordinated, can contribute to a more coherent and more nearly comprehensive pattern of primary medical care. Although more than 20,000 public health nurses are employed by public health departments and visiting nurse services,[18] and although they have many primary-care functions, they operate parallel to primary medical services rather than as a coherent part of a coordinated system. We must give attention to ways of better using this valuable, available resource.

Our fragmented ambulatory-care system is very much influenced by the fact that most care is rendered by solo practitioners, partnerships, and small independent units and is largely separated from other supporting and related services. The economic base of such practices does not permit the effective use of nutritionists, social workers, outreach personnel, clinical pharmacists, or a host of other health workers who can contribute to the quality, comprehensiveness, and efficiency of care. Physicians are not only unable to arrange for supporting services at the site of ambulatory care, but they are also generally uninformed about what services exist in the community and how to enlist them properly for the patients' benefit.

Part of the difficulty in implementing comprehensive primary-care programs has been the concept of the physician service. Once we conceive of medical care as an array of services provided by teams of specially trained personnel, the options and possibilities greatly increase. A facility for first-contact care may include not only doctors, nurses, technicians, and physicians' assistants, but also nurse practitioners, health educators, psychologists, and group leaders. To the extent that the population being cared for is sufficiently large, it becomes more economical than in smaller practices to provide supporting services that facilitate not only comprehensive care but also care more attuned to patients with less common needs, such as the excessive drinker and the parents of retarded children. Although every source of first-contact care need not replicate every facility or program, it must be tied in some way to sources of help for patients with more nearly unique health-related problems.

Since medical care has comprehensive functions and since patients seek care for varied problems, the initial assessment of the patient and his needs constitutes a problem of great complexity. The initial assessment, often described as triage, requires considerable sophistication, not only about physical illness, but also about people and how they respond to their difficulties. The issue of who should perform the triage has received much discussion in recent years, but there is no simple solution. Many physicians dislike triage because they feel that many of the problems that patients present are relatively simple and do not require the physician's specialized skills. They maintain that most of such complaints can be managed appropriately by a nurse or a specially trained assistant. An opposing view is that many serious and complicated problems appear in common and innocuous forms, and it requires considerable skill on the part of the clinician to make a proper assessment. The meaning of a complaint may, moreover, be difficult to interpret without consideration of the patient's entire medical and social history, and this is probably a task for the physician.

We believe then that basic triage should be performed by a suitably trained physician, although some services such as care for minor trauma and preventive care might be filtered off before reaching the doctor. The most appropriate uses of assistants and other paraprofessionals are for performing more routine aspects of the medical consultation, for taking some responsibility in the continuing management of chronic patients, and for offering particular specialized services relevant to the overall care of the patient.

At this juncture, a word on the successful implementation of care is essential. We have already defined access to include the initiation of the appropriate management of the patient. Appropriate management requires that the patient reasonably conform with medical advice, that he return to the physician when necessary, and that he assume some responsibility for getting well. It is perhaps symptomatic of the difficulties in medical care that physicians go through considerable efforts to locate disease, make the correct diagnosis, and prescribe appropriate management but give relatively limited attention to the conditions facilitating responsiveness to medical advice and follow-up on treatment. But if management is not implemented successfully, all the earlier steps are of little avail.[19]

Various studies show that failure to follow medical advice is extremely common, and patients frequently fail to follow up on their care. Although all the reasons for such failures are not known, various studies indicate that such noncompliance is often a product of disruptions in doctor–patient relationships and communication.[20] Whereas patients dissatisfied with the care and concern they receive are less likely to respond to suggested advice, failures also result from the complexity of medical advice, incomplete or inappropriate instructions, or the tendency of many patients not to hear or remember what the physician said. Many patients do not feel comfortable in asking questions and seeking clarification, and they frequently give the false impression that they understand the physician's instructions.

Patients with complicated medical problems may have a particularly difficult time in understanding and responding to medical advice. Such patients may have a variety of medications—each requiring different instructions—and confusion may easily occur. Various studies demonstrate that, as the number of medications increases, so do errors and failure to follow advice. The importance of careful instruction of the patient and of the opportunity to ask questions is clear. What is not so clear is how to provide such instructions within the context of a busy ambulatory-care practice.

More recently, a great deal of attention has been given to the rubric "family medicine," but there has been little conceptual clarification of the specific role of the family in medical care. Most usually "family medicine" refers to little more than that the practitioner is trained to assume a wider scope of responsibility than the usual specialist, including responsibilities in general medicine, obstetrics, pediatrics, and psychiatry. Although under some circumstances medical care may be enhanced by the same practitioner's looking after all members of a family, this is not always true and is frequently impractical. First, family members are often geographically separated and may, in any case, have varying preferences in medical care. Second, some family members, like adolescents, may find it more difficult to be frank with a physician close to their parents. Third, if physicians function as agents of the patient, and family members are in conflict with one another, the physician under some circumstances may feel conflicting loyalties and have difficulty in performing his role.

A more reasonable use of family medicine in ambulatory medical care is to guide information. The family is the most intimate group in modern society, and the individual's genetic, psychological, and social proclivities are linked to family history and family process. Moreover, many of the stresses and strains that affect people's lives, and many of the supports that they depend on, are found within the family structure. Effective medical care must take place within consideration of the familial context and family interaction processes. This requires, not that the physician treat the whole family, but that he understand the manner in which family difficulties and family supports affect the patient's health and the implementation of his medical care.

In recent years considerable evidence has shown that ill people experience stressful events and traumatic life changes more frequently than control populations do.[21] Changes in life circumstances and social and psychological tensions may result in modifications of habits, activities, and diet and in exposure to trauma and infection. Such changes are also frequently related to modifications in mood and other physiological changes directly mediated by the central nervous system.[22] And unpleasant life events may also lead persons to focus on illness and to use their symptoms to escape the burdens of their life situations. These factors may affect the incidence of illness, its severity or recurrence, its progression and associated disability, and its responsiveness to medical intervention.

Although the precise impact of social events on disease is not fully understood, studies show that medicine must come to terms with the role of life situations in the occurrence of perceived illness and its development. This is not to suggest that such factors are easily amenable to intervention or that the physician endorsing such an approach knows how to deal with the problems recognized.

THE RESPONSIVENESS OF MEDICAL CARE
AND MEDICAL EDUCATION

It is usually maintained that the physician's perspectives and patterns of work are molded by medical education, and it is here that efforts at reorganization of work must begin. Although a great deal has been written about the influence of medical education, most of it is conjectural and reliable findings are difficult to obtain. Among the problems in obtaining hard data is the fact that medical schools vary, and the characters of students who choose to be physicians, or who are recruited, differ by school and from one student cohort to another. A physician's choice of practice and method of work generally results from four groups of factors: (1) the abilities, attitudes, and other personal qualities he brought to medical school; (2) the processes and content of medical education and postgraduate training and their influence on him; (3) the character of his practice, the demands it makes on him, and factors influencing his daily work; and (4) extrinsic factors such as family and peer-group pressures.

Most is known about the relative success of medical schools in selecting students with high aptitude and good academic performance. Medical schools in the United States have been successful in recruiting highly capable students. Prior undergraduate and Medical College Aptitude Test (MCAT) scores have been reasonably good predictors of the way students will perform academic tasks. MCAT scores tend to predict grades, although only to a limited degree, but they are modestly good predictors of results on National Board Examinations.[23] They are not, however, good predictors of clinical performance.

For some years medical schools have overselected students who are male, of higher socioeconomic status, and of urban origins. In more recent years greater efforts have been made to recruit more nonwhites and other minority group students, and there is decreasing prejudice toward women. Although many schools use interviews as a means of screening on personality criteria and indications of character and commitment, such screening is notoriously unreliable. There is some evidence that medical schools tend to choose students who are high on achievement motivation and endurance and low on needs for change and autonomy.[24] In general, few consistent trends emerge in respect to recruitment except in regard to sociodemographic characteristics and academic criteria. There tends to be little agreement beyond the academic area about how to screen effectively or even about the appropriate criteria. Although many believe in the value of locating prospective physicians dedicated to the public good and willing to work on tasks where they are most needed, no reliable selection techniques exist for prior identification of such persons, and it is unlikely that adequate criteria will be available as useful tools in the near future.

One reason for the difficulty in screening for motivation is that prospective physicians have only a very limited understanding of the nature of medical work or knowledge of the possible choices with which they will eventually be confronted. Many come to medical school with a naive idealism and a stereotyped motivation to help people.[25] Initially, many desire to be general practitioners and to help solve community medical-care problems.[26] But medical school and postgraduate education confront students with a complex reality to which they have to make a continuing series of personal, social, and academic adjustments.[27] As reality tends to diminish their naive idealism and makes them aware of difficulties in academic work and of troublesome medical problems, they begin to take on a more professional and limited perspective.

This process continues throughout the internship and residency, and as the student confronts new experiences he is constantly faced with choices and possibilities. The structure of medical education and postgraduate training has a significant effect on the character and scope of such choices.

Despite the existing diversity in medical education, certain generalizations are possible. In the post-World War II era the research capacities of medical schools became highly elaborated, and the degree of specialization and subspecialization in medical work was very much encouraged.[28] Medical education—concentrated largely in specialized teaching hospitals—emphasized the less common and more complex disorders and the most advanced medical technologies. Teaching was increasingly done by specialists and subspecialists, each concentrating on his particular concern. Students quickly learned that medicine was highly complex, that it was impossible to master in whole, and that choosing a limited specialty was the only way of achieving intellectual mastery of the subject or control over one's future work life. Such choices were reinforced by the educational process and the career commitments of the faculty, and only a very small proportion of those freshman medical students who wished to be general practitioners retained this wish by their senior year. Few medical schools, if any, offered any reasonable model or encouragement for primary medical practice.

Since medical students were trained almost exclusively within a teaching-hospital context, the training strongly influenced their selection of a specialty. The structure of primary medical care, as it existed in the community, offered limited opportunity to make use of the sophisticated model of medical care taught in the teaching hospital, but the training failed to provide an adequate alternative for work as a primary-care physician. And even if it did, the community structure of medical care was not particularly suited to modern primary-care practice.

Most medical students thus sought a medical or surgical specialty. The models of practice they had learned required a hospital, related specialties, and a host of supporting services. Physicians became more concentrated in urban and suburban areas and less available to many segments of the general population. The practice of a specialty was accompanied by more regular hours, less responsibility for continuous care, and less willingness to deal with the larger context of medical ills. From a consumer point of view this trend resulted in less access, greater difficulty in finding a personal physician who took an interest in one's problems, and more deterrence to obtaining medical care at night, on weekends, or in the home. Although such care was at a higher technical level than ever before, it was increasingly fragmented and frequently limited to the site of the specialist's concerns.

Many physicians who moved from the training context to primary care and who viewed their patients in a narrow way were disturbed by their practice, which seemed to involve much that was trivial and hardly a test of their technical skills and knowledge. Indeed, from a more technical and limited view, many of these problems were trivial, but they were important to the people who had them and constituted most of the ordinary demand for physicians' services.

Many physicians who went into general practice would be prepared to deal with the problems as best they could, but such physicians were exposed to a very heavy work load. Although general practitioners constitute less than one-fifth of physicians in office-based practice,[29] they perform almost three-fifths of all office consultations.[30] General practitioners report an average of 173 patients a week, in contrast to internists, who report 123.[31] General practitioners and pediatricians in solo practice or small partnerships were faced with a steady pressure of patients that made it difficult either to practice the high standards of technical quality they learned in medical school or to give patients the time they required for adequate care and sustenance. Such practice often became a treadmill, draining the doctor of his energy and motivation for further developing his skills. Prospective physicians who observed such practice, or who tried it for themselves, frequently received further encouragement for concentrating on a specialty.

If we are to develop realistic options for improved primary medical care, it would be wise to be fully aware of the influences of recruitment, medical education, and practice pressures on the viewpoints of the primary-care physician. Recruitment and the concentration of training in urban areas reinforced a pattern of urban practice. Those recruited from urban areas to begin with, or those exposed to urban hospital medicine and other social and cultural amenities, were less willing to settle in small communities that offered few medical supporting services or educational and cultural opportunities for their families. Educated, urban, middle-class physicians and their families sought the same community opportunities and amenities sought by other educated, urban, middle-class people.

Some alternatives were available to young physicians, such as prepaid group practice or other organized forms of care that provided greater opportunity to practice in a more coordinated way. However, these alternative forms were located in only some areas of the country, and in general they were not particularly innovative in how they organized services, they were not competitive financially, they had little prestige, and they were often harassed by the medical community. It is not surprising that most young doctors did not select such practices.

In sum, physicians came from their medical training poorly prepared to practice primary medical care. The models of diagnosis and treatment taught in the teaching hospital were ill fitted to the practices the physicians faced, but other models or experience with more common problems had not been part of their education. Physicians were oriented to disease rather than concerned with health, knew almost nothing about the behavioral and psychiatric aspects of disease, had little experience in working with primary-care paraprofessionals, knew little about community problems or social services, and were poorly equipped to deal with many of the more common chronic problems seen in ambulatory medical care. They focused on the identity and treatment of specific disease entities but saw the rarer conditions infrequently enough so that it is doubtful that they provided optimal medical management for such conditions.

More recently, many significant changes have been initiated in medical education. Increasingly, schools are developing models for primary care and are teaching students how to work appropriately and effectively in such contexts. Family-practice programs and residencies are developing at a rapid rate. Schools are giving serious consideration to how to train physicians for working in teams and to how to integrate some of the educational and training experiences of varied health professionals. The medical curriculum has undergone extensive change, giving students both greater flexibility and new learning opportunities. Although the existing situation is chaotic, it is a constructive chaos, and many useful trends are likely to emerge. In considering how best to influence these trends, we now turn to a more specific discussion of problems in making existing services congruent with patients' needs and expectations.

MAKING AMBULATORY SERVICES RESPONSIVE
TO PATIENTS' NEEDS AND EXPECTATIONS

The adequacy of the number of doctors in the United States cannot be reasonably determined apart from issues such as their geographic distribution, the allocation of tasks among medical specialties, the use of other health workers, and the general scope of medical care. The number of physicians relative to the population is generally an uninformative statistic by itself. For example, the number of primary-care physicians necessary to provide coherent basic medical-care services depends on the scope of responsibility of first-contact care, the number and types of supporting personnel, and the special needs of the population at risk. In poor populations with sociocultural and linguistic orientations different from those of the providers, more effort will be necessary in supplying translators, outreach workers, and the like. Given appropriate supporting services and a well-organized use of paramedical health workers, it might be possible for a single primary-care physician to care properly for at least a couple of thousand patients; in problem populations without an adequate health-care structure, a primary-care physician may have difficulty providing care to as few as 700 or 800 patients. In England and Wales the typical general practitioner has responsibility for approximately 2500 patients; in Kaiser groups in Oakland and Los Angeles, primary-care physicians look after 2000 patients.[32] In short, numbers in the absence of other considerations are quite meaningless. The number of physicians in the United States at present would probably be more than adequate under optimal organizational conditions.

Given our pluralistic and democratic system, it is highly unlikely that we can achieve an optimal situation even in the long-range future. It is thus necessary to assess the need for physicians in general, given varying assumptions, and to understand that special policies will be necessary to distribute services adequately on a geographic basis or achieve a more reasonable balance among the varying medical specialties. Moreover, since we cannot seriously predict medical discoveries or their impact on medical demand, we need a policy-making process capable of monitoring existing activities and likely trends and responsive to changing needs.

The most appropriate way of assessing manpower requirements is to examine the distribution of need in the community. We assume that, however medical care is financed, the fulfillment of basic medical needs will not be dependent on income. One aspect of need is objectively definable, while the other is highly subjective. First, we must be aware of the actual distribution of diseases, defects, and disabilities in the population for which medical services are relevant either because they cure or alleviate the condition or mitigate pain or suffering. This objective assessment must also take into account the necessary preventive measures amenable to individual or community application. On a more subjective level, the effective demand for medical care not already accounted for by the objective definition must be estimated. Thus, "medical need" has three components: (1) those needs recognized by medical personnel and also by the recipients as requiring care; (2) those needs recognized by medical personnel as needing care but not so recognized by the recipients (here outreach work and health education are particularly significant); and (3) those needs defined by the consumer but not evident in medical screening or community assessments.

Obviously, these judgmental assessments involve many matters on which both physicians and consumers disagree. For example, physicians disagree on the value of many treatment modalities and preventive procedures, and consumers may strongly disagree about whether care for certain complaints and problems is a legitimate part of medical services. Judgments of need at any time must be tied to the level of technology available and to prevailing social ethics and perspectives. Although these often pose knotty problems, it is both possible and desirable to plan for medical services on the basis of epidemiologic intelligence. Resources are scarce, and an adequate information system is necessary for establishing priorities.

Because problems vary widely in their prevalence, services should be organized and different types of manpower provided in a reasonable relationship to the frequency and complexity of various diseases. Services designed for more common illnesses and problems should be organized close to the source of need and be readily available. But as diseases occur less commonly and are more complicated, specialized services should be based on larger populations and geographic areas. Services should be organized along principles that maximize (1) the accessibility of the service; (2) the probability that those who perform the service are best qualified to do so by either training, practice, or both; and (3) the use of financial resources. Because these principles are sometimes competing, planning requires some balancing.

It is useful to specify criteria for balancing principles in relation to accessibility to services. In planning we must distinguish between first-contact medical services and secondary and tertiary ones. In general, secondary and tertiary services—which are also more specialized and more expensive—tend to be later links in referral. In balancing criteria, consumer accessibility should be given highest priority in first-contact services, since only after entry can the necessary or appropriate services be assessed. After entry into the medical-care system, the health professional at the level of first contact can arrange accessibility to more specialized services. To achieve this, first-contact care must be well integrated and coordinated with other services and must have the resources necessary to ensure that the patients in need can reach more specialized levels of care. Ensuring this accessibility on a larger geographic basis may from time to time involve transportation assistance, homemaker help, child care, or other resources. Planning should take into account possible barriers to necessary care at all levels of service and make provision to overcome them.

THREE

Toward a Coherent and Coordinated Health-Care Policy:

ISSUES FOR THE DEVELOPMENT OF POLICY OPTIONS

As stated at the outset, solving the crisis in medical care requires a coordinated health strategy. Issues such as financing, manpower, and the organization and distribution of facilities are interlinked in numerous ways, and any policy change in one of these areas usually has broad implications. The incentives implicit in one or another financing scheme affect what procedures health professionals are willing to perform and how they organize their practices. The need for physicians and other health personnel depends on how medical activities are organized, how facilities are distributed, and how functions are allocated among different types of physicians and between physicians and other health workers. The number and types of physicians and facilities available affect both the quantity and character of the procedures performed and the costs generated by such activities.

Because the interests that sustain the existing system of priorities and the organization and distribution of medical-care services are both powerful and entrenched, single measures to deal with one or another aspect of the problem are easily diluted or deflected from achieving significant modification of the overall pattern of services. If we are to overcome the inertia characteristic of so many components of the system, if we are to provide adequate incentives to the involved parties who are fearful or suspicious of the consequences of change, and if we are to bring about forceful new organizational forms, innovative manpower policies, changes in medical education, improved financing, and responsive care, then we must carefully construct a system of coordinated incentives that are internally consistent and reinforce one another. One of the important lessons gained from recent governmental efforts to increase entitlement is that modifications of one aspect of the system (such as financing) without attention to the context in which change will be introduced results in enormous costs relative to the benefits.

In encouraging the development of new organizational forms for increasing access to primary medical care, it is prudent to keep in mind that we are developing incentives for human systems. Administrative logic often fails in planning because persons frequently do not behave in accord with the rational assumptions imputed to them. Often their preferences or their needs are radically different from those implicit in organizational schemes. It is thus essential that we examine how the systems we design really work, how both professionals and consumers behave in response to the systems, and whether or not they promote and maintain health and limit disease and disability.

Because the existing structure of medical organization and distribution is consistent with the needs and satisfaction of many parties involved in medical care, significant change will not come easily. Medical schools focus on research and care of the very sick and emphasize the training of specialists and superspecialists unless there are constraints or strong incentives for them to do otherwise. Physicians, while disliking many simple and repetitive tasks that they regard as an underuse of their time and training, resist the reallocation of such work to other health workers unless they are confident that this does not threaten their position. Hospitals, in the face of pressures from the community, physicians, organized labor, and other interests, do what they can to sustain their present position unless new incentives have clear direction.

In considering the formulation of a national health strategy we need a policy that will achieve our goals within the context of our values and orientations. We need to be forceful and effective without being coercive. Although we require new and more effective ways of meeting our goals, we wish to do so within conceptions that retain choice and maximize the performance of both providers and consumers. In charting a proper course, it is necessary to inquire why—despite a perception of need and a desire to respond—the Congress has been unable thus far to cope with the perceived crisis in medical care. It is also necessary to take into account the special characteristics of the medical-care marketplace that make it so resistant to modification by single initiatives.

Moving from the existing chaotic pattern of ambulatory-care services to one more coherent and coordinated involves the implementation of policies that require choices. Part of the present difficulty is our reluctance to make necessary decisions that focus incentives for a more organized design of ambulatory health care. Although it is essential to preserve choice and provide encouragement for innovation in any model we advocate, we must at the very least be clear on the assumptions we are promoting and the risks we are willing to assume.

Decision-making in any area requires balancing alternatives—each of which has certain advantages and disadvantages. Although the choices may not be easy, they must be made or we may find ourselves perpetuating our present dilemma of going in every direction at once and creating conflicting incentives. If we think through the choices and examine them thoroughly, we have better opportunity not only to pursue a coherent policy but also to correct for whatever risks such a course may involve. This can be illustrated by asking what type of primary medical service is best equipped to handle the ambulatory-care needs of the future.

Central to this issue is whether we should ask what makes a good primary-care physician as contrasted with asking what constitutes a good primary health service. The first question, as usually posed, perpetuates the assumption that such care will be primarily delivered by a single professional, and his training and competence are the key issue. The latter question leads to inquiries about the needs of populations and about how they might be met by a variety of possible approaches. Public policies would be dramatically different, depending on whether one assumes that every patient ought to have either a personal physician for continuing health care or at least a source of care responsible for his health. Under the first criterion we are likely to have a very large and continuing "shortage" of such physicians, owing to maldistribution; under the second, we can do a great deal more with the physician manpower we already have.

This confusion extends as well to the support and financing of medical education. Although the definition of a personal primary-care physician for all would suggest that as many as one-half or two-thirds of all new physicians be trained for primary care, our system of medical education largely produces medical specialists.[1] In recent years we have significantly increased the number of students entering medical school, on the assumption that most medical functions should be performed by doctors, but despite this focus, most of these physicians are being trained as consulting specialists rather than as primary-care practitioners. If, indeed, the role of the physician is to be primarily a consulting specialist, the emphasis on increased output of physicians is excessive.

Concurrent with these developments has been a trend toward encouraging family-practice programs to train physicians for a more nearly comprehensive understanding of the parameters of illness and to improve their skills in combining medical, obstetric, pediatric, and psychiatric knowledge. But it is inevitable that altering the physician's training without changing the conditions under which he works will ultimately produce frustration and disappointment. Although family-practice programs conceive of medicine as a team effort, they still tend to conceptualize medical practice as the skills inherent in the physician as opposed to the effective organization of professional and paraprofessional manpower roles.

Concurrent with these trends, moreover, has been a great deal of activity in training a variety of paraprofessionals. The concepts of extenders are highly varied, and only rarely are they considered explicitly relative to training physicians. Although some thought has been given to the joint training of varying personnel in the primary-care team, such ideas have not been extensively implemented. The choices are not fully clear nor are they easy. But it is difficult to conceive of a course more confused than the current situation of going in every direction at once in the hope that it will somehow all jell in the end.

In statistical decision-making we distinguish between the risks of accepting a hypothesis as true when it is false and of accepting it as false when it is true. In health-care policy we frequently face situations where the course is uncertain, and we must decide what risks are potentially less damaging for individuals and for the maintenance of our social system. Each choice we make increases some options and closes others. If we make services more accessible to the population, we obviously increase the risks that some in the population may use them carelessly. But if we allow significant barriers to access, we make it more likely that persons who need care and attention will not receive it. Although we seek some balance that minimizes both risks, we cannot eliminate them and must choose. For many reasons, we believe the proper choice is to maximize entry into the system and impose controls on the extensiveness of the care that follows.

Another area of weighing risks involves the incentives for the professional. Some structures of organization and remuneration increase risks of unnecessary surgery and other types of care.[2] Under fee-for-service arrangements and cost reimbursement there is little incentive for limiting unnecessary work. In contrast, capitation models—particularly those that provide for sharing of unexpended funds—provide incentives that may discourage necessary care, particularly at the margins. Here we must weigh economic costs against possible dangers to the patient. A cautious approach removes incentives to perform unnecessary work initially in areas where the quality of care can be evaluated. It would thus be possible to evaluate undertreatment as well as overtreatment.

In promoting some types of access to care we often restrict others, this dilemma being inherent in the provision of health-care services. The consumer's access to initial care is enhanced when medical facilities are highly decentralized and when the source of care is physically close and convenient to entry. But to the extent that services are disaggregated, they are less than comprehensive and less capable of using specialized personnel or effective manpower arrangements. Once again, choice is necessary; it is probable that the most appropriate choice would depend on the characteristics of the population being served. In populations with sociocultural characteristics and environmental difficulties that create barriers to medical care—as among many disadvantaged groups—ready access and outreach are essential features of care. In such situations, highly decentralized health stations associated with a more central and more nearly comprehensive facility are desirable. In providing care for more advantaged populations (those who have greater means and accessibility to easy transportation and who are better informed and more motivated to use medical facilities), a somewhat greater physical distance to a facility is more tolerable and probably advantageous in terms of the ability to aggregate more nearly comprehensive resources.

A related issue concerns the observation that under capitation-type practices, where physicians are more attuned to the organizational structure of which they are a part, they tend to be less responsive to patients than in practices where client controls are more influential.[3] Moreover, the bureaucratization of practice may establish new barriers to access—difficulties in reaching the physician, getting an appointment, or obtaining service outside regular hours. Some critics, observing these trends, defend the more traditional patterns of independent, office-based practice with fee-for-service incentives.

More organized types of practice are, however, both desirable and inevitable. Rather than respond to possible abuses of organized practice by looking backward, we must develop new mechanisms allowing us to take advantage of increased organization, complexity, and aggregation of facilities while protecting us against the known abuses that accompany such forms of practice. Education offers an excellent analogy. No one would seriously respond to the abuses of bureaucracy in education by insisting that we return to the individual tutor. Instead, institutions attempt to develop new services for advising, counseling, and assisting students with problems that are associated with the scale of the institutions themselves or that may be neglected because they are less visible in a complex and heterogeneous environment. In many ways, the traditional general practitioner is as antiquated as the tutor-educator.

***

In the second part of this book, various programs instituted in recent years to increase access to medical care are examined. The previous discussion has suggested the following seven general areas of medical-care service in which barriers to access develop: (1) excessive cost, (2) insufficient supply, (3) poor distribution, (4) inadequate scope, (5) ineffective coordination, (6) psychological and sociocultural impediments to effective use, and (7) inadequate organizational arrangements and poor use of technology. In considering interventions that deal with each of these barriers, it becomes clear that action can be taken to affect the behavior of consumers, providers, or both. For example, one difficulty in meeting medical demand involves what some perceive as an inadequate number of physicians. Alternatives on the production side include increasing the number of physicians trained, changing the distribution of physicians or the specialty mix, introducing physician extenders to increase the physician's productivity, and providing incentives for physicians to work longer hours. At the level of the consumer, the problem might be attacked by patient-education programs inducing consumers to use physicians more wisely or gaining acceptance of physician extenders. Table 1 shows examples of interventions at the level of production and consumption of services for each of the seven barriers to care previously identified.

An examination of Table 1 reveals many different ways of improving access to care—some of which are as yet unexploited. For example, the inadequate scope of services available is seen almost exclusively from the production side, but many medical and medically related problems can be assisted by community self-help groups. Problems such as obesity, alcoholism and other addictions, and anxiety and fear are helped by supportive group relationships provided by others who have shared similar problems. Many persons either are reluctant to contact such groups or have difficulty in knowing how to contact them. Although there is a tendency among professional workers to stay aloof from such community-generated groups, these can be a valuable adjunct to a comprehensive medical-care facility. Such a facility could provide its premises for meetings of such groups and even organize them around special problems that occur commonly in the surrounding population. Here exists a simple and unexploited opportunity to extend greatly the efforts of medical facilities in areas where they have done a notoriously inadequate job.

In Part III of this book various policy options affecting the organization and provision of ambulatory medical care are presented. These options are more narrowly stated than the range of problems discussed, since policy-making in a democratic society must depend on more limited means than those theoretically available. The single most influential opportunity to affect the structure of care is government financing and the incentives built into this process. Limited funds, prudently invested and directed at structuring the incentives associated with financing schemes, offer possibilities of having an impact far greater than the absolute amounts expended.

In developing policy options it is also realistic to work under the assumption that only alternatives consistent with dominant American values are likely to receive a serious hearing. Although such an approach is expedient, there is danger of misgauging what these dominant values are or what their susceptibility to change is even within limited time periods. Looking back over the past

Table 1   Approaches to Decreasing Barriers to Access to Medical Care

Types of Barriers	Interventions Affecting Consumption	Interventions Affecting Production
1. Cost	Medicare and Medicaid	Peer review
		Professional Standards Review Organization
		Capitation payments with incentives against unnecessary use
2. Supply	Health-education programs	Physician extenders
	Obtaining acceptability of physician extenders	Nurse practitioners
		Capitation payments to medical schools
3. Distribution	OEO health centers	National Health Corps
	Subsidy of transportation to health facilities	Loan-forgiveness programs
4. Inadequate scope	Patient groups	Family-practice programs
	Convenience enhanced by aggregating services at one location	Cross-specialty educational programs
		Health-care teams
5. Coordination	Single-route access	Experimental systems
	Medical ombudsman	Medical information systems
		Conjoint funding
6. Psychological and sociocultural factors	Outreach	Models of medical education
	Use of indigenous workers	Student recruitment and selection
	Home visits	Behavioral science and language training
7. Organizational arrangements and uses of technology	Easy phone communication	Automated screening
	Patient "rights" to service	Intramural staff education and consultation
	Achieving acceptability of new technologies	

decade, one could not have predicted either the surge of events or the changing attitudes of the population toward them. In this short period the attitudes of the population toward sex roles, family, youth, personal rights, modes of political expression, and many other matters underwent dramatic shifts. In medical care, impressive changes in the population took place in respect to contraception, abortion, the concept of the "right to medical care," and the willingness to support government financing and regulation of the health sector. Policy options that are too far ahead of the American people are unlikely to be acceptable, but it is equally true that attitudes are changing, and an approach that is insufficiently bold may find itself following instead of providing leadership.

Policy options must be developed within some broad context involving assumptions of the directions in which the nation is headed. It is better to make these assumptions explicit and subject them to criticism and review than to have them lie submerged below the surface. In the discussion of options we assume that the nation is moving toward a system of financial entitlement to health-care services, with third parties of one sort or another paying the vast majority of medical-care bills. We anticipate that the medical-care organization will be characterized by increasing pressures toward specialization and aggregation of facilities and that cost pressures will continue to persist as a result of the implementation of expensive medical technology increasingly elaborated by new advances. We expect that the government and the American people, faced with these growing pressures, will be prepared more and more to apply firmer regulation and control over the medical-care sector. We further anticipate that physicians, hospitals, and other providers of health service will respond to growing government involvement by offering new models of care and developing new professional controls as a means of resisting government intervention and gaining greater public support.

There are many uncertainties in deciding on policy options. Many medical-care and other health-care services have uncertain effects, and we lack full knowledge of their impact and potentialities. Many questions in both the biomedical sciences and the evaluation of effective health-care delivery require research and development. And the incentives we develop for the systems of care in the future must be sensitive to, and cognizant of, the need to encourage the expansion of the knowledge base of medical practice and to find better ways of making it applicable to the health problems of the community.

PART TWO

PAST HISTORY

CHARLES LEWIS

FOUR

Eleven Programs for Increasing Access to Primary Care

Access to health care has become a part of the American Dream. The right to care and freedom from disease, disability, and discomfort are part of the endowment of every inhabitant of the richest nation of the world. Equal opportunity to health has joined education as the means whereby all men, created equal, may achieve the promise of a better life.

Not everyone would subscribe to these tenets, but we, as a nation, have come a long way from the posture that medical care is a privilege, a commodity purchased in a free-enterprise market by those with the means to do so. In the not too distant past, the poor of body and purse received free care, doled out through a separate and unequal system of public-health clinics and hospitals, often staffed by physicians operating on the principles of Robin Hood. Although concern over the inequities produced by this dual system of care has been expressed for many years, only recently have significant changes in public policy occurred that are supportive of, but not completely consistent with, the view that health care is a right.

The various efforts mounted during the past two decades to improve access to primary care in the United States have differed widely in their target populations, their methods, and the motivations of their sponsors. They range from the actions of citizens in small rural communities who build offices for the free use of any doctor who will live with them and care for them to the laws created by the 89th Congress that have affected the health care of millions of people.

Several of these efforts have been examined to assess their impact on access to primary care, for whom, and at what cost. This exercise traces the origins of programs and searches for evidence of their effects. It has not been easy, since few, if any, of these programs were viewed as social experiments. If more concern for evaluation had been evident at their conception, the conclusions might be more precise, if not more valid.

Before these are discussed further, the classification scheme described by Mechanic in Part I will be reviewed for the criteria used in selecting certain programs for examination.

THE CLASSIFICATION SCHEME

Access implies both ability and opportunity. Although the term could be defined operationally in ways susceptible to measurement, this has not been done adequately, and so no measures of access to care are generally available. Access is *not* utilization. Use of services is evidence that access has been achieved, but use rates do not permit estimation of the degree to which services were not used, for a variety of reasons. Availability of care must also be differentiated from access. Availability describes the existence or presence of sources of care, without reference to the barriers (costs, transportation, or attitudes of the consumer, for example) inhibiting access.

In examining the impact of programs to influence access to primary care, it has been necessary to describe the extent to which specific barriers were eradicated or diminished (frequently manifested by changes in rates of use), rather than indicate the numbers of individuals with increased access to care as a result of this intervention.

In Table 1, barriers to access were separated into those related to the consumption and to the production of services. These were further subdivided into those concerned with costs, supply and distribution of services, scope of services and their coordination, and psychosocial and technical–organizational factors.

Many of the efforts examined do not fit into one specific cell within the 2 × 7 matrix described. For example, neighborhood health centers affected consumption of services by eliminating the financial barrier. These centers also dealt with geographic maldistribution of physicians by making these resources available in underserved areas. They expanded the scope of services, and some made transportation available for those needing it. Indigenous health workers and aides attempted to influence patients' health and illness behavior patterns. The same multibarrier approach is also evident in Children and Youth projects.

Most efforts focused, however, on only one barrier. Medicare and Medicaid were designed to influence access by reducing financial barriers to care, without affecting other aspects of the system. Other programs had as their goal an increase in the numbers of practitioners, without reference to their location or type of practice.

CRITERIA FOR SELECTION OF PROGRAMS

It was not feasible to review in depth all the major activities mounted during the past two to three decades to improve access to primary care. Three criteria were defined for selecting the efforts to be examined in some detail:

1. The means used to affect access should be explicit. It was deemed important to be able to identify the principal independent variable or treatment applied.
2. A sufficient period of time should have elapsed so that effects might be observed. Although this is a laudable criterion, many of the most important efforts of this type were initiated in the late 1960s. The effects of some may not be observed for at least a decade. Moreover, many of these programs have been in constant flux since their creation. There have been expansions, cutbacks, and even cancellations of funds, as well as changes in policy and personnel. Effects are, therefore, difficult to attribute to any level or type of intervention.
3. Sufficient data should be available to permit an analysis of impact. It soon became apparent, however, that this criterion also could not be applied too vigorously, because plans for evaluation were not established at the initiation of most of the programs. The data collected for analysis are, therefore, drawn from a variety of sources, frequently using different definitions and time intervals of observation.

In a purely experimental sense, no program can be evaluated in terms of its impact. There is adequate information to permit a formative evaluation or description of the processes by which each was implemented. If there is any one lesson to be learned, it is that this error—the failure to require any formal evaluation of their efforts—must not be repeated in future legislation of the magnitude now under discussion.

With the latter two criteria applied sparingly in some instances, 11 programs were selected for in-depth study. Six were directed at affecting the supply of primary-care services: practice-agreement/loan-forgiveness programs for medical students; rural preceptorships for medical students; increasing the number of family practitioners; increasing the number of physicians; producing new health practitioners (physicians' assistants and nurse practitioners); and the National Health Service Corps. The other five were primarily concerned with reducing barriers to consumption: Medicare, Medicaid, Neighborhood Health Centers, Children and Youth projects, and Health-Maintenance Organizations.

Some readers may feel there is evidence of bias in overselection in the study of efforts to increase the number of primary-care providers and to alter their geographic distributions. If this is true, it is related to a conviction that, until the production of providers can be altered to deal more effectively with barriers to care, there will be little hope of improving access to services.

The focus of these analyses was access to primary care. Many programs had far greater impact on access to secondary and tertiary care provided by specialists and subspecialists in hospital settings than on first-contact services rendered primarily to ambulatory patients. The absence of any discussion and documentation of these effects reflects the specific objective of this review, rather than the lack of importance or impact of these programs on the other levels of care.

Information about these programs was collected during the latter half of 1973 and the first half of 1974. The information presented *was* current as of mid-1974. Many changes will have occurred between the time of preparation of these reports and their publication. The magnitude and frequency of future changes, that is, the rate that these studies become "out-of-date," will only serve to document the degree of flux that has characterized the history of these programs.

The case studies are presented in a sequence related to the classification scheme and to their historical evolution. The first group comprises programs concerned primarily with the provision of services. The second set of case studies includes efforts directed at the consumption of services. In each case, the following format is observed: (1) reasons for development of the program, (2) the nature of the intervention, (3) sources of data for the study, (4) a description of the program, (5) evidence of effectiveness, (6) costs, (7) secondary (unintended) effects, and (8) overall impact on access to primary care.

FIVE

Practice Commitment
Plus Loan Forgiveness:

AN INCENTIVE FOR RURAL LOCATION OF MEDICAL PRACTICE?

REASONS FOR DEVELOPMENT OF PROGRAMS

Considerable attention is being given at the federal level to the development of incentives to encourage physicians and other health manpower to enter practice in the areas of manpower shortages. One such incentive, with which several states have had considerable experience, is the provision of loans to those who agree to practice for a specified time in underserved areas.

The nature of this incentive makes its consideration particularly important at this time. The legislation authorizing federal support of medical education to the extent of more than $200 million a year expired at the end of FY 1974.[1] At present, there is uncertainty about which sections of the Comprehensive Health Manpower Training Act, Nurse Training Act, Public Health Training Act, and the Allied Health Professions Personnel Training Act will be renewed, if any. Policy changes that reduce federal support could prove a severe blow to medical schools that have relied increasingly on federal funds (particularly capitation payments) during the past decade and would force them to seek alternative sources of operating funds.

One suggested source of support is tuition, which now represents only a small portion of the actual costs of medical education.[2] However, almost one-third of all medical students now require major financial support to meet tuition payments, and the Association of American Medical Colleges estimates that two-thirds to three-fourths of all students would need such financial assistance if tuitions were to increase significantly.[3] There is some question about whether sufficient loan funds would be available from the private sector to meet such a demand. Substantial increases in tuition could, therefore, result in discrimination against certain subgroups of qualified applicants and in the long run could threaten the viability of medical schools.

One option included in pending manpower legislation would establish a federally insured medical-student loan program. Acceptance of financial support from the government would bind the student to governmental policies and priorities in health care. Given the current interest in reducing problems of access to health-care services related to a geographic maldistribution of physicians, such a program would very likely make loans conditional upon students' commitment to future practice for a specified period of time in designated shortage areas. Some or all of the loan principal and interest could be forgiven in exchange for short-term service, a practice that would subsidize medical education while placing physicians in underserved areas. A loan-forgiveness program was part of the reorganization of the Department of Health, Education, and Welfare proposed in 1972 by Elliott Richardson, who was Secretary then, and was also prominent in the administration's FY 1974 budget proposal. Although this provision was not part of the budget finally authorized early in 1974, it has been incorporated in the new legislation proposed to replace the recently lapsed federal authority for financing medical education.[4]

NATURE OF INTERVENTION

Practice-agreement/loan-forgiveness programs are designed to affect the distribution of physicians' services by offering financial incentives to encourage practice in rural or medically underserved locations. The intervention has two components: (1) a tuition loan, granted to medical students agreeing to practice for a specified length of time after graduation in areas designated as having shortages in health services; and (2) "forgiveness," or cancellation of all or part of the loan in return for fulfillment of the practice agreement. The amount loaned, years of practice required for cancellation, and options to "buy out" or pay back the loan in cash rather than practice vary from state to state. Fulfillment of the practice agreement is obviously a short-term solution to the problem of maldistribution of physicians. Most programs operate, however, on the assumption that this temporary experience can influence physicians to locate their practices permanently in these areas of need.

SOURCES

Although few of the practice-agreement/loan-forgiveness programs have published evaluations of their impact in encouraging physicians to practice in rural or underserved areas, two recent studies of several programs provided useful background material on their short-term success. In 1970 and 1971, Henry R. Mason, at the American Medical Association, reviewed the experience of 11 state programs, 10 incorporating loan-forgiveness provisions. In 1972, the CONSAD Research Corporation, under contract to the Office of the Secretary, Department of Health, Education, and Welfare, evaluated the short-term impact of loans granted between 1960 and 1965 by 10 state programs, and of existing federally supported loan-forgiveness programs through 1972. Since Mason's data covered longer time periods, information from the CONSAD report has been used chiefly to supplement descriptive information from Mason's study. Neither study provided information on long-term success, that is, the numbers of borrowers remaining in practice in shortage areas after their commitments had been fulfilled. Additional information on federal programs was derived from an "option" paper prepared and made available by William Christoffel, Director, Program Development and Implementation Branch, Bureau of Community Health Services, Health Services Administration.

We tried to update the descriptions of the state programs and the data on their short- and long-term effectiveness through 1973. Not all programs responded, and some that did failed to provide complete data. Hence, a more current assessment of their overall effectiveness as of 1974 is not possible. The information has been used to indicate program costs.

DESCRIPTION OF PROGRAMS

State Programs

Most of the experience with practice-agreement/loan-forgiveness programs has been at the state level. Programs now in operation postdate World War II; many were established during the 1940s and 1950s, and at least seven began during the 1960s and 1970s. The majority are in midwestern and southern states with sizable rural populations. By 1970, 27 states had loan programs and 18 had scholarship programs, many designed for the same purpose as loan programs.

Of the 17 programs incorporating loan-forgiveness provisions, the majority require borrowers to promise to practice in a state-defined rural or health-services-shortage area for a specified length of time, regardless of the total amount borrowed. Borrowers are usually expected to begin practice in these areas within one to three years after graduation from medical school. For each year of service, 10 to 25 percent of the loan is forgiven. *Almost all programs give the borrower the option to buy out of the practice commitment by repaying the loan principal plus interest.* (In some programs, buying out is not offered as an option directly but is a requirement made upon default in the practice obligation; the option here is one of defaulting, but the results are the same.) Loans provide from $3000 to $20,000 to each borrower over a four- or five-year period. Usually, these are available only to state residents, and frequently only to those enrolled at the state university's medical school. Most programs are sponsored either by the state government or state medical society; in some states, these agencies are joint sponsors.

Federal Programs

Federally sponsored programs are of far shorter duration, and practice commitment was not incorporated in legislation until 1971. In 1965, Congress added to the Health Professions Educational Assistance Act of 1963 (P.L. 88–129) what was described as a "hard-won landmark"[5]—the provision that students with HPEA loans could have up to 50 percent of their loans forgiven, 10 percent each year, for practice in federally designated scarcity areas. The first loans were available in 1965 and 1966, and unlike state loans, were not contingent upon a promise for future practice. The 1966 Allied Health Professions Personnel Training Act (P.L. 89–751) increased the loan-cancellation rate to 100 percent, 15 percent for each year of service, for physicians and other health manpower practicing in rural, low-income areas. In 1971, the Comprehensive Health Manpower Training Act (P.L. 92–157) changed earlier loan-cancellation provisions to allow repayment of up to 85 percent of any educational loan (not only HPEA) for at least three years of practice in a federally designated shortage area. Sixty percent of the loan is canceled after a minimum of two years of practice; another 25 percent is forgiven for a third year of practice. Repayment extends over a 10-year period after all advanced training is completed, with interest computed at 3 percent. This law also raised the annual sum available to each HPEA borrower from $2500 to $3500.

In addition, Congress has authorized two scholarship programs to encourage rural practice, both conditional upon commitment to future practice. The Physician Shortage Area Scholarship program was established in 1971 as part of the Comprehensive Health Manpower Training Act and is now administered by the Bureau of Health Resources Development. In program regulations adopted this year, students who promise to provide primary care either where physicians are in short supply or where many patients are migrant workers are eligible for scholarships of up to $5000 annually. Preference is given to applicants from low-income families living in underserved areas who agree to return to those areas to practice. One year of practice is required for each year of scholarship support. Recipients who fail to fulfill the complete obligation are credited for half the time actually spent in practice, and the balance of the scholarship must be repaid, with interest, in proportion to the remaining obligation. As amended in 1972, the Emergency Health Personnel Act of 1970 (P.L. 91–623), which established the National Health Service Corps (see Chapter 10), now incorporates the National Health Service Corps Scholarship Training Program as a recruitment device for Corps physicians. One year of practice is required for each annual scholarship with the added condition that at least half the practice must be in a "critical manpower shortage area." This program has not yet begun, because funds were not requested until the current fiscal year.[6]

EXTENT OF EFFECTIVENESS

Since all these programs permit borrowers to "buy out," or pay back their loans in cash rather than with practice, the numbers and proportions of recipients who select the practice option are one of the best indicators of effectiveness.

State Programs

In 1971, Mason analyzed 10 of the 17 state practice-agreement/loan-forgiveness programs operating as of 1970, as well as the Illinois program, which did not offer loan forgiveness. Six programs beginning in 1965 and thereafter had not been in operation long enough to permit assessment. Mason did not include Mississippi, placing it in his list of programs that had terminated by 1970. Information from the Mississippi State Medical Education Scholarship Loan Program indicates, however, that the program has not terminated but that the forgiveness provision was dropped in 1960. Its 14-year experience prior to 1960 has, therefore, been included in this analysis, and information on the Illinois program has been excluded (see Table 2).

Mason concluded that "the majority of states are fortunate if 60 percent of the borrowing physicians follow through by practicing in the rural areas of

Table 2 Experience of 11 State Practice-Agreement/Loan-Forgiveness Programs (Borrowers Available to Practice by 1970)

	Number of Borrowers	Borrowers Available for Practice by 1970 (%)	Physicians Repaying Loan With Rural Practice[a] (%)	Physicians Buying Out of Practice Commitment (%)	Physicians in Default of Payment (%)	Borrowers Unavailable to Practice for Other Reasons (%)
Arkansas	96	57.2	32.8	56.4	10.9	0.0
Georgia	639	45.2	50.2	49.8	0.0	7.0
Iowa	62	4.8	66.7	0.0	33.3	0.0
Kentucky	331	61.0	96.0	0.0	4.0	11.5
Minnesota	22	54.5	66.7	25.0	8.3	0.0
Mississippi	611	93.6	74.4	25.5	0.0	6.4
North Carolina	301	47.5	58.0	42.0	0.0	4.3
North Dakota	40	35.0	71.4	28.6	0.0	0.0
South Carolina	160	37.5	66.7	33.3	0.0	0.0
Virginia	291	83.8	44.7	55.3	0.0	3.4
West Virginia	22	27.3	66.7	33.6	0.0	0.0
Total:	2575 Average:	62.0%	63.0%	34.1%	2.0%	5.7%

Total:

[a] Base number for percentage is the total number of borrowers available to practice by 1970. Includes those borrowers fulfilling practice commitment in 1970 and those who had completed either the entire commitment or that portion for which they were legally liable before buying out of remainder.

their states. In all of these programs, one-third of physicians chose to buy out of their obligation to practice in a small community."[7]

On the average, 62.0 percent of all borrowers were available for practice by 1970; 32.2 percent were still in school, advanced training, or military service; and almost 6 percent were unavailable for other reasons. By 1970, 63.0 percent of *all* borrowers, on the average, had begun or completed their practice obligations, and 34.1 percent had elected to repay the loan principal plus interest.

On the basis of experience, the program in Kentucky emerges as one of the most successful. This program ranked third in total numbers borrowing and close to the top in the proportion of borrowers available for practice. A majority of all borrowers and 96.0 percent of *available* borrowers had entered practice in rural areas, and none had bought out of their practice obligations. The effort in Mississippi (1946 to 1960) achieved considerable success in the proportion of borrowers (74.4 percent) available for practice who fulfilled practice obligations.

With the exception of Iowa, states with older programs usually had higher proportions of borrowers available for practice, as would be expected. Although duration of the program was not necessarily associated with higher rates of repayment through practice, Illinois, Iowa, Minnesota, North and South Carolina, North Dakota, and West Virginia had larger, but not always strikingly larger, practice-repayment than buy-out rates. Georgia's program had similar proportions electing to practice and repay the loan, but in Virginia and Arkansas, larger proportions of borrowers chose to buy out rather than enter rural practice.

There is nothing in these statistics, nor in Mason's analysis, that explains either the apparent success of programs in Kentucky and Mississippi nor the variations among programs in practice-repayment and buy-out rates. The CONSAD evaluation suggests two factors that may be associated with the success or failure of these loan programs:

1. *The total dollar amount of the loan available* to each borrower during medical school. The more money available, the larger the potential loan and thus the larger the amount to be forgiven through practice or to be repaid if the borrower buys out of the practice agreement. In either case, the assumption is that the larger the loan available, the higher the rate of the practice repayment will be.

2. *The stringency of the loan-forgiveness provision.* A program requiring at least three years of practice before a loan is canceled at the rate of one year of practice for each annual loan is more stringent than a program demanding simply a year of practice for each annual loan. If the terms of forgiveness are important, they should be related to practice-repayment rates.

Size of Total Loan Available. The loan programs, ranked by the percent of borrowers *available* for service by 1970 who elected to fulfill their practice obligation and by the amount of the total loan available, are compared in Table 3. Inspection of the data, confirmed by calculation of rank-order coefficient (r_s), shows there is *no* relation between success of the program, in terms of practice-repayment rates, and the size of the total loan available to each borrower.

The incentives provided by these programs may be outweighed by other considerations at the time the physician–borrower is making decisions about

Table 3   Comparison of State Loan Programs

State	A Rank by Percent of Borrowers Available for Practice by 1970 Who Chose to Fulfill Practice Agreement	B Rank by Total Loan Available to Each Borrower	C Rank by Stringency of Forgiveness Provision[a]
Kentucky	1	2.5	2.5
Mississippi	2	6.5	6
North Dakota	3	6.5	8.5
Iowa	5.5	11	11
Minnesota	5.5	9	8.5
South Carolina	5.5	9	2.5
West Virginia	5.5	9	6
North Carolina	8	4	2.5
Georgia	9	2.5	10
Virginia	10	5	2.5
Arkansas	11	1	6

[a] The stringency ranking was done as follows: programs in Kentucky, North Carolina, South Carolina, and Virginia, requiring only a year's service for each annual loan to be forgiven, were ranked as least strigent; next were ranked Mississippi, West Virginia, and Arkansas, each requiring a minimum period of service before the loan was forgiven at the year of service for year of loan rate; Minnesota and North Dakota ranked next, since they demanded five years of service for four annual loans; Georgia, which adds a minimum period of service before forgiving four annual loans over five years ranked next; the five-year period required to forgive 50 percent of a loan from Iowa, 10 percent being forgiven each subsequent year, ranked most stringent.

r_s for A and $B = 0$

r_s for A and $C = 0$

SOURCE.   Based on information in table 2.

location and type of practice. It has been argued that no loan has been so large that a physician's expected income could not easily cover its repayment within several years after graduation. Whereas the total amounts available through these loan programs ranged from $3000 to $10,000 in the years reviewed, the total amounts actually loaned ranged from $4800 to $6000, debts not large enough to prohibit cash repayment by most practicing physicians.[8] Examination of the limited data on demographic characteristics of those who select practice versus cash repayment shows that the relative affluence of the medical student may be a determinant of the "effectiveness" of the loan program.[9] If only students from disadvantaged families (and communities) cannot afford the buy-out option, then these programs may have unintended and undesirable discriminatory side effects.

Stringency of Loan-Forgiveness Provision.   Comparisons of the programs' ranks by available borrowers electing to fulfill their practice obligations to their ranks on the stringency of loan-forgiveness provisions are also shown in Table 3; calculation of the "stringency" ranking is explained in table footnotes. Calculation of rank-order correlation coefficient (r_s) shows no relation between stringency of loan-forgiveness provisions and success as measured by practice-repayment rates for these 11 programs.

These findings cannot be interpreted as demonstrating that loan forgiveness is not an incentive to fulfillment of the practice commitment. They do suggest, however, that the incentive may be weak and that the relative ease or difficulty of obtaining forgiveness through practice has little impact on the decision to practice or to buy out. Apparently, this decision may be secondary to that of whether to buy out or not.

Some insights into the effectiveness of loans as such versus forgiveness of loans as an incentive to rural service may be found in data comparing the experiences of the Mississippi program before and after termination of the loan-forgiveness provision of 1960.

In the 14 years from 1946 to 1960 when loans were canceled in exchange for rural practice, an average of 43 students borrowed from the program annually. Each incurred a practice obligation of five years. Two of these years *had* to be completed before any practice time was credited to forgiveness or before borrowers could legally buy out of the remaining commitment. In the 14 years since changes in terms were made, loans have been made to an average of six borrowers annually. Borrowers since 1960 had the same practice obligations as earlier borrowers. They also agreed to repay the entire loan plus interest within eight years after beginning practice, since no forgiveness was offered.

Since there was no reduction in the amount of money available that might have prompted a curtailment in lending, program administrators attribute the sizable decline in borrowers to the termination of the forgiveness provision.

Before 1960 a larger proportion of the borrowers than of more recent borrowers chose to fulfill both the basic two-year practice obligation and the full five-year term of practice. More of these individuals, who did not have forgiveness as an option, have paid off the entire amount, defaulting on their practice commitments. These data suggest that cancellation of all or part of the loan seems to provide a real incentive for fulfilling rural practice commitments, but they give no indication of its relative strength. Such findings support the inference drawn earlier, that although forgiveness of loans may act as an incentive to locate in rural areas, it does not appear to be as important as other considerations in influencing a decision to fulfill the commitment or to buy out of the obligation.

Another confounding variable in the Mississippi experience is time. Changes in the orientations of entering students, the curriculum of the medical school, and the relative values of a $1000 loan in 1954 and 1974 have undoubtedly affected the effectiveness of the program.

Federal Programs

The comparatively recent federal loan-forgiveness programs, coupled with the length of the training period that precedes entering practice, preclude any evaluation of their success in increasing the number of physicians serving in target areas. The information available documents, however, the demand for these loans.

Despite their recent origin, the federal loan-forgiveness programs grew quickly. By 1968 and 1969, they represented almost 75 percent of all loan funds available to medical students, ample evidence of initial federal commitment to the goals of the program. Federal budget cuts in the 1970s forced more medical schools to increase the amount of school funds made available for student loans. At the same time, loans provided through the AMA's Educational and Research Fund and from sources other than medical-school funds increased rapidly.

In spite of the almost $10 million increase in federal funds for loans since the 1971 provisions of the Comprehensive Health Manpower Training Act, the dollar amount of loans made available from medical-school and "other" funds, which include state loan program funds, has continued to increase.[10] Although the number of dollars and sources of money for loans have increased, the demand for loans from states that require practice commitments has remained fairly steady, despite the fact that terms for federal loans are far less demanding.

Data available on federal loan programs that do not require prior practice agreements indicate that loans themselves are far more attractive than any options for the forgiveness of those loans.[11] Of an estimated 3800 HPEA loan recipients graduating from medical school in 1965 and 1966, only 42 physicians canceled their loans through shortage-area practice by November 1972. Presumably, this six- to eight-year period would allow for time required for postgraduate training and decisions regarding practice location.[12] Although the Bureau of Health Resources Development claims it is impossible to obtain data on the effects of more recent federal practice-agreement and loan or scholarship programs on geographic location of health manpower,[13] the requirement of prior commitment to practice is expected to increase the success of federal loan programs.[14] This expectation is supported in part by the greater overall success of the state loan programs than of federal programs to date. Apparently, the practice obligation (regardless of length) combined with a forgiveness provision may be a stronger incentive to locate in rural practice than the simple forgiveness of loans for such location, even when buy-out options exist.

PROGRAM COST

Overall costs to operate practice-agreement/loan-forgiveness programs vary from program to program, depending on the level of funding available from the sponsoring agency and the length of program operation. Three of the programs, two state supported and one funded by a state medical society, provided enough financial data to permit calculation of average program expenditures per borrower for loan funds and administrative costs (see Table 4). These expenses are not strictly comparable and cannot be generalized to other programs; they are presented only to provide examples of program cost.

Table 4   Program Operating Expenses, Selected Programs and Years

	Minnesota (1952–1953 to 1972–1973)	Mississippi (1946–1965)	North Carolina (1946–1969)
Number of borrowers	26	674	964
Total amount loaned	$104,000	$2,481,190	$2,463,941
Total administrative expenses	10,000	207,525	310,325
Average loan per borrower	4,000	3,681	2,556
Average administrative expenses per borrower	385	308	322

SOURCE.   Based on information and estimates provided by the Minnesota State Association's Rural Family Practice Scholarship program; by Lucille Hardy, at the Board of Trustees of State Institutions of Higher Learning, for the Mississippi Medical Education Scholarship Loan Program; and by Janet Procter, Administrator, Educational Loan Program, State of North Carolina Department of Human Resources.

Total loans ranged from $2500 to $4000 per borrower, and administrative expenses per borrower ranged from $308 to $385. In comparison, the average loan to medical students from the federally sponsored Health Professions Educational Assistance Act from FY 1965 through FY 1969 was $1120, considerably smaller than that available from these three state programs. During those four years, almost $60 million was loaned to some 53,000 medical students by the federal government.[15] No information on the administrative expenses of the federal program was available. If, however, administrative costs are as low as for the state programs illustrated in Table 4, the annual costs would be between $4.5 and $5 million.

SECONDARY EFFECTS

Perhaps the confidence that something effective was being done to influence the location of physicians might be considered an undesirable secondary effect of these programs; otherwise, none is evident.

OVERALL IMPACT ON ACCESS TO PRIMARY CARE

Examination of 11 state practice-commitment/loan-forgiveness programs suggests that they have had limited success in locating small numbers of physicians in rural or medically underserved areas for short periods. Several were substantially more effective in achieving their short-term goals than others. Analysis of the data has, however, failed to isolate any factors conclusively related to their differential success. The availability of loan-forgiveness options for federal tuition loans has done little to date to encourage physicians to locate in rural areas, but further analyses are necessary.

Evidence to date suggests the following:

1. The decision to practice in a rural or shortage area, with subsequent cancellation of all or part of a tuition loan, may be related primarily to factors other than any agreement to practice in an area as a condition of receiving a loan, the size of the loan, and the ease of obtaining such forgiveness.
2. The availability of loans at the time of need and the subsequent availability of money to buy out of the practice commitment may be more important than options for forgiveness of the loan.
3. A commitment to practice in a shortage area, combined with a provision for forgiveness of the loan, may encourage practice repayment more than the option of forgiveness alone.

4. The option of "buying out" greatly reduces the effect of this incentive, since practice commitments are not legally binding.
5. The buy-out option may discriminate in that it seems to be most effective in coupling students with the greatest financial needs to communities with the least purchasing power.

Other factors in the success of these programs, such as the extent of prior disposition of borrowers toward locating their practices in rural areas, cannot be measured by the available data.

Experiences to date cannot predict the potential success of practice-commitment/loan-forgiveness programs on a national level, now being proposed as part of legislation to extend federal funding for medical education and to alter the geographic distribution of physicians. Data are based on loan programs that supply only a small portion of tuition to a few medical students. These programs certainly provide positive reinforcement for those medical students who intend to practice in rural and underserved areas of the United States.

If the tuitions paid by students, loans, and amounts potentially forgiveable were to increase to only twice their present levels, the relationships suggested above might no longer hold. What is clear and what has already been predicted is that the demand for loans, regardless of practice commitment or forgiveness features, will rise sharply if tuitions increase. Furthermore, elimination of buy-out options would obviously result in increased effectiveness of these programs in achieving their short-term goal of placing physicians for a defined period of time in shortage-area practice. The relation of the achievement of this short-term goal to the long-term goal of securing more permanent sources of care for these areas can only be speculated on at this time.

SUMMARY

The effectiveness of loan-forgiveness programs as a redistributive mechanism depends on many factors. The experiences of several state programs in placing recent graduates in nonurban areas have been variable. Almost nothing is known about their long-term effectiveness, that is, the extent to which physicians remain in these communities after their obligations have been met. In all probability, the effectiveness of a loan-forgiveness program depends on the degree to which the students involved are *predisposed* to practice in smaller communities. The effects of this intervention seem to be indirect and reinforce preexisting tendencies rather than directly affect students' plans. Buy-out options reduce the impact of the intervention considerably. Apparently, no legal actions have been recorded to date involving physicians who have defaulted on their obligation.

Despite this rather negative analysis, loan forgiveness could be an effective mechanism. The costs of medical education are enormous and seem likely to increase. The demand for loans among medical students (already high) will increase as tuitions are raised unless these costs are directly assumed by government. Practice-agreement/loan-forgiveness programs should become more effective as the financial stakes increase.

Their impact could be greatly amplified if *carefully* coupled to incentives for schools to accept a significant proportion of their students from among those with orientations toward practice in nonurban areas, and given the enormous pool of qualified applicants, this should be possible. Such incentives must be carefully constructed to avoid creating a dual system of admissions and passing on to the medical schools the onerous and difficult responsibility for enforcing and administering this effort. To cope with these problems a variety of mechanisms, ranging from volunteerism to regional lotteries for designated assignments, could be established.

Loan-forgiveness programs, in their past form, had limited promise; as part of a more nearly comprehensive policy for health manpower, they could be an effective and relatively inexpensive tool.

SIX

Rural Preceptorships:

IMPACT ON THE DECISION TO LOCATE IN RURAL PRACTICE

REASONS FOR DEVELOPMENT OF PROGRAMS

Considerable attention is being given to different ways of altering the urban–rural distribution of physicians and other health manpower. Rural preceptorship programs have been suggested as one means of affecting this distribution.

NATURE OF INTERVENTION

Preceptorships expose medical students to the delivery of ambulatory, nonhospital medical-care services within the context of a physician's practice and a particular community. These programs have been introduced into medical curricula for two related reasons, which have shifted in importance over time. Initially, this preceptorship was an alternative to in-hospital clinical rotations focusing on acute medicine, designed to sensitize students to the social parameters of illness. More recently, the location of this experience, as well as the type of practice, has taken on greater importance.[1] Exposure to general medical practice in rural or medically underserved areas is intended primarily to influence the decisions of participants about location of practice in favor of rural areas. Some influence on specialty choice is intended as well, since family practitioners make up the largest proportion of physicians in underserved and rural areas. If the preceptorship is an effective influence, increased numbers of physicians will locate in rural areas and thereby enhance the availability and accessibility of services to the residents.

Rural preceptorships, in themselves, represent "add-ons" to the medical-school curriculum; that is, as electives they offer to those interested an opportunity to participate in the provision of primary care in nonurban areas. They are *not* an *essential* part of the education of the medical student. The preceptorships or clerkships in smaller communities that are part of the decentralized medical-education effort of the Washington–Alaska–Montana–Idaho (WAMI) program based at Seattle are quite different. They are an integral and essential part of that unique educational effort. It is not appropriate, therefore, to compare the impact of such "preceptorships" to the traditional "add-on" experiences that bear this label.

SOURCES

Significant contributions to the background research for this case study came from unpublished sources, since the literature describing rural preceptorships and their effectiveness in encouraging rural practice location is not extensive. Several people assisted us in locating and making use of these sources.

Ellen Sax, at the Manpower Distribution Project, National Health Council, Inc., allowed us to use materials from files developed during the Project's ongoing survey of efforts to alter the distribution of health manpower. Particularly helpful were the responses from health professions schools to the second part of the survey, detailing efforts to influence the decisions of student health professionals about specialty and location of practice. During discussions in San Francisco and at National Health Council headquarters in New York, Ms. Sax suggested several other sources for this research and was first to call our attention to the unpublished studies based on the Rand–AMA 1972 survey of influences affecting location of practice of physicians graduating in 1965 from U.S. medical schools.

Bruce and Carolynn Steinwald, in the Health Programs Research Department, Center for Health Services Research and Development Department, American Medical Association, gave permission to use as resource material their unpublished study of the effects of preceptorship and rural-training programs on physicians' practice locations based on data from the Rand–AMA survey. Conversations at the Center in Chicago with Ms. Steinwald and with

John McFarland, also in the Health Programs Research Department, provided helpful insights into the literature and problems of studying physicians' decisions about location.

Karen Heald, research associate at the Rand Corporation based in Washington, D.C., provided a draft version of the final report on the Rand study of physician location for the Department of Health, Education, and Welfare (Contract HEW-OS-71-125), which includes analysis of the Rand–AMA survey results.

DESCRIPTION OF PROGRAMS

Characteristics of Rural Preceptorship Programs

Rural preceptorships train medical students under the tutelage of physicians in private practice, usually family practitioners. Many, but not all, of these preceptors are located in rural or medically underserved areas. The programs are most frequently offered as elective opportunities during the clinical (the last two) years of medical school.

Extent of Effort

The first significant move to incorporate preceptorships into medical curricula came in the 1920s, after establishment of the "Flexner curriculum." Their development, admittedly uneven, continued during the late 1940s and 1950s. In 1949, 13 medical schools offered preceptorships. This number increased to 21 in 1952, and to 27 by 1955. During this six-year period, 8 schools terminated preceptorships, 3 of which were later reinstated. Students participating in these programs numbered 400 in 1949, 700 one year later, and 1400 by 1955.[2]

During the 1960s and 1970s, preceptorships in rural or medically underserved areas have become common features of curricula in schools with a commitment to influence geographic distribution of health manpower.[3] By 1964, 34 of the 84 medical schools offered preceptorships, most as electives; 70 percent were in state-supported medical schools. Participation had, however, fallen off to 1000 students, 400 less than the number participating in 27 programs in 1955.[4] Review of information collected by the Manpower Distribution Project of the National Health Council, Inc., in response to their recent survey of ongoing efforts to affect manpower distribution in health professions schools, shows that at least 12 medical schools have initiated rural preceptorship/clerkship programs since 1964 and that several others contemplate introduction of such programs.[5] Participation rates for these newer programs were not available.

Federal support of efforts to redistribute health manpower dates from passage of the 1971 Comprehensive Health Manpower Training Act (P.L. 92–157). That act expanded the purposes of special projects grants authorized in 1966 and 1968 amendments to the Health Professions Educational Assistance Program to include assistance to schools developing programs to improve the distribution of manpower. It also added three new categories of assistance to the program, the principal one being a series of health-manpower educational-initiative awards to improve the distribution (by specialty and geography), supply, quality, utilization, and efficiency of health personnel.[6] Information from the Bureau of Health Resources Development, which administers the program, reveals that 69 medical and osteopathic schools have received federal support specifically for preceptorships in primary care or in rural and underserved areas, or both, since 1971.[7] Participation rates for these programs were not available.

EVIDENCE OF EFFECTIVENESS

Extent of Self-Evaluation by Preceptorship Programs

For all such programs, the chief detriment, as noted by the Steinwalds and others, is lack of evaluation of their influence on location of physicians. Several schools pointed out to the Manpower Distribution Project survey that evaluations are under way or planned. The extent to which the results of such evaluations are shared with other schools is unknown, but certainly very few have been made public. Available program descriptions generally focus on developmental problems: difficulties of integrating such an experience into the hospital clinical rotation period, of finding qualified practitioners to act as preceptors and coordinating them with the teaching institution and of framing educational objectives that can be both attained and measured. In most instances, outcome analysis has been limited to measurement of students' and preceptors' satisfaction with the program and of attainment of certain educational goals, such as descriptions of the range of ambulatory problems dealt with, understanding and use of community health-care referral systems, and appreciation of the social parameters of disease.[8–16]

Where concern over effects on geographic distribution is included, it is often presented in numbers of participants later located in or planning careers in rural areas or primary-care practice, or both. Any positive influence of preceptorship on such actions is presumed. For example, evaluations of the rural preceptorship program at the University of Washington, an elective clinical rotation in the family-medicine curriculum and the initial part of the WAMI experiment in regionalized medical education, have noted to date that 64 percent of the 97 students participating are pursuing primary-care careers (particularly family medicine) and that 6 percent are already in rural and small-town practice.[17]

Relationship of Participation in Rural Preceptorship Programs to Later Rural Location

Awareness of the many personal, professional, and community factors associated with physicians' decisions about location of practice makes isolating the singular influence of the preceptorship a complex exercise.[18-22] Two recent efforts have, however, been made to determine specifically the impact of preceptorship on later location.

SAMA–MECO Project

The Student American Medical Association (SAMA) has reviewed annually the experience of students participating in the SAMA–MECO (Medical Education and Community Orientation) Project, the preceptorship it has coordinated nationally since 1970. MECO was developed with a primary goal of redistributing physician manpower. Through this project, preceptorships based at community hospitals and group practices in nonurban settings are offered to students during summer between their preclinical and clinical years in medical school. The evaluations have concluded that "after participating in MECO and becoming aware of community-type medicine, the students are much more likely to consider community practice as a career possibility."[23] Upon questioning after participation, more than two-thirds of the participants in 1970 and 1971 expressed a desire to practice eventually in the same or similar communities; 89.5 percent of the 1972 group expressed a strong desire to do the same.[24-25]

The influence of the program on participant location was further explored in the 1971 analysis by comparing prior location plans to those held after participation. Before their preceptorship, 100 students intended to practice in the same state as that of their SAMA–MECO program; 22 planned practices in other states; and the majority, 212 students, had no plans for location of practice. After participation, 35 percent of those with no prior plans expressed a desire to return to the same community to practice; 61 of that group wanted to practice in the same or a similar community. Similar questions to the group as a whole found 41 percent desiring to return to the same community, and 65 percent, to the same or a similar community.[26] Preceptorship evidently made a sizable impact on the plans for practice location of those with no prior plans.

In 1972 SAMA investigated the location plans of the 70 student participants in the pilot MECO project of 1969, most of whom graduated from medical school in 1972; 34 responded. Of the 20 respondents who had chosen the type of area in which to locate, 1 had chosen Illinois (the state in which the 1969 project took place), and 15 had chosen rural, small, or medium-sized communities for future practice sites. Although their immediate pre- and post-preceptorship location plans are not included for comparison, the majority indicated that MECO experiences had had a significant effect on their choices.[27] It must be remembered, however, that participants in this program are self-selected and that intentions rather than behaviors are being measured, and the results must be interpreted accordingly.

Rand–AMA Survey of Influences on Location Decisions.   In 1972 the Rand Corporation, assisted by the American Medical Association, surveyed medical school graduates of 1965 ($N = 6978$), and the wives of the married male graduates, to investigate factors important in their decisions about location of practice. That class was chosen specifically to ensure that a large proportion of the graduates would have completed postgraduate training and military service if required and would have located their practices by the time of the survey. Of the 76.3 percent responding, 70.9 percent had made decisions about practice location ($N = 3773$). These physicians were either in nonfederal patient-care practice in fall 1972 or planned to be by September 1973 and were fairly certain of their practice location. There is no way to distinguish further those already located from those "fairly certain" of future locations.

Physicians were questioned about specialty, type of community chosen for practice, time of deciding location of practice, whether they had seriously considered rural location (for those who had chosen urban practice), and whether they had participated in rural training programs. The specific question on that participation read: "In your medical education or training, did you participate in a rural preceptorship program or other experimental rural health program?"[28] In addition, they were asked to check factors, from a list of 26, that had been important to them in making location decisions. These factors are listed below as they appeared on the questionnaire. Full analysis of the influence of participation in rural training programs on later practice location is enhanced by the availability of information for respondents on many other personal, professional, and community influences.

List of Twenty-six Factors Potentially Influential in Physician Location of Practice, Used in 1972 Rand/AMA Survey

1. Income potential
2. Climate or geographic features of area
3. Having been brought up in such a community
4. Payment of "forgiveness loan"
5. Influence of wife or husband (his/her desires, career, etc.)

6. Influence of family or friends
7. High medical need in area
8. Influence of preceptorship program
9. Having gone through medical school, internship, residence, military service near here
10. Advice of older physician
11. Organized efforts of community to recruit physicians
12. Opportunities for social life
13. Recreational and sports facilities
14. Quality of educational system for children
15. Prospect of being more influential in community affairs
16. Cultural advantages
17. Prosperity of community
18. Preference for urban or rural living
19. Availability of clinical support facilities and personnel
20. Availability of good social service, welfare, or home care services
21. Opportunity for regular contact with a medical school or medical center
22. Opportunity for regular contact with other physicians
23. Opportunity to join desirable partnership or group practice
24. Availability of loans for beginning practice
25. Opportunity to work with specific institution
26. Access to continuing education

SOURCE.   Physician Questionnaire, Survey of 1965 Medical School Graduates, in K. A. Heald, J. K. Cooper, and S. Coleman, *An Analysis of Two Surveys of Recent Medical School Graduates* (Washington, D.C., Rand Corporation, January 1974), Draft Appendix A.

The subgroup of these respondents on which the Steinwalds base their analysis are those physicians who had chosen practice locations *and* who answered the question relating to participation in rural training programs.[29] This subgroup represented 98.3 percent of all those who had made location decisions ($N = 3729$). Of this number, 17.8 percent had opted for rural practice; 13.1 percent had participated in rural preceptorships; and 33.5 percent were in or about to enter primary-care practice (see Table 5). The Steinwalds' findings for this subgroup of 1965 medical graduates are reviewed here along with additional information from the final report on the survey prepared at Rand.[30]

The Steinwalds point out several key attributes of the 482 participants in rural preceptorships who had chosen practice locations. They were more likely to have entered family practice than nonparticipants; nearly twice as many participants than nonparticipants were reared in rural areas; and those attending public (state-supported) medical schools were far more likely to have participated in rural programs (see Table 5).

The relationship of participation alone to later rural location being considered, participants were more likely to have chosen rural practice loca-

Table 5   Selected Characteristics of 1965 U.S. Medical School Graduates Who Had Made Practice Location Decisions as of 1972 and Provided Information on Participation in Rural Training Programs, and of Rural Program Participants (in percent)

Characteristics	Graduates for Whom Location and Participation Information Was Available (N = 3729)	Rural Program Participants (N = 482)
Specialty		
General and family practice	13.2	22.4
Internal medicine	17.0	12.0
Pediatrics	7.0	7.3
Obstetrics and gynecology	7.8	8.3
Surgery	27.0	22.8
Psychiatry	9.0	7.3
Hospital based[a]	14.3	15.6
Other	4.7	4.3
	100.0	100.0
Primary care	33.5	41.3
Nonprimary care	66.5	58.7
	100.0	100.0
Practice type		
Group practice	13.3	16.6
Nongroup practice	86.7	83.4
	100.0	100.0

SOURCE.   Bruce Steinwald and Carolynn Steinwald, *The Effect of Preceptorship and Rural Training Programs on Physicians' Location Decisions* (Chicago: AMA Center for Health Services Research and Development, draft, 1973), Table 2, p. 9.
[a] Includes anesthesiology, radiology, and pathology.

Table 5   (*Continued*)

Characteristics	Graduates for Whom Location and Participation Information Was Available (N = 3729)	Rural Program Participants (N = 482)
Practice location		
Urban location	82.2	72.3
Rural location	17.8	27.7
	100.0	100.0
Place of rearing		
Urban reared	75.9	56.8
Rural reared	24.1	43.2
	100.0	100.0
Time of location decision		
Before medical school	13.4	10.9
During medical school	7.5	11.8
After medical school	79.1	77.3
	100.0	100.0
Type of medical school attended		
Private school	51.1	24.3
Public school	48.9	75.7
	100.0	100.0

tions than nonparticipants (27.7 percent versus 16.3 percent).[31] They were also slightly more likely to acknowledge its influence on their decisions (4.7 percent versus 2.6 percent). Of the 134 participants actually locating in rural areas (27.8 percent of all participants), 20.1 percent stated that their participation was influential in their decision.[32]

Relationship of Intervening Variables to Participation in Rural Preceptorship Programs and to Later Rural Location

The bias of self-selection for those who elected rather than were required to serve such preceptorships cannot be either dismissed or assessed. As the Steinwalds demonstrate in their analysis, it is virtually impossible to separate completely the effects of participation in rural preceptorships from other factors that may increase the likelihood of choice of rural practice. Since information on several of those factors is available for the subgroup of Rand–AMA survey respondents whose experience in rural preceptorships is under consideration, their combined impact on rural location can be studied. The five intervening variables isolated for discussion in the Steinwalds' analysis are as follows: (1) place of rearing (primary place of residence up to age 18); (2) specialty type; (3) time of decision to locate practice; (4) type of practice chosen (group versus nongroup); and (5) urban physicians who considered rural practice locations.

Place of Rearing.   Participation was found to have a notably different association with later rural location, depending on place of rearing. Of the rural-reared physicians, 36.7 percent of participants, as compared to 34.9 percent of nonparticipants, located in rural practice. This suggests that factors other than participation influenced the location decisions of rurally reared physicians. Physicians growing up in urban areas present a very different picture: 20.7 percent of urban-reared participants, as opposed to 11.2 percent of the urban-reared nonparticipants, chose rural practice locations, a difference significant by Chi-square analysis at the .01 percent level.[33]

Specialty Type.   Interestingly enough, the influence of participation appears to be particularly strong for urban-reared nonprimary-care physicians: 19.2 percent of these participants located in rural practice as compared to 9.2 percent of nonparticipants with the same characteristics.[34] This is a striking finding, for urban rearing and nonprimary-care specialty practice are generally considered factors predisposing to urban practice location. Indeed, place of rearing was found to be strongly predictive of urban location, as were several professional considerations, such as nearby training and contact with medical centers, which were frequently concerns of specialists.[35] Further analysis to explain this finding was not done.

Primary-care physicians were more likely to have participated in rural training programs than all respondents (16.2 percent versus 13.0 percent),[36] and participants later practicing primary care were more likely to locate in rural than urban areas (32.7 percent versus 12.8 percent).[37]

Time of Decision to Locate Practice.   Analysis of the times at which this group of respondents had decided to locate in urban or rural areas showed that the majority had made their decision *after* medical school (see Table 5). The results are, however, somewhat different for rural program participants when considered separately. Although a positive association was found for each decision time (before, during, and after medical school) and participation, the strongest association exists for those participants deciding to locate in rural areas *prior* to medical school.[38] This further supports the Steinwalds' inference that many rural preceptorship participants are predisposed to rural practice before this exercise, a fact that may be related to selection of this experience when it is an elective.

The primary-care respondents were also more likely to have decided on a rural location before or during medical school, suggesting that participation may have had some influence on their choices. In fact, a larger proportion of primary-care physicians acknowledged the influence of participation in rural training programs on their location decision than all graduates did (3.4 percent versus 2.6 percent).[39] Rural primary-care physicians were more likely to state its influence than urban primary-care physicians (7.6 percent as opposed to 2.0 percent),[40] a tendency that tends to support this inference. The extent of acknowledged influence is, however, low for all subgroups.

Type of Practice.   The Steinwalds considered the relationship between choice of group or nongroup practice and preceptorship participation in a rural location in their evaluation, for creation of rural-group practices is a policy alternative frequently mentioned as enhancing the desirability of rural practice. Although nongroup practice was the choice of far more respondents, a strong association was noted between all group practitioners and rural practice: 25.2 percent of group practitioners had chosen rural practice over 16.6 nongroup practitioners in rural areas.[41] This association was even stronger for those who participated in preceptorships and subsequently chose rural locations: 43.6 percent of them chose group practice in rural areas, as compared to 21.6 percent of nonparticipants who chose rural-group practice, significant at the .01 level.[42] The opportunity to join a desirable partnership or group practice figured prominently among the factors mentioned as influences on decisions: 56.6 percent of all respondents noted it, making it the fifth most frequent factor listed.[43]

Urban Physicians Who Considered Rural Practice Location.   Finally, analysis was directed at the physicians in this group who had seriously considered rural location before locating in urban practice. These physicians are regarded, in both the Rand and Steinwald analyses, to be probably those most readily influenced by efforts encouraging physicians to enter rural practice. It was discovered that 44.1 percent of all urban-located physicians had seriously considered rural practice; 63.7 percent of preceptorship participants subsequently locating in urban areas had done so. Furthermore, for participants who located in urban areas, location of rearing and specialty choice made little difference on whether they considered rural practice; preceptorship may well have been a significant influence on their considerations.[44]

Factors Associated with Effectiveness
of Rural Preceptorship Programs

It seems clear from the foregoing discussion that the success of rural preceptorships in influencing participants to locate in rural areas may relate more
closely to the characteristics of the participants themselves than to any direct
influence of the program. In particular, participants who grew up in rural
areas, who are interested in primary-care practice, and/or who have already
decided on rural-practice location enhance a program's "success rate," since
they are more likely to locate in rural areas than other participants and than
nonparticipants.

Not enough data are available yet to permit us to compare and contrast individual rural preceptorships in terms of program features, holding constant the
characteristics of their participants. Until such information becomes available,
program features that enhance the program's influence on later location will
remain unknown.

PROGRAM COST

Since passage of the Comprehensive Health Manpower Training Act in 1971,
the federal government has supported 69 rural preceptorship or primary-care
training programs, or both, in schools of medicine and osteopathy. The amount
of support through the end of the 1973 academic year totaled just more than
$11.7 million, an average of almost $17,000 per program during the interval,
or about $8500 per program per year.[45] Because the number of students par-
ticipating in these programs is not known, no estimate of the cost per student
can be made.

Rough estimates have been developed for the cost per student participating in
the University of Washington's rural preceptorship in family practice. The
program pays instructional costs for the time of physicians and staff in the
preceptorship unit. These are negotiated on the basis of experience showing
that the preceptor loses about 1.5 hours of each productive day while instruct-
ing the student. The program reimburses the physicians for the overhead for
that time at the rate of about $20 per hour. Thus, the instructional costs for the
program over a nine-month period, on the assumption that two students are in
the program full time, come to approximately $17,000, or about $8500 per
full-time student equivalent. Since individual students are in the program for
six-week periods, the program estimates instructional costs for individual
students at about $1400.

In addition to instructional costs, the program has also undertaken to pay for
rental of student housing in the community, transportation for students to the

community and back to school, transportation for faculty site visits, and some equipment on a start-up basis. Including these items, each unit costs from $25,000 to $35,000 annually. With each unit handling two full-time student equivalents, the overall cost per full-time equivalent approaches $12,000 to $15,000 annually.[46]

SECONDARY EFFECTS

Somewhat unintended secondary effects have stemmed from the advocacy of rural preceptorships in certain schools. With the expansion of medical science and increased demands for time and curriculum, many preceptorship experiences have been identified as "expendable," unless specific educational objectives can be identified for such programs. Frequently, the specification of these objectives requires a reexamination of the preceptors involved in the program. For example, many rural preceptors are highly qualified general practitioners who are the only physician in a community of less than 5000 and are also extremely visible in medical-society politics within the state.

A suggestion that preceptorships should follow "delivery system trends" and be located in somewhat larger communities (5000 to 20,000) and in group practices has created political problems for medical-school administrations. Without more nearly definitive descriptions of preceptors, their location, and data about these programs than are available, one can only speculate about the prevalence of this problem or the degree to which it may be of future concern to the deans of medical schools.

OVERALL IMPACT ON ACCESS TO PRIMARY CARE

Rural preceptorship appears to have some influence on later rural-practice location for most participants, or at least *reinforces* prior tendencies toward rural location. Evaluations of the SAMA–MECO preceptorships show the immediate impact of the program, perhaps in combination with other factors, on participants' location *plans* and suggest its apparent continuing effect over time. The Rand–AMA survey, which investigated influences on physician location close to the actual time of location, further documents the continued influence of preceptorship on location decisions.

This influence or reinforcement appears to be particularly strong for urban-reared physicians and for that group choosing primary-care specialties. For participants later entering urban practice, preceptorship apparently encourages their serious consideration of rural practice while making location decisions but is outweighed by personal and professional considerations.

These analyses point up two factors important in determining the impact of preceptorship participation and later location on relieving access problems related to uneven geographic distribution of physicians: small numbers of medical students are ever exposed to preceptorship, and despite participation's having been a predictor of later rural location,[47] *few participants either perceive or credit its influence on their later location decisions.* Of the subgroup of respondents ($N = 3728$) to the Rand–AMA survey whose preceptorship and later location were reviewed, only 13.1 percent had ever participated in rural-training programs, and only 2.6 percent stated that participation in a rural preceptorship had influenced their decision on location practice.[48] Although these specific proportions clearly apply only to the survey respondents, there is little to indicate they are not suggestive of overall medical-student exposure to preceptorships, particularly since participation rates appear to be decreasing as these programs are reclassified as senior "electives."

These facts offer support for the conclusion that rural preceptorships in themselves have not increased the numbers of physicians in rural practice. There are definite areas of potential influence on particular groups of student physicians, but since numbers participating thus far have been so small, the experience cannot be said to have significant impact on relieving access problems in medically underserved areas. Newly operating programs, with an apparently stronger emphasis on redistributive goals than many of those operating before 1965, may have more of an impact, particularly if participation rates can be increased. Until the impact of specific or more current programs, or both, can be investigated, the conclusions and inferences drawn from the available data must be taken into consideration by proponents of rural preceptorships as a redistributive device. Such consideration need not lead to termination of such programs, since they undoubtedly have educational value and can reinforce interests in rural practice for some students.

SUMMARY

Rural preceptorships have existed for many years. The number of schools offering such experiences has increased and the number of participants has decreased as these experiences have become elective rather than required. They have always represented "add-ons" to, rather than integral parts of, the medical curriculum.

As such, it should not be surprising that the meager evidence suggests that they reinforce preexisting orientations toward rural practice. They seem to have little direct effect on decisions regarding location of practice. The early experiences from a decentralized effort in medical education, the Washington–Alaska–Montana–Idaho (WAMI) program, point out the differences that may be achieved when such experiences are an essential *part* of a global educational policy.

Preceptorships, as presently constituted, represent marginal efforts that deserve to be available for students with appropriate interests. They should not be expected to alter the effects of a system of education–socialization that emphasizes institution-based specialized medical practice.

SEVEN

Family Practice:

THE PRIMARY-CARE SPECIALTY

REASONS FOR DEVELOPMENT OF PROGRAMS

Decline of the Generalist

The continued reduction in the numbers of general or family physicians in the United States over the past quarter of a century has been well documented and much deplored. For a variety of reasons discussed at length elsewhere, the number of physicians choosing careers in specialty and subspecialty practice has increased and the number entering general practice has declined, resulting in a drastic reduction in the total number of practicing general physicians.[1] This trend began in the mid-1940s, and recent figures illustrate its continuing severity. Between 1968 and 1973, the number of physicians in general or family practice decreased by almost 2000 annually. This rate was twice as high in urban areas as in rural areas.[2]

This decline has been not only in numbers, although that is the most pressing public concern, but in professional stature as well. Increasing specialization has resulted in identification of the generalist by what he lacks—advanced training and specialty certification—rather than by whatever unique knowledge and capabilities he brings to the provision of care. Because of decreasing numbers, many of his functions have been assumed by so-called primary-care specialists—internists, pediatricians, obstetrician–gynecologists, and surgeons who do not restrict their practices to the subspecialty concerns of their respective fields. Defined by default and without a unique or separate field of clinical knowledge and practice, the general or family physician, once the mainstay of American medical practice, was fast becoming an anachronism of his own profession.[3]

Impact on Health-Services Delivery

The seriousness of this decline and its impact on health-care delivery were clearly evident to the public and to the medical profession by the late 1950s. By then, it was becoming more difficult to secure the services usually provided by the family physician: first-contact care, point of entry to other health-care services, and continuity of care across illness episodes—all provided with an understanding of the patient's family and social context. As a result, health-care services were described more and more frequently as fragmented, episodic, impersonal, disease-oriented, inaccessible, and too complex. The need for providers of family, primary, or personal medical-care services (the terms are often used interchangeably) was obvious. Huntly described the centrality of their role in health-services delivery:

. . . the adequacy of care available from the family physician, and his sense of responsibility, will in large measure determine the effectiveness with which the whole structure of medical care serves the patient.[4]

Failure of Initial Attempt to Upgrade Residency Training

The earliest attempt to halt the decline of the family physician focused on creating opportunities for more extensive and intensive training for such practitioners. Before World War II, the postgraduate training for most general practitioners was a one-year rotating internship. A few hospitals offered a two-year residency in general practice that resembled the rotating internship in structure and content. Believing this type of preparation inadequate for the general practitioner of the future, the American Medical Association's House of Delegates established in 1956 a committee to "analyze and make recommendations as to the best background preparation today for general practice." A second charge directed the committee to "give full consideration to the importance of a broad background of training and experience for all physicians in the care of the patient as a whole, and of the family as a unit."

The committee, composed of representatives of the AMA's Council on Medical Education and Hospitals, the Association of American Medical Colleges, the American Academy of General Practice (AAGP), and of specialty societies, made its final report in June 1959. Although recognizing the changes in medical knowledge and practice and the marked trend toward limited specialty practice, the committee noted a continuing need for provision of comprehensive care over broad areas of medicine to patients of all ages. To prepare physicians to meet the future demands of that role, the committee considered two possible approaches: (1) designing new, high-quality graduate programs specifically for the preparation of family physicians and (2) broadening the training available in existing residencies in internal medicine. Although the program proposed in the final report dealt with the former, the committee urged consideration of the second approach, arguing that it might be advantageous to develop both simultaneously.

Minimal course requirements for the proposed graduate program included a basic 18-month rotation in medicine and pediatrics, at least 4 months in obstetrics–gynecology for those who planned to include it in their office practices, continuous and extensive exposure to ambulatory and outpatient care, and regular periods of emergency service, including minor surgery. Physicians who planned to undertake more than uncomplicated obstetrical procedures or minor surgery were expected to take additional advanced training.[5]

After the committee's recommendations, the House of Delegates approved establishment of 20 pilot family-practice programs in June 1959. The following June, the House agreed to consider for approval other two-year programs that included a required rotation in surgery and an elective obstetrics–gynecology rotation in addition to the basic medicine and pediatrics services. To distinguish these latter programs from existing general-practice residencies (those resembling extended rotating internships) and the newly recommended family-practice programs, they were termed "general-practice programs."[6]

The experience of these pilot family-practice programs during the decade following their recommendation is summarized in Table 6. In the mid-1960s, 17 of the authorized 20 pilot programs were in operation, an average of 5 residency positions being offered by each. The American Medical Association commented on their status in its 1963–1964 report on graduate medical education, noting that ". . . because of their pilot status, the program directors have been reluctant to substitute these programs entirely for their other existing internships, and thus the available positions per program have remained small."[7] Inability to fill a majority of available residency positions made expansion of the programs seem unwise. By the mid-1960s, they were still unable to fill more than half of the available positions, and plans were made to decrease the size of future programs. Affiliation with teaching hospitals did not affect the

Table 6 Experience of Pilot Family-Practice and General-Practice Programs, 1960–1969[a]

Year	Approved Programs	Positions Offered	Percent Filled
1960–1961	5	11	9.1
1961–1962	9	30	20.0
1962–1963	14	29	62.1
1963–1964	17	52	51.9
1964–1965	14	72	51.4
1965–1966	17	81	54.3
1966–1967	17	85	42.4
1967–1968	16	75	48.0
1968–1969[b]	—	—	—

SOURCES. American Medical Association, "Thirty-fifth through Forty-third Reports on Graduate Medical Education, Inclusive," *Journal of the American Medical Association* **186:**671 and Table 20 (1963); **190:**621 (1964); **194:**765 (1965); **198:**875 (1966); **202:**764 (1967); **206:**2025 (1968).

[a] All program data are as of September 1 in the academic year noted.
[b] Programs were being discontinued by the end of 1967–1968, or converting to the new three-year family practice residency programs.

proportions of positions filled or vacant during those years for which data are available.

Apparently, their status as pilot programs adversely affected the ability of these 17 programs to secure more than tentative support in teaching centers and hospital programs, in comparison to established internships and residencies in other fields. This, in turn, may well have contributed to the recruitment problems encountered. The pilot programs may also have failed, as Haggerty has suggested, since they did not "demonstrate decisively what it is that the family physician can do better than the specialist."[8] Dr. Robert Graham, Assistant Director, Division of Education, American Academy of Family Physicians, confirms Haggerty's analysis, noting that, despite the ambitious educational objectives outlined in the program proposals, the clinical and educational experiences offered by the pilot programs actually differed very little from those of rotating internships and general-practice residencies.[9]

The Specialty Issue

With the acknowledgment that the pilot programs were unsuccessful in attracting and producing adequately trained primary-care physicians so badly needed, efforts were renewed in the mid-1960s to develop programs that would fulfill the original objective. An additional objective, enhancing the professional status of the family physician, figured prominently in these discussions. Renewal of the generalist's role in medical-care delivery was not to imply a simple return to past values and models. The generalist had to "come of age." As Silver put it, succinctly: "Efforts to restore the general practitioner are wholly against the current of modern medical knowledge and scientific development. We must create a situation in which one of the specialties will be family practice."[10]

A major catalyst in the development of support within the medical profession for such a specialty was the 1966 report of the AMA Council on Medical Education's Ad Hoc Committee on Education for Family Practice, better known as the Willard Report. This Committee noted other specialists' neglect of preventive medicine, of personal health maintenance, and of the impact of social, environmental, and psychological factors on health in their delivery of care. It also pointed to the lack of effectiveness of the pilot family-practice programs. To correct the situation, the report called for a new *specialist,* educated to provide comprehensive, personal health services; and for augmentation of the numbers of physicians, particularly the number and proportion of physicians practicing family medicine.[11] At almost the same time, the report of the Citizen's Commission on Graduate Medical Education, chaired by John S. Millis, was issued. Assessing the situation in terms similar to those used in the Willard Report, the Millis committee also called for more physicians trained to deliver primary-care services.[12]

Opinion on specialty status for family practice was by no means as united as these reports might have implied. Many physicians believed strongly that the type of medicine practiced by the generalist was anachronistic to developments in contemporary medicine, regardless of its designation as a "specialty." Others supporting this view argued further that there was no area of clinical expertise that the family practitioner could claim as his particular province. This question of delineating clinical "boundaries" was of particular concern to surgeons, who objected to the family physician's practice of general surgery without completing the training required of those specializing in that field.

These objections were not (and have not been) completely overcome as the effort to develop training programs in family practice moved forward. Answering them became, however, a secondary concern as other events made recognition of family medicine as a specialty more likely. The passage of legislation creating Medicare and Medicaid resulted in rapid increase in the public's effective demand for all types of medical-care services. That demand exposed major limitations in the ability of the delivery system to respond with the necessary services, particularly primary-care services. State legislators, faced by constituencies without physicians, and by appropriations bills for state medical schools that produced everything but an adequate supply of family doctors, began to demand a return on their investments. In addition, an increasing number of medical students, concerned that medicine should be more responsive to public demands, began to express an interest in practicing family or "community" medicine and called for educational preparation in these fields.

In response to these forces, and to untold "politicking" within the organized medical profession, family practice was recognized as the 20th medical specialty field by the American Medical Association's House of Delegates in February 1969. In the following year, the American Academy of General Practice proposed changing its name to the American Academy of Family Physicians, a change that became official in 1971.

NATURE OF INTERVENTION

Attempts to increase the number of primary-care physicians represent an extremely complex intervention into the incompletely understood process of medical education. Family practice was recognized as a specialty for a variety of reasons. As previously indicated, the need to enhance the prestige of this type of practice was important to many. This step also created and formalized postgraduate residency training sequences of known quality for those planning careers in this field.

Most students, however, make decisions about postgraduate training long before graduation from medical school. This decision-making process is influenced by the students' prior interests, backgrounds, personalities, and school experiences. These experiences are not limited to course work but are also related to the impact of role models that are the students' personal embodiments of a certain type of practitioner.

Proponents of family practice have long recognized the political realities created by the departmental structure of medical schools. As a result, considerable effort has been expended in creating separate departments of family practice. These entities have their own faculty members (role models), budgets, space, and representation on the various committees in the school concerned with curriculum, research, and the like. To date, less attention has been paid to the importance of the selection of students with orientations toward primary care, perhaps because there are fewer objective data on this topic and because the issue is so sensitive.

Thus, a variety of interventions have occurred and are occurring. These differ both in their nature (creation of a department or a residency program) and scope (national, state, or local). Nationally, a specialty board has been created. Legislation that would have provided special funding for departments and programs training primary-care physicians was passed but vetoed. Considerable legislation that would stimulate schools to create departments, programs, and courses to encourage students to enter this type of practice is now pending. National foundations have given grants to support different models for training such physicians. Professional associations, such as the American Academy of Family Physicians and the Student American Medical Association, have mounted promotional campaigns and extracurricular programs to involve students in primary care.

Many state legislatures have mandated creation of departments of family practice and residency training programs at tax-supported medical schools. These and other states have also provided funding for the developing programs. Within medical schools different approaches have been employed to sensitize students to family practice, some beginning in the first week of medical school.

The rapid rate of development of these interventions and the number of permutations and combinations that exist make it impossible to inventory or classify those now occurring. This inability to describe in detail the specific approaches used in different settings makes it impossible to assess the relative effectiveness of each one. Of the interventions described, only the development of residency programs is subject to partial assessment, in terms of time lapsed and the availability of data. The subsequent sections deal primarily, therefore, with effects of *residency training programs* on access to primary care. Because of the importance of undergraduate educational efforts, these are discussed briefly, without reference to their demonstrated (or potential) impact.

SOURCES

Since family medicine is of current importance to medical education and health-services policy, a review of the literature provided many of the sources used in this case study. Suggestions for additional sources and information regarding the issues behind development of the specialty came from personal conversations with Thomas L. Stern, M.D., Director, Division of Education, American Academy of Family Physicians (fomerly Director, Residency in Family Practice, Santa Monica Hospital, Santa Monica, California), and with Robert Graham, M.D., Assistant Director of the AAFP's Division of Education. Information on the status of family-medicine programs at the graduate and undergraduate levels came from the American Academy of Family Physicians, the American Medical Association's Council on Medical Education, and annual reports on medical education published in the *Journal of the American Medical Association*.

DESCRIPTION OF PROGRAMS

Requirements for Residency Training

Core contents for residency programs in each specialty are recommended by the American Medical Association in the *Essentials of Approved Residencies*. The requirements for family-practice residencies aim to enable the family physician "to fill a unique and specific functional role in the delivery of modern comprehensive health services." The definition used in the *Essentials* describes that role as follows, identifying the family physician as one who

1. serves as the physician of first contact with the patient and provides a means of entry into the health care system;
2. evaluates the patient's total health needs, provides personal medical care within one or more fields of medicine, and refers the patient when indicated to appropriate sources of care while preserving the continuity of his care;
3. develops a responsibility for the patient's comprehensive and continuous health care and when needed acts as a coordinator of the patient's health services; and
4. accepts responsibility for the patient's total health care, including the use of consultants, within the context of his environment, including the community and the family or comparable social unit.[13]

With such a role in mind, residency requirements identify six areas in which clinical preparation is necessary for the family physician during a three-year residency following graduation from medical school. A major part of the program is devoted to family medicine, practiced in a "model family-practice unit." The unit, a clinical service geared to the medical needs of the patient population rather than to the particular skills of the physician, serves as a base of operations for the resident. It enables him to accumulate a panel of patients for whom he can provide and coordinate comprehensive care during his training period. Basic to the clinical preparation of the family-practice resident is experience in general internal medicine, pediatrics, and psychiatry. In addition to these clinical foundations, it is recommended that the resident acquire skill in management of antepartum and postpartum obstetric care and in medical and office gynecology, competence in recognizing surgical emergencies, and technical proficiency in performing the surgical procedures required from a physician of first contact. (Residents planning to include more obstetrics–gynecology or surgery in their practices are cautioned to obtain further training in those specialty areas.) Community medicine, the sixth area, is termed one of the unique components of family medicine. A background in this field is required to give the physician an understanding of the principles of epidemiology and environmental health, and a familiarity with the organization of community health resources.[14]

Undergraduate Programs

Most programs offer clerkships or preceptorships in family practice during the last two or three years of medical school, most frequently on an elective basis.

In many family-medicine programs, the faculty are an integral part of under-graduate teaching as well, participating in such interdisciplinary courses as "Introduction to Clinical Medicine" and "Physical Diagnosis."[15] Beyond this description, developed by the AMA Council on Medical Education during a survey of family medicine programs at university medical schools in 1972 and 1973, there has not been a systematic assessment of the content of programs, their educational objectives, methods of teaching, or number of hours of teaching time.

EXTENT OF EFFECTIVENESS

Graduate Programs

Since family practice achieved specialty status in 1969, development of residency programs has proceeded rapidly. As illustrated in Table 7 the period 1968–1969 was transitional, as the pilot family-practice programs were phased out or converted to three-year family-practice residencies, and these new residency programs qualified for AMA approval. Development of the new programs also accelerated the decline in numbers of two-year general-practice resi-

Table 7   Experience of Three-Year Family-Practice Residencies, 1970–1974[a,b]

Year	Approved Programs	Positions Offered	Positions Filled (%)	Positions Filled by U.S. or Canadian Graduates (%)	Positions to be Offered 2 Years Later
1970–1971	62	548	48.4	89.1	1024
1971–1972	103	1109	57.0	89.2	1877
1972–1973	151	1755	59.3	88.3	2701
1973–1974	164	NA		90.8	NA

SOURCES. 1970–1971 through 1972–1973 data: American Medical Association, "Forty-fourth through Forty-sixth Annual Reports on Graduate Medical Education, Inclusive," *Journal of the American Medical Association* **218:**1235 (1971); **222:**98 (1972); and **226:**929 (1973). The 1973–1974 data from: American Academy of Family Physicians, "Final results: Survey of Family Practice Residency Programs, July 1973," AAFP Reprint 614A (August 29, 1973).
[a] Pre-1970 data not available, since the American Medical Association did not tabulate family-practice residencies separately in 1968–1969, during which year the first few were established, and did not publish an annual report on graduate medical education during 1969–1970.
[b] Program data for 1970–1971 through 1972–1973 as of September 1 in the academic year noted; data for 1973–1974 as of July 1973.

Table 8 Status of Programs in Family Medicine at 113 University Medical Schools, May 1974 (Including Four Two-Year Schools)

Status of Program			Number of Schools
Operating formal program			70
Graduate and undergraduate		63	
Department	42		
Division	21		
Undergraduate only		6	
Graduate only		1	
Operating informal program			2
(training available only through programs at affiliated hospitals, both are considering development of formal program at university)			
Developing Program			4
Program under active consideration			19
(educational level unspecified)			
No action known			18
Total:			113

SOURCE.   American Academy of Family Physicians, *Medical School Family Practice Programs.* Reprint No. 164 (May 2, 1974).

dencies. The exact numbers of pilot programs and rotating general-practice programs that have converted to three-year family-practice residencies and received AMA approval are unknown.

Seven years after the Willard Committee's report, the AMA's Council on Medical Education surveyed 110 four-year medical schools to "assess the progress being made in the preparation of physicians for Family Practice." Graduate programs had been established in fewer than one-third of the schools, chiefly within the previous three years. The newer programs were usually administered by free-standing departments of family practice/medicine. Eleven other schools were developing programs; whether these were at the graduate or undergraduate level was not known. Thirty-eight schools had made no commitment to family medicine at the graduate level.

Development of graduate programs at university medical schools continued more rapidly in the next two years, with only a small number still not committed to or considering a family-practice graduate program by 1974. The American Academy of Family Physicians reviewed the status of family-medicine programs in 113 university medical schools (including 4 two-year schools) as of May 1974. Those data are summarized in Table 8. By that date, more than half of the schools had graduate training programs in the new specialty. Two were developing residency programs at their university medical centers, and another two, affiliated only with residency programs at outside hospitals, were considering programs at their own hospitals. Many of the remaining schools were actively considering inclusion of family-medicine programs in their curricula also, although the educational level was not specified.

A majority of the schools with graduate training programs administered them through free-standing departments of family medicine. Whereas programs in the remaining schools had divisional status, many were operated in a quasi-departmental fashion, rather than as divisions within clinical departments. In at least 44 states, legislative action had been taken to require development of family-practice programs in state-supported medical schools or to offer financial aid to the new programs, or both.[16]

About a third of the 211 programs approved as of May 1974 were located in university medical centers. Military hospitals sponsored 13 programs, and the remainder were in other hospitals. Approximately a third to a half of the programs in other hospitals were affiliated with those run by university medical centers, although the exact number cannot be determined from available listings.[17]

As indicated in Table 7, family-practice residency programs have had success in filling the residency positions offered. Almost 90 percent of these trainees are graduates of United States and Canadian medical schools.

The full extent of their success is not completely revealed in these figures; however, the figures in Table 7 are based on the total number of residency positions approved for all years of the programs. Many programs in early status of development have available posts in all three years but actually attempt to fill only their first-year positions. Data on first-year residency positions offered for July 1973 reflect more accurately the extent of these programs' success in attracting physicians. A total of 874 first-year resident positions were offered by the 145 approved programs in operation; 756, or 86 percent, were filled.[18]

There is no one curriculum identifiable as "the" family-practice residency program. The basics of each approved program necessarily conform to those outlined in the *Essentials*. One thing common to almost all the programs is the development and operation of a model family-practice unit, usually apart from the existing outpatient clinics.[19] The specific preparation offered by each program varies considerably, as recommended in the *Essentials,* depending on the particular strengths of each school or hospital and the identified health-care problems of patients seen in the model family-practice units.[20]

Undergraduate Programs

According to the data for 1972 and 1973 reported by the Council on Medical Education, more schools were involved in some type of education in family medicine at the undergraduate rather than the graduate level. Forty-nine schools had formal family-medicine programs, 33 at both undergraduate and graduate levels and another 16 at the undergraduate level only. In a majority of these schools, the undergraduate clerkships in family medicine were offered as electives. Most of these had experienced recent increases in the number of students selecting these options.[21] Another 10 schools offered some kind of elective clerkship or preceptorship in family medicine at the undergraduate level, although they did not have operating programs.

By 1974, 61 schools had undergraduate programs in family medicine, most still offering them as elective opportunities. Fifty-five of the schools with graduate programs included family medicine in undergraduate curricula, and 7 schools with residency programs were developing programs at the undergraduate level. Another 6 schools offered family medicine to undergraduates only, although 2 of them were currently developing residency programs. As with graduate programs, the majority of the undergraduate programs were based in departments or divisions of family medicine.

Specialty Boards

A major step in the recognition of family practice as a specialty was the establishment of a specialty board in that field, offering the family physician the opportunity to become board certified in a particular area of clinical and medical expertise. Development of the American Board of Family Practice (ABFP), which began in 1968, was undertaken by what was then the American Academy of General Practice in cooperation with members of other specialty boards.

The first examination for the Board was held in September 1970. It has been given annually since then. The 3286 physicians who passed the first two board examinations became charter diplomates of the ABFP. Another 1284 physicians were certified in April 1972, bringing the total of Board-certified family-medicine specialists to 4750.[22] Although the numbers of those passing the two most recent examinations were not available, it is known that there were more than 7000 fellows of the ABFP by October 1973; fellows must attain diplomate status in family medicine or complete more than 600 hours of accredited continuing education.[23] Physicians registering for the earliest examinations had generally received training in the two-year pilot or rotating general-practice residencies, or in one-year rotating internships. Increasing numbers of those sitting for the more recent examinations have completed three-year residency programs in family medicine.

Unlike other specialty boards, the ABFP requires that diplomates be periodically recertified. Every six years, diplomates will be tested on medical advances since they last took the examination, must offer proof of continuing education in the interim, and must submit to a medical audit of their office and hospital practices. The recertification process is now in the planning stages. It will be implemented in 1976, when the initial groups to be certified are scheduled for reexamination.

None of these process or throughput measures—number of diplomates, programs, residents, students—indicate the impact of these efforts on access to primary care. If these trends continue, there should be a gradual and significant increase in the number of primary-care services available. These programs are not, however, designed in themselves to affect productivity of physicians, their geographic distribution, or other barriers preventing access to care.

PROGRAM COST

Estimates of the funding required to support a three-year residency program of average size (12 residents) for one year place costs at approximately $20,000 per resident, for a total annual cost per program of $250,000. This estimate uses an average annual resident salary of $12,305, based on 1973 data, plus an average administrative cost per resident of $7500. These administrative costs for faculty and secretarial support, secretarial supplies, and office equipment amortized over a three-year period are estimated by use of a minimal figure of one full-time equivalent teacher–administrator for every six residents. This also assumes adequate volunteer faculty support. Basic administrative costs for a program with 1 to 6 residents are estimated to be $48,000. A program supporting from 6 to 12 residents would require the basic sum plus an additional $8000 for each resident above the original 6. With these figures, programs having from 12 to 18 residents might expect to incur administrative costs of $90,000 for the first 12 residents and another $7500 for each additional resident.[24]

Not included in these estimates are funds necessary to support construction or maintenance, or both, of the model family-practice unit required for the clinical training of residents. Although the charges for services provided by residents and staff in the unit can be a source of some of the funds required to maintain the unit, there is no satisfactory formula for projecting this income. Obviously, these units cannot pay for themselves, since practice productivity is reduced markedly by the inexperience of the residents and the teaching functions of the unit.[25]

The AMA's Council on Medical Education requested funding information from the family-practice programs it identified as in operation during the 1973–1974 academic year. Virtually all the programs depended on funding from multiple sources, including general university funds, grants from federal and/or state governments and private foundations, gifts, and earned income. Those programs organized as departments were more likely to receive financial aid from general university funds than those organized as divisions within departments were.[26]

The new family-practice programs have not benefited, as training programs did in many other fields, from the availability of extensive federal funding. At about the same time the current drive to develop educational programs in family practice began, federal funds for medical education decreased markedly. Furthermore, despite the frequently voiced governmental concern with increasing the availability of primary care, only limited federal funding has been earmarked specifically for family practice. A major family-practice funding measure, authorizing $425 million over a five-year period to finance construction of facilities, education and training of medical personnel to teach in or administer departments of family practice, and operation of residency programs, was introduced into Congress early in 1970. The proposal, known as S. 3418, met heavy opposition from the Nixon Administration. Receiving strong support from Congressional leaders and family-practice proponents in the medical profession, however, it passed late in 1971. The much-publicized pocket veto of this measure by President Nixon was contested, and two years later judicially overturned, but so far as is known, few of the funds authorized by that bill have ever been made available.

The 1971 Comprehensive Health Manpower Training Act did contain authorization for federal support of hospital training in family practice. The amounts obligated under that authority have been far lower than those sought under S. 3418. The original grant of $5 million in FY 1971 went to 51 hospitals in 28 states and the District of Columbia to support residency training. Another $5 million was obligated in FY 1973, chiefly for continuation grants to the original recipients. Proposals in 1973 requested a budget of $25 million for FY 1974, but the Labor/HEW appropriations bill finally signed late in 1974 included only $10 million for family-practice programs.[27]

SECONDARY EFFECTS

Efforts to increase the number of family practitioners by creating residency programs and undergraduate teaching programs have been resisted by practitioners and organizations who felt that these activities threatened their own spheres of influence. The principal and most critical resistance has been within schools of medicine, although for many reasons this opposition has not been overt.

The creation of any new department implies sharing of precious resources and teaching time in the curriculum. In addition, the presence of the generalist in a tertiary-care environment creates opportunities for invidious comparisons between subspecialist and generalist. For the first time, medical-school faculty members had little or no control over the forces that generated a new department within their midst. As a result, they have reacted predictably. The extent of the rejection reaction of faculty members to these "foreign bodies" transplanted into their organization may well determine the ultimate fate of these interventions in medical education.

OVERALL IMPACT ON ACCESS TO PRIMARY CARE

As suggested in previous sections, it is far too early to predict the overall impact of training programs for family practice/primary care on access to primary care. Many issues remain to be resolved. There is still considerable resistance from many groups, including medical-school faculty members, to family medicine as a specialty. Specialists still control not only medical education but also staff privileges at community hospitals and reimbursement formulas that do not favor the generalist. It is also too early to determine if the increased interest in family practice among medical students is transient.

The establishment of the Specialty Board, the rapid increase in training programs at undergraduate and graduate levels, and the manifestations of support from state governments would augur well for the success of these efforts. How great their impact will be may be determined by the degree of federal support of future manpower legislation specifically designated to reinforce the interventions necessary in the production process.

SUMMARY

The creation of departments of family medicine in schools of medicine that have identifiable and significant offerings in the required curricula of the preclinical and clinical years, and responsibility for postgraduate training programs, represent the only contemporary, nonmarginal intervention into medical education designed to increase the number of primary-care practitioners.

The effectiveness of these programs will, however, depend on the extent to which they can meet the expectations of those students and physicians who see in them the solutions to a host of problems. Despite the systematic effort (undergraduate/graduate/Board Certification), they still must deal with current admission policies, reimbursement schedules, and practice and academic environments that do not share their *Weltanschauung*. The next few years will be critical. The quality of their output, in terms of the second generation of faculty members for such departments, and their teaching, research, and clinical competencies, may be the principal determinant of their future. In any event, these "transplants" will require considerable fiscal nurturance by governmental agencies if their promise is to be realized.

EIGHT

Efforts to Increase
the Number of Physicians:

IMPACT ON ACCESS TO MEDICAL CARE

REASONS FOR DEVELOPMENT OF EFFORTS

Concerted efforts to increase the numbers of medical students in the United States began in the mid-1960s. By encouraging that increase, the federally funded programs were intended to have a direct, if delayed, impact on alleviating problems of access to care caused by what was perceived as a nationwide shortage of practicing physicians. Arguments supporting the existence of a shortage took two forms. A series of government-sponsored reports, published during the 1950s and 1960s and calling for increased physician/population ratios, argued primarily that there was an overall numerical shortage of physicians in the United States. By the late 1960s and early 1970s, arguments acknowledged the complications of geographic distribution patterns that left rural areas with few physicians, and of specialty-choice career patterns that resulted in ever-decreasing numbers of physicians providing primary care.

Direct federal support of undergraduate medical education through the programs described in this case study represented a significant change in focus from earlier types of support. During the late 1950s and early 1960s, federal financial support in medicine went chiefly to biomedical research and to post-graduate fellowships in the biomedical sciences. Such funding was part of a broader federal involvement in support of education and manpower develop-ment concentrated in the sciences generally, spurred by Russia's 1957 launch of Sputnik I. Major legislative programs underwriting this support were the National Defense Education Act (1958) and the Manpower Development and Training Act (1962).[1] Although organized medicine fully supported federal support of postgraduate research, it remained opposed to the involvement of federal funds, and thus to federal priorities for medicine, in support of under-graduate medical training throughout the 1950s.

The shift in policy began in the early 1960s: an editorial in the 1960–1961 medical education number of the *Journal of the American Medical Association* called specifically for federal funds for construction of new medical schools dur-ing the next decade to alleviate shortages in health manpower.[2] Medicine had begun to support efforts already called for in earlier government-sponsored reports. By 1969, the Association of American Medical Colleges and the American Medical Association had held joint meetings to consider the national shortage. Statements issued in March and April called for substantial increases in enrollments of existing U.S. medical schools to a level permitting all qualified applicants to be admitted.[3] Their joint statement issued in September 1969 called for marked increases in federal financial support for medical educa-tion, noting the precarious financial status of many medical schools attempting to increase enrollments and to renovate or construct facilities.[4]

The uneasy financial position of medical schools in the late 1960s related directly to severe cuts in federal support of biomedical research. Since much of that support had actually financed education, rather than strictly research endeavors, these reports represented open recognition by organized medicine of both the de facto federal involvement in medical training and the need for that support. By 1971, the American Medical Association was committed to easing specialty and geographic maldistribution of physicians, and in 1973, the AMA president-elect included among organized medicine's priority goals an increase of primary-care physicians and a better geographic distribution of health professionals, especially to deprived areas.[5, 6]

NATURE OF INTERVENTION

The federal programs encouraged medical schools and medical educators to increase the numbers of first-year students, increase the numbers of medical schools, and shorten the length of medical curricula as means of increasing the numbers of practicing physicians. The programs were thus designed to affect access by increasing the availability of physicians in general. At the outset, it was assumed that increasing the number of physicians would have a direct impact on more effective geographic and specialty distributions of physicians. Later versions of the legislation dropped this assumption in favor of direct support for redistributive efforts.

SOURCES

A review of the literature provided much of the material for this section. Major sources of information and statistics included the *Distribution of Physicians in the U.S.* series, compiled annually by the American Medical Association's Center for Health Services Research and Development, and several volumes from their Special Statistical Series; the American Medical Association's annual reports on medical education, published in mid-November issues of the *Journal of the American Medical Association*; and annual studies of U.S. medical-school applicants published in mid-year issues of the *Journal of Medical Education* by the Association of American Medical Colleges (AAMC).

In addition, this topic was among several discussed during meetings in Washington, D.C., with AAMC staff members, including August G. Swanson, M.D., Director, Department of Academic Affairs; James B. Erdmann, Ph.D., Director, Division of Educational Measurement and Research; Davis G. Johnson, Ph.D., Director, Division of Student Studies; and Ayres D'Costa, Ph.D., Principal Investigator, AAMC Longitudinal Study Project, Division of Educational Measurement and Research.

DESCRIPTION OF PROGRAMS[7]

The federal effort to increase the numbers of medical students in the United States began with the Health Professions Educational Assistance Act of 1963 (P.L. 88–129), establishing the Health Professions Educational Assistance (HPEA) program, intended to increase the numbers of graduates from health-professions schools and to improve the quality of their education. Initially administered by the Bureau of Health Manpower Education, National Institutes of Health, Department of Health, Education, and Welfare (HEW), the program is now under the direction of the Bureau of Health Resources Development, Health Resources Administration, HEW.

The 1965 amendments to this legislation (P.L. 89–290) created the Health Professions Educational Improvement (HPEI) program, the heart of the effort to increase numbers, which received initial funding in FY 1966. Most of the funds under this program were disbursed in institutional grants requiring the applicant school's assurance that the first-year class would increase in size and were calculated on a formula reflecting the school's total enrollment. Other types of assistance provided under other parts of the overall HPEA program were matching grants for construction or renovation of teaching facilities, loans for student-health professionals, and scholarships for health-professions students with exceptional financial need. (The student loan program is more extensively described and evaluated in another case study.)

The Health Manpower Act of 1968 (P.L. 90–490) made significant changes in the HPEI program. The purposes of the special project grants (unfunded under the original legislation until FY 1968) were expanded to include efforts at further increasing the supply of trained personnel, assisting schools with severe financial problems, and affecting significant improvements in curricula. The following criteria were established for use in determining priorities among special project grant applications: (1) the extent to which the project will increase enrollment of full-time students; (2) the relative need of the applicant for financial assistance to maintain or provide for accreditation or to avoid curtailing enrollment or reducing the quality of training provided; and (3) the extent to which the project may result in improved curricula or methods of training or help to reduce the period of required training without adversely affecting the quality of training.

Among these expanded purposes, which became effective with the FY 1970 grants, was a special Physician Augmentation Program announced by HEW in 1969. The program sought to increase first-year enrollments in schools of medicine and osteopathy by 4000 over the next four years. This annual increase of 1000 was to be over and above new first-year places already committed under other federal programs.[8]

By June 1971, more than half of the HPEI institutional grants and two-thirds of the special projects grants—more than $125 million—had gone to medical schools, testimony to the federal government's particular concern with increasing numbers of physicians.

After legislative authority expired in June 1971, the program was renewed in the Comprehensive Health Manpower Training Act of 1971 (P.L. 92–157). This law greatly increased support to health-professions schools through capitation grants, which replaced the institutional grants, providing incentives for shortened curricula as well as increased enrollments. It also significantly altered the purposes of the special projects grants, including for the first time specific authorization for grants to assist in improving distribution of health manpower. Three new categories of assistance, apart from the special projects grant awards, were (1) health-manpower-education initiative awards to improve distribution (by specialty and geography), supply, quality, utilization, and efficiency of health personnel and the health-services distribution system; (2) start-up grants for new schools of medicine, dentistry, and osteopathy; and (3) grants to assist schools in financial distress (formerly authorized under special projects grants).

EVIDENCE OF PROGRAM EFFECTIVENESS

Increases in Numbers

Evaluated in terms of their goal, these programs certainly were effective in increasing the overall numbers of first-year students, enrolled students, and graduates from medical school. (Achievement of the program goal, increase of the quality of education in the health professions, is not included in this evaluation.) Since the first academic year in which effects of the program funding were felt, 1966–1967, the entering classes and total enrollments have generally continued to increase faster than those of the 1960–1966 period.

The special effort of the Physician Augmentation Program did not achieve an additional thousand students above previously committed increases beginning with the 1970 entering class. In that year, 29 schools received grants to add a proposed 448 places; inability of other schools to respond within the time limit for grant applications inhibited further increases.[9] The funds authorized under this program undoubtedly contributed, however, to the doubling of previous increases that was seen in the entering classes of 1970, 1971, and 1972.

Larger numbers of graduates began to be seen at the end of the decade. By the 1973–1974 academic year, the number of entering students had increased 41 percent over the 1960–1961 level, the total student body was 57 percent larger, and the estimated graduating class of 1974 was more than 60 percent larger than that of 1961. For complete figures, see Table 9.

The number of medical schools increased from 86 in 1960–1961 to 112 by 1972–1973. In the academic year 1973–1974 another 2 schools enrolled students. Most of the increase has been among schools with a four-year M.D. curriculum, and several two-year basic-science-curriculum schools have been converted to M.D.-granting institutions. For the first time in more than a decade, the 1972–1973 academic year saw no schools in developmental status, that is, with a formal commitment by sponsors to establish a school, firm assurance of construction and operating funds, and the appointment of a dean or executive officer.[10] In 1972–1973, however, some 16 efforts at planning or implementing plans for new medical schools were announced.[11]

The development of new medical schools was owing in large part to the availability of HPEA construction funds. Reporting on construction grant activity from FY 1963 through the end of FY 1969, HEW noted that 20 new

Table 9   First-Year Medical Students, Total Students, and Graduates of U.S. Medical Schools, 1960–1974

Academic Year	First-Year Students	Total Students	Graduates
1960–1961	8,298	30,228	6,994
1961–1962	8,391	31,078	7,168
1962–1963	8,642	31,491	7,264
1963–1964	8,842	32,001	7,336
1964–1965	8,836	32,428	7,409
1965–1966	8,760	32,835	7,574
1966–1967	8,991	32,423	7,743
1967–1968	9,473	34,538	7,973
1968–1969	9,863	35,833	8,059
1969–1970	10,422	37,669	8,367
1970–1971	11,348	40,487	8,974
1971–1972	12,361	43,650	9,551
1972–1973	13,667	47,546	10,391
1973–1974	14,044	50,636	11,250–11,682

SOURCES.   1960–1961 through 1972–1973 data from studies of student applicants by the Association of American Medical Colleges, as reported in mid-year issues of the *Journal of Medical Education*. The 1973–1974 data on first-year students and total students from AAMC fall enrollment questionnaires, as reported in W. F. Dubé, "Datagram. U.S. Medical School Enrollment, 1969–1970 through 1973–1974," *Journal of Medical Education* **49**:302–307 (1974). About the 1973–1974 data on the number of graduates: the AAMC estimates that between 11,200 and 11,300 will graduate in the class of 1974; the Bureau of Health Resources Development, formerly the Bureau of Health Manpower Education, in the National Institutes of Health, estimates 11,682 graduates, including 1015 three-year graduates, based on requests for capitation payments. (Davis G. Johnson, Ph.D., Director, Division of Student Studies, AAMC, personal communication, February 25, 1974.)

health-professions schools, 12 of them medical and osteopathic schools, had been constructed with federal funds. Another 113 had expanded, renovated, or remodeled teaching facilities under the program.[12] Half of the new medical and osteopathic schools received awards for basic science facilities only; half received funds for both basic science and hospital facilities. Of the existing schools, 49 received construction grants: 18 for major basic-science construction, 7 for major hospital construction, and 11 for construction of both facilities; 13 had varying amounts of construction aid, including small amounts for basic science and hospitals.[13]

Approximately 4800 new first-year places were added in health-professions schools as a result of these construction funds, 2900 of them occupied by the

1968–1969 academic year. Another 8600 first-year places were maintained through funds for expansion and renovation. HEW reported that grants to schools of medicine and osteopathy between 1963–1964 and 1970–1971 had increased first-year places by an estimated 1685 (35.6 percent), and schools without federal construction funds increased first-year enrollments by 656 (14.6 percent).[14]

The financial incentives for shorter curricula built into the special grants section and into the capitation mechanism, combined with general interest in curriculum experimentation on the part of many medical educators, stimulated a move through the late 1960s and 1970s to three-year M.D. programs. In 1973 the AMA collected curriculum information from 106 degree-granting institutions, several of which were in development, in an effort to document the shift to shorter curricula. In 1972–1973, at least 12 schools either permitted or required 90 to 100 percent of their students to obtain degrees in three years, twice as many as in the previous year. Another 14 offered a three-year curriculum that between 10 and 90 percent of their students took advantage of, an increase of 8 over the previous year. In addition, another 20 schools reported offering three-year programs; however, less than 10 percent of their students elected that option.[15]

It is not possible to credit the federal programs with effecting *all* of these numerical increases; however, from the magnitude and timing of the increases it is certain that the financial incentives provided by the programs were responsible for most schools' ability to respond to the calls for increased numbers of physicians, as well as to pressures from the well-documented increase in the numbers of qualified students applying to medical school over the past decade.

Impact of Increased Numbers on the Physician Shortage

Evaluating the impact of increased numbers of graduates on physician shortages is problematic. There is a four-year lag between increased first-year enrollments and larger graduating classes; the now usual internship and residency training adds at least another three to five years. Until 1973, two further years were required for military services, and many graduates of the late 1960s have yet to complete their military obligations committed under the Berry and other deferment plans. Although the numbers of physicians in internship and residency programs burgeoned in the late 1960s and early 1970s (see below, "Activity Distribution," for further discussion and figures), the enrollment increases beginning seven years ago will very likely not be reflected in increased numbers of physicians in nonhospital patient care for another two to three years.

In addition, it is not yet possible to measure the extent to which the increased numbers of physicians produced by the federal programs will reduce a shortage of physicians' services once they enter practice. As the U.S. Comptroller General noted in his 1972 review of the HPEI program, HEW and the National Institutes of Health had never established the annual increase in enrollments required to eliminate the shortages of health professionals in the United States. Although various estimates had been made, inadequate and conflicting estimates of what the desirable supply of health personnel should be confounded their efforts.[16] If those estimates had been issued, the inability to measure a reduction in shortages would have persisted nonetheless. The physician/population ratio, much used in arguments supporting the existence of a nationwide physician shortage, is under deserved attack as an indicator both of the relative need for physician manpower and of physician availability, since it cannot take into account differing health-care needs of populations varying on sociodemographic parameters, or the several types of services produced by physicians in different specialties. Although methodologies for calculating the relative need for physicians are under continual discussion and testing, none has yet emerged that would permit measurement or prediction of reduction in physician shortages resulting from the programs under consideration.

Impact of Increased Numbers on Physician Distribution

It is clear that specialty and distribution patterns undoubtedly aggravated problems of access to primary care, whatever the effects of an actual physician shortage may have been. Given this, it would be unwarranted to assume that a simple increase in the number of physicians, of any realistic degree, would ease access problems related to maldistribution. As Mattson has reported: "The number of physicians who can practice in upper- and upper-middle class communities without seriously reducing opportunities for adequate incomes appears to be greatly beyond any production capacity of U.S. medical schools."[17]

It has been noted that efforts to increase the number of physicians made it necessary as of 1971 to add specific provisions directed at redistribution of health manpower. It was no longer assumed that an increase in number would force physicians into needed specialties and underserved areas. However, the full effects of "redistributive" encouragements on those students comprising the increases in enrollment are yet to be felt, because most have not yet entered practice.

Evidence of shifts in specialty and geographic distribution patterns toward primary-care specialties and/or location in underserved areas that occur along with the documented increase in numbers is necessary to determine any redistributive effects of manpower support efforts before 1971 on access to primary care. To determine such shifts, the specialty, geographic, and activity distribution patterns for the five calendar years prior to full program funding, 1963–1967 (1963 being the first year for which physician distribution statistics are available in the AMA series), have been compared to those patterns evident between 1967 and 1972, the most recent year for which distribution data are available from the AMA.

Specialty Distribution.   Although already declining in numbers, general practitioners still comprised the largest proportion, somewhat more than one-fourth, of all U.S. physicians in 1963. Surgical specialists followed closely at about one-fourth; medical specialists and other specialists (including the categories of "unspecified" and "not recognized") each represented about one-fifth of the total. Although they increased only 16.6 percent between 1963 and 1967, surgical specialists represented more than one-fourth of all specialties by 1967. There was a 30.7 percent increase for other specialties and a 21.8 percent rise among the medical specialties during the same period. By 1967 other specialties had risen to represent almost one-fourth, and medical specialties to more than one-fifth, of all physicians; general practitioners had decreased to equal medical specialties in proportion. During the next five years, surgical specialists posted the smallest percentage increase over 1967 figures (10.8 percent) but still made up the largest proportion of physicians. In the same period, medical specialties grew 22.1 percent and other specialties increased 22 percent. The proportion of physicians in other specialties and in medical specialties thus continued to increase. As indicated in Table 10, by 1972, general practitioners represented only 15.5 percent of the total number of physicians in the United States.

Some of the changes between 1967 and 1972 are due to a reclassification of physicians' specialties in the 1968 AMA physician survey, especially affecting the counts of general practitioners and those in other specialties.[18] See Table 11 for complete figures on specialty proportions, numeric changes, and percentage increases.

Table 10   Comparison of Percentages of Total U.S. Physicians in Major Specialty Groups, 1963, 1967, 1972

		Specialty Group		
Year	General Practice	Medical Specialties	Surgical Specialties	Other Specialties[a]
1963	26.7	20.6	25.6	20.6
1967	22.3	22.3	26.6	24.0
1972	15.5	23.6	25.5	25.3

SOURCE.   Based on Appendix Table 6.
[a] Includes "not recognized" and "unspecified" specialty categories.

Those specialties considered to be the "primary-care specialties"—internal medicine, pediatrics, and obstetrics–gynecology—have continued to hold their own and attract a sizable number of physicians. The number of physicians practicing medical and surgical subspecialties, most notably cardiovascular disease specialists and diagnostic radiologists, increased at the expense of broader specialty groups such as general surgery and radiology.

After initiation of the programs under consideration, there was a shift toward subspecialty practice, particularly to those classified as "other" specialties. This is revealed in both proportional and numeric changes, although less clearly in the latter. In addition, the percentage increases among these subspecialties posted between 1967 and 1972 were sizably larger than those during 1963–1967. Primary-care specialties continued to increase, but at slower rates than those recorded in the earlier period. Certainly many of these large percentage gains in the subspecialties reflect growth from rather small base numbers; however, the acceleration of these rates of change in 1967–1972 over 1963–1967 levels, seen for almost all other specialties and several medical specialties, is not due merely to an additional year of growth (6 years versus 5). Accelerated rates of change among these subspecialties, coupled with lower rates of increase among surgical specialties and primary-care specialties, indicates fairly clearly the increased attraction of subspecialty practice for physicians from 1967 to 1972.

Geographic Distribution. The geographic distribution of physicians is closely related to their specialty and activity distribution, owing largely to the demands of medical specialization itself. The delivery of specialized medical-care services requires the support of other personnel and technology, as well as access to other specialists. With increasing medical specialization, medical practice has become more closely affiliated with hospitals and teaching institutions, usually located in urban and suburban areas. This phenomenon, coupled with the replacement of some general practitioners, whose practice was less restricted geographically, by primary-care specialists, has resulted in the loss of practicing physicians from rural areas.

The uneven urban–rural distribution of physicians is clear in the pattern for the 1963–1967 period, shown in Table 12. (These figures, and those discussed in this section, refer only to nonfederal physicians. Definitions of urban and rural follow those employed in the AMA physician surveys: urban = all SMSAs* and potential SMSAs; rural = all non-SMSA areas.) Although 1963 figures for each category are not available (indeed, these categories were not adopted until the 1966 survey), comparison of the rates of increase of all non-federal physicians—12.3 percent for urban areas as opposed to a 0.4 percent

* Standard Metropolitan Statistical Areas.

increase in rural areas—illustrates the differential growth pattern. By 1967, 85 percent of all nonfederal physicians practiced in urban areas, as did well more than 80 percent of all physicians engaged in patient care and more than 90 percent of physicians in hospital-based practice and other professional activities.

In general, this pattern prevailed between 1967 and 1972. The total number of nonfederal physicians in both areas rose at increasing rates, close to 18 percent in urban areas and 9 percent in rural locations. Although this represented a far larger gain for rural areas than in the preceding five years, the *proportion* of nonfederal physicians in rural areas continued its decline below the 1963 level. Nonfederal physicians in patient-care categories also increased more rapidly in urban than rural areas. Most of this was due to loss of general practitioners.

Although a larger proportion of office-based general practitioners were in rural areas in 1972 than in 1967, the majority of them continued to practice in urban locations. Similar proportional increases in rural areas were seen between 1967 and 1972 among the other office-based nonfederal patient-care physicians and hospital-based practitioners, and although numbers are small, they showed growth somewhat higher than those for the same group in urban areas. Not surprisingly, the number of physicians in medical training, administration, and research continued to increase more rapidly in urban areas.

Activity Distribution. The AMA physician surveys request physicians to classify their major activity, as well as their specialty. Main categories are patient care, including office- and hospital-based practice, and other professional activities, comprising medical-school faculty, administrators, and researchers. Shifts in activity distribution between 1963–1967 and 1967–1972 are associated with changes in the site and type of medical practice. The trends away from primary-care practice already noted in specialty distributions are illustrated in Table 12.

Between 1963 and 1967, the proportion of physicians in patient care declined, chiefly owing to the decreasing proportion of doctors in office-based practice. Hospital-based practice, particularly of interns, residents, and fellows, had grown considerably, as had medical-school faculties. The largest percentage increases, owing to small base figures, were seen in other professional activity designations, particularly medical-school faculty and research. Many of the changes noted after 1967 were due to the alterations in the 1968 AMA survey, which requested activity designation by the number of *hours* devoted thereto in a typical week, more accurately reflecting major activity than earlier classifications had. These changes are particularly significant since they indicate shifts *away* from patient care, both in office-based and in-hospital practices, toward nonpatient-care activities, chiefly administration

Table 11 Urban and Rural Distribution of Nonfederal U.S. Physicians by Major Activity in 1963, 1967, and 1972, with Numerical and Percentage Changes for 1963–1967 and 1967–1972

Activity	1963	Percent	1967	Percent	Change 1963–1967	Percent Change	1972	Percent	Change 1967–1972	Percent Change
			Urban							
Total physicians	212,016	83.7	238,043	85.2	26,027	12.3	280,629	86.1	42,586	17.9
Total patient care			211,629	84.9			230,184	85.5	18,555	8.8
Office-based practice										
General practice			43,398	69.2			33,208	67.4	-10,190	-23.5
Medical specialties			36,167	90.2			42,046	89.4	5,879	16.3
Surgical specialties			49,129	86.7			54,037	85.7	4,908	10.0
Other specialties			27,477	89.9			35,390	89.3	7,913	28.8
Hospital-based practice			55,458	93.7			65,503	93.4	10,045	18.1
Other professional activities			16,036	93.0			22,584	93.2	6,548	40.8
			Rural							
Total physicians	41,210	16.3	41,375	14.8	165	.4	45,160	13.9	3,785	9.1
Total patient care			37,644	15.1			38,911	14.5	1,267	3.4
Office-based practice										
General practice			19,359	30.8			16,057	32.6	-3,302	-17.1
Medical specialties			3,946	9.8			4,980	10.6	1,034	26.2
Surgical specialties			7,507	13.3			9,018	14.3	1,511	20.1
Other specialties			3,096	10.1			4,238	10.7	1,142	36.9
Hospital-based practice			3,736	6.3			4,618	6.6	882	23.6
Other professional activities			1,211	7.0			1,644	6.8	433	35.8

SOURCES. 1963 data from C. N. Theodore and J. N. Haug, *Selected Characteristics of the Physician Population, 1963 and 1967* (Chicago: American Medical Association, 1968), Table 14, p. 76, and text table, p. 11. The 1968 data from J. N. Haug and G. A. Roback, *Distribution of Physicians, Hospitals, and Hospital Beds in the U.S., 1967* (Chicago: American Medical Association, 1968), Table H, p. 14. The 1972 data from G. A. Roback, *Distribution of Physicians in the U.S., 1972,* Volume 1: *Regional, State, County* (Chicago: American Medical Association, 1973), Table 1, p. 21.

Table 12 Activity Distribution of U.S. Physicians in 1963, 1967, and 1972, with Numerical and Percentage Changes for 1963–1967 and 1967–1972

Activity	1963	Percent	1967	Percent	Change 1963–1967	Percent Change	1972	Percent	Change 1967–1972	Percent Change
Total physicians	275,140	100.0	308,630	100.0	33,490	12.8	356,534	100.0	47,904	15.5
Patient care	246,951	89.9	274,190	88.8	27,239	11.0	292,210	82.0	18,020	6.6
Office-based practice	179,449	65.2	190,079	61.6	10,630	5.9	201,302	56.5	11,223	5.9
Hospital-based practice	67,502	24.2	84,111	27.3	16,609	24.6	90,908	25.5	6,797	8.1
Intern	9,517	3.5	10,549	3.4	1,032	10.8	11,496	3.2	947	9.0
Resident and fellow	28,999	10.5	36,307	11.8	7,308	25.2	42,055	11.8	5,748	15.8
Physician staff (full-time)	28,986	10.5	37,255	12.1	8,269	28.5	37,357	10.5	102	.3
Other professional activity	14,777	5.4	19,882	6.4	5,105	34.5	26,000	7.3	6,118	30.8
Medical school faculty	8,190	3.0	11,166	3.6	2,976	36.3	5,636	1.6	-5,530	-49.5
Administration	3,222	1.2	4,121	1.3	789	23.7	11,074	3.1	6,953	168.7
Research	3,255	1.2	4,595	1.5	1,340	41.2	9,290	2.6	4,695	102.2

SOURCES. 1963 data from C. N. Theodore, and J. N. Haug, *Selected Characteristics of the Physician Population, 1963 and 1967* (Chicago: American Medical Association, 1968), Table A, p. 5. The 1967 data from J. N. Haug and G. A. Roback, *Distribution of Physicians, Hospitals, and Hospital Beds in the U.S., 1967* (Chicago: American Medical Association, 1968), Table 1, p. 21. The 1972 data from G. A. Roback, *Distribution of Physicians in the U.S., 1972*, Volume 1: *Regional, State, County* (Chicago: American Medical Association, 1973), Table 1, p. 21.

and research. In addition, the reclassification resulted in a significant shift away from medical-school teaching, more accurately reflecting the time faculty spends in administration and research.

The number of physicians providing patient care continued to increase after 1967, but the rate of increase was only half of that noted between 1963 and 1967 (despite a 15.5 percent increase in the number of physicians nationwide). Most of the primary medical-care services are provided by physicians in office-based practice. This group posted the largest gains in overall numbers in both periods, and continued to increase at a similar rate after 1968, in spite of the AMA reclassifications; however, the *proportion* of all physicians in office-based practice declined greatly between 1968 and 1972. As indicated earlier, interns and residents continued to increase in numbers and residency–fellowship programs gained proportionately as well. Many of these residents and interns were training in nonprimary-care specialties.

PROGRAM COST

From FY 1964 through FY 1971, approximately $1.8 billion was authorized by Congress for the Health Professions Educational Assistance Program as a whole. By FY 1970, the latest year for which figures are available, not quite $1.1 billion (61.1 percent) had been appropriated for use by the various programs (see Table 13). In most of the program categories, actual obligations ran below appropriations throughout the period for which figures are available.[19]

Authorizations, appropriations, and obligations for the HPEI institutional and special project grants in support of expanded enrollments are given in Table 14. By 1971, 79.9 percent of authorized funds had been appropriated, but only 24.7 percent had actually been obligated. Following Congressional recommendations that funds be concentrated on schools of medicine and dentistry, these schools received a combined total of $313.4 million between FY 1966 and FY 1971, 83.9 percent of obligated funds. Authorizations for the HPEI program rose markedly when the Comprehensive Health Manpower Training Act's provisions became effective in FY 1972, as did appropriations for the initial year under that legislation. More recent appropriations and obligations under that authority have not been published.

Although the HPEI program was regarded as the central feature of the effort to increase the number of physicians, funding information indicates that the construction program probably contributed far more to that effort. The financial experience of the HPEA construction program appears in Table 15. By FY 1969, 85.5 percent of authorized funds had been appropriated, and 82 percent had been obligated.

HEW calculations of the contribution of the construction program to the

Table 13   HPEA Authorizations and Appropriations,
FY 1964–FY 1971[a]

Fiscal Year	Authorization	Appropriation
1964	$ 30,100	0
1965	85,200	$ 100,200[b]
1966	113,178	101,082
1967	204,855	194,355
1968	279,200	249,700
1969	287,800	167,219
1970	338,000	262,422
1971	443,000	NA
Total:	$1,781,333	$1,074,978

SOURCE. Office of the Secretary, Department of Health, Education, and Welfare, *Report to the President and the Congress: Health Professions Educational Assistance Program* (Washington, D.C.: Department of Health, Education, and Welfare, September 1970), Appendix Table 1, p. 141.
[a] Authorizations and appropriations under Comprehensive Health Manpower Training Program not available.
[b] Based on cumulative 1964 and 1965 authorizations.

increase in first-year enrollments in the health professions indicate that, on the average, the federal programs paid $112,000 for each new first-year place. The sum paid varied considerably with the type of school funded. At a combined sum of $186,000 per new place, increases at schools of medicine and osteopathy were by far the most expensive, more than $50,000 greater than the cost at schools of dentistry, the second most expensive. As HEW's review of the program points out, however, this is a one-time cost. If one assumes that the facilities (teaching and, in some instances, the hospital) are used for a minimum of 30 years, the federal capital investment is about $6,000 per entering student in 1965–1969 dollars.[20] In further breaking down this investment, HEW notes that the federal one-time share was actually $81,000 per added student for basic-science facilities and $105,000 for hospital facilities, clinical teaching space, and administration.[21]

These figures can be used to provide a very rough estimate of the cost of doubling the output of physicians (both M.D.s and D.O.s). The present graduating class of M.D.s and D.O.s being estimated at 12,000,[22] it would require at least $1 billion to build facilities enabling 12,000 new spaces to be created.

This is a one-time cost, in 1965–1969 dollars; it does not include maintenance support for the positions already established, nor does it provide for financing additional faculty.

SECONDARY EFFECTS

Perhaps the major unintended effect of the efforts to increase the number of physicians in the United States was the program's demonstration that it was no longer possible to assume that the force of numbers would encourage physicians to make specialty and location choices more consonant with national health needs. It became readily apparent that "interference" in the actual distribution of physicians by specialty and geography is necessary if health-services delivery is to be "rationalized." The federal government acknowledged this necessity on a small scale when it began to encourage redistributive efforts under the HPEI

Table 14   HPEI Authorizations and Appropriations, FY 1966–FY 1974 (in thousands)

Fiscal Year	Authorization	Appropriation
1966	$ 20,000	$ 10,482
1967	40,000	30,000
1968	60,000	52,500
1969	80,000	66,000
1970	117,000	105,000
1971	168,000	124,000
1972	427,000	255,000
1973	503,000	NA
1974	590,000	NA
Total:	$1,421,503	$642,982

SOURCE. Office of the Secretary, Department of Health, Education, and Welfare, *Report to the President and the Congress: Health Professions Educational Assistance Program* (Washington, D.C.: Department of Health, Education, and Welfare, September 1970), Appendix Table 4, p. 144. U.S. Comptroller General, *Report to the Congress: Program to Increase Graduates from Health Professions Schools and Improve the Quality of their Education*, National Institutes of Health, Department of Health, Education, and Welfare. B-164031(2) (Washington, D.C.: General Accounting Office, 1972), pp. 9 and 10.

Table 15   HPEA Construction Program Authorizations and Appropriations, FY 1964–FY 1971 (in thousands)

Fiscal Year	Authorizations	Appropriations
1964 ⎫		$ 0
1965 ⎬	$ 175,000	100,000
1966 ⎭		75,000
1967	160,000	135,000
1968	160,000	175,000[a]
1969	160,000	75,000
1970	170,000	118,100
1971	225,000	NA
Total:	$1,050,000	$678,100

[a] The 1965 Amendments provided a cumulative authorization, that is $160 million for 1967, $320 million through 1968, and $480 million through 1969.

program in 1971. Since 1971 government involvement in this area has proceeded apace, at least in draft legislation. For example, bills have been introduced calling for a National Advisory Council on Post-Graduate Physician Training, and eventually, for a mandatory allocation of residency training posts by geographic area and by specialty.[23] More recently, the Administration has introduced a bill proposing major changes in federal financing of medical education, stressing primary-care training and service in shortage areas.[24] Several of the specialty societies have acknowledged the need for direct intervention in physician distribution and are beginning to curtail the number of approved residencies in their fields in an attempt to guard against "overproduction."

OVERALL IMPACT ON ACCESS TO PRIMARY CARE

Federal programs to increase the number of physicians achieved their immediate goal of increasing first-year enrollments, encouraging shortened curricula, and increasing the number of medical schools. Most of these new physicians have not yet entered practice, and there is as yet no way to measure to what extent they will reduce a physician shortage when they begin practice. However, consideration of specialty, geographic, and activity distribution patterns before and after the inception of the programs demonstrates that the force of numbers has not affected trends toward increasing specialization and urbanization of medical practice.

There were recognizable redistributions among the specialties after initiation of the programs but not in favor of primary care. Those redistributive efforts encouraged by the special projects grants were not effective in encouraging physicians to enter primary care, nor has the force of numbers made specialty choice more responsive to contemporary public demands for more primary-care services.

If the 1968 AMA physician survey reclassifications reflect more accurately the actual time spent by practicing physicians in different activities, the increase in the number of physicians did *not* increase access to primary care, as the decrease in physicians in office-based practice demonstrates. Although office-based practice did hold its own, increasing at the same rate between 1967 and 1972 as it had in the earlier period, it continued to decline proportionately; hospital-based practice and nonpatient-care activities continued to increase.

Whether the proportional increases and larger rates of growth for nonfederal office- and hospital-based patient-care practitioners in rural areas between 1967 and 1972 represent the beginning of a trend is of major interest. A full analysis is complicated by the unavailability of 1963 figures; therefore, shifts in proportion and percentage increases for the 1963–1967 period are not available for comparison. Given that fact, it is clear that these programs had no effect on access problems related to specialty and activity distributions. Because geographic distribution is so closely related to specialty practice and the types of activities performed by physicians, it seems very unlikely that these changes, if they represent a true shift, are related to programs designed to increase the number of physicians in the United States.

SUMMARY

Federal intervention in medical education began after World War II. Support of biomedical research had an indirect but enormous impact on medical schools. In the 1960s policy changed, and a series of health manpower training bills was enacted that provided direct financing for construction of new facilities and expansion of the size of classes in existing medical schools. This second era was characterized by an assumption that any shortage of physicians in the United States (either absolute or relative) could be remedied by increasing the number of medical graduates.

During the fiscal years 1966–1971, more than 1.9 billion dollars were spent in this quest. The results include (1) a 16 percent increase in the number of medical schools, (2) a 25 percent increase in the number of students enrolled, and (3) 40 percent increase in the size of graduating classes. Over (almost) the same interval (1967–1972) almost 48,000 physicians were added to the medical manpower pool in the United States.

During this interval, the following changes occurred in the distribution of physicians, by location and type of practice. The number practicing in urban areas increased by 42,500; those in rural areas increased by 3785. The number of family practitioners decreased by 13,500, while medical specialties gained 15,200, other specialties 16,000, and surgical specialties 8900. Of this increase of nearly 48,000 physicians, almost one-third went into direct patient-care activities.

In summary, there is little evidence that merely increasing the output of physicians by medical schools, that is, altering the supply, will have the desired effects of redistributing physicians among specialties or geographic areas, or both. The principles of the free-enterprise market do not apply to the workings of health services.

We are now entering the third phase of federal intervention. Various proposed bills are being debated. The major contribution of the second phase may be an awareness that, if the distribution of physicians is a concern, then more intrusive (and, from the viewpoint of schools of medicine, more specific) mechanisms must be embodied in future legislation supporting the education of health professionals.

NINE

New Health Practitioners:

A SOLUTION FOR THE PROBLEMS OF OLD HEALTH PRACTITIONERS?

REASONS FOR DEVELOPMENT

The provision of medical care by persons other than physicians is not new. Throughout history, physicians have trained individuals to assist them in their practices and have delegated various tasks and functions to these persons. Within the past 15 years, however, the feasibility and effectiveness of this process have been demonstrated in a variety of settings, and formal training programs have been established to prepare "new health practitioners" to function in these roles. Thus, in a very brief period, an informal and highly individualistic activity has been institutionalized and formalized.

The objectives of those concerned with the initial demonstration projects of the 1960s were quite different from those who developed the first training programs. The first formal demonstrations involved nurses in extensions of the roles and functions of clinical-nurse specialists and public-health nurses. These activities occurred in settings providing care to pregnant women, to infants and children, and to adults with chronic disease.[1-4] All were located in health

111

departments or hospital clinics, and the concern of those responsible for these efforts was to improve the quality of care provided to the recipients of services.[5] Although there were some occasional references to the relief of physicians from these types of activities, and thus some saving of physician manpower, the primary objective of these projects was not replacement but improvement.

The development of programs to prepare individuals to perform as extenders of physicians or to serve as intermediate-level or new health practitioners began soon after the demonstration activities. Most training programs developed in settings quite apart from places where demonstration activities were occurring. In historical perspective the initial training programs seem to have developed without regard to the findings of the demonstration activities.

The first training programs were concerned with the preparation of physicians' assistants. Organized nursing rejected the role of the "nurse practitioner" as not within the scope of nursing until the late 1960s. Since that time, there has been a rapid increase in the number of programs preparing various nurse practitioners to function in extended/expanded roles.

NATURE OF THE INTERVENTION

As indicated, there are several subspecies of new health practitioners. Their effects on the health-care system are related to the roles for which they have been prepared and the services they provide. Although there have been changes in the philosophies of the original training programs, at least three separate streams, or types of training programs, can be identified with reasonable clarity: (1) physicians' assistants (including Medex); (2) nurse practitioners; and (3) "other," such as the child-health associate. Each of these will be discussed separately.

One principal difference among these training programs, as of the early 1970s, was the extent to which students were prepared to function independently/interdependently/dependently. The first programs preparing assistants to the physicians placed heavy emphasis on this individual as an extender of the physician's abilities to collect data through history and physical examination and to perform routine tasks. Physicians were expected to supervise their actions, to review the data collected by them, make all decisions, and prescribe all the necessary treatments, which might (depending on their complexity) be carried out by an assistant.[6]

Another emphasis in these early training programs was on the preparation of the individuals to perform certain "tasks." Many of these were similar to those performed by corpsmen in the Vietnam war, such as suturing wounds and applying casts. Their curricula stressed the performance of activities that required psychomotor skills, rather than in-depth preparation for evaluation of clinical data or decision-making.

There have, however, been rather dramatic changes in the philosophy and assumptions underlying educational programs for physicians' assistants, so that the characteristics described are no longer evident. Graduates are being prepared to process information and make decisions, as well as to collect data and perform certain skills.

Nurse-practitioner programs have emphasized aspects of patient care that involve psychosocial interventions, such as health education and counseling. The first nurse practitioners functioned as public-health nurses endowed with the additional medical skills required for the collection of data by physical examination of the patient. Very little emphasis has been placed on the surgical aspects of medical practice. As with programs for the training of physicians' assistants, there has been a considerable shift in their orientation. Increasing numbers of programs are emphasizing courses for clinical nursing specialists, supplemented by training in physical diagnosis and medical management.

"Other" new health practitioners are reasonably recent additions to the field. They include the child-health associate, the family-planning specialist, and the primary-care associate. These practitioners possess a blend of the skills and abilities of physicians' assistants and nurse practitioners. But some of these programs take students directly from high school or college and do not require any prior experience in any of the health-science fields. Their curricula reflect this lack of prior training or experience in terms of requiring course work in the basic sciences and medical terminology.

The interventions provided by these individuals have been characterized in a variety of ways. Many studies have sought to describe the tasks and services performed by them. Elaborate task inventories have been developed (some containing more than 500 items) to describe the types of services provided and the frequency of their performance.[7] Another way of categorizing their roles is to examine the types of problems cared for or services provided by them, and their degree of independence from or dependence on physicians:

• What problems—medical, surgical, psychological, social—do they deal with?
• What is the extent of the data base they can collect validly and reliably?
• What decisions can they make without first consulting a physician?

In examining the interventions provided by new health practitioners, it is important to recall that the initial demonstration programs were concerned with quality of care, and yet the first training programs prepared individuals to cope with the shortage of physicians. More recently, these programs have been suggested as a means of controlling the cost of care by providing cheaper manpower and womanpower, as well as by training individuals who would function in geographic areas short of physician manpower. The data available indicate that the interventions provided by new health practitioners depend on: (1) the prior work experience of the student; (2) the philosophy of the training program preparing the practitioner, particularly with regard to their proposed relation to the physician; and (3) the specific setting and physician with whom the new health practitioner is associated.

SOURCES OF DATA

Within the past decade various publications have appeared describing demonstration projects and training programs. Various studies have been conducted on the impact of these individuals on the quality of care, their scope of functions, and their performance capabilities.[8-10] Few of these studies have, however, attempted to measure the new practitioners' impact on access to primary care.

Additional sources of data, other than the literature, were the American Medical Association's Division of Health Manpower, including data on their accreditation activities for programs preparing assistants to the primary-care physician; personnel from the Division of Nursing, Bureau of Health Manpower Education, Health Resources Administration; and various reports from the National Center for Health Services Research.

DESCRIPTION OF THE PROGRAMS

Training Programs

Most programs for physicians' assistants began with the assumption that many of their students possessed a wealth of practical experience but lacked in-depth preparation in the basic sciences.

In the late 1960s four organizations, the American College of Physicians, the American Academy of Pediatrics, the American Academy of Family Practice, and the American Society of Internal Medicine, evidenced interest in developing a means of accrediting programs preparing assistants to the primary-care physician (Type A Physicians' Assistant). As a result of these activities, a formal accreditation mechanism has been developed. The Joint Committee on Accreditation reviews applications, conducts site visits, and recommends actions to the Joint Council on Medical Education of the American Medical Association, which has recently been recognized by the Office of Education as the official body for accrediting these training programs.

As of mid-1974, 43 programs had received such approval. As a result of this accreditation mechanism, programs preparing assistants to primary-care physicians have relatively similar formats in terms of content of curricula, extent of clinical experiences, and evaluation mechanisms. This standardization has also been reinforced with the development, by the National Board of Medical Examiners, of a certification examination for graduates of these programs. This examination was administered to more than 700 registrants in late 1973. It was given a second time in December 1974. At that time registration was open not only to those who had graduated from accredited programs but also to individuals who had worked on the job in such a role for four years and who could provide appropriate documentation of this fact. The examination, given in December 1974, also included a competency assessment of the skills of the applicant.

The curricula of physician-assistant programs have evolved rapidly, from task-oriented training for previous corpsmen, to well-developed, soundly based educational programs preparing individuals to function in roles according to the guidelines set forth by the Joint Review Committee.

Guidelines

Primary-Care Physicians' Assistant. The description of the primary-care physicians' assistant from the *Essentials* prescribed by the Council on Medical Education includes the following:[11]

The assistant to the primary care physician is a skilled person, qualified by academic and clinical training to provide patient services under the supervision and responsibility of a doctor of medicine or osteopathy who is, in turn, responsible for the performance of that assistant. The assistant may be involved with the patients of the physician in any medical setting for which the physician is responsible.

The function of the assistant to the primary care physician is to perform, under the responsibility and supervision of the physician, diagnostic and therapeutic tasks in order to allow the physician to extend his services through the more effective use of his knowledge, skills, and abilities.

In rendering services to his patients, the primary care physician is traditionally involved in a variety of activities. Some of these activities, including the application of his knowledge toward a logical and systematic evaluation of the patient's problems and planning a program of management and therapy appropriate to the patient, can only be performed by the physician. The assistant to the primary care physician will not supplant the doctor in the sphere of the decision-making required to establish a diagnosis and plan therapy, but will assist in gathering the data necessary to reach decisions and in implementing the therapeutic plan for the patient.

Intelligence, the ability to relate to people, a capacity for calm and reasoned judgment in meeting emergencies, and an orientation toward service are qualities essential for the assistant to the primary care physician. As a professional, he must maintain respect for the person and privacy of the patient.

The tasks performed by the assistant will include transmission and execution of physician's orders, performance of patient care tasks, and performance of diagnostic and therapeutic procedures as may be delegated by the physician.

Since the function of the primary care physician is interdisciplinary in nature, involving the five major clinical disciplines (medicine, surgery, pediatrics, psychiatry, and obstetrics) within the limitations and capabilities of the particular practice in consideration, the assistant to the primary care physician should be involved in assisting the physician provide those varied medical services necessary for the total health care of the patient.

The ultimate role of the assistant to the primary care physician cannot be rigidly defined because of the variations in practice requirements due to geographic, economic, and sociologic factors. The high degree of responsibility an assistant to the primary care physician may assume requires that, at the conclusion of his formal education, he possess the knowledge, skills, and abilities necessary to provide those services appropriate to the primary care setting. These services would include, but need not be limited to, the following:

1. The initial approach to a patient of any age group in any setting to elicit a detailed and accurate history, perform an appropriate physician examination, and record and present pertinent data in a manner meaningful to the physician;

2. Performance and/or assistance in performance of routine laboratory and related studies as appropriate for a specific practice setting, such as the drawing of blood samples, performance of urinalyses, and the taking of electrocardiographic tracings;

3. Performance of such routine therapeutic procedures as injections, immunizations, and the suturing and care of wounds;

4. Instruction and counseling of patients regarding physical and mental health on matters such as diets, disease, therapy, and normal growth and development;

5. Assisting the physician in the hospital setting by making patient rounds, recording patient progress notes, accurately and appropriately transcribing and/or executing standing orders and other specific orders at the direction of the supervising physician, and compiling and recording detailed narrative summaries;

6. Providing assistance in the delivery of services to patients requiring continuing care (home, nursing home, extended care facilities, etc.) including the review and monitoring of treatment and therapy plans;

7. Independent performance of evaluative and treatment procedures essential to provide an appropriate response to life-threatening, emergency situations; and

8. Facilitation of the physician's referral of appropriate patients by maintenance of an awareness of the community's various health facilities, agencies, and resources.

Nurse Practitioners.   In contrast to the relative order that exists among programs training type A (primary care) physicians' assistants, the preparation of nurse practitioners resembles the status of medical education prior to the Flexner report. Programs for training nurse practitioners vary in duration from six weeks to two years. This variability is a function of the type of practice for which the students are being prepared (adult medicine, family practice, pediatrics); of the location of the program (in a graduate program of the school of nursing, or continuing-education division of a university); as well as of the basic philosophy of those responsible for their development.

The majority of these training programs include a formal didactic phase that may range from three weeks to six months or longer, as well as a preceptorship involving practical on-the-job experience. Recently, however, some training programs for nurse practitioners have provided only the didactic course work and required that students arrange for their own clinical experiences. These programs also differ in the extent to which the disciplines of medicine and nursing are involved. In many instances, the initial training efforts were dominated by physicians; the reverse is now generally true. Nurse practitioner programs also vary in the relative emphasis placed on medical skills versus more in-depth preparation in nursing activities, such as counseling and health teaching. Various statements about the roles of nurse practitioners have been made, but the Report of the Secretary's (HEW) Committee to Study Extended Roles for Nurses, "Extending the Scope of Nursing Practice," issued in November 1971, represents the most nearly definitive statement to date.[12] Scope of functions is defined for primary care, acute care, and long-term care:

Primary Care Functions for Which Many Nurses Are Now Prepared and Others Could Be Prepared:

- Routine assessment of the health status of individuals and families.
- Institution of care during normal pregnancies and normal deliveries, provision of family planning services, and supervision of health care of normal children.
- Management of care for selected patients within protocols mutually agreed upon by nursing and medical personnel, including prescribing and providing care and making referrals as appropriate.
- Screening patients having problems requiring differential medical diagnosis and medical therapy. The recommendation resulting from such screening activities is based on data gathered and evaluated jointly by physicians and nurses.
- Consultation and collaboration with physicians, other health professionals, and the public in planning and instituting health care programs.

Assumption of these responsibilities requires that nurses so engaged have knowledge and requisite skills for:

- Eliciting and recording a health history;
- Making physical and psychosocial assessments, recognizing the range of "normal" and the manifestations of common abnormalities;
- Assessing family relationships and home, school, and work environments;

- Interpreting selected laboratory findings;
- Making diagnoses, choosing, initiating, and modifying selected therapies;
- Assessing community resources and needs for health care;
- Providing emergency treatment as appropriate, such as in cardiac arrest, shock, or hemorrhage; and
- Providing appropriate information to the patient and his family about a diagnosis or plan of therapy.

Acute Care Functions for Which Many Nurses Are Now Prepared and Others Could Be Prepared:

- Securing and recording a health and developmental history and making a critical evaluation of such records as an adjunct to planning and carrying out a health care regimen in collaboration with medical and other health professionals.
- Performing basic physical and psychosocial assessments and translating the findings into appropriate nursing actions.
- Making prospective decisions about treatment in collaboration with physicians, e.g., prescribing symptomatic treatment for coryza, pain, headache, nausea, etc.
- Initiating actions within a protocol developed by medical and nursing personnel, such as making adjustments in medication, ordering and interpreting certain laboratory tests, and prescribing certain rehabilitative and restorative measures.

Two examples of these actions are

1. a coronary care nurse recognizes sinoatrial arrest or block, discontinues the maintenance dose of digitalis according to standing orders, notifies the physician, and prepares to assist with such measures as transvenous pacing or Isoproterenol drug therapy, and
2. a nurse administers postural drainage, clapping, and vibrating as a part of the treatment cycle for patients with chronic pulmonary problems caused by bronchiectasis, emphysema, or fibrocystic disease.

Long-Term Care Functions for Which Many Nurses Are Now Prepared and Others Could Be Prepared:

- Assessing physical status of patients at a more sophisticated level than is now common in nursing practice.
- Securing and maintaining a health history.
- Within protocols mutually agreed upon by medical and nursing staff—make adjustments in medications; initiate requests for certain laboratory tests and interpret them; make judgments about the use of accepted pharmaceutical agents as standard treatments in diagnosed conditions; assume primary responsibility for determining possible alternative for care settings (institution or home) and for initiating referral.

- Conducting nurse clinics for continuing care of selected patients.
- Conducting community clinics for case findings and screening for health problems.
- Assessing community needs in long-term care and participating in the development of resources to meet them.
- Assuming continuing responsibility for acquainting selected patients and families with implications of health status, treatment, and prognosis.
- Assuming responsibility for the environment of the care setting as it affects the quality and effectiveness of care.

As of mid-1976, the American Nurses Association had appointed committees to begin the job of establishing mechanisms for accrediting programs preparing nurse practitioners and certifying their graduates.

Other Health Practitioners.   The curricula of programs for other health practitioners reflect the special roles for which graduates of these programs are being prepared. They generally prescribe a broader course of education related to the background of the students accepted for these programs.

There seems to be a gradual convergence of the educational objectives of these three types of programs, and it would seem quite possible that at some time in the future (professional organizations notwithstanding) there may be common curricula for new health practitioners with different "tracks" for specific types of providers.

Scope of Function

The scope of functions of physicians' assistants has been fairly clearly defined, as a result of the activities of the Joint Council on Medical Education.

The scope of functions of nurse practitioners depends on the type of practitioner. In the case of the pediatric-nurse practitioner, the scope of functions is relatively clearly defined by the nature of pediatric practice as well as by the roles performed by clinical specialists in pediatric nursing. There has been considerably more difficulty in defining the scope of functions of adult medical-nurse practitioners (and therefore, family-nurse practitioners), because of the depth as well as breadth of problems and activities encompassed within the practice of internal medicine.

Growth of the Programs

Because of the accreditation activities described for physicians' assistant programs, there is a means of readily inventorying the number of these programs. Since these programs have been supported primarily through federal funding, there is an additional source of data to assist in their enumeration. Unfortunately, the situation is quite different with regard to nurse practitioners. There have been various sources of funding for these programs, including the Division of Nursing (Bureau of Health Manpower Education), the National Center for Health Services Research, Regional Medical Programs, and private foundations, among others. The lack of any certification mechanism or accreditation activities makes it difficult to do more than estimate the number of programs and graduates. An inventory has been commissioned by the Division of Nursing to collect data on nurse-practitioner programs, but as of this date it is still being compiled.[13]

After review of the data available from the sources listed, estimates of the numbers of programs for these two types of practitioners are presented in Figure 1.

Estimates of the numbers of graduates of these two groups of programs are depicted in Figure 2.

The number of nurse practitioners produced per annum is increasing and already exceeds the number of graduates of the physician-assistant programs in the United States. This trend reflects the relative number of schools of nursing

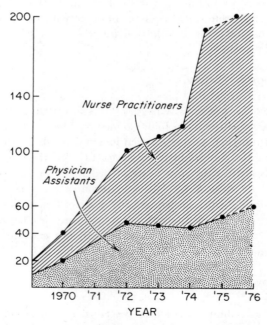

Figure 1. New health practitioner programs. (Developed from information provided by the Bureau of Health Resources Development and the Bureau of Health Services Research, Department of Health, Education, and Welfare, and by other funding sources noted in Table 16.)

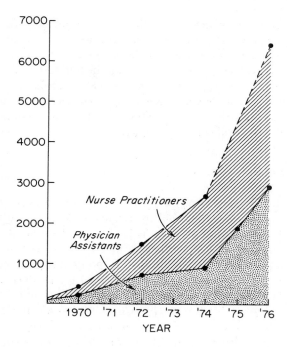

Figure 2. Total health practitioner graduates. (Developed from information provided by the Bureau of Health Resources Development and the Bureau of Health Services Research, Department of Health, Education, and Welfare, and by other funding sources noted in Table 16.)

in the United States versus the number of academic health centers with medical schools that can support physician-assistant programs.

THE EXTENT OF EFFECTIVENESS

The impact of new health practitioners on access to primary care can occur through their effects on a variety of barriers such as finances, geographic distribution of manpower, and patients' reluctance to seek services or comply with recommendations (psychosocial factors). Each of these areas will be discussed separately.

Financial Barriers

Any effect on financial barriers is contingent upon a reduction of the cost of services billed directly to patients when these services are provided by new health practitioners. There are no national data to allow generalizations on this point. In some instances patients, or their insurance carriers, are billed at 50 to 75 percent of the prevailing relative-value schedule for the same services when provided by physicians' assistants. In the majority of instances, however, it appears that few distinctions have been made in billing for services, whether rendered by "new" or "old" practitioners. The outcomes of deliberation regarding guidelines for reimbursement for such services under the Social Security amendments will have a profound effect on the volume and types of services that will be provided by these practitioners.

Geographic Barriers

Few if any of the developers of these training programs have contended that their graduates could solve the problems related to the geographic distribution of physicians. In fact, such a proposal is inimical to the general concept of the interdependent roles of such practitioners, that is, their need for backup physicians. Certain programs, notably the Medex programs, have operated on the assumption that physicians interested in employing the products of their training program should be identified and matched with individual trainees. This strategy seems to have been very effective in facilitating the education and employment of these students.[14] The extent to which students in various kinds of programs are enrolled on a nonsponsored basis, that is, without having a specific physician–sponsor who agrees to serve as a preceptor and subsequently as their employer, is quite variable.

There are no national data to describe the impact of these graduates on access to primary care by reducing barriers to geographic distribution of manpower, but there is no reason to believe that new health practitioners will or should want to choose to practice alone in areas where old practitioners have elected not to serve. Their impact on geographic barriers is quite dependent on the setting of their practice. Those who have been placed in storefront clinics or located with family practitioners in rural areas have had significant impact on access, although there are no national data to describe the extent of their effects.[15] The location of these practitioners in outpatient departments of teaching hospitals or organizations more highly endowed with personnel would seem to produce less dramatic effects on access to primary care. Again, there are no data to document this assumption.

Psychosocial Barriers

One of the hopes expressed by those preparing new health practitioners was that they would prove more effective than physicians in dealing with patients' behaviors necessary to ensure the optimal outcomes of care. Presumably, these effects would be achieved through different styles of interactions with patients and a reduction in the social distance between provider and consumer, as well as through their orientations toward these aspects of patient care.[16] Although only anecdotal data are available, apparently the vast majority of new health practitioners (including those with nursing backgrounds) are interacting with patients very much in a traditional mode. There may be several reasons for this: (1) the self-selection process attracting certain types of individuals to these programs; (2) the training programs, which have emphasized the acquisition of skills in physical diagnosis, medical management, and so forth; (3) the general lack of preparation, either in previous education or practice experiences, of students predisposed to different styles of interacting with patients; and (4) the nature of the system and its financial reinforcements, that is, what is paid for.

As of 1976, there is little reason to believe that more than a fraction of the new health practitioners are providing the kinds of patient care that will affect psychosocial problems associated with barriers to access.

PROGRAM COSTS

Since their inception in 1965, an increasing number of sources have provided an increasing amount of money to support training programs for new health practitioners. As indicated in Table 16, at least 9 federal agencies, several states, and 10 foundations have been sources of funding.

As might be suspected, there is no way of specifying the exact amount spent for training, in contrast to research and evaluation, or even of estimating the degree of completeness of this listing.

Whereas early funding for training came primarily from foundations, the federal government has supported the training of nurse practitioners and physicians' assistants for six years. The amounts provided, by fiscal year and type of program, are summarized in Table 17.

The development and support of physicians' assistant programs preceded that of programs for nurse practitioners; however, the rate of growth of the latter, both in the number of programs and of graduates and in level of support, has already exceeded that for physicians' assistant programs.

Because of the degree of variability in length of curricula (three months to four years) and the extent of clinical (medical) supervision provided, it is impossible to estimate the costs of graduating various types of new health practitioners (cost/graduate). Individual estimates from specific programs suggest that, whereas the total costs of education are less than those for physicians, this is so only because of the relative length of training periods.[17] The costs per month would seem to be not dissimilar for these programs and those preparing "old" health practitioners (physicians).

Table 16 Agencies and Groups Supporting the Training of New Health Practitioners

Source	Type of Program		
	Physician Assistant	Nurse Practitioner	Other
Federal			
Office of Economic Opportunity	x		
Defense	x	x	
Housing and Urban Development	x		
Labor	x	x	
Veterans Administration	x		
Indian Health Service	x		
Bureau of Health Resources Development	x	x	
National Center for Health Services Research and Development	x	x	x
Regional Medical Programs	x	x	
States	x	x	x
Foundation			
Boeltcher		x	x
Brunner	x		
Carnegie	x	x	x
Commonwealth	x	x	x
Ford	x		
Hoffman-La Roche		x	x
Kellog	x		
Johnson	x		x
Macy	x		
Rockefeller	x		

SOURCE. Developed from information provided by the Bureau of Health Resources Development and the Bureau of Health Services Research, Department of Health, Education, and Welfare, and from the other funding sources noted.

SECONDARY EFFECTS

Perhaps the greatest unintended or initially unanticipated effect of new programs of health-manpower training has been to bring a high degree of scrutiny to educational programs for old practitioners as well as "new" ones. As studies have examined the quality of care, productivity, scope of services, and cost of education for graduates of these programs, it has been difficult not to collect comparable data on the physicians with whom they are associated. These side effects, or secondary benefits, are certainly to be applauded.

A somewhat less beneficial side effect—at least from the perspective of certain disciplines or sexes—has been an association of nurse-practitioner activities with the feminist movement in the United States. All of the appropriate questions of equal pay for equal work, and opportunities for advancement, have been raised by graduates of these programs. These programs seem to have attracted a large number of women who are competent, bright, and aggressive and who speak eloquently for women's rights and patients' rights. This can certainly be viewed as a very positive side effect, but for a male-dominated medical profession that has viewed nurses as totally dependent, the shock of confrontation with these concepts, issues, and graduates has, in some instances, further polarized their views and resulted in a more adamant stand by physicians in opposition to these activities.

OVERALL IMPACT ON ACCESS TO PRIMARY CARE

Despite the facts that these programs have been in existence for almost a decade and that there are several thousand graduates in practice, the enormous variability in output of training programs and the failure of funding agencies to impose any standard evaluation methods make it impossible to arrive at an overall conclusion about their impact on access to primary care. In all

Table 17   Federal Expenditures for Training New Health Practitioners, FY 1969–FY 1974

Fiscal Year	Nurse Practitioners	Physicians' Assistants
1969	$ 83,000	—
1970	158,000	$ 300,000
1971	420,000	1,000,000
1972	1,070,000	6,700,000
1973	7,500,000	6,900,000
1974	6,900,000[a]	7,500,000
Total:	$16,131,000	$22,400,000

SOURCE. Developed from information provided by the Bureau of Health Resources Development and the Bureau of Health Services Research, Department of Health, Education, and Welfare, and by other federal agencies listed in Table 16.

[a] Does not include all training funds included in 25 Special Project training grants.

probability it has been positive in terms of making additional primary-care services available to specific population groups such as children and those in certain urban areas.

The marketplace for these practitioners has been rather sluggish in terms of demand for them, particularly in those areas and settings where their placement will ensure the greatest impact on access. Without a doubt, the current deliberations on reimbursement under the Social Security amendments will determine the impact of these practitioners on access to primary care. All evidence to date suggests they are subject to exactly the same forces that impinge on physicians and further emphasizes the importance of making them part of a systematic effort to increase access to care.

SUMMARY

The ultimate impact of new health practitioners on access to primary care will be determined by the outcomes of interorganizational struggles related to how these practitioners will be reimbursed and regulated. Undoubtedly, their future will depend also on the success of efforts to increase the number of physicians entering postgraduate training programs emphasizing primary care.

The evidence available as of 1976 indicates that these individuals are subject to the same forces that affect physicians. There is every reason to believe that, given the opportunity, they can expand greatly the scope of the services available and improve the quality of care provided. There is little reason to believe that, independently, they will affect any of the primary problems of the health-care system. The key question is, Will they be marginal additives or embellishments for the present system, or will they be part of an overall strategy for improving the quality and quantity of primary-care services available? In view of the rate by which programs preparing new health practitioners are proliferating, definition of their future roles is of some importance.

A considerable sum has been spent in the development of educational programs to prepare new health practitioners. This investment could pay handsome dividends if certain innovations related to instruction and evaluation created by these programs were adopted by institutions preparing "old" health practitioners.

TEN

National Health Service Corps:

INCREASING ACCESS IN AREAS OF HEALTH-MANPOWER SHORTAGES

REASONS FOR DEVELOPMENT OF PROGRAM

Like many of the programs considered in these case studies, the National Health Service Corps resulted from growing national and Congressional concern about the adverse effects of geographic maldistribution of health manpower on access to care, particularly for low-income rural and inner-city populations. By 1970 it seemed apparent to some that the efforts of state-sponsored loan-forgiveness/service-commitment programs were of limited effectiveness in encouraging physicians to locate in shortage areas. The possibility that national health insurance would give shortage areas the purchasing power to draw needed health professionals was both remote and questionable. Earlier federal programs to increase access, most notably Medicare and Medicaid, had only guaranteed financial access to health-care services for specific age and income groups, without concomitantly supplying personnel and services. Some additional mechanism to intervene directly in the distribution of physicians seemed needed.

127

The Corps concept, characterized by Redman as a "'marriage bureau' for doctors and needy areas," had been advocated by organizations representing student-health professionals. It was recommended by the President's Advisory Commission on Rural Poverty in its 1967 report, *The People Left Behind,* and received increased attention from the medical profession in the early 1970s. Earlier attempts to create a corps of federal physicians in shortage-area practice had focused on the largest group of physicians in federal employ, those fulfilling their military obligations in the uniformed services. These attempts had not met with success, and in the legislative proposal for the Corps, the problem was circumvented by making it part of the Public Health Service (PHS). Corps physicians would thus be drawn from the pool of PHS physicians, who serve their draft obligations outside the uniformed services. The PHS was a logical choice for another reason. Its physicians were already delivering health care to populations, other than the military, for whom the federal government had assumed the responsibility of guaranteeing these services, namely American Indians, merchant marine, and federal prisoners.[1]

Although it was not the federal government's first venture into direct provision of health services, creation of the National Health Service Corps represented its recognition of the need to intervene in physician distribution at least temporarily. Programs to intervene in the developing stages of physician distribution through influences during medical school would not be enacted until 1971, and then only in a suggestive, rather than mandatory, fashion.

NATURE OF INTERVENTION

Passage of the Emergency Health Personnel Act of 1970 (P.L. 91–623) established within the PHS a National Health Service Corps (NHSC), mandated to "improve the delivery of health services to persons living in communities and areas of the United States where health personnel and services are inadequate to meet the health needs of the residents of such communities and areas."[2] The National Health Service Corps' matching of federally employed physicians, nurses, dentists, and allied health personnel with geographically defined areas of health-services shortage is aimed at alleviating immediate needs. NHSC support is not intended to be a long-term or permanent solution to scarcity and related access problems. Support is designed to help establish a viable medical practice and to encourage the community and assignee to continue the practice arrangement after NHSC support ends. In addition, the community's assistance in identifying its needs and its role in determining the success of the NHSC practice are intended to enable it to understand and meet its needs better once formal NHSC support terminates.

SOURCES

The NHSC has been described in medical journals and the lay press, but little of its operational experience has been documented or analyzed in the health-services literature. Consequently, personal interviews with NHSC administrators and outside consultants in Rockville, Maryland, and Washington, D.C., provided the bulk of the information used in this case study.

Howard Hilton, Ph.D., Deputy Director, National Health Service Corps, provided much information about recruitment. As one of the few administrative personnel with the Corps since its inception, he also provided a valuable perspective on the Corps' overall operations. William Christoffel, formerly Director, Office of Program Planning, Evaluation, and Legislation, NHSC (now Director, Program Development and Implementation Branch, Bureau of Community Health Services) provided information about the Corps' newly implemented site-review mechanism, which he was instrumental in developing. David Kindig, M.D., the Corps' first director of professional services, discussed the earliest matches of scarcity areas and personnel.

The Problem Oriented Management Institute (POMI), Family Health Care, Inc., in Washington, D.C., is under contract to advise NHSC physicians on office-management problems and procedures and consults with the NHSC on community–assignee matches. From this experience, POMI staff members Douglas Stafford and James Norris provided much anecdotal evidence on the Corps' operations in the field and on characteristics of NHSC physicians.

In addition, Eric Redman's recent book *The Dance of Legislation* details the issues behind creation of the NHSC and traces the legislative process through which the Corps concept was developed and modified before passage of the bill. His analysis was helpful in documenting the reasons for development of the program; its wealth of information could be only partly reflected.

As emphasized in the introductory chapter, data were collected for these case studies during the latter part of 1973 and the first several months of 1974. All these programs have been in flux since their inception, and the National Health Service Corps is no exception. The data and discussion relate to activities prior to mid-1974.

DESCRIPTION OF THE PROGRAM

The Corps, a Public Health Service program, is administered by the Bureau of Community Health Services in the Health Services Administration, Department of Health, Education, and Welfare (HEW). Since its inception, it has been run primarily as a demonstration project. The NHSC sends personnel into areas of "critical health manpower shortages" for two-year assignments and occasionally supplements manpower in other ongoing federal programs for increasing access to care, such as the Indian Health Service, community mental-health centers, neighborhood health centers, Migrant Health Service, and Model Cities health projects. Although it is primarily a supply program, concern for both supply and financial barriers to access was apparent in the 1972 amendments to the NHSC program (P.L. 92–585), which stated: "Corps personnel shall be assigned . . . on the basis of the extent of an area's need for health care and services and without regard to the ability of the residents of an area to pay for health care and services."[3] Consequently, although NHSC operates on the fee-for-service model, collecting clinic fees through direct payment and from third-party insurers, it subsidizes some services by using a sliding scale for those who cannot pay the full cost.

Scarcity-Area Designation

The original legislation called for creation of an advisory board to develop criteria for identifying areas with "critical health manpower shortages." In the earliest matches of personnel and sites, NHSC administrators identified areas for approval and subsequent assignment of personnel. The legislative request prompted, by mid-1972, establishment of the Health Service Scarcity Area Identification Program, and its companion, the Master Health Service Scarcity Area Data Base by spring 1973. These information banks use program- and ratio-free definitions of scarcity, determining shortages of health and related services by (1) quantitative lack of resources, (2) inaccessibility of existing resources, and (3) ineffective use of existing resources. The focus is on primary-care resources. Although prompted by NHSC legislation, these programs and their information are designed for use by all HEW programs concerned with placement of resources in areas with shortages of health manpower and service. Preliminary findings on data from 520 areas reported into the systems by September 15, 1972, showed that, whereas quantitative lack of manpower and services was a larger problems than lack of facilities, inaccessibility and ineffective use of resources were larger problems than numerical manpower shortages. By December 1972, more than 1300 shortage areas had been identified by these programs alone, and they were expected to contain information on approximately 1500 such areas by the initial update, scheduled for summer 1973.[4] As of mid 1974, 1609 had been listed.

Nominations are sponsored by community boards and endorsed by local physicians, if there are any. The board coordinates the application and commits the community to provide and equip office space for NHSC personnel, to cooperate with assignees in providing effective health services, and to encourage adequate use of Corps services by community members. HEW regional office staff visit the site of each applicant community, coordinating sociodemographic and health-services data available in the scarcity-area identification material and on the application with personal knowledge of the site.

Approval of a community for designation as an NHSC site and assignment of potential personnel are based in part on the determination that a viable practice can be established by the end of two to four years. Another important consideration is the prospect that the community–assignee match may prove successful enough to encourage continuation of the practice arrangement after formal NHSC support terminates.

Personnel Recruitment

For physicians and dentists, service in the NHSC for a two-year period as a PHS Commissioned Officer fulfills the military obligation of the "doctor draft." Although the Senate Committee on Labor and Public Welfare noted that it "did not feel that service in shortage areas is motivated solely, or even significantly, by considerations of military service," the attractiveness of the NHSC program as a draft alternative was considered to be a significant factor in recruitment, as well as in the program's success, particularly by student health professionals.[5,6]

By recruitment the NHSC capitalizes on health professionals' interest in shortage-area service and, together with the community, subsidizes the establishment of the practice, eliminating financial risk to the new practitioner. In addition, the Corps assists the assignee in developing hospital and physician referral networks and offers additional training and educational programs. For the past two years, through a contract with POMI, the Corps has offered consultation and assistance on practice-management problems and use of the problem-oriented medical record to its field physicians, many of whom are fresh out of hospital internships and inexperienced in office-based practice.

Until recently, the major source for NHSC physicians was the pool of applicants to the PHS Commissioned Officers Corps. Since the recent abolition of the "doctor draft," the possible applicant pool has broadened to include all graduates from medical school. Nurses and intermediate health personnel (physicians' assistants and nurse practitioners) are usually hired locally for NHSC practices.

Matching Community and Assignee

There are no formal guidelines or criteria for matching community with assignee. According to the NHSC Deputy Director, nonquantifiable factors such as the community's expectations, preferences for particular medical services, and willingness to support the NHSC practice must be estimated and balanced alongside impressions of the assignee's style of medical practice, commitment to shortage-area practice and location, expectations of success, and adaptability to solo or partnership office-based practice from hospital-based training programs. Important, too, are the pairing of assignees, usually sent in tandem unless there is a local physician, and the expectations and acceptance of living in shortage areas on the part of the assignee's family. At present, interviews, site visits, and assessments of the information and impressions gathered are used. Recently, the Corps contracted with outside consultants to assist in identifying personnel likely to remain in shortage-area practice for selection as NHSC physicians and to coordinate preassignment interviews and assessments between communities and potential assignees.

EXTENT OF PROGRAM EFFECTIVENESS

Determination of NHSC success rests on three factors, the first two related to the program's impact on shortage areas, and the third to impact on Corps assignees:

1. Relief of access problems related to geographic maldistribution of health manpower, particularly physicians.
2. Development of viable practices to ensure their continuation after NHSC support ends.
3. Encouragement of the assignee's continuation in shortage-area practice beyond NHSC service.

Evaluation of these points is, however, seriously inhibited by lack of any data beyond rough estimates and anecdotal evidence. Certainly, since the NHSC is a young program, it cannot be expected to produce comparative data over a period of time adequate for assessing its full impact on either communities or assignees. But statistics that would usually be considered necessary to operation of the program and would partly indicate the impact of NHSC, such as rates of use of service before and during Corps assignment, information on practice management (beyond monthly financial statements), and sociodemographic and performance data on physician assignees, have not yet been made part of a continuous NHSC reporting system. Some summary information on utilization and practice management has been developed as an adjunct to consultation provided by POMI. NHSC recruitment staff are beginning to collect data on Corps physicians through intake and debriefing questionnaires, but very little is publicly available.

Since the success of recruitment is crucial to the NHSC's ability to influence both the shortage areas and the personnel serving in them, evidence of its effectiveness is discussed before the available anecdotal evidence of the Corps' impact on shortage areas and on personnel is presented.

Effectiveness of Recruitment

With the incentive of a draft alternative to NHSC service operating for physicians, recruitment was not a major problem. During the late 1960s, 3500 to 4500 medical-school graduates applied annually for the 700 Commissioned Officer Corps positions then available. The ceiling on these positions was raised to 900 in 1971, the first year of NHSC operation, and applications continued at former levels. Applicants could request assignment to a specific PHS program, and the NHSC was apparently one of the most popular among those entering the Commissioned Officer Corps. Originally having 300 positions to fill, the NHSC currently has 405 field positions budgeted; these are not included in totals for the Commissioned Corps.[7]

Intimations of the coming abolition of the "doctor draft" were apparent when the initial NHSC legislation passed. The Senate Committee on Labor and Public Welfare, when reviewing the bill, commented on the probable effect on the draft's abolition on the Corps' recruitment as follows:

. . . abolition of the "doctor draft" would not seriously impair National Health Service Corps recruitment. At the very least, those trained young health professionals who desired to serve in physician deficient areas would still find the program a great aid to such service; by reducing the cost of such service and capital outlay required by an individual practitioner, the program will encourage more trained doctors and health professionals to consider this type of service.[8]

Contrary to the Senate Committee's rather naive predictions, the draft alternative has proved a major incentive to NHSC service. Whereas NHSC service would continue to fulfill the selective-service obligation, anticipation of the end to the physician's draft obligation in July 1974 resulted in a considerable decrease in the numbers of medical students applying for Commissioned Corps positions.[9] This loss of available candidates led the NHSC to mount a major recruitment campaign, appealing to young physicians to join the Corps and "cure a community." Although they acknowledge that loss of the draft alternative may have seriously hurt their recruitment, NHSC administrators suggest that the physicians who now join will be more committed to the NHSC concept and goals than those looking only for alternatives to military service. They are thus focusing their efforts on those most likely to be interested in rural practice and attracted by the lack of personal financial risk required to establish or take over such a practice under NHSC auspices. Key targets in this campaign are primary-care physicians, particularly those training in family practice.

NHSC recruitment officials have worked with representatives of the Student American Medical Association, Physicians' National Housestaff Association, and the American Medical Association to identify and recruit interested students, interns, and residents. They have toured medical-school campuses across the country to speak with potential candidates. Letters describing NHSC program goals and attractions have been sent to all housestaff and senior medical students, further encouraging interest. In addition, news stories, usually based on interviews with NHSC physicians who have decided to continue in shortage-area practice, appear frequently, focusing on the advantages of rural medical practice.

The goal of this recruitment was set at 200, double the number of new physicians placed in the previous July. A majority of them would have replaced the approximately 140 physicians whose two-year assignments ended in June 1974. The NHSC planned to place only 117 new personnel in scarcity areas in July 1974.[10]

Despite the lack of marked success in this recruitment drive, the NHSC expected to grow to twice its present size by 1976, pending renewal of its legislation. In 1974, projections for 1976 placed field strength at more than 700 health professionals, including 450 physicians, in some 350 communities. In fact, as of February 1976, 315 physicians and 159 other health professionals were in the field. To achieve those levels, the plans were to broaden the pool of eligible physicians so as to identify and place mid-career physicians willing to relocate their practices.[11] The Corps would also have a new incentive to aid its upcoming recruitment campaign. Congress recently passed a military pay bill, bowing to the Defense Department's efforts to counter the adverse effects of the end of the "doctor draft" with the promise of higher pay. Physicians in the Commissioned Corps of the Public Health Service, and thus in the NHSC, were also included.[12]

Physician recruitment has not been the only problem for NHSC personnel administrators. Table 18 presents NHSC field-employment figures by personnel category and HEW region as of January 7, 1975. Some vacancies reflect difficulties in finding an adequate number of nurses and other nonphysician professionals in or near the shortage areas; the impact of reduced physician recruitment was not noticeable at that time.

Impact on Shortage Areas

Resolution of Problems of Scarcity of and Access to Health Services. As yet, there is no way of knowing whether problems of access have been resolved by

Table 18   National Health Service Corps

Region	Manpower in Field				
	Total	MD	DDS	PE	Other
I	15	10	3	1	1
II	30	25	1	4	0
III	85	58	17	9	1
IV	104	56	22	21	5
V	36	29	3	2	2
VI	49	27	8	12	2
VII	18	10	3	4	1
VIII	58	38	10	9	1
IX	42	32	3	6	1
X	51	28	4	17	2
Total	488	313	74	85	16

an increase in available health services because of NHSC presence in shortage areas or by the proven viability of medical practices begun under NHSC auspices. Communities that have lost their designation as shortage areas as a result of NHSC support have not been identified. There is some evidence of increased availability of services; NHSC practices provided more than a million visits during 1974.[13]

The impact of the program on access in areas of shortages appears to have been rather limited. The Corps' director estimated a nationwide total of 5000 shortage areas in 1972, and yet only 136 areas had been approved for personnel assignment by that date.[14,15] The newness of the program does not explain this initial low figure, because fewer areas have received NHSC approval in each succeeding year. In FY 1973, 128 areas were designated as NHSC sites, and another 74 were designated by April of FY 1974. The total by *June 1974* stood at 329; 290 were rural sites and 39 were in urban areas. Rural sites generally represent shortage areas, and urban sites are usually those with ongoing federal programs to enhance access that need additional personnel. Of the 329 approved areas, 211 had been staffed with NHSC personnel as of April 15, 1974 (64.1 percent), whereas 118 had never been staffed (35.9 percent).[16]

The "demonstration project" status of the program, funding at lower levels than authorized by Congress, and frequent changes in NHSC administrative staff have undoubtedly constrained the number of sites approved. The even lower number of sites ever staffed results in part from lack of complete funding and very likely from problems in matching assignees to some of the less desirable sites. Continued inability to fill all NHSC field positions in each personnel category and current problems with physician recruitment are related factors.

The 1973–1974 recruitment drive did not maintain present NHSC strength in the field, and it is unlikely that available personnel will permit an expansion of NHSC service into shortage areas that have not yet received their first NHSC assignees.

Impact on Perceptions of Health-Services Scarcity. Anecdotal evidence from POMI consultants suggests some positive impact on communities and their perceptions of scarcity of health services. They believe that many NHSC sites more realistically appraise the range of their health-services needs as a result of the application process, instead of believing all services are immediately necessary, as many had during their initial requests for NHSC support. In addition, their determining the range and availability of existing health services within each community and its surrounding "medical trade area" seems to have discouraged the "one doctor for every community" outlook. Further evidence for this impact is reflected in the following comment:

. . . while [the NHSC] has not done much to alleviate the maldistribution [of health personnel], it has at least forced the communities to look rather objectively at their need and their resources, and in some instances has stimulated a county-wide, or multicounty approach to recruitment which may be more effective in the long run.[17]

Impact on Personnel

Retention Rates. Before 1973, approximately 1 or 2 percent of assignees remained in NHSC service at the practice site or developed independent practices there after their tours of duty; in 1973, this figure rose to 3 percent. Estimates for the group of 140 physicians who completed NHSC service in June 1974 placed retention at 25 percent; 25 physicians extended their duty tours and 10 developed independent practices in their assignment locations (see Table 19).

These increasing retention rates confirm the belief of Corps officials that elucidating factors for success in matching has improved with each round of assignments. They also suggest that Corps practice has had a more positive effect on the location of recent assignees in rural areas and that current assignees are more frequently chosen for their predisposition to rural practice.

Despite this apparently increased impact on location plans, the majority of Corps physicians continue to leave the NHSC and shortage-area practice after their two-year tours of duty, usually to continue residency training. The NHSC Deputy Director estimates that only five assignments have proved to be "absolute failures," but anecdotal evidence collected by POMI practice consultants during site visits in late 1972 and 1973 suggests that all practices have problems that can reduce the success of the match and probability of

Table 19   Physician Continuation in NHSC Practice and Independent Practice Development, by HEW Region (July 1, 1974)

HEW Region		Extensions	Developing Practices	
I	Boston	1	1	
II	New York	1	3	
III	Philadelphia	6	2	
IV	Atlanta	6	–	
V	Chicago	1	3	(1 practice with 2 M.D.s)
VI	Dallas	2	–	
VII	Kansas City	1	1	
VIII	Denver	1	–	
IX	San Francisco	1	–	
X	Seattle	5	–	
	Total:	25	10	Grand total: 35

SOURCE.   Unpublished information provided by Howard Hilton, Ph.D., Deputy Director, NHSC.

retention. The most frequently identified problem was that the assignee had no intention of remaining beyond two years; this was found to be true of new assignees as well as of those near the end of their duty tours. Other problems were incompatibility of assignee and community, and lack of community support of the practice.

Impact on Practice Plans.   In terms of the NHSC practice's influencing future plans, approximately half of the original 20 assignees changed residency plans during or after their NHSC service to enter family medicine.[18] Although no estimates have been made of such changes among more recent assignees, POMI consultants report that many express active interest or commitment to future primary-care training and practice. This undoubtedly reflects the Corps' recent efforts to recruit primary-care physicians.

Evaluation Plans

Gaps in readily available data on the operations and experience of the NHSC were identified at the outset of this section. Inhouse evaluations of the impact of NHSC support on shortage-area problems of availability and access have begun, and the first round has been made. None of the information is yet available, but a description of the evaluation indicates the types of data to be collected, making possible more extensive analyses of the NHSC in the future.

In April 1973, the Corps took its first action to implement the review and evaluation required in the memorandum of agreement jointly signed by the NHSC and each NHSC community. Its purpose is to determine whether the NHSC will continue to provide assistance to communities beyond the initial two-year commitment, based on assessment of the program's effectiveness in alleviating scarcity problems in health services. All NHSC sites are to be reviewed and their progress is to be evaluated between the 6th and 18th month of operation.

After development of the review procedure and criteria for evaluation, the Corps focused its efforts on projects scheduled for termination in July 1974, attempting to determine by October 1973 whether they would receive continued support. The review requires each community to update information in the original application, paying particular attention to resources that have not increased or decreased since that application. The guidelines given below list the types of information suggested for inclusion in this update. In addition, the Corps asks assignees and HEW regional program directors to assess the practice and its progress, collates practice information developed by outside consultants, and visits sites to verify information and make on-the-spot assessments through interviews and observation. Particularly important to this interview and observation is evidence of adequate service utilization; continued community support of the practice, including assistance in obtaining professional backup and in collecting fees; financial viability; and continuing efforts by the community to correct its shortage situation.

GUIDELINES FOR UPDATED INFORMATION REQUIRED FOR NHSC SITE REVIEW AND EVALUATION

Statement of Health Plans

- immediate
- long range (type of delivery system envisioned)

Local Project Personnel

- number
- type
- full- or part-time

Service Area Population

- total patients seen in preceding three months
- breakdowns by age, sex, race, and residence

Transportation

- general public and private resources in area
- transportation to NHSC practice site
- emergency services
- no change or decrease in transportation resources since original application

Health Manpower Available in Area

- numbers
- types
- descriptions of practices
- no change or decrease in health manpower since original application

Health Facilities Available in Area

- numbers
- types (e.g., hospital, ECF, family planning, etc.)
- no change or decrease in health facilities since original application

Project

- utilization
- professional backup
- financial operation
- administrative structure
- facilities, equipment, and supplies
- volunteer support
- outside professional relationships

Progress to Date

- operation to date
- reception of NHSC practice/assignee by community
- changes in health patterns
- related community improvements, such as added employment, new pharmacy, increase in health-insurance coverage

After this process is completed, the site-visit team recommends one of the following four actions:

1. Terminate projects in those areas no longer considered scarcity areas because of additional health services in the community or contiguous areas, or because of incorrect identification as a shortage area initially.
2. Provide limited support for one year or less to communities requesting it or for communities that could become self-sufficient in a short time.
3. Provide additional support for up to two years, without requiring reapplication, for communities that have tried to correct their maldistribution problems and have received a majority of positive ratings on evaluation.
4. Terminate current assignment and request community to reapply for NHSC support, for those communities that would continue to be shortage areas were NHSC support to terminate but that received negative ratings on evaluation.[19]

PROGRAM COST

Since its inception, the NHSC has continually received less operating funds than those authorized by Congress. The original legislation called for initial funding of the demonstration project at $60 million over three years. The Administration chose not to request any funds for the program's FY 1972 operations in its January 1971 budget. Funds were diverted from other PHS programs to enable the first personnel to be sent into the field in January and July 1971. Under pressure from Congressional leaders and student-health professionals, the Administration requested $10 million to begin implementation of the NHSC in its 1972 budget for FY 1973. By FY 1974 the operating budget had increased to $13.4 million, and the Administration requested a budget cut, to $12.3 million, for FY 1975 operations.[20]

POMI consultants estimate that approximately half of these funds were used in site operations during FY 1974. They placed expenditures for the delivery of health services, maintenance of NHSC practices, and salaries of field personnel at about $6 million. The $6 million purchased approximately 1 million health-care visits, for an average cost of $6 per visit to the patient. As a result, the delivery of health-care services through the NHSC is, according to both the NHSC Deputy Director and the POMI consultants, the least expensive delivery-system demonstration run by the federal government. (Their estimate does not take into account the more than $6 million of administrative expenses required to support the Corps' delivery of services. Including those costs, the average overall cost per visit is closer to $12.) Given the recently increased salaries of NHSC physicians under the new military pay bill, this cost may not continue; however, the recent budget cut has decreased administrative personnel from 55 to 12, which may release more funds for site operations.

SECONDARY EFFECTS

The National Health Service Corps was heralded as the new solution to the problem of access to care, especially for those in rural areas. To the extent that their expectations were increased, and then unmet, the program may have created an untoward side effect. No other manifestations of adverse reactions are apparent.

OVERALL IMPACT ON ACCESS TO PRIMARY CARE

With so few "hard" data on NHSC operations and their effectiveness available, full determination of the Corps' impact on access problems in shortage areas must wait until the NHSC establishes a more nearly complete and continuous reporting system, and either performs an overall self-evaluation or makes information available for others to do so. Implementation of site-review procedures will add considerably to the amount of information available for evaluation, so long as it is made public. In addition, the sociodemographic, educational, and practice-performance information now being collected on physician intake and debriefing questionnaires will aid in determining the influence of NHSC experience on later location and specialty choices.

On the basis of the anecdotal evidence and data available, it is apparent that NHSC's efforts to place health personnel in shortage areas and thereby relieve access problems have been seriously constrained by administrative and funding difficulties. These problems have prevented the approval of larger numbers of sites. If the specific criteria used in site approval were known, they might indicate other factors preventing approval for additional areas. One factor may have been the Nixon Administration's efforts, contradicting the legislative provision exempting ability to pay from consideration in assignment of personnel, to ensure that the Corps pay for itself by recovering full fees for services rendered.[21] Since lack of adequate funds to purchase health insurance or medical-care services is common in shortage areas, the number able to qualify on this basis is clearly limited. In addition, it has been suggested that site approvals for the earliest NHSC assignments were prompted more by their political appeal than by evidence of actual scarcity of health services, further limiting the Corps' achievement of its legislative intent.[22]

The small number of sites approved for NHSC support, relative to the number of defined shortage areas, coupled with funding and recruitment problems, has curtailed the number of sites for which NHSC support has been available. Recruitment remains the Corps' most pressing problem; unless recruitment achieves greater success than indicated by current estimates, the ability to reach more shortage areas will be jeopardized, if not inhibited entirely.

Matching, a central feature of the Corps concept, has become more effective over time, and this improvement, along with recruitment focused on primary-care physicians, has achieved somewhat better retention rates for physicians in NHSC practices and for those developing independent practice in scarcity areas. The majority of physicians continue, however, to leave NHSC practice and shortage-area locations after two years, contrary to the key goal of matching.

Despite these factors, the Corps has been able to provide more than a million health-care visits to persons in areas where few of those visits would have been available without NHSC support. These visits have been produced at a cost that is not prohibitive, either to most of the patients or to the federal sponsors. The possibility that the federal government can deliver health-care services at costs lower than those incurred by other demonstration projects is generally regarded as one of the most significant achievements of the NHSC program. Another achievement, relating directly to the goal of community education in health needs, is evidence of the communities' more realistic perception of their health-services needs. Their apparent willingness to work with other shortage areas to solve those needs, rather than continue the "one doctor for one town" demand, is seen as further evidence of the Corps' educational impact.

The impact of the Corps' experience on health personnel, particularly on physicians, has not yet met expectations. Indications are, however, that new recruitment methods and the focusing of recruitment on primary-care physicians have somewhat more success in encouraging physicians to remain in shortage-area practice. An even greater impact may be seen if the Corps secures for NHSC physicians credit toward residency and board eligibility requirements in primary-care specialties. Such credit might also encourage higher shortage-area practice-retention rates, since NHSC practice would no longer represent an interruption in specialty training for all assignees.

SUMMARY

The concept of voluntarism has permeated the American approach to problem solving. The National Health Service Corps represents such an effort, and as such may be the last nonlegislatively mandated attempt to increase the availability of primary-care services. Similar "brokerage" operations have been carried out in the past by various individuals, communities, and organizations, with limited success.

In less than three years of existence the Corps has experienced most of the problems affecting older efforts to improve access to care: (1) changing or ambiguous goals/policies; (2) reduced and uncertain funding; (3) difficulty in retaining competent administrative personnel, as a consequence of (1) and (2);

and (4) lack of continuity in program operations and evaluation, owing to all of the preceding.

Despite these afflictions, services have been provided to people in underserved areas at reasonable costs, and (apparently) matching has become more effective. The program's effectiveness depends, however, on the existence of physicians interested in providing primary care in certain types of settings. This democratic approach has great popular appeal, but past experiences with programs depending on individual incentives that run counter to group expectations and reinforcements suggest that the Corps, as presently defined, will have limited impact.

ELEVEN

Medicare:

ELIMINATION OF FINANCIAL BARRIERS TO CARE FOR THE AGED?

REASONS FOR DEVELOPMENT OF PROGRAM

Between 1900 and 1963, the number of persons aged 65 and older in the United States increased five and one-half times, from 3 to 17.5 million, and was expected to reach 25 million by 1980. The rate of growth for this segment of the population was almost three times that of the nation as a whole. As it grew in numbers and in proportion, this subgroup of the population grew older as well, the highest percentage increase being seen among those aged 75 and older.

Health Needs of the Aged

In the early 1960s, attention was focused on this older group's special health and economic problems. The elderly were twice as liable to have chronic illnesses than those under 65 and were far more often limited in their range of activity. Since the prevalence of chronic illness and frequency of activity limitation increase after age 65, and the aged population was growing older, illness and disability were increasing as well. Not surprisingly, use of health-care services by the aged was far greater than that of younger persons. They were more likely to visit a physician, and they were admitted to the hospital more frequently, where their length of stay was several times longer than that of persons under 65.[1]

Problems of Financing Health Care

Because of their greater need and use of health-care services, the elderly incurred far higher costs. In 1962 the average personal expenditure for all health-care services for all age groups was $119. This included an average of $33 for hospital care. For those aged 65 and over, average personal expenditures for health care were $244, and the portion spent on hospital care averaged $78. At 1963 prices an aged couple (one or both of whom were hospitalized during the year) spent approximately $1200 for their annual medical expenses; a single person hospitalized during the year incurred a total bill of more than $900.

A major problem for the elderly was their difficulty in meeting these higher-than-average health-care costs from limited incomes, far lower than those of the younger and healthier population. In 1960 most elderly persons lived in one- or two-person family units, and the economic status of these families was far lower than similar family units in which the head of the family was under 65. During that year the median income of a two-person family headed by an individual over 65 was $2530, less than half that of the two-person families with a head of the household younger than 65 ($5314). The elderly living alone or with nonrelatives were at even more of a disadvantage. Their median income in 1960 was $1050, compared to $2570 for single persons under 65.[2]

Financing Health Care for the Aged:
A Matter of Social Policy

During the 1950s and 1960s, the escalating costs of care for the aged, afflicted with ill health and lower-than-average income, made it clear that they faced serious financial barriers in attempting to obtain health-care services and that these would increase in the future. Whether some financial assistance would be provided and the form that assistance would take became topics of major social and political concern.

The issue was not new. The financing of health care, and particularly the federal government's participation, has been a political issue of varying importance throughout the twentieth century. Discussion of compulsory national health insurance, with significant government financing, began in earnest about 1912. It reappeared during the Depression, when the federal government first financed health-care services for a significant part of the population, the indigent. The Depression also saw passage of the Social Security Act of 1935, creating a series of social-insurance, public-assistance, and social-service programs and expanding public-health activities. Although the Committee on Economic Security, whose report proposed the Social Security program, favored inclusion of national health insurance in the program, political considerations kept the committee from doing more than endorsing the concept.

Throughout the 1930s and 1940s, national health insurance remained a potent political issue, but the enormous difficulties in reaching consensus on the issue, particularly with organized medicine, stalemated the passage of any legislation. By the early 1950s comprehensive national health insurance had been replaced as a political issue by discussion of health insurance for the elderly population alone. Transforming that issue from a social concern into an operative program of medical insurance took 15 years, culminating in passage of the legislation authorizing the Medicare program.[3]

The complexity of that evolution and its significance to contemporary health politics make its adequate description too lengthy for this background statement. Others have detailed the draft bills introduced between 1951 and 1965, their varied provisions, the positions of supporters and opponents, and the political compromises required to enact the Medicare legislation. Their work should be referred to for a more nearly complete background analysis.[4-6]

NATURE OF INTERVENTION

Title XVIII of the 1965 Social Security Amendments (P.L. 89–97) authorized a federal program of health insurance for the aged known as Medicare. The explicit goal of Medicare was to reduce the financial barrier to access to health care for those aged 65 and over, aiding them in reaching needed services. Medicare was intended to serve as a financing mechanism alone. It was not designed to influence directly either the supply or organization of services. In fact, Section 1801 of the legislation states:

"Nothing in this title shall be construed to authorize any federal officer or employee to exercise any supervision or control over the practice of medicine or the manner in which medical services are provided, or over the selection, tenure, or compensation of any officer or employee of any institution, agency or person providing health services. . . ."[7]

SOURCES

Most of the data on trends in Medicare enrollment were drawn from annual program reports issued by the Social Security Administration. Several sources provided ambulatory- and hospital-care utilization rates for the aged. The Current Medicare Survey, based on a 5 percent sample of Medicare Part B enrollees, is compiled and issued by the Office of Research and Statistics, Social Security Administration. Other surveys used were reported in the *Social Security Bulletin,* including Medicare Control Records, a census based on the experience of enrollees in Medicare Part A; the 1965 and 1967 surveys by the National Opinion Research Center on Medicare's impact; the American Hospital Association's annual survey of community hospitals; and the Hospital Discharge Survey of short-stay hospitals issued by the National Center for Health Statistics.

Other sources used were topical studies, some unpublished and several presented in the *Social Security Bulletin,* covering Medicare program experience during varying time periods. Especially helpful have been several papers written by Karen Davis, Ph.D., Research Associate, The Brookings Institution, that analyze the utilization rates of ambulatory services under Medicare by different socioeconomic groups. Paula A. Piro and Nancy L. Worthington, both researchers in the Office of Research and Statistics, Social Security Administration, were also contacted during the preparation of this study.

DESCRIPTION OF PROGRAM

Medicare is a federal health-insurance program for the aged. As part of the Social Security program, it is administered by the Bureau of Health Insurance, Social Security Administration (SSA), in the Department of Health, Education, and Welfare (HEW).

Entitlement

All persons aged 65 years and older who are citizens or permanent residents of the United States and who are Social Security recipients are entitled to Medicare coverage. Qualified Railroad Retirement program beneficiaries, and other individuals uninsured by the Social Security system in 1966, when Medicare began operation, were allowed to file for coverage during a transitional period.

Coverage

Medicare Part A, the hospital insurance (HI) section of the program, covers hospital, nursing home, and home health services. Medicare Part B, a supplementary medical insurance (SMI) program, covers outpatient physician and other ambulatory health-care services. HI coverage is compulsory for Medicare beneficiaries, and enrollees can voluntarily elect SMI coverage at the time of filing.

Financing

The HI section of Medicare is financed by compulsory contributions of employers and employees through the Social Security system, with a separately earmarked payroll tax and trust fund. SMI is funded by premiums paid by the covered individual and matched by the federal government from general revenues. As in many private health-insurance policies, the Medicare beneficiary must meet a deductible and cost-sharing requirements for certain services received under both HI and SMI. Under a "buy-in" provision in the Medicaid legislation, state Medicaid programs have the option to pay SMI premiums and copayments for aged public-assistance recipients.

Physicians are reimbursed for delivery of Medicare services by fiscal intermediaries, usually health-insurance carriers, at a level determined to be "reasonable," defined as the customary and prevailing costs for institutions and charges for physicians in each local area. Under the original hospital reimbursement formula, hospitals were allowed 2 percent above their costs of providing services to Medicare beneficiaries.

Program Changes

Subsequent amendments to the original Medicare legislation have changed provisions in several program areas. The 1972 amendments (P.L. 92–603) extended Medicare protection to disabled persons receiving Social Security and to Railroad Retirement beneficiaries for at least 24 months. As of 1972 all Medicare beneficiaries are enrolled automatically in the SMI program but may subsequently decline coverage. Uninsured individuals who file for HI pay a $33 filing premium and must file for SMI coverage as well.

Specific provisions in the extent of coverage available have undergone several changes. At present, HI coverage includes, for each spell of illness, up to 90 days in a hospital, 100 days of home health services, and a lifetime reserve of 60 additional hospital days, as well as inpatient laboratory and X-ray services. Outpatient and emergency-room services, medical supplies and diagnostic services, outpatient laboratory and X-ray services, and 100 home health visits are covered under SMI. SMI does not cover preventive-care services such as routine physician checkups, hearing and vision examinations, immunizations unrelated to injury, and prescription drugs.

Other changes have established requirements for Medicare service providers to control costs and provide for quality of care. The 1965 amendments required that participating hospitals be accredited by the Joint Commission on the Accreditation of Hospitals (JCAH) and establish utilization review for Medicare services. In 1970 the Secretary of HEW announced that fiscal intermediaries for the Medicare program were to assess as "reasonable" charges falling within the 75th percentile of customary charges in effect during the calendar year preceding each fiscal year. The 1972 legislation permitted changes in the prevailing charge level after 1974, depending on changes in costs of medical practice and physicians' earning levels in each locality. Also in 1972 a limit was placed on the amount the insured individual would have to contribute for the SMI premium.

The 1972 amendments allowed suspension of hospitals from the Medicare program, despite a JCAH accreditation, if they did not meet the requisite performance guidelines established by HEW. It also permitted individuals eligible for both parts of Medicare, or for SMI only, to enroll after July 1973 in health-maintenance organizations—prepaid group practices or independent practice associations that had met prescribed standards. The Secretary of HEW was authorized to initiate demonstration projects implementing prospective reimbursement to determine the efficacy of this method of payment in reducing costs. In a further effort to monitor costs and utilization, it was required that the Secretary of HEW designate, by January 1974, areas in which local physicians would organize Professional Standards Review Organizations to review the necessity and quality of all Medicare (and Medicaid) services delivered in institutional settings.[8]

EXTENT OF EFFECTIVENESS[9]

Enrolled Population

Extent of Enrollment: HI and SMI.   The SAA estimated that 98.5 percent of the aged population was eligible for HI benefits under Medicare in 1970. Since the figure for total Medicare enrollment exceeds the U.S. Census Bureau's figure for the total aged population, it is difficult to estimate the proportion of the eligible aged actually enrolled in the program.[10] Migrant workers and domestic laborers are commonly excluded from Social Security Insurance coverage and are not, therefore, likely to be enrolled.

The enrollments for HI and SMI have increased since 1966, reflecting the growth of the aged population. By 1971, HI enrollment had increased by 8.7 percent and SMI by 12.6 percent (see Table 20). In 1966, 93 percent of all HI enrollees were also enrolled in the SMI program. This increased to 95.5 percent in 1971.[11] The greatest difference in the proportion of HI enrollees also covered by SMI was by race. In 1971, 96 percent of the white HI enrollees were in the SMI program, as compared to 90.3 percent of the nonwhite HI enrollees.[12]

Table 20   Medicare Enrollment and Annual Percentage Increase by Type of Coverage, FY 1966–FY 1971 (in thousands)

Type of Coverage	1966	1967	1968	1969	1970	1971
Hospital insurance (HI)	19,082	19,494	19,770	20,014	20,361	20,742
Supplementary medical insurance (SMI)	17,736	17,893	18,805	19,195	19,584	19,975
HI and SMI	17,710	17,866	18,754	19,107	19,455	19,802
HI only	1,373	1,628	1,016	908	907	940
SMI only	26	27	51	88	130	173
		Annual Percentage Increase				
HI	—	2.2	1.4	1.2	1.7	1.9
SMI	—	0.9	5.1	2.1	2.0	2.0
HI and SMI	—	0.9	5.0	1.9	1.8	1.8
HI only	—	18.6	−37.6	−10.6	−0.1	3.7
SMI only	—	2.7	88.2	73.3	46.9	33.1

SOURCE.   Office of Research and Statistics, *Medicare: Health Insurance for the Aged, 1971, Section 2: Persons Enrolled in the Health Insurance Program.* DHEW Publication No. (SSA) 73-11704 (Washington, D.C.: Government Printing Office, August 1973), based on Table A, p. ix.

According to a report to Congress by the U.S. Comptroller General based on a survey of six states, the Medicare buy-in arrangement for Medicaid recipients has not been fully implemented. As of December 1971, about 2 million aged were enrolled in Medicare through the buy-in program, and yet three large stages had failed to enroll significant number of eligible elderly: in New York, 25,000 eligible public-assistance recipients were not enrolled; in California, 42,000; and in Pennsylvania, 9500. Although old-age public-assistance recipients are eligible for coverage under Medicaid, it is frequently not as nearly complete as that under Medicare.[13]

Characteristics of the Enrolled Population.   The distribution of HI enrollees by race and sex has been stable since Medicare began in 1966.

In 1971, 90 percent of the enrolled population was known to be white and 8 percent nonwhite, the highest proportion of nonwhites (15 percent) residing in the South. The larger proportion of women than men, 58.4 compared to 41.6 percent, is related to the greater longevity of women. The median age of the population was fairly constant, although nonwhites were slightly younger than whites. The trend in SMI enrollment from 1966 to 1971 resembles that of HI for race, sex, and median age.[14]

Changes in Utilization

By subsidizing the medical-care demands of the elderly, Medicare was intended to affect their utilization in two ways. It was expected that use of health-care services by covered persons would increase relative to that of other persons and that it would reflect health status (needs) rather than financial or other factors.[15]

Hospital Utilization under Medicare. The effect of Medicare on the use of hospital care provides some measure of its overall success in meeting its aim of increasing access to *all* health-care services. Several surveys demonstrate differences in use rates before and after Medicare and during the program's career.

According to data collected by the National Opinion Research Center (NORC), the *proportion* of the aged population using short-stay hospitals—although rising slightly—did not change significantly from 1965 to 1967. The mean number of days per stay did increase 12 percent, resulting in a 25 percent increase in the total number of days of hospital care per person, 3.9 days in contrast to 3.1 days before Medicare.

Not all segments of the aged population experienced uniform increases. A significantly larger increase in days of care per 1000 persons occurred for persons aged 75 and over, nonwhites, residents of the South, residents of urban areas other than metropolitan, and persons in one-member family units with low incomes.[16] Although the substantial gap in the number of hospitalization episodes per 1000 persons between whites and nonwhites was not closed, nonwhites did have a growth in the number of days of care.

Data from the National Center for Health Statistics (NCHS) Hospital Discharge Survey demonstrate that increases in the days of hospital care per 1000 up to 1967–1968 were owing primarily to an increased average length of stay. Thereafter, a lower rate of increase, or an actual decrease, occurred (see Table 21). This calendar-year trend in hospital use rates, excluding the discharge rate, is roughly similar to trends demonstrated by fiscal year data for the same period from the American Hospital Association's (AHA) community-hospital survey and the Medicare Control Records (MCR) census of claims for hospitals certified for participation in HI.

The trend in hospital use exhibits three distinct periods. Between 1967 and 1968, hospital use increased substantially because of several factors: an epidemic of respiratory infection, the fulfillment of previously unmet demands, and the addition of a lifetime reserve of 60 days with the ratification of the 1967 amendment. The 1968–1969 period was marked by a stabilization of hospital use. In the 1969–1971 period, this pattern was reversed; use declined, perhaps

Table 21   Short-Stay Hospital Utilization Rates for Persons Aged 65 and Over, CY 1965 and CY 1967 (NCHS Hospital Discharge Survey Data)[a]

Measures of Utilization	1965	1966	1967	1968	1969	1970
Discharges, rate per 1000	264	277	289	301	305	306
Days of care per 1000	3444	3712	4086	4272	4276	4015
Average length of stay (days)	13.0	13.4	14.1	14.2	14.0	13.1
Annual Percentage Changes						
Discharges, rate per 1000		4.9	4.3	4.2	1.3	0.3
Days of care per 1000		7.8	10.1	4.6	0.1	−6.1
Average length of stay (days)		3.1	5.2	0.7	−1.4	−6.4

SOURCE.   Julia Pettengill, "Trends in Hospital Use by the Aged," *Social Security Bulletin* **35**:3–15 (July 1972); based on Table B, p. 12. Annual percentage changes calculated from data.
[a] Since 1967, federally owned hospitals eliminated.

owing to exhaustion of initial demand, more rigorous application of utilization review limiting the number of days in a hospital, and increases in cost-sharing requirements.

The AHA, MCR, and NCHS surveys do not provide breakdowns for hospital utilization rates on socioeconomic or demographic variables. Karen Davis, using regression analysis on data from the 1969 Health Interview Survey conducted by the National Center for Health Statistics, found that use of hospital services increased with income and that nonwhite aged in the South had lower use rates than their white counterparts.[17]

Ambulatory-Care Utilization under Medicare: Overall Changes in Use.   The NORC survey data on rates of ambulatory care for those 65 years and over reveal no significant changes in the percent of persons making visits or in the number of visits per year between 1965 and 1967. A substantial shift in place of care was evident, however; a larger proportion saw a physician in the office, and fewer had home visits. Fewer persons reported visits to a clinic after Medicare; the relative decline was greatest for those in rural areas and smallest for residents in metropolitan areas. Nonwhites also exhibited a decline in the use of clinics: 25 percent used clinics in 1965, dropping to 14 percent in 1967. Medicare did not, however, eliminate the disparity in use of clinics by race. The percent of whites using clinics in 1965 was 13 percent, dropping to 8 percent in 1967.[18]

Data from the Current Medicare Survey show that, although the number of persons enrolled in SMI has grown since 1967, the proportion of enrollees using covered services has been fairly constant at 79 percent.[19] The proportion meeting the deductible has, however, increased slightly from 45.8 percent in 1967 to 50.3 percent in 1971. Whereas the proportion of SMI enrollees using all covered services has remained essentially constant, the number of persons per 1000 with visits in a physician's office decreased during the 1967–1970 period, as did the number of persons per 1000 with home visits. The number of persons using outpatient services increased during the same period. The average number of visits for all three ambulatory services also increased during this time, although at differing rates.

Although these data from the Current Medicare Survey are not strictly comparable to the NORC survey data, it appears that a decline in the proportion of persons with physician visits in the home has continued since Medicare began but that the proportion using outpatient services increased during the 1967–1970 period, contrary to the pre-Medicare experience.

Differential Use of Ambulatory Care.   Studies by Karen Davis at The Brookings Institution demonstrate that use of SMI services, the best proxy for use of primary care under Medicare, has varied considerably by income, race, and region. In 1968, persons with higher incomes received more services and more reimbursable services at higher charges, reflecting both greater utilization and price differential (see Table 22). Although low-income persons ranked lowest in utilization and reimbursement rates, those receiving public assistance used 30 to 40 percent more services than other low-income persons, factors such as health status, age, sex, race, and education being held constant.[20]

Physician visits per person aged 65 and over do not increase uniformly by income as might be expected:

Under $5000	6.4
$5000–9999	6.1
$10,000–14,999	6.8
$15,000 and over	9.4

When health status is taken into account, the pattern of physician visits exhibits an almost uniform progression. In each health-status category, use increases with income. Within each income group, however, use increases with poor health (see Table 23). The effect of public assistance on utilization is again reflected by the larger average number of physician visits for this group compared to the aged with incomes under $5000 who are not public-assistance recipients. A smaller proportion of nonwhites than whites received SMI services in 1968, but use of outpatient services by nonwhites was greater than that of the white population (see Table 24).

The aged in the South, regardless of race, had low utilization rates for physicians' services when compared to those in other regions. When use is com-

Table 22 Reimbursements for Covered Services and Persons Served under SMI, by Income, 1968

Family Income	Reimbursement per Person Enrolled	Persons Receiving Reimbursable Services per 1000 Enrollees	Number of Reimbursable Services per Person Receiving Reimbursable Services	Reimbursement per Reimbursable Service
Average	$ 88.60	460.1	26.6	$ 7.27
Under $5000	78.77	431.7	26.0	7.02
$5000–9999	103.87	475.0	26.6	8.21
$10,000–14,999	115.10	527.2	27.5	7.95
$15,000 and over	160.30	552.3	27.9	10.40
Ratio, over $15,000 income to under $5000 income	2.04	1.28	1.07	1.48

SOURCE. From calculations based on unpublished tabulations from the 1968 Current Medicare Survey, in Karen Davis and Roger Reynolds, *Medicare and the Utilization of Health Care Services by the Elderly* (Washington, D.C.: The Brookings Institution, December 1973, unpublished), Table 1, p. 3.

Table 23 Average Physician Visits for the Elderly, by Health Status and Family Income, Adjusted for Other Morbidity Indicators

Family Income	Health Status[a]		
	Perfect	Average	Poor
Under $5000			
No Aid	2.78	5.64	10.47
Aid[b]	3.86	7.52	13.42
$5000–9999	3.14	6.60	11.70
$10,000–14,999	3.75	7.27	12.98
$15,000 and over	5.35	9.53	16.98

SOURCE. From calculations based on 1969 Health Interview Survey in Karen Davis and Roger Reynolds, *Medicare and The Utilization of Health Care Services by the Elderly* (Washington, D.C.: The Brookings Institution, December 1973, unpublished), Table 5, p. 14; see Table 4, p. 13, for other morbidity indicators used in adjustment.

[a] Perfect health status is defined as without any chronic conditions, limitation of activity, or restricted activity days. Average and poor health status is defined at the mean and twice the mean level of the three morbidity indicators used.

[b] Aid indicates public assistance recipients.

Table 24   Reimbursements for Covered Services and Persons Served under SMI, by Race, 1968

Race	Persons Receiving Reimbursable Services per 1000 Enrollees	Reimbursement per Person Served	Reimbursement per Enrollee
	Physician Services		
White	394.9	$199.44	$78.76
Other	279.4	$173.37	$48.44
Ratio: white to other	1.41	1.15	1.63
	Hospital Outpatient Services		
White	75.7	$ 39.02	$ 2.79
Other	89.8	$ 50.43	$ 4.53
Ratio: white to other	0.84	0.77	0.62

SOURCE.   Karen Davis, *Financing Medical Care: Implications for Access to Primary Care.* Paper presented at the Sun Valley Forum on National Health, Sun Valley, Idaho (June 28, 1973), unpublished, Table 3, p. 20.

pared to reported presence of a chronic illness, residents of the South seemed to have the greatest unmet need for medical services. The percents of elderly persons with some activity limitation due to chronic illness for 1968–1969 by region were as follows: South, 49.5 percent; Northeast, 39.4 percent; North-Central, 39.6 percent; and West, 38.9 percent.[22] The aged in the North-Central region had the lowest utilization rate, but their health status was superior to that of the aged in the South, and also in the West, where use was the highest. Low utilization rates in both the South and North-Central regions are partly explained by low concentrations of physicians and difficulties in access owing to unavailability of physicians.

Impact on Financial Barrier

Initial Decrease in Personal Expenditures.   Since implementation of Medicare (and Medicaid) in 1966, government's share of personal health-care expenditures has risen sharply, from 22 percent in 1966 to 37 percent in 1972.[23] Although these proportions are based on figures that include state and local government expenditures, as well as those of the federal government, virtually the entire shift was due to increased federal expenditures.[24] Moreover, almost all of the shift from private to public spending since 1966 has been in the financing of health care for the aged, chiefly through Medicare. Since 1966, the private portion of health-care costs for those aged 65 and over—costs met by out-of-pocket payments, private health insurance, philanthropy, and industry—

has been cut in half, from 70 percent in 1966 to 34 percent in 1972.[25] By 1968 government's share in health expenditures for the aged reached a high of 67.6 percent, from the 1966 low of 29.8 percent before full implementation of Medicare. Out-of-pocket payments made by the elderly declined sharply as a proportion of their personal health-care costs, from 53.2 percent in 1966 to 26.4 percent in 1968 and a low of 25.5 percent by 1969.

Partial Rebuilding of Financial Barrier. Despite increasing total and per capita government expenditures on health care for the aged, the portion of health-care bills for the aged paid for by Medicare has declined in recent years, from 46 percent in 1969 to 42 percent in 1971 and 1972.[26] Several factors are responsible for this decrease, all of which suggest a partial rebuilding of financial barriers for the aged. Since 1969, cost-sharing requirements under both the HI and SMI programs have risen. HI cost-sharing provisions have doubled in all categories, and whereas the annual deductible for SMI services has increased only $10 (20 percent), the monthly premium has doubled since 1966. Medicare contributions to payments for physicians' services have dropped, as a result of more stringent reimbursement regulations and the decreasing number of claims for which physicians agree to accept Medicare's "reasonable" charges as full payment. The proportion of hospital charges paid by Medicare has decreased since 1969 also, since the length of stay for the elderly has shortened and since many hospital services used by the aged are covered only partly if at all. In addition, significant reductions have been made in Medicare payments for services in extended-care facilities, owing to utilization and cost controls imposed in 1970.[27]

Despite the decreased proportion of costs paid by the elderly in out-of-pocket payments. the absolute value of those payments has increased since 1968, partly as a result of increased cost sharing. By 1970 their direct payments equaled those paid before full implementation of Medicare. By 1972 they were more than $40 higher, up almost 18 percent. At the same time, the proportion of payments met by private health insurance, declining after 1966, had not increased to fill this gap. A significant portion of the aged population is not, however, protected by private health insurance to supplement Medicare payments and must themselves pay for expenses not covered by the program. In 1972, 47 percent of those 65 and over were not insured for hospital care, 80 percent were not covered for ambulatory-care services such as physician office visits and home visits, and 83 percent had no insurance for the costs of out-of-hospital prescription drugs.[28]

Differential Effects of Cost-Sharing Provisions on Ambulatory Care. An extensive analysis of the socioeconomic and demographic characteristics associated with differential rates of utilization of SMI services was conducted by Peel and Scharff to determine the effect of cost sharing on use of ambulatory services. The investigators divided the 1969 SMI population without hospital stays (N = 15 million) into the following categories: those receiving public medical assistance, 12.7 percent; those possessing private insurance covering out-of-hospital services, 17.2 percent; persons with high annual family income but no supplementary insurance, 9.2 percent; those with low to moderate family incomes without additional insurance, 51.3 percent; and those with financial background not reported, 9.6 percent.[29]

The public-assistance category had twice as many individuals aged 80 and over than the other groups and also the largest proportions of women and non-white persons.[30] These individuals were the heaviest users of SMI-covered services and had the largest number of services per user. A large proportion of users in high-income families met the deductible and incurred charges of $100 or more. The low-to-moderate income group had the largest proportion of enrollees who failed to use any covered services. This group also had the lowest percent using enough services to meet the deductible of $100.

The low-to-moderate income group (excluding those on public assistance) had the largest proportion of persons with less than seven years of education and significant numbers of nonwhites (9 percent) and rural residents (18 percent).[31] Of those who claimed their health to be worse than others their age, 20 percent did not use covered services, and 57 percent used services to the extent that they met the deductible.[32] In comparison 12 percent of the respondents with private insurance who assessed their health as worse than others their age did not use covered services, and 67 percent used enough services to meet the deductible.[33] This middle-income group also perceived themselves to have a high level of unmet medical needs (30 percent, as compared to 19 percent of those with insurance and 17 percent of the high-income families)[34] and felt the deductible to be a heavier burden and a more formidable deterrent to seeking medical care than other income groups did.

Distribution of Medicare Expenditures

The majority of Medicare expenditures have been directed toward the provision of institutional care. The proportion of total expenditures devoted to SMI services, or ambulatory care, has remained consistently under one-third of all expenditures. Annual proportions (in percent) since 1967 are as follows:[35]

1967	23.5
1968	28.7
1969	27.9
1970	30.7
1971	29.0

When a claim is submitted for payment under Medicare, the full amount is not necessarily reimbursable. The percent actually reimbursed of the amount claimed was slightly higher for HI claims, 75.9 percent in calendar year (CY) 1972, than for SMI, 73.2 percent.[36]

Whereas the proportion of Medicare expenditures for service benefits distributed by state is predominantly influenced by the proportion of aged in a state, other factors intervene, such as the availability of medical facilities and services and the prices for such services. The proportions of Medicare expenditures distributed to each region in 1969 were 28 percent each to the Northeast and North-Central, 25 percent to the South, and 19 percent in the West.[37] By that year Medicare was the largest public source of health-care funds in 45 states. It was an especially important component in health-care spending in the South, where federal expenditures in 1969 represented 75 percent of a total of $4.39 billion as compared to 56 percent of a total of $5.726 billion in the Northeast.[38]

PROGRAM COSTS

Program costs for Medicare appear in Table 25. In examining total expenditures from FY 1967 through FY 1973, most striking is the rate of increase between FY 1967 and FY 1968 for total expenditures and benefit payments under HI and SMI. After FY 1968, the rate of increase fell off sharply in all categories of expenditures except administrative expenses. These decreasing rates of growth have continued for total SMI payments, but SMI benefit payments, as well as HI total and benefit payments, have shown larger rates of increase since FY 1970.

Administrative expenses for both HI and SMI in FY 1967, the first year of program operation, represented a larger proportion of total expenses than in any other year, as might be expected (3.4 percent of total HI expenses and 16.8 percent of total SMI expenses). Since 1968, administrative expenses for the HI program have remained between 2 and 3 percent of total expenditure. Those for the SMI program are more sizable, representing between 9 and 11 percent of total expenditures since 1968.

The relatively low figure for the first year was due to an initial lag in the processing of bills for reimbursement and payment of extended-care benefits for the latter half of the fiscal year. The subsequent decline in rate of growth has been attributed to a reduction in the backlog of medical-care needs of the enrolled population, the adoption of utilization controls, discontinuance of the 2 percent cost-plus reimbursement to hospitals, restriction of reimbursement of physician services, and increasing cost-sharing requirements. The impact of the Economic Stabilization Program further limited the rate of increase as of 1972.[39]

SECONDARY EFFECTS

The secondary effects of Medicare are multiple, many running counter to original goals. In general, these unintended consequences have either reinstated financial barriers or affected the availability of services.

Medicare and Medical Price Inflation

The American economy has had periods of inflation during the last 25 years; however, the rise in medical-care prices has been greater than other items measured by the Consumer Price Index. Between 1960 and 1965, consumer prices rose at an average annual rate of 1.3 percent, whereas medical-care prices rose 2.5 percent annually. After the introduction of Medicare in 1966, medical-care prices rose at an increased average annual growth rate of 6.1 percent through 1970, while consumer items rose at a rate of 4.2 percent. Both increases slowed considerably in 1972 as a result of the August 1971 freeze on wages and prices and subsequent economic controls.

Factors cited as contributing to a rise in hospital prices are increased demand, rising costs of labor, and increased capital outlays and expansion of outpatient departments. Increased physician fees also contributed to the overall rise of medical-care prices. Medicare, by expanding the demand for physicians' services, has given impetus to the rise in physicians' charges. The initial method of physician reimbursement for Medicare services, on the basis of customary and prevailing charges, added to this growth in prices. Before Medicare many physicians employed a sliding-fee scale for the needy elderly but abandoned this mechanism when given the prospect of full reimbursement with the advent of Medicare.[40]

Imbalance of Supply and Demand

This insurance program created a sudden increase in effective demand in a system or marketplace with a fixed quantity of manpower and services available. The results were manifested by increased prices, rationing of services, and exposure of the extent of the shortages of physician manpower, especially in certain geographic areas and types of practice.

Impact of Rising Program Costs

Continually and rapidly rising program costs have been the major impetus for legislative changes in the program. The Senate Finance Committee's report on the fiscal impact of Medicare in 1970 concludes that this program had led to "serious financial trouble." In documentary evidence supporting this contention, the report cited revisions made in the projections of Health Insurance

Table 25 Total Medicare Expenditures, FY 1967–FY 1973; Total and Per Capita HI and SMI Expenditures, FY 1967–FY 1971

Program	Fiscal Year						
	1967	1968	1969	1970	1971	1972[a]	1973[a]
	Amount (in millions)						
Total	3,395	5,347	6,598	7,149	7,875	8,819	9,478
HI	2,597	3,815	4,758	4,953	5,592		
Benefit payments	2,508	3,736	4,654	4,804	5,443		
Administrative expenses	89	79	104	149	149		
SMI	798	1,532	1,840	2,196	2,283		
Benefit payments	664	1,390	1,645	1,979	2,035		
Administrative expenses	134	143	195	217	248		
	Per Capita Amount						
HI	136	196	241	245[b]	272		
Benefit payments	131	192	236	238	265		
Administrative expenses	5	4	5	7	7		
SMI	45	85	98	113[b]	116		

160

Benefit payments	37	77	87	102	103	7.5
Administrative expenses	8	8	10	11	13	12.0

Percentage Change from Preceding Fiscal Year

Total	—	57.5	23.4	8.4	10.2
HI	—	46.9	24.7	4.1	12.9
Benefit payments	—	49.0	24.6	3.2	13.3
Administrative expenses	—	−11.5	32.5	42.7	.6
SMI	—	92.0	20.1	19.4	3.9
Benefit payments	—	109.2	18.4	20.3	2.8
Administrative expenses	—	6.7	36.5	11.5	14.1

SOURCE. For 1967–1971: Howard West, "Five Years of Medicare—a Statistical Review," *Social Security Bulletin* **34**:17–27 (December 1971); based on Table 5, p. 20. For 1972 and 1973 totals: Barbara Cooper, Nancy L. Worthington, and Paula A. Piro, "National Health Expenditures, 1929–1973." *Social Security Bulletin* **37**:2–19 (February 1974); based on Table 3, p. 8 and Table 3, p. 7. Percentage change calculated for 1972–1973.
a Breakdown by HI and SMI is not available. Includes benefit payments, administrative expenses, and premium payments for SMI by or on behalf of enrollees.
b Corrected totals.

program costs[41]:

Year Actuarial Estimate Made	Billions of Dollars
In: 1965 for 1970	3.1
1967 for 1970	4.4
1969 for 1970	5.0

Legislative cost consciousness led to the enactment of controls, such as restrictions of the reimbursement levels for medical-care providers and increased rates of cost sharing. These regulatory measures reduced use and increased out-of-pocket health-care expenses, and hence reduced access.

Despite uniform coverage for all eligible persons, disparities in the use of SMI services persist because of uniform cost-sharing requirements that weigh most heavily on low-income and nonwhite aged. In 1971 approximately 25 percent of the aged population was below the official poverty level. (The aged constitute 10 percent of the total population, and they represent 20 percent of the poor.)[42] Lack of coverage for all low-income persons for SMI services through the Medicaid program's "buy-in" option contributed to their lower use.

Reaction of Health-Care Providers.   The reaction of health-care providers to Medicare cost controls created additional financial and supply barriers for the aged. Under Medicare, a physician has the option to be reimbursed by assignment or by the patient. In the former instance, full payment is made at the reasonable charge level according to regulation. In the latter, the physician's charge may exceed this level, and the patient must then pay whatever portion Medicare will not reimburse. The proportion of physicians accepting assignment has declined from 61 percent in FY 1969 to 53 percent in 1973.[43] In New York it was recently reported that differences between physicians' bills and Medicare reimbursements paid by the patient totaled $70 million in 1973.[44]

Whereas some physicians have responded to Medicare by refusing to accept assignment, other health-care providers have withdrawn from the program entirely. According to a government auditor's survey of hospitals and nursing homes in California, Texas, and Massachusetts, 10 institutions dropped out of Medicare by the end of 1971, 3 owing to governmental demands that they return millions of dollars in overpayments.[45] This situation apparently evolved because the federal government, through the fiscal intermediaries, had overestimated the actual level of hospital costs considered reimbursable.

Withdrawal from Medicare participation was not the only response from providers of care. Inclusion of extended-care services in HI coverage and the prospect of a ready-made market of elderly persons who could pay hospital bills in full resulted in a large increase in the number of nursing homes, many of them for-profit concerns.

Program Impact on the Nonaged Population

Cost and Availability of Care.   Many of Medicare's secondary or unintended effects have had a significant impact on that part of the population not covered by the program. Through its contribution to medical-care price inflation, Medicare generated higher medical costs for the entire population. Furthermore, rising program costs owing to inflation necessitated a higher payroll tax to finance the increase. Some of the inflation was due to an inadequate supply of providers to meet the demand prompted by Medicare coverage, and there is some evidence that Medicare may have been a factor in the rationing of health-care services, both ambulatory and inpatient, resulting in lower utilization rates for the younger population.[46]

OVERALL IMPACT ON ACCESS TO PRIMARY CARE

It is difficult to evaluate Medicare's impact on access to primary-care services alone. As an insurance mechanism, its major purpose was to eliminate financial barriers associated with the use of all health-care services, and the primary focus of its coverage was on more costly hospital care. Coverage under HI is compulsory for all Medicare enrollees: SMI, as its name suggests, is a supplement to HI's basic protection against financial barriers, and participation in SMI is voluntary. Consequently, the program has been most successful in providing assistance with costly institutional care. Even though Medicare has considerably improved the access of the aged to hospital care, nonwhites and lower income groups with poorer health use fewer services than their health levels warrant.

Despite the optimal nature of SMI coverage, which reflects coverage of primary-care services under Medicare, most enrollees in Medicare also have protection against financial barriers associated with use of ambulatory-care services. Although there does not appear to have been an increase in the proportion of the elderly with physician visits or in the number of physician visits per person overall, noticeable shifts in the location of ambulatory care have taken place. The immediate impact of SMI was to lower the use of outpatient clinics and home visits in favor of visits to physicians' offices the greatest relative improvement being experienced by nonwhites and rural residents. This apparent increase in the availability of personal physicians shifted again in the early 1970s, visits to outpatient clinics replacing those to office and home.

Contrary to expectations, use of services under SMI does not always reflect health status but is somewhat more closely associated with income. More high-income aged use SMI services and receive more costly services, as reflected in proportionately higher reimbursement rates. The low-income aged on public assistance, generally with poorer health, *do* tend to use SMI services in relation to their health status and use more of them than low-income aged with no public aid or those in the low-to-middle income bracket. For this latter group, with few outside resources to pay the costs of services not covered by Medicare, the imposition of higher cost sharing has interfered considerably with their use of ambulatory services. For other groups of the aged population, particularly nonwhites and those living in the South, possible gains in use of ambulatory-care services have been offset by the interplay of factors such as the maldistribution of providers of care[47] and the cost-sharing features of the program itself.

The positive impact of Medicare's subsidy of use of health-care services by the aged has been confounded by unexpected rises in costs and subsequent imposition of utilization and cost controls. Since institution of these controls, the payments made by the elderly for their services have increased. Some aged are able to meet these personal payments or have commercial health insurance to aid them. The impact on other elderly persons of this partial rebuilding of a financial barrier is reflected in stabilization or decreases in use of all types of services under Medicare. Medicare's subsidy of demand without any concomitant concern with supply revealed the imbalance between demand and supply of services and *may* have reduced the volume of care available to those under 65 years of age.

SUMMARY

The passage of Public Law 89–97 eliminated financial barriers inhibiting access to institutional care for the aged in the United States. Because of deductibles and subsequent increases in the costs of the coverage for Part B that must be paid by the beneficiary, its effects on access to ambulatory care have been somewhat less dramatic. Medicare also created secondary and unintended effects on the health-care system. Various efforts have been designed to cope with these, including programs to increase the supply of provider services, systems for monitoring the quantity and quality of services rendered, and other attempts at cost control. Medicare probably has had the greatest direct impact of any program to date on access to primary care; its indirect effects on access may, however, prove to be even greater.

TWELVE

Medicaid:

ELIMINATION OF FINANCIAL BARRIERS TO CARE FOR LOW-INCOME PERSONS?

REASONS FOR DEVELOPMENT OF PROGRAM

Medical Assistance Programs Before Medicaid

Financial barriers inhibit access to health care for low-income persons, who as a group are in poorer health than those with higher incomes. For many decades some form of public assistance has been provided to low-income persons in the United States to aid them in obtaining health-care services. Traditionally, such assistance was the concern of local authorities and of state governments and was usually provided in the form of services available without charge at publicly owned hospitals and outpatient clinics.

The federal government first became involved in financing health services for low-income persons during the economic depression of the 1930s. Provisions in the 1935 Social Security Act offered federal funds to match state payments for medical expenses made directly to welfare recipients, subject to state and federal matching maximums. No federal funds were available for matching payments made to those providing services to public-assistance recipients. State participation in this matching program was optional, as were the standards chosen by each state for entitlement and coverage.

Medical assistance remained a minor part of overall public assistance until 1950. Amendments to the Social Security legislation in that year established a federally supported program of direct medical-vendor payments, making federal matching funds available to state public-assistance programs for payment of charges directly to physicians, hospitals, and others who had provided health services to those qualifying for public assistance. By 1960 more than four-fifths of the states participated in the program, which disbursed more than $500 million annually in medical-vendor payments to all public-assistance categories.[1]

Passage of the Kerr–Mills Act in 1960 signaled a major increase in federally supported medical assistance to low-income persons, particularly to the low-income aged. Also of major importance in the legislation was establishment of a new aid category, the "medically needy," those whose incomes were too high for them to be eligible for public assistance but were too low to cover their health-care expenses. Again, state participation was optional, and each state determined its own standards for medical and financial need as well as the scope of services covered. By the end of 1965, most states had set up programs under the new regulation. These programs spent slightly more than $100 million per month for services provided to some 7.5 million persons, including 3.5 million children and more than 2 million elderly persons.[2]

Inadequacies of the Kerr–Mills Program

Despite the sizable federal, state, and local funds committed to the Kerr–Mills program, the disadvantageous position of low-income persons, as reflected by lower rates of use of health-care services, persisted. A survey of the use of personal health services of a sample of the United States population in 1963, reported by Andersen and Anderson in 1967, documented these differences. Low-income families (less than $4000 annual income) were more likely to use outpatient clinics or to have no regular source of care than families with higher incomes. When personal physicians were named by low-income families as a regular source of care, they more often tended to be general practitioners, rather than specialists, and these doctors were considerably older than physicians seen by higher income families.

The proportion of persons making visits to a physician in 1963 increased in direct relation to income (see Table 26). Low-income children were at a particular disadvantage. Whereas young children from middle- and upper

Table 26   Percent of Persons Visiting a Physician During 1963, by Age and Family Income[a]

Age	Income		
	$0–3,999	$4,000–6,999	$7,000 and Over
1–5	52	76	87
6–17	41	53	70
18–34	57	67	70
35–54	54	64	69
55–64	69	70	66
65 and over	68	66	71
	—	—	—
Total:	56	64	71

SOURCE.   Ronald Andersen and Odin W. Anderson, *A Decade of Health Services: Social Survey Trends in Use and Expenditure* (Chicago: The University of Chicago Press, 1967), Table 2, p. 29.

[a] Based on multistage area probability sample of total noninstitutionalized population of United States in 1963; percents calculated only on those in sample for entire 12-month period.

income families were most likely to have made visits to a doctor than any other group, those aged 1–17 years in the low-income group were the least likely to have seen a physician during the year. The income–use relation did not hold for those over 55 years of age. Similar proportions of older persons in all income groups made physician visits. Higher income persons reported, however, more illness episodes during the year than those in the low-income group. The investigators noted that low-income persons were less likely to respond to selected symptoms by visiting a physician. The data indicate the effects of financial and psychosocial barriers on access to care. Predictably, expenditures for personal health services reflected this differential use, low-income families spending the least during the year. Low-income families devoted, however, a larger proportion of their total annual incomes to health care than any other group did in 1963, and that proportion increased far more rapidly for the lowest income group (less than $2000 annual income) than for other groups during the preceding five years.[3]

Such findings indicated to analysts that coverage of medical-care costs of the low-income population under Kerr–Mills was incomplete and inadequate. Yerby, describing the status of health care for the needy in mid-1965, found that comprehensive health-care programs for low-income persons existed in less than one-fourth of all states and that similar programs for the medically needy were virtually nonexistent. He noted that administrative concern with increasing costs and fiscal accountability under the Kerr–Mills and general public-assistance programs, rather than the provision of adequate and high-quality health-care services, had led to programs of care he characterized as "piecemeal, poorly supervised, and uncoordinated." Services available were "frequently inadequate, sometimes quite poor, and rarely related to the total needs of the individual or to the family."[4] Similar findings, in terms of administrative and financial problems, were reported by the Senate Special Committee on Aging during subcommittee investigations into the administration and effectiveness of the Kerr–Mills program for the elderly, Medical Assistance for the Aged.[5]

Political response to the administrative inadequacies and the lack of demonstrated effectiveness in reaching and assisting all low-income persons, not only the elderly, was evident in amendments to the Social Security Act proposed in the 89th Congress. Their passage significantly increased the involvement of the federal government in financing health care for low-income persons under a program known as Medicaid.

NATURE OF INTERVENTION

Title XIX of the 1965 Social Security Act amendments (P.L. 89–97) authorized establishment of a jointly funded and administered federal–state program of medical assistance known as Medicaid. The program was designed to reduce financial barriers to access to health care for low-income and medically needy persons by subsidizing their use of services with direct payments to the providers. As in Medicare, Medicaid was designed to be only a financing mechanism and was not intended to affect or alter directly the supply or distribution of health-care services. As described in the legislation, Medicaid was to

furnish medical assistance on behalf of families with dependent children, and of aged, blind or permanently and totally disabled individuals whose income and resources are insufficient to meet the costs of necessary medical services, and rehabilitation and other services to help families and individuals attain or retain capability for independence.[6]

The intent of Medicaid was to broaden the eligibility and scope of covered services of each state's medical-assistance program then operating under Kerr–Mills legislation, with federal participation contingent on "maintenance of effort"; that is, federal funds were to supplement, not supplant, the states' medical-assistance programs. By mandating a minimum level of eligibility coverage and covered services, Title XIX was to eliminate existing inequities in the Kerr–Mills programs owing to differing state standards.

SOURCES

Aggregate financial data on state Medicaid programs are collected and published periodically by the National Center for Social Statistics (NCSS), Social and Rehabilitation Service, Department of Health, Education, and Welfare. The primary source of trend data on the distribution of Medicaid payments by assistance category and type of service was the NCSS Report B-5 series for FY 1968–1971. These data were supplemented by information from other NCSS series where fiscal-year reporting did not provide specific data, and with an advance copy of the reporting for FY 1972. Lack of continuity in the data used in this case study is owing to changes and gaps in reporting and to the unavailability of data collected in recent years.

Aggregate data on trends in the utilization of health-care services under Medicaid are not readily available from NCSS, since state programs are not required to collect and report them. Some states do so, however, although collection and reporting requirements are not uniform. Two recent unpublished studies on use of ambulatory care by Medicaid recipients for specific time periods include available data. These studies, by Karen Davis at Brookings and by John Holahan at the Urban Institute, are the best sources (in lieu of aggregate trend data), for estimating the impact of Medicaid on use of primary-care services. Both investigators were contacted during preparation of the case study, as was Jack Ebeler, program analyst for the Medical Services Administration, Social and Rehabilitation Service, Department of Health, Education, and Welfare, who discussed the operation of Medicaid.

DESCRIPTION OF THE PROGRAM[7]

Medicaid comprises 50 federal–state programs of medical assistance for low-income and medically needy persons. Each state program is administered by local and state agencies responsible for operation of the state public-assistance program. The federal portion of each is administered at the national level by the Medical Services Administration, a branch of the Social and Rehabilitation Service in HEW. Although participation in Medicaid is voluntary, the original legislation exerted considerable pressure on each state to participate by providing that no federal matching funds under the categorical titles for public-assistance programs and under Kerr–Mills would be available after December 31, 1969.

Entitlement

Eligibility for Medicaid benefits is determined at the state level, following federal guidelines defining those groups whose coverage is required or optional. As established in the original legislation, these categories were as follows:

1. *Required* inclusions—*money payment recipients*: persons receiving public assistance payments in the four public-assistance categories—Old-Age Assistance (OAA), Aid to the Blind (AB), Aid to the Permanently and Totally Disabled (APTD), and Aid to Families with Dependent Children (AFDC).
2. Optional inclusions—*medically needy recipients*: the aged, blind, disabled, and mothers with dependent children who were not eligible for public-assistance money payments but whose incomes were not sufficient to pay for health-care bills (as determined by income levels set by each state), as well as poor children under 21 who were not members of AFDC families.
   —"other" medically needy: adults aged 21 to 64 who were not eligible for public-assistance money payments and whose incomes were inadequate to cover their medical bills.

Coverage

The original legislation required each state program to cover inpatient and outpatient services, other laboratory and X-ray services, nursing-home services, and physicians' services for all money-payment recipients. Coverage of these basic services for other eligibles, and of any optional services, such as prescribed drugs; additional screening, diagnostic, preventive, and rehabilitative services; or emergency services, was at the state's discretion.

Financing

Financing for medical-vendor payments through Medicaid comes from state medical-assistance funds matched by the federal government at levels of 50 to 83 percent, depending on the state's per capita income. The higher the state's per capita income, the lower the level of matching funds. Under the original legislation, matching funds were available only for medical-vendor payments made in behalf of money-payment recipients and medically needy recipients. In addition, the federal government provided 75 percent of the administrative costs of payments to all recipient categories, including those for which it did not match vendor payments. Each state chose at the outset a fiscal intermediary to make payments according to the Medicare principle of reimbursement of providers on a basis of reasonable costs and charges. A "buy-in" provision allowed the states the option of paying for Supplementary Medical Insurance premiums and copayment requirements under Medicare for OAA recipients and the aged medically needy.

Program Changes

Amendments to the original Medicaid legislation have been made most often in response to escalating costs. These have resulted in restrictions on entitlement, coverage, and levels of reimbursement. Testimony to the impact of this concern on program goals is evident in the shifting target dates for attaining coverage of comprehensive health-care services for a substantial portion of the low-income population. The 1965 legislation established a target date of 1975, and the 1969 amendments postponed this deadline to 1977. In the 1972 amendments, this goal was abandoned entirely.

The 1967 amendments (P.L. 90–248) set federal guidelines for definition of income eligibility in the medically needy category by matching only those payments made for the medically needy whose incomes did not exceed 133.33 percent of the AFDC income eligibility ceiling. At the same time, utilization review of services in participating institutions was required, in an attempt to institute some controls over services paid for by the program. The 1967 amendments also added to the basic services covered, requiring all states to institute an "Early and Periodic Screening, Diagnosis, and Treatment Program" for eligible children by 1969.

In 1970 the Secretary of HEW declared that payment of physician fees under Medicaid and Medicare would be limited to 75 percent of the physician charges in effect during the calendar year preceding each fiscal year. The 1972 amendments (P.L. 92–603) legislated this limitation on physician reimbursement. State programs were required to collect an enrollment premium from medically needy recipients and were allowed to require copayments for all services from the medically needy, as well as for optional services from money-payment recipients. Additional sections of these amendments established Professional Standards Review Organizations to review the quality and necessity of services rendered, and standard regulations for nursing facilities. Strengthening the requirements for coverage of children's services, the 1972 amendment imposed a penalty, the loss of 1 percent of federal matching funds, if states did not provide pediatric screening services and inform all AFDC recipients of such services.

The most recent changes in the Medicaid program relate to the Federal Supplementary Security Income (SSI) program for adult public-assistance recipients, authorized for introduction in January 1974 under P.L. 93–66. To ensure Medicaid coverage for all SSI beneficiaries (the categorically needy), states may authorize the federal government to administer their Medicaid eligibility procedures for this group of recipients.

EXTENT OF EFFECTIVENESS

Enrolled Population

According to the 1968 Tax Foundation Survey of 37 state Medicaid programs, the most important change made after the introduction of Medicaid was the extension of financial coverage to those previously ineligible for public medical-vendor payments. Fifty percent of the states cited moderate expansion in their medical assistance programs, 25 percent a considerable expansion, and 25 percent no expansion.[8]

Despite an initial increase in the number of recipients of publicly financed medical assistance under Medicaid, these increases have not continued nor have they been uniform for all categories. The rate of growth slowed considerably in 1969 after the initial spurt, and preliminary estimates for 1972 predicted the first reversals of this trend with a drop of 5.2 percent in the total number of recipients from the preceding year (see Table 27). National cutbacks legislated in 1967 limiting the definition of medically needy are not readily apparent in these figures, because of the addition of 14 new state programs between 1968 and 1969, and yet the lower growth rate in 1969 probably reflects these cutbacks. National totals are particularly affected by changes in eligibility in the states with liberal programs, such as New York and California, since these two programs make nearly a third of all medical-vendor payments.[9]

Not all the categories of recipients experienced increases of the same magnitude. Some of the increases in the number of persons categorized as money-payment recipients were related to expansions in the public-assistance rolls between December 1968 and December 1970. Other changes related to the addition of new state programs, and their individual definitions of eligibility for recipient categories (see Table 28).

Although Medicaid has provided medical assistance to more low-income persons, particularly those already on public assistance, not all of the potentially eligible population has received Medicaid coverage. There have been substantial regional variations: in the Northeast and the West a larger proportion of the low-income population was covered in all age groups. The five programs with the broadest coverage were New York, California, the District of Columbia, Connecticut, and Pennsylvania. States with the smallest proportion of low-income populations covered were Arkansas, Louisiana, Texas, South Carolina, and Alabama—all low per capita income, Southern states.

Table 27 All Medical Assistance and Medicaid Expenditures, Number of Recipients, and Number of Programs, FY 1966–FY 1972

	1966	1967	1968	1969	1970	1971	1972
Total medical assistance expenditures (in millions)[a]	—	$2,271	$ 3,484	$ 4,273	$ 4,808	$ 5,939	$ 6,299
Title XIX expenditures (in millions)	$ 372	$1,944	$ 3,236	$ 4,042	$ 4,691	$ 5,939	$ 6,299
Recipients[b] (in thousands)	1,600	5,200	11,500	12,900	15,500	19,300	18,300
Medicaid programs[c]	9	29	40	43	45	52	52

Annual Percentage Change in Total Medical Assistance Expenditures, Title XIX Expenditures, and All Medical Assistance Recipients

	1966	1967	1968	1969	1970	1971	1972
Total medical assistance expenditures	—	—	53.4	22.7	12.5	23.5	6.1
Title XIX expenditures	—	422.6	66.5	24.9	16.1	26.6	6.1
Recipients	—	225.0	121.2	12.2	20.2	24.5	-0.5

SOURCE. The 1967 total medical-assistance expenditures figure is from National Center for Social Statistics, *Medicaid and other Medical Care Financed from Public Assistance Funds, 1951–1969, Selected Statistics.* Report B-6 (Washington, D.C.: Government Printing Office, 1970), p. 55. The 1966 and 1967 Title XIX expenditures and number of programs and the 1968 figure for recipients are based on material provided by Jack Ebeler, Program Analyst for the Medical Services Administration. The 1966 and 1967 figures for number of recipients are from Tax Foundation, Inc, *Medicaid: State Programs after Two Years.* Research Publication No. 15 (New York: Tax Foundation, Inc., 1968), p. 31; these data were not available in NCSS Reports. All 1972 figures are from National Center for Social Statistics, *Number of Recipients and Amounts of Payments under Medicaid, 1972,* Advance Copy (Washington, D.C.: Government Printing Office, April 25, 1974). All other data for 1968 through 1971 are from annual FY reports issued by National Center for Social Statistics, *Medicaid and Medical Care Financed from Public Assistance Funds.* NCSS Reports B-5 (Washington, D.C.: Government Printing Office, 1968, 1969, 1970, 1972). Percentage changes were calculated from the data.
All expenditure and recipient figures rounded.
[a] Includes all medical-vendor payments financed from federal-state Public Assistance programs but does not incorporate SMI premium payments paid by the states under "buy-in" arrangement for Medicare recipients also entitled to Medicaid.
[b] The 1966 and 1967 figures are estimates of all Title XIX recipients only; the 1968 through 1970 figures are estimates of all medical-assistance recipients, the majority of whom were Title XIX recipients; 1971 and 1972 figures are estimates of all Title XIX recipients.
[c] Includes jurisdictions of Guam, Puerto Rico, District of Columbia, and Virgin Islands, as well as states.

Table 28 Estimated Numbers of Recipients for Whom One or More Medical Bills Were Paid, on the Basis of Eligibility, and Annual Percentage Changes, FY 1969–FY 1972[a]

Recipient Category	1969 Number	1969 Percent	1970[b] Number	1970[b] Percent	1971 Number	1971 Percent	1972 Number	1972 Percent
Total (in thousands)	12,900	100.0	15,515	100.0	19,323	100.0	18,312	100.0
Age 65 and over	2,900	22.5	3,200	20.6	3,600	18.6	3,417	18.7
Blind	75	0.6	107	0.6	123	0.6	109	0.6
Permanently and totally disabled	960	7.5	1,200	7.7	1,500	7.8	1,673	9.1
Children under 21	5,900	45.9	6,500	41.9	8,300	43.0	8,376	45.7
Adults in families with dependent children	2,225	17.3	3,500	22.6	4,700	24.3	3,196	17.5
Other Adults	800	6.2	1,008	6.5	1,100	5.7	1,542	8.4

Percentage Change

	1969–1970	1970–1971	1971–1972
Age 65 and over	10.3	12.5	−5.1
Blind	42.7	15.0	−11.4
Permanently and totally disabled	25.0	25.0	11.5
Children under 21	10.2	27.7	0.9
Adults in families with dependent children	57.3	34.3	−32.0
Other Adults	26.0	9.1	40.2

SOURCE. National Center for Social Statistics, *Medicaid and Other Medical Care Financed from Public Assistance Funds*. NCSS Reports B-5 for fiscal years 1969, 1970, and 1971 (Washington, D.C.: Government Printing Office, 1969, 1970, 1972), Table 2 for 1969, Table 1 for 1970, and Table 1 for 1971. National Center for Social Statistics, *Numbers of Recipients and Amounts of Payments under Medicaid, 1972*, Advance Copy (Washington, D.C.: Government Printing Office, April 25, 1974), Table 2. Percentage changes calculated from data.

[a] Federally aided assistance programs only; data are not available on numbers aided under state general assistance programs. Excludes recipients for whom only monthly per capita amounts were paid into Social Security Administration system.

[b] The 1970 figures presented are the revised preliminary estimates shown in National Center for Social Statistics, *Medicaid and Other Medical Care Financed from Public Assistance Funds*. NCSS Report B-5 (FY 1971) (Washington, D.C.: Government Printing Office, November 7, 1972), p. 2.

174

Much of the state-by-state variation in the degree of coverage of the low-income population results from variations in how states determine the eligibility of the medically needy. The most recent complete state-by-state figures for the Medicaid coverage, those for 1972, demonstrate this variation. Of the 49 states and jurisdictions with Medicaid programs in 1972, 23 states, the District of Columbia, and Puerto Rico extended benefits to the medically needy in addition to money-payment recipients; however, New York and Puerto Rico together accounted for close to 50 percent of all medically needy recipients covered nationally. In the same year, only 9 states and 2 jurisdictions included "other" medically needy low-income persons as beneficiaries. In this category also, the spread of coverage was extremely uneven, New York providing assistance for just under 50 percent of the 1.4 million "other" medically needy persons enrolled in the United States in 1972.[10]

Cutbacks in Medicaid financing and in eligibility requirements have reduced the number of those who qualify only for assistance in their payment of medical bills. The proportion of the medically needy categories in the total population covered by Medicaid has declined as follows: calendar year (CY) 1968, 40 percent; CY 1969, 32 percent; CY 1970, 27 percent, FY 1972, 27 percent.[11] Although eligibility of public-assistance recipients in the four money-payment categories was mandated in the original legislation, subsequent changes have decreased the number of eligibles in these groups as well.

Covered Services

The range of services for which direct medical-vendor payments are made in each state varies as much as the coverage of low-income persons. All programs offered coverage for the 5 required services in 1972, and 25 programs extended that coverage to the medically needy as well. Coverage for the 17 optional services noted in federal legislation, many of which represent ambulatory services, was spotty. Many states offered a partial range of optional services only to money-payment recipients; others covered some optional services for the medically needy as well. Very few states covered the entire range for both recipient categories.

Some programs may appear similar in the range of services for which vendor payments were made, but the similarities mask great disparities in the extent of coverage, for example, number of days for which reimbursement is available or limitations on reimbursable charges. These discrepancies lead to wide variations in the value of the "benefit package" for each beneficiary. Estimates of these values per eligible money-payment recipient in the permanently and totally disabled category (only one of the four categories whose coverage is required) in 1970 ranked California, Wisconsin, Minnesota, New York, and Connecticut as providing the most valuable "package" for these beneficiaries.

States with the lowest benefit-package values were Arkansas, Mississippi, Tennessee, Louisiana, and West Virginia.[12]

Impact on Utilization of Ambulatory Care

Changes in Utilization.   The impact of Medicaid on the *proportion* of low-income persons using ambulatory services appears to have been considerable. In 1963, 56 percent of low-income persons (less than $5000 annual income) saw a physician, but 65 percent did so in 1970.[13] When compared to the use of physicians' services by other income groups, which experienced stable or declining rates of use during 1964–1969, this proportionate increase in use for low-income persons was appreciable. By 1969, their use of ambulatory services surpassed that of middle- and upper-income persons.

This increase in use was not uniform for all portions of the low-income population. The number of physician visits by low-income persons in the medically needy and "other" medically needy categories was lower than that for money-payment recipients. Very likely this reflects uneven coverage of the two optional categories. However, the apparent advantage of the low-income population with respect to use of ambulatory care disappeared entirely when adjustments for health status were made in the 1969 figures. After adjustment, use of physicians' services increased with income, and persons with less than $5000 annual income in the medically needy and "other" medically needy categories had the lowest utilization rates (see Table 29).

In 1969 Roghmann et al. conducted a study in Rochester, New York, to determine if the introduction of Medicaid resulted in any changes in the type of medical care received by low-income children as compared to children covered by private health insurance. Using rates of immunization and dental checkups as indicators, the study analyzed differences in the nature of care received by Medicaid children and by children covered by Blue Cross insurance between 1967 and 1969. Rates of immunization increased during the period for Medicaid children but did not reach the immunization rates of non-Medicaid children by 1969. The proportion of Medicaid children receiving dental checkups actually declined from 57 percent in 1967 to 43 percent in 1969. In contrast, 72 percent of non-Medicaid children received dental checkups in 1967, increasing to 78 percent by 1969. This decrease in dental care among children covered by Medicaid was due, according to the investigators, to a 20 percent reduction in dental fees paid, causing many dentists to withdraw from the program.[14]

Changes in the Availability of Care.   One of the implicit objectives of Medicaid was to broaden the range of providers available to low-income persons, who generally received care through outpatient departments and emergency rooms.

Table 29   Physician Visits by Family Income, 1969[a]

	All Persons	
Income Level	Unadjusted	Adjusted for Health Status
All family incomes	4.6	4.6
Under $5000	4.9	3.7
Public assistance	6.6	4.5
No public assistance	4.7	3.6
$5000–9999	4.2	4.6
$10,000–14,999	4.4	4.9
$15,000 and over	4.8	5.2

SOURCE. Estimated from the 1969 Health Interview Survey, National Center for Health Statistics, in Karen Davis and Roger Reynolds, *Impact of Medicare and Medicaid on Access to Medical Care* (Washington, D.C.: The Brookings Institution, 1974, unpublished), Table 2, p. 7.
[a] Excluding individuals reporting family income unknown; those under 17 for whom head of household's education was unknown; and those 17 and older for whom individual education was unknown.

Available data suggest that Medicaid coverage may have allowed some recipients to use private physicians as a source of care, at least at the outset, but that it has not produced major changes in the sources of care available to or used by Medicaid recipients.

National data on trends in the use of outpatient clinics and emergency-room services during the 1960s, as interpreted by Piore et al., illustrate some changes in the use of these services immediately after introduction of Medicaid (and Medicare). During this period, there was a sizable increase in the volume of ambulatory visits made to these sources of care. Between 1962 and 1964 the number of visits increased by 30 percent. Increases have continued since 1964 but at a much slower pace. A low growth rate of 7.1 percent between 1966 and 1968 has been attributed in part to a decline in the use of these services resulting from Medicaid and Medicare coverage and increased access to private practitioners. After 1968 the rate of increase began to accelerate again. Much of the 17 percent growth between 1968 and 1970 came during 1969, perhaps, as the authors suggest, as a result of cutbacks in Medicaid coverage and reimbursement levels.[15]

As part of Roghmann's 1969 study comparing the utilization patterns of children covered under Medicaid and Blue Cross in Rochester, New York, changes in the source of care were examined to assess the impact of Medicaid in this area. The shifts in the source of medical care for Medicaid children included a decrease in the percent of these children served by private physicians, no change in their use of outpatient clinics, and an increase in the percent having no regular source of medical care:

Source of Care	1967	1969
Private physician	45	30
Outpatient clinic	33	31
No regular source	22	39

The investigators cited inadequate transportation, reimbursement at lower than usual and customary fee levels, and shortages of available manpower as factors influencing these shifts.[16]

Olendzki et al. also investigated the possibility of shifts in source of medical care as a result of Medicaid coverage. This study compared the preferred sources of care of two panels of welfare recipients in 1961–1962, prior to Medicaid, to those in 1968–1969. Although an increase in the use of private physicians' services did occur—12 percent of the respondents cited a private physician as their usual source of care in the follow-up study as compared to 1 percent in the initial study—neither group exhibited a marked shift in preference for a private physician. The investigators speculated that the high quality of care available to the study group in hospital clinics prior to Medicaid was a factor in the low degree of shift from clinics to private physicians. Another factor is, however, revealed in the evidence that many individuals who preferred a private physician used other sources of care, apparently expecting physicians to reject Medicaid recipients as patients.[17]

Factors Affecting Differential Use of Ambulatory-Care Services. Using regression analysis on data for 1969 and 1970, Holahan examined the use of ambulatory-care services under Medicaid by different socioeconomic and demographic groups, and in relation to variables representing the local supply of physicians' services.[18] Ambulatory care was defined as outpatient hospital care and office-based physicians' services.

The primary determinants of utilization of outpatient services were availability of physicians, per capita income of Medicaid eligibles, and location of residence. Greater availability of outpatient services tended to reduce patient delay in obtaining care and was related to increased use. High per capita incomes were related to significantly increased rates of utilization, particularly among children. Since children were likely to receive more preventive care than other Medicaid recipients, cost considerations may have been more important in determining their use of outpatient services. Utilization was affected positively by residence in urban areas, reflecting the effect of proximity to services.

No relationship was found between the availability of services by physicians, as measured by the ratio of office-based physicians to total population, and use of their services. Noting that an abundant supply of office-based physicians is characteristic of areas with sizable numbers of hospital-based physicians, Holahan hypothesized that the latter (hospital) group may be more accessible to eligible Medicaid populations. Income was positively related to use of physicians' services, but place of residence demonstrated no such relation.

In their study of the impact of Medicaid on access to medical-care services, Davis and Reynolds attempted to sort out the factors determining use of ambulatory-care services, as measured by use of physician services.[19] (Use of outpatient services was not considered in their study.) Their analysis revealed health status to be a major determinant; utilization increased as health status deteriorated. Family size negatively affected utilization: the larger the family, the lower the use of physician services. The availability of physicians and hospitals in an area did not have a significant effect on use. The lack of a relation here may be the effect of inappropriate measurement (exclusion of outpatient services), which, the authors conjecture, did not adequately reflect the narrow range of providers generally available to the poor.

Whites and nonwhites outside the South used significantly more services than whites and nonwhites in the South. Although there was a tendency for whites to use more services than nonwhites throughout the United States, the differences in rates of use between whites and nonwhites in the South were smaller than those between whites and nonwhites residing in other regions.

Effect of Program Administration on Utilization.   The utilization of services under Medicaid is at least partly dependent on the extent to which state social service agencies inform and instruct eligible persons about the procedures for receiving Medicaid benefits. In 1970–1971 the Community Services Administration surveyed three social service agencies administering Medicaid in states representing urban, rural, and semiurban areas. The objective was to assess the effectiveness of current practices of the administering state and county agencies in promoting proper use of services under Title XIX. Money-payment recipients and caseworkers were interviewed regarding their knowledge of Medicaid benefits; 42 percent responded that no one had ever explained Medicaid to them. Those who did have caseworker assistance received proportionately more guidance about nursing-home care (29 percent) and hospital inpatient care (24 percent) than for physician services (18 percent). Social service assistance was viewed as vital to the optimal functioning of Medicaid: two-thirds of the recipients using health service did so with caseworker assistance, stating they would not have received care without this help.

Sixty-nine percent of the caseworkers felt that they had explained Medicaid to recipients; 38 percent felt it was difficult to provide supportive health services because of complex and changing entitlement regulations and other procedures. All caseworkers expressed the opinion that the lack of provision for transportation was a major obstacle to use of medical services by their clients. Other sources of difficulty in coordination were the amount of "red tape" and administrative delays, infrequent contact with physicians, and misunderstanding of the "buy-in" provision for Medicare recipients.[20]

Distribution of Medicaid Expenditures

Reimbursement by Type of Service.   Distribution of medical-vendor payments by type of service reflects use of services as well as differentials in prices. For the most part, expenditures under Medicaid have been heavily weighted toward institutional inpatient care as opposed to ambulatory care. The distribution of total expenditures for 1967 through 1972 shows the preponderance of payments for inpatient hospital and nursing services (see Table 30). These payments represented about two-thirds of total expenditures in 1972, a decline of 8 percent since 1967. Although payments for "other" services, including outpatient and physicians' services, increased during this period, they represented only a small proportion of total outlays (10.8 percent) in 1972.

Reimbursement by Recipient Category.   The proportion of the total medical-vendor payments for services used by the aged declined from 45 percent in 1968 to 31 percent in 1972, chiefly as a result of their coverage under Medicare. The proportion of payments in their behalf was still, however, almost twice the proportion of aged in the total population, which had also decreased from 22.5 percent in 1969 to 18.7 percent in 1972. The proportion of medical-vendor payments for the permanently and totally disabled was also twice that of their proportion in the recipient population for this period. Children represented 48 percent of the recipient population; however, payments for pediatric care accounted for only 18.6 percent of the total medical-vendor payments in 1972. The greater relative outlays and higher-than-average payments for the aged and the permanently and totally disabled may be attributed to both greater use of services and cost variations in the type of services used by these groups.

The medically needy and "other" medically needy used medical-vendor payments roughly in the same proportion as their respective representation in the recipient population. The proportion of medically needy covered under Medicaid declined from 40 percent in 1968 to 27 percent in 1972, and the proportion of medical-vendor payments on their behalf declined as well, from 48 percent in 1968 to 39 percent in 1970. In 1972, however, the trend reversed, and reim-

Table 30   Medical Assistance: Expenditures by Type of Service, FY 1967–FY 1972[a]

Type of Service	1967	1968	1969	1970	1971	1972
	Amount (in thousands)					
Total	$2,270,996	$3,451,376	$4,273,439	$4,807,533	$5,939,236	$6,299,050
Inpatient hospital care	912,662	1,360,947	1,586,092	1,887,438	2,288,384	2,669,494
Nursing-home care	766,120	1,063,950	1,291,363	1,321,000	1,673,999	1,470,939
Physicians' services	224,543	379,551	516,404	577,745	717,104	794,005
Dental care	72,246	190,000	208,688	168,653	181,315	170,286
Prescribed drugs	179,424	235,218	301,341	395,402	473,020	511,877
Other services[b]	115,261	220,970	369,298	457,153	604,414	682,447
Not reported	740	740	253	142	1,000	—
	Percentage Distribution					
Total	100.0	100.0	100.0	100.0	100.0	100.0
Inpatient hospital care	40.2	39.4	37.1	39.3	38.5	42.4
Nursing-home care	33.7	30.8	30.2	27.5	28.2	23.4
Physicians' services	9.9	11.0	12.1	12.0	12.1	12.6
Dental care	3.2	5.5	4.9	3.5	3.1	2.7
Prescribed drugs	7.9	6.8	7.1	8.2	8.0	8.1
Other services[b]	5.1	6.4	8.6	9.5	10.2	10.8

SOURCE.   National Center for Social Statistics, *Medicaid and Other Medical Care Financed from Public Assistance Funds*. NCSS Report B-5 (FY 1971) (Washington, D.C.: Government Printing Office, 1972), Table 4. For 1972 figures, see: National Center for Social Statistics, *Numbers of Recipients and Amounts of Payments under Medicaid, 1972*, Advance Copy (Washington, D.C.: Government Printing Office, April 25, 1974), Table 5.

[a] Expenditures from federal, state, and local funds under federally aided programs, as of 1971, Title XIX only. Excludes per capita payments into Social Security Administration system.

[b] "Other" services includes other practitioners' services, outpatient hospital services, clinic services, laboratory and radiological services, home health services.

181

bursements for services represented 45 percent of all medical-vendor pay-ments.[21] A greater incidence and severity of illness among the medically needy accounted for their greater use of services and higher medical payments, despite uneven coverage of care for them. The average payment for this group in 1970 was $427, compared to $249 for the money-payment recipients.[22]

Reimbursements by Region and State. Medicaid has substantially augmented the level of publicly financed health-care spending. In fiscal year 1973, $8.9 billion (26 percent) of the $34.0 billion publicly financed health-care budget was spent under the Medicaid program.[23]

The massive increase in medical-assistance spending created by Medicaid has not, however, altered the distribution of public health-care expenditures by region. The proportion of total federal Medicaid expenditures by region in 1969 were as follows: Northeast, 36 percent; North-Central, 22 percent; West, 22 percent; and South, 20 percent.[24] And the proportions of the population liv-ing in these areas in 1969 were as follows: Northeast, 24 percent; North-Central, 28 percent; West, 17 percent; and South, 31 percent. The regions that spent the most or the least per person for health care were the same in 1969 as in 1966 before the full impact of Medicaid. Medicaid payments by region varied considerably for all age and recipient groups. This variation is a com-bination of price differentials, varying utilization rates, and differences in services and recipient categories covered. Whereas Medicaid payments per recipient were highest for the Northeast and North-Central regions, the pay-ments per low-income person were considerably higher in the Northeast and West because of the extensive coverage of the medically indigent in New York and California.

Another factor explaining the regional variation in Medicaid benefits is the rate of federal matching in state Medicaid programs. These matching rates as of 1972–1973 are shown in Table 31. Although a strong relation did in fact exist between state per capita incomes and the rate of matching—Mississippi, Alabama, Arkansas, and South Carolina, all low-income states, had high rates of matching funds—the largest proportion of the expenditures flowed to a rela-tively small number of states. New York alone received more than 28 percent of the total federal Medicaid expenditures, and California received 17 percent. Both of these high-income states also disbursed high average per capita pay-ments. In 1969 the average per capita payment nationally was $22, but averages in New York and California were $68 and $40, respectively. The pro-portions of all welfare recipients in these two states were 7.3 percent and 7.4 percent, respectively. In contrast, Louisiana, with the largest proportion of welfare recipients (8.7 percent), received only 1.2 percent of federal Medicaid expenditures and averaged $14 per capita payment in 1969.[25]

Table 31   Federal Matching Rates for State Medicaid Programs, FY 1972–FY 1973

State	Federal Medical Assistance Percentage[a]	State	Federal Medical Assistance Percentage[a]
Alabama	78	Nebraska	58
Arkansas	79	Nevada	50
California	50	New Hampshire	59
Colorado	58	New Jersey	50
Connecticut	50	New Mexico	73
Delaware	50	New York	50
District of Columbia	50	North Carolina	73
Florida	61	North Dakota	71
Georgia	70	Ohio	54
Hawaii	51	Oklahoma	69
Idaho	72	Oregon	57
Illinois	50	Pennsylvania	55
Indiana	55	Rhode Island	50
Iowa	58	South Carolina	78
Kansas	59	South Dakota	70
Kentucky	73	Tennessee	74
Louisiana	73	Texas	65
Maine	69	Utah	70
Maryland	50	Vermont	65
Massachusetts	50	Virginia	64
Michigan	50	Washington	50
Minnesota	57	West Virginia	77
Mississippi	83	Wisconsin	58
Missouri	60	Wyoming	63
Montana	67		

SOURCE.   Based on Table 4, John Holahan, *Financing Health Care for the Poor: The Medicaid Experience*. Working Paper No. 976-01 (Washington, D.C.: The Urban Institute, 1974), p. 25.
[a] Rate of federal financial participation in a state's medical vendor payment expenditures on behalf of individuals and families eligible for Medicaid coverage. Percentages are rounded.

PROGRAM COST

Increased federal spending on direct medical-vendor payments authorized under Medicaid greatly increased the amount of funds spent for publicly financed medical assistance. In FY 1965, before the enactment of Medicaid, these expenditures totaled $1.2 billion for all states.[26] In 1967, with only 29 programs participating in Medicaid, total expenditures for publicly financed medical assistance had almost doubled to $2.3 billion. Six years later, and with all but one state participating in Medicaid, expenditures had quadrupled, reaching $8.9 billion in FY 1973.

The levels of these expenditures have been affected markedly by the increasing cost consciousness evidenced in legislative amendments to the original program legislation. Title XIX expenditures jumped between 1966 and 1967, as the program went into full swing. Cutbacks in eligibility, enforcement of utilization review, and limitation in reimbursement of physician charges resulted in a significantly slower growth rate for expenditures in 1968 and 1969. By 1972 the level of expenditures had begun to decline below that of earlier years, despite the continuing introduction of new state programs and eligible persons into the program.

SECONDARY EFFECTS

Impact of Rising Costs

As indicated in the discussion of Medicare, medical-care prices have risen much faster than other items in the Consumer Price Index during the past decade, and especially after Medicare and Medicaid were introduced in 1966. Both programs contributed markedly to this escalation by increasing the demands for health care in the face of a fixed supply of services. As with Medicare, however, the rapidly rising program costs consequent to the medical-care price inflation and spending at levels far above original estimates became the major stimulus for subsequent legislative changes. To curtail use of services and subsequent payment, the program restricted coverage, imposed cost-sharing requirements, placed limits on reimbursement of physicians' fees, and instituted utilization review for costly inpatient services.

With these restrictions, and the subsequent shifts in the recipient categories and services covered, Medicaid withdrew from its original goal of financing comprehensive care for a majority of low-income persons. Retrenchment from another goal, that of making a wider range of providers and services available to low-income persons through subsidy, was made clear in 1969 when Dr. Roger O. Egeberg, then Secretary of Health and Scientific Affairs, HEW, asserted that the slogan "Let's get everybody into the mainstream" should never have been used in connection with Medicaid.[27] According to a Medical Services Administration representative, the present goal of Medicaid, or at least its federal administering agency, is the promotion of management efficiency and elimination of ineligible persons from Medicaid rolls.[28]

Impact of Program Administration

The aspect of Medicaid administration with perhaps the most serious unintended effects was the delegation to the states of the authority to determine the extent of their participation in Medicaid. A primary intent of this program was elimination of inequities in the Kerr–Mills program resulting from differing state rules and regulations. Although the termination of matching funds under Kerr–Mills and categorical assistance were effective in prompting all states to enter Medicaid, no other features have worked effectively to encourage uniform eligibility requirements and covered services.

The differential matching-grant formula, which was to have encouraged uniform coverage of services by distributing greater costs to states with higher per capita incomes, has not had that effect. Cooper and Worthington assessed its effectiveness by developing cost–benefit ratios for each state program, comparing the amount of state taxes financing the Medicaid program to the total medical-vendor payments made for state residents. They found that benefits exceeded costs in 10 states, almost all rated as high-income states with liberal Medicaid programs, whereas the low-income states bore a relatively heavier cost burden. The overall impact of this method of financing, they concluded, was a redistribution of medical-assistance income from lower to higher per capita income states.[29] Thus, those states whose high per capita incomes had encouraged more liberal coverage of the low-income population and of optional services were even better able to provide that coverage as a result of Medicaid, while low-income states with a preponderance of low-income population provided less than adequate coverage for their recipients.

Other studies have documented problems arising in individual programs or areas from program administration. These problems also frequently arose as a result of the payment mechanism or cost-control devices.

S. M. Davidson traced the pattern of hospital utilization of one Chicago community with a lower rate of physician visits than the national average and an inpatient hospital utilization rate twice the national average. Despite the preponderance of nearby community hospitals, many residents (45 percent of whom were Medicaid recipients), traveled outside the area to a teaching hospital for medical care. The explanation resides, according to the investigator, in the rejection by community hospitals of those individuals unable to demonstrate ability to pay. Lack of coordination with the Public Aid Agency, reimbursement at less than full cost, delays in payment, and cumbersome billing procedures also made these individuals less desirable than other patients. Traveling outside the community resulted in higher Medicaid costs and delays in seeking medical care.[30]

Failure of the states to comply with the 1967 legislation mandating Early and Periodic Screening, Diagnosis, and Treatment programs for eligible Medicaid children has been attributed to the unwillingness of the states to increase Medicaid expenditures further. Federal officials estimated that 12 million children were eligible for this program in 1971 but that only 1.2 million (10 percent) had actually been screened. The lapse of three years between legislation requiring screening and HEW's promulgation of regulations in 1970, a year after the programs were to have gone into operation, was also a factor in their slow development. Another administrative factor was the logistical problem of locating and informing eligible children of the availability of the program.[31]

Impact on Non-Medicaid Beneficiaries

The medical-care price inflation, the surge in demand for services, and attendant exposure of the system's inability to respond to that demand have affected virtually all segments of the population in their efforts to gain access to care. Low-income persons not eligible for Medicaid benefits as a result of state definitions of income limitation or restrictions in eligibility requirements have suffered most from rising medical-care costs. If, as national statistics suggest, they have increasingly resorted to outpatient and emergency rooms as usual sources of care, they have also been confronted with higher charges precipitated by the Medicare and Medicaid policy of reimbursement of hospitals at full cost. Customary charges for clinic visits in voluntary hospitals nationwide rose rapidly after the introduction of these programs. For example, typical charges in New York for a clinic visit before the enactment of Medicaid ranged from $0.50 to $5. After Medicaid began, these charges jumped to $20, $30, and even $50 per visit.[32]

OVERALL IMPACT ON ACCESS TO PRIMARY CARE

An overall assessment of Medicaid's impact on access to primary care illustrates vividly the problems resulting from an effort to ensure access without intervening in the supply of services and without imposing on the states uniform guidelines for participation. Medicaid, by augmenting the level of medical-assistance expenditures, did make publicly financed coverage of medical-care costs available to many persons previously ineligible for such aid;

however, inequities in that coverage persist nationwide. The medically needy, in particular, are unevenly covered, owing to variations in determinations of income levels for eligibility by states. Low-income persons in the South are at a relative disadvantage in both use of services and coverage, with a lower value of Medicaid benefits per recipient in those states. Many of these persisting inequities have been further reinforced by changing eligibility requirements and restrictions on service benefits, which have affected the medically needy individuals and lower income states most directly.

Although Medicaid provided a somewhat broader medical-assistance program, in terms of coverage and benefits, it has not resulted in a uniform program nor, apparently, in a significant decrease in financial barriers to access to primary care for low-income persons.

SUMMARY

Before Medicaid there was great variation in the availability of medical care to the recipients of welfare in the United (but individual) States of America. This legislation was designed to ensure that a minimum set of benefits would be available to all those in need. This was to be done in a way that would not interfere with the rights of the individual states or with the private practice of medicine. As a result there were significant increases (not uniform) in the accessibility of primary care for these less fortunate members of society. Data indicate, however, that the benefits were not equitably distributed among and within states, the rich/white receiving more benefits than the poor/nonwhite, even when adjusted for severity of medical problem. These differences apply to both states and individuals. As with Medicare, there were many unanticipated and unintended side effects. The consequences of increasing effective demand, given a fixed supply of services in a system without effective financial control mechanisms, have also been evident. The lessons learned at considerable expense will, we hope, be useful in designing the next generation of interventions designed to improve access to primary care for *all*.

THIRTEEN

OEO Neighborhood Health Centers:

COMPREHENSIVE HEALTH CARE FOR LOW-INCOME INNER-CITY RESIDENTS

REASONS FOR DEVELOPMENT OF PROGRAMS

The decade of the 1960s was characterized by social upheavals. Deteriorating social and economic conditions in most inner-city areas, the locus of migration of rural Southern blacks, coupled with tense racial relations, led to sporadic but serious disorders in some cities in the early 1960s.[1] Political awareness of the problems contributing to those upheavals, particularly of the "vicious circle" of poverty characteristic of most central cities, was evident in the legislative programs of the Kennedy and Johnson administrations. The keynote legislation in the "War on Poverty" was the Economic Opportunity Act of 1964, creating the Office of Economic Opportunity (OEO) and within it the Community Action Program to serve as a link between the federal government and local communities in eliminating poverty. As envisioned, the variety of OEO programs, through federal funding and decentralized decision-making, would allow community residents to participate in determining specific goals within the broader aim of fighting poverty.

The 1964 OEO legislation did not earmark a specific program or funds for health care. Given the well-documented lower health status of low-income persons, however, provision of health care was soon accepted as an integral aspect of raising the standard of living, along with job training, educational opportunities, and housing. In 1965 and 1966, funds were channeled into health care, and demonstration projects were organized. A formal comprehensive health-services program was included in the OEO repertory in 1966.

Baseline studies were made in nine low-income inner-city areas on the East and West coasts between 1968 and 1969, before the development of OEO health-services projects in each. National data on utilization of medical-care services by low-income groups from the 1969 Health Interview Survey were compared to those developed during the OEO baseline surveys. This comparison pointed up the greater need of inner-city residents for health care.[2]

As revealed in the baseline studies, the average number of ambulatory-care visits by low-income residents in all but three of the nine sites was somewhat higher than that of low-income persons nationwide. Their combined average was virtually the same as the nationwide average for low-income persons. But the usual location of care for low-income persons in those nine inner-city areas was far more likely to be hospital outpatient clinics, contrary to the experience of low-income populations nationwide. This was particularly true for those with chronic health problems. For those with less than $5000 income nationally, 10 to 11 percent of the white population used clinic services predominantly, and 20 to 30 percent of the nonwhite population did so. In the baseline study areas, use of clinic services as a usual source of care ranged from 13.2 percent to 89.9 percent.

The time spent in reaching sources of care underlined even more dramatically the disadvantageous position of low-income inner-city residents. In six of nine areas, a larger proportion of residents traveled more than 20 minutes to reach their usual source of care as compared to a national sample of persons with incomes of less than $5000 per year, 42 percent of whom traveled less than 15 minutes. Those with a private physician as a usual source of care usually spent less time in travel, but for the majority of inner-city residents who received their care in hospital clinics, from 59 to 83 percent traveled longer than 20 minutes.

The large proportion of these baseline populations using hospital clinics as a primary source of care reflects financial barriers to other sources of care; the small proportion traveling less than 20 minutes points to geographic barriers to access. In other inner-city areas, travel time and costs were even more extreme. In 1966, before the Montefiore Medical Care Demonstration was organized in the Bronx, New York, area residents traveled 45 minutes by bus to a clinic, whereas in Los Angeles, virtually no public transportation was available to residents of Watts.[3, 4]

NATURE OF INTERVENTION

In 1966 an amendment (P.L. 89–749) to the OEO legislation formalized the Comprehensive Health Services program, focusing "upon the needs of persons residing in urban and rural areas having high concentrations of poverty and a marked inadequacy of health services."[5] The amendment provided for grants to public and nonprofit organizations or institutions to cover a part of the cost of health services for geographically defined poverty populations and established guidelines for delivery. Thus, unlike the insurance of Medicare and Medicaid, the OEO Comprehensive Health Services entailed a dual intervention in the delivery of medical care, subsidizing provision of services, rather than demand for them, through direct grants to the agencies contracting to provide comprehensive services.

The neighborhood health center, one of the health-care delivery models used in Comprehensive Health Services, actually originated in the early 1900s during another period of social reform. The model represents an active, multifaceted intervention in the health-care system, including efforts to reduce barriers related to finances, geography, supply of providers, fragmentation, and even psychosocial factors. Implicit in the adoption of this model by OEO was the belief that

[the] basic institutional arrangements—governmental and private—whereby health services were made available to the poor were defective, and to the extent that health services were relevant to health status, the health of the poor could not be improved without fundamental changes in the arrangements whereby health services were organized and delivered.[6]

SOURCES

The major source of information for this case study was the *Study to Evaluate the OEO Neighborhood Health Center Program at Selected Centers,* Volume 1, prepared by investigators at Geomet, Inc., under contract to OEO. Unpublished OEO baseline data for NHC target areas and comparable national statistics for low-income populations from the Health Interview Survey by the National Center for Health Statistics were used with permission from Gail Wilensky's as yet unpublished study for the Urban Institute entitled

Utilization of Ambulatory Care. These were supplemented by other studies focusing on specific issues relating to particular neighborhood health-center models. More recent material concerning the current operation and funding of the OEO centers since their transfer to HEW was obtained in telephone conversations with William White, Deputy Associate Bureau Director for Community Health Centers, Bureau of Community Health Services, Health Services Administration, Department of Health, Education, and Welfare, and with Nick Campagnoli, program analyst for the Bureau. Clifton Cole, Director of the South Central Multipurpose Health Services Center in Watts, Los Angeles, California, and former president of the National Association of Neighborhood Health Centers, was contacted during the preparation of this case study.

DESCRIPTION OF PROGRAM

The NHC program, established as a demonstration project in OEO's Comprehensive Health Services in 1966, was administered by that agency in the Executive branch until OEO began to be phased out entirely. Between 1970 and 1973, administration of the NHC network was gradually transferred to HEW. The program is now under the jurisdiction of HEW's Bureau of Community Health Services, Health Services Administration.

Program Guidelines

Befitting a demonstration program, guidelines for development and operation of health-services centers were stated in a broadly descriptive manner, since it was OEO's intention that they be free to respond to local health problems within the context of each community's goals and priorities for health care and the alleviation of poverty.

Guidelines specified that NHCs (and other delivery models) were to be located in rural or urban areas characterized by concentrations of low-income populations without adequate health services. Centers were to serve from 10,000 to 30,000 eligible persons in each target area, providing a broad range of outpatient health and related services. These were to include preventive health services, diagnostic services, treatment, family planning, in-home care of the chronically ill and other home health services, rehabilitative services, dental care, and mental-health services. Additionally, the projects were required to arrange for care that was beyond their individual capabilities, such as hospitalization and referral to medical specialists at cooperating facilities.

The provision of comprehensive services was to be achieved by maximum feasible use of existing health and health-related agencies and resources.

Furthermore, the delivery of health care was to be coordinated with social, educational, employment, and related services. Community members were to be informed of available services through active outreach efforts and to participate directly on community boards in the administration of each center. Further community involvement was to be encouraged through training programs that were to add indigenous health-care workers to the staff at each center.[7]

Extent of Effort[8]

Before formal establishment of OEO health programs, demonstration projects were initiated in eight neighborhood health-center models between 1965 and 1966. By 1968, 30 NHC projects were in operation. Between 1970 and 1973, 40 OEO centers were transferred to HEW administration, 12 in rural areas, 26 in urban areas, and 2 in urban–rural areas. As a result of changing political priorities and budgetary constraints, the extent of the program has not been expanded, and HEW has concentrated instead on maintaining existing centers and increasing the sizes of target areas. The estimated target-area population to be served by the 40 existing NHCs in 1974 is 720,000.

EXTENT OF EFFECTIVENESS

Extent of Program Evaluation

The neighborhood health-center concept has been extensively described and debated in the literature during recent years, but overall operation and effectiveness of the program has been less documented. Particular areas of performance in the delivery of services have occasionally been described for individual centers, both those sponsored by OEO and by other public and private agencies. One factor inhibiting overall self-evaluation of the program was the unavailability of comparable program-wide operating statistics. Many centers were not able to collect such data because of expense of installing reporting systems.[9]

A comprehensive study and evaluation of the NHC program was commissioned in May 1970 by OEO to determine the extent to which its legislative mandate had been fulfilled. The evaluation, performed by Geomet, Inc., was based on an analytic construct that delimited areas of a center's performance in meeting the basic program objectives. Dimensions of performance, such as utilization and continuity of care, were related to an organizational and functional analysis to identify the features most characteristic of a "successful" center.

The 21 NHCs surveyed by Geomet during 1970 and 1971 represented about half of the existing centers, usually the more senior programs. Consonant with the intent of the program as a demonstration project, they also represented a wide range of delivery systems, serving varied communities and target populations (ranging from an urban housing project to a multicounty rural area), under several types of sponsorship. Data for the evaluation were developed through site analyses, household interviews of nearly 10,000 families, and a review of records at each center. The families interviewed represented center *users* and *nonusers* in the target area and a *control* group matched to the target area population on socioeconomic and demographic characteristics but *residing outside* the area.

The user group did differ from the nonuser and control groups in several respects, many of which indicated greater needs for available health services. Users were more likely to be younger, members of larger families, persons with lower per capita incomes, and receivers of Medicaid or welfare assistance. They also tended to perceive their health as worse than other groups and had greater perceived needs for both health and related social services, as reflected in recent demand for or use of such services, than nonusers or controls did.

Selected data from Geomet's year-and-a-half-long survey, supplemented by relevant information from other sources, form the basis of the following discussion of the extent to which OEO–NHCs have successfully increased access to care.[10]

Penetration of Target Area

The centers served an average of 55 percent of the eligible families and 66 percent of the eligible individuals in the target areas (range for families, 21 to 93 percent; for individuals, 33 to 97 percent). Active registration figures for the centers ranged from 2856 to 40,854, with a mean registration of 17,135. Although OEO guidelines specified that the centers serve from 10,000 to 30,000 eligible registrants, only 11 centers had active registrations in that range; 5 centers were below the minimum, and 3 were over the maximum.

An average of 72 percent of user families considered the center as their usual source of care. Usual sources of care for users before the opening of the centers had been hospital clinics (47 percent) and private practitioners (24 percent). This pattern was fairly similar to the current one for nonusers: 36 percent used hospital clinics and 53 percent used private physicians. Almost one-fourth of the user population had had, however, no usual source of care before using the centers, and less than 10 percent of nonusers reported no usual source of care. Data reviewed by Moore and by Hochheiser confirm that neighborhood health centers had replaced emergency rooms, which provide more crisis-oriented care than routine health care, as a regular source of care for many target-area residents.[11]

Whereas an average of 63 percent of the nonusers was aware of the existence of the centers, only 17 percent had been contacted by center staff, as compared to 31 percent of the users. Only 29 percent of nonusers had been directly asked to use center services, as opposed to 77 percent of the users. Similar proportions of nonusers and users were aware of center eligibility requirements (79 percent and 83 percent, respectively).

Failure to reach a substantial portion of the eligible population seemed related to lack of resources and personnel in several centers; however, since the centers were serving that segment of the target population with relatively more need for medical care and with significant financial and supply barriers to access to care, the investigators concluded that the centers were generally successful in reaching their target populations and supplementing available health services.

Scope of Services Offered

To determine the scope of services available at the NHCs surveyed, the Geomet evaluation studied four different types of efforts: clinical and supportive care, preventive services, family-planning programs, and training programs. Most centers had implemented a wide range of clinical services, some providing most of them directly. Other centers offered only primary care and relied on referral facilities to complete their range of services. Nineteen centers provided care by all three "primary-care specialties" (internal medicine, pediatrics, and obstetrics–gynecology), and all 21 had a broad base of medical specialties available on referral. The 6 rural centers ranked below the median on availability of medical specialties, and the urban centers ranked higher.

Nineteen centers offered a wide range of dental services. Most centers provided some mental-health services, although few had a staff psychiatrist to run the program. When centers could not provide mental-health services, referrals were readily available and usually within 20 minutes from the center. Alcoholism and drug-abuse services were less frequently provided. All centers had social service programs supporting other clinical services, although most depended on outside agencies to provide these on referral.

Although few centers initiated appointments for periodic adult physical examinations, most regularly provided them on request by patients. In contrast, the majority did initiate dental-care checkup appointments and provided regular dental care. Most automatically scheduled newborn examinations. Thus, performance of the centers on scope of preventive care was not uniform for all types of services.

Most centers implemented a full range of family-planning services, provided by the center physician and offered routinely to all women of child-bearing age.

Although the majority also offered training programs to community residents in health-related careers, insufficient data precluded more extensive analysis of training programs.

To test the comprehensiveness of services actually delivered by NHCs, user families were compared to nonusers and controls to determine whether they received a more nearly comprehensive range of services. The parameters for analyzing the dimension of comprehensiveness are shown below. Users generally received more of all types of services considered, although some of the differences between their use and that of nonusers and controls were explained by age variations between the groups.

PARAMETERS USED TO INDICATE COMPREHENSIVENESS OF SERVICES USED BY NHC USERS IN COMPARISON TO NONUSERS AND CONTROLS, GEOMET EVALUATION OF OEO–NHCS

Medical Examination (Adult)

- Examined at all
- Blood test
- Urinalysis
- Chest X-ray
- Blood pressure
- Body examination
- Vision test
- Hearing test

Dental Care

- Dental checkup
- Teeth filled
- Teeth pulled

Prescribed Devices

- Eye glasses obtained
- Hearing aid obtained

Prenatal and Postnatal Care

- Month of first visit
- Number of prenatal visits
- Postnatal checkups

Social Services

- Services received for perceived needs

BASED ON: Joann H. Langston et al., *Study to Evaluate the OEO Neighborhood Health Center Program at Selected Centers,* Volume 1. PB–207–084. (Springfield, Virginia: National Technical Information Service, January 1972), Table 7, p. 89.

Continuity of Care

Centers employed a variety of methods to coordinate their services with those of other agencies. These included direct referral, joint programs or meetings, and data transfer. Most centers were fairly well coordinated with local health and welfare departments and made extensive use of state mental hospitals for referral services, as well as of back-up hospitals and private physicians. Coordination of back-up services with a local hospital depended on whether NHC physicians had staff privileges. This in turn related to factors such as proximity of the hospital, the existence of a full-time hospital staff, and the supply of physicians at the center. Coordination was not markedly affected by the type of NHC sponsorship, that is, hospital or nonhospital.

Almost two-thirds of the surveyed centers used a team approach in the delivery of care and family-oriented record systems to facilitate continuity. They were judged to perform adequately in eliciting appropriate user behavior in completing referrals to specialists and making return visits. Users made and kept more appointments for care than nonusers or controls but were not as likely to see the same provider as the other groups were. Seeing more than one physician did not in itself indicate a barrier to continuity of care for NHC users, since they did not express as strong a preference as other groups did for seeing a single physician.

Accessibility of Services

Most centers surveyed provided a nearly comprehensive range of health and health-related services and had adequate coordination with outside agencies for back-up services. In almost all instances, urban centers ranked higher on these measures than rural centers did. Accessibility can be indicated by data on several different variables, including eligibility of patients, availability of services, waiting time, availability of transportation, travel time, and cost of services.

Eligibility of Patients.   Most centers had registered a majority of their eligible populations, ranging from 31 to 100 percent with a median of 65 percent. Centers registering a higher percentage of their eligible populations were most likely to have closed their registration rolls at some time to prevent case overload in the face of insufficient resources.

Availability of Services.   Centers were open from 8 to more than 12 hours a day; a majority provided services approximately 9 hours a day. Centers with shorter service hours generally had extensive after-hours arrangements for service, whereas those with longer open hours did not provide for these services.

Waiting Time.   For patients with appointments, waiting time for services at the centers ranged from approximately one-quarter to two-thirds of an hour. The shorter the waiting time for service, the longer the waiting time before obtaining the appointment. By using appointment systems, centers generally reduced waiting times and crowding.

Availability of Transportation.   Registrants in the urban NHCs generally had adequate public transportation available, in terms of operating hours, frequency of operation, and coverage of the target area. The cost of this transportation made it somewhat less than adequate as a resource for urban NHC populations. Public transportation was not as nearly adequate for rural NHC registrants and in three areas was not available at all. These rural centers were also judged to have less than adequate transportation available through the center.

Travel Time.   Average travel time to center services reflected the urban–rural differences in availability of transportation. Travel distances were generally less for smaller urban target areas. Urban users generally traveled 16 minutes, and rural registrants spent 27 minutes in travel to the center. Travel time for NHC users in urban areas was less than that for nonusers, indicating the greater proximity of urban centers to their eligible populations; users and nonusers in rural areas traveled about the same length of time.

A survey of satisfaction of Medi-Cal beneficiaries in Watts, Los Angeles, the location of an OEO neighborhood health center, indicates the impact of that urban center on geographic accessibility of services. For persons using the center as their usual source of services, 43 percent expressed satisfaction with their health care because the center was located within walking distance of their homes.[12]

Cost of Services.   The 21 centers surveyed by Geomet provided all services free of charge, but other NHCs are known to use sliding fee scales. In both instances, the financial barrier to care, excluding the cost of transportation to care, was minimal, enhancing accessibility of NHC services.

The barriers to access, when represented organizationally as long waiting times and closed registrations, or geographically as lack of transportation, were not equally present at each center. Their presence depended on particular characteristics, such as location of the center, and varied according to the strength of other barriers measured by factors such as availability of the resource and percent of the population registered.

Utilization Experience

The Geomet evaluation compared NHC users to nonusers and controls to determine if they were using health services more appropriately. (Use of services by nonusers and controls indicates, of course, utilization of resources other than the NHC's.) The measures used to indicate appropriateness of utilization are listed below.

Questions Used to Indicate Whether NHC Users Used Care More Appropriately than Nonusers or Controls, Geomet Evaluation

1. Do users seek care for their most limiting conditions more often than nonusers or the control group?
2. Do users follow instruction for this care better than nonusers or the control group?
3. Do NHC users complete referrals more often than nonusers or the control group?
4. Do users break fewer appointments than nonusers or the control group?
5. Do more users report receiving preventive health care (shots) more often than nonusers or the control group?
6. Do more NHC users report receiving physical exams (including vision exams and hearing exams) than do nonusers or the control group?
7. Do users report receiving prenatal care earlier than do nonusers or the control group?
8. Do more users report receiving postnatal care than do nonusers or the control group?
9. Do users report seeing a dentist more recently than nonusers or the control group?
10. Do more users report requesting home care than do nonusers or the control group?
11. Do more users report receiving social and health-related services than do nonusers and the control group?

12. Do users seek emergency/weekend care less often than do nonusers or the control group?

13. Are there fewer reported perceived health needs that are untreated among NHC users than among nonusers or the control group?

BASED ON: Joann H. Langston et al., *Study to Evaluate the OEO Neighborhood Health Center Program at Selected Centers,* Volume 1. PB-207-084 (Springfield, Virginia: National Technical Information Service, January 1972), pp. 68–73.

Users were found to seek care more often than nonusers, but at the same level as controls; these comparisons persisted when differences among groups were adjusted for variations in demographic characteristics. Users had received more preventive health care (immunizations) than either nonusers or controls and significantly more physical examinations and vision and hearing tests than nonusers and controls. None of these differences were influenced by demographic variables. Users also had visited a dentist more recently than the nonusers or controls and sought less emergency and weekend care than either of the other two groups. Little or no difference was found among the three groups on other measures of appropriate utilization, such as completion of referrals, use of prenatal and postnatal care, and use of social and health-related services.

Strauss and Sparer studied the utilization rates of eight OEO comprehensive health-service projects, five organized as neighborhood health centers and three as prepaid group practices that enrolled OEO-sponsored low-income populations. The registered populations were estimated from a group of persons using at least one service in the center during the preceding 18 months and having resided in the target area approximately one year. Active registrants represented an estimated 80 percent of the total registrant population. Registrants were so defined to avoid the effects of inflating registration figures by including all those who had *ever* used center services.

The number of encounters per year, including those with physician, nurse, and public health nurse, ranged from 3.6 to 6.3 per person, averaging 4.7 per person for all centers. The center with the lowest encounter rate had registered chiefly young and large families, and the one with the highest rate had selectively registered the medically deprived as a priority population.

The urban projects in this study had average annual physician visit rates somewhat higher than the national average for urban areas of 4.5 per person. Annual encounters for registrants in the four urban NHCs studied were 4.6, 4.9, 5.0, and 5.3 per person, averaging 4.95. This average, if generalized to other urban NHCs, would indicate a slightly higher utilization rate after opening of NHCs than that in the OEO baseline survey areas (4.7) before the opening of centers there.

The utilization rates for the three rural projects did not differ significantly from those of the urban projects and were thus sizably larger than the national average of 3.3 encounters per year for rural areas. This higher rate may be influenced by the fact that two of the three rural centers were prepaid group practices, rather than the NHC model.[13]

Attitudes Toward Health Care

Significant barriers to access to care are those attitudes toward health care that predispose people to delay or forgo seeking care. Although health education *may* be helpful in affecting these attitudes, in most instances it is not sufficient to induce a positive change, especially if other barriers to access persist.

Bellin and Geiger's analysis of health behaviors and attitudes of the Columbia Point, Boston, NHC users, as revealed in a 1967 follow-up survey to the 1965 baseline study, illustrates this point. Comparison of survey results indicated an increase in the proportion of respondents who appreciated the value of asymptomatic checkups and in the proportion who believed less serious symptoms of illness required medical care. For example, in 1965, 30 percent of the respondents thought a sore throat needed medical care, increasing to 50 percent by 1967. Analysis showed that these changed behaviors and attitudes were *not* the product of an active health-education campaign but the consequences of the organized health-care delivery system of the NHC, which reduced other barriers of supply, distance, and cost.[14]

The extent to which these particular results can be generalized in relation to other NHCs, organized in varying fashions and located in differing areas, is unknown, but a review of patient satisfaction in the Geomet survey indicated other areas of positive influence on the attitudes of users.

Patient Satisfaction

Patient satisfaction was measured in the Geomet survey on a series of variables relating to the personal, convenience, and technical-performance dimensions of services received by the three groups. A summary of the variables used to measure each dimension appears below.

MEASURES USED TO MEASURE PATIENT SATISFACTION, GEOMET EVALUATION OF OEO–NHCS

Human Dimension

Personal and Respectful Service
- Personal
- Physicians respectful
- Other staff respectful

Do you Like:
- Treatment?
- Physician?
- Other staff members?

Complaints
- Too many questions asked initially
- Rushed through
- Other complaints
- Complain to persons outside family

Convenience Dimension

Waiting Times
- Waiting time
- Wait too long

Crowded

Accessibility
- Access time
- Convenient time

Cost

Appointments
- Appointment for last service
- Usually make appointments
- Missed appointment within last year

Technical Performance Dimension

Range of Needed Services

Perceived Quality
- Chance to explain problems
- Explanation of health matters
- Received care you went for
- Condition improved

Recommended Source to Others

See Same Person

Preference for Same Person

SOURCE: Joann H. Langston et al., *Study to Evaluate the OEO Neighborhood Health Center Program at Selected Centers*, Volume 1. PB-207-084. (Springfield, Virginia: National Technical Information Service, January 1972), table 5, pp. 77–78.

NHC users did not differ from nonusers or controls in reporting general satisfaction with receiving respectful and dignified treatment from NHC staff, and they liked the staff and treatment received as much as those receiving care from other sources. Users did complain more often about being rushed through the center and being asked too many questions than nonusers did, and they reported more complaints on all four indicators than controls did. Few differences appeared among the three groups on convenience factors. Where there were differences, nonusers were somewhat more apt to think the cost of services was too high but reported their source of care to be open at more convenient times than users did. All three groups reported substantial satisfaction with the range of services available and the quality of care received. NHC users were far more likely to have recommended the center to others as a source of care.

Personnel Resources

The characteristics of NHC physicians and the stability of their employment have been examined by Tilson.[15] Center physicians had a median age below 40; they were more likely to be foreign medical graduates; one-half were licensed less than six years; and two-thirds were not certified by a specialty board. When compared to a control group of non-OEO physicians, the OEO sample contained twice as many women, four times as many black physicians, and more primary-care specialists, especially pediatricians.

Based on probability calculations, 48 percent of center physicians were expected to remain two or more years and 37 percent three or more years. High retention rates were correlated with high community participation, demonstrated continuity of care, and the use of team-care arrangements and allied personnel in an NHC. Physicians more likely to be retained by a center were older, board-certified, black, and not working on a full-time basis.

Measures used to indicate supply of personnel resources and the ranges for the 21 NHCs surveyed by Geomet were (1) ratio of staff per 1000 registrants, 4.1 to 28.4; (2) ratio of professional staff per 1000 registrants, 1.9 to 6.7; and (3) ratio of physicians per 1000 registrants, 0.3 to 1.9. Ten centers had fewer than 25 percent of their physicians working part-time and four centers had 50 percent or more part-time physicians. Centers with high ratios of staff per thousand registrants had a low ratio of part-time to full-time physicians. In these centers, the mean separation rate for physicians during a specified time period (the percent of physicians who left a center) was 26.8 percent, ranging from 2.6 to 59.4 percent. Five of the six rural centers were above the median level for staff separation rates. These wide variations in the level of personnel resources and frequent turnovers contributed to the inability of many centers to reach and serve the range of eligible persons stipulated in the OEO guidelines.

Outreach

Outreach programs, one of the distinctive features of the NHC delivery model, were assumed to be a means of increasing accessibility of services by actively encouraging eligible persons to use NHC facilities and services. All centers had developed outreach programs, including services such as case finding, home health care, follow-up, community health education and training, transportation, social service support, eligibility determination, and counseling. The extent of the programs varied considerably, depending on size of target area and urban or rural location.

The number of outreach personnel in the 21 centers studied ranged from 9 to 64 persons per center, and from 0.2 to 4.6 per thousand eligible persons. Five of the high-density-population urban centers were at or above the mean level for outreach activities, primarily because of smaller target areas, and all six rural centers ranked lower on most measures of outreach.

In a majority of centers, 50 percent or more of the outreach time was allocated to service activities, rather than to administrative tasks. Most of the outreach activities related to home health care. The number of households visited per week ranged from 15 to 55; half of the centers made between 20 and 40 visits per week. All centers routinely contacted new mothers and supervised maternal and child health care, and despite their lower level of outreach activity, rural centers did so more frequently.

Community Involvement

Involvement of community residents in center activities, both the delivery of care and administration, is another characteristic of the NHC model. All centers had community boards, and the percent of community residents on these policy-making boards ranged from 25 to 100 percent. Nineteen centers had community boards composed entirely of consumers; when nonusers were removed from consideration, seven centers had community boards composed entirely of users. On most boards, consumers reflected the ethnic mix of the target area. The most common activity of these boards was handling patient and employee grievances. The more often the project director or administrator attended board meetings, the more involved the board became in decision-making activities.

Overall Center Evaluation

When the centers were ranked by overall performance on the four dimensions used, those ranking above the median generally achieved high scores on continuity of care and patient satisfaction and lower scores for comprehensiveness of care and appropriate utilization. Although the existence of NHCs enhanced the availability of providers in all areas, lack of preexisting medical resources in rural areas was not a barrier readily overcome by rural centers. Only two rural centers ranked above the median on organizational and functional ratings. This confirmed the disadvantageous position of the rural centers vis-à-vis supply of resources, since the most common feature of centers ranking above the median on this rating was a high level of personnel resources.

One of the primary aims of the Geomet evaluation was to identify characteristics of "successful" centers, those that had come closest to fulfilling OEO guidelines for comprehensiveness and continuity of services, appropriate utilization, patient satisfaction, and other organizational variables as operationalized for measurement in the evaluation. Successful centers had more personnel in all professional categories per thousand registrants than less successful centers did and served smaller active registrant populations, spending more on each active registrant in delivery of services. They were also characterized by high levels of community involvement, outreach activities, good community-staff relations, and commitment of administrative personnel to the NHC concept.

PROGRAM COST

Complete figures for annual OEO–NHC program authorizations, appropriations, and obligations were not readily available, for the program was one of the many funded by OEO (and later by HEW), and its financial experience could not easily be distinguished from among complete program figures. The FY 1967 appropriation for the program in its first full year of operation was $50 million (for between 8 and 30 centers).[16] By FY 1974, for the 40 centers transferred from OEO to HEW administration, the budgetary appropriation stood at $92.3 million; the amount actually obligated for program use is not known.[17]

Individual center budgets vary considerably, as demonstrated in the Geomet data. For the 21 centers surveyed between 1970 and 1971, total 1969–1970 budgets provided by OEO, including categories such as personnel, facilities, and equipment, ranged from $1.08 to $7.33 million. Budget size per active registrant ranged from $72 to more than $400, with an average of $201 per registrant. Five of the six rural centers fell below the mean budget size of approximately $2.9 million, but all rural centers had higher-than-average budgets per person actively registered.[18]

Although the primary funding agency, OEO, was not the only source of money for its neighborhood health centers, 15 of the centers in the survey had between two and five non-OEO sources of income, excluding third-party sources such as Medicare, Medicaid, health insurance, and workmen's compensation. In 1969–1970, 11.6 percent of the centers' funds were derived from third-party sources.[19] In 1974, between 13 and 20 percent of NHC costs were reimbursed through these third-party sources.[20] This increase in the proportion of funds from third-party sources reflects an HEW policy decision to shift funding of the centers away from federal sources to the centers themselves, which must seek alternative funds or charge for services, or both.

According to the Deputy Associate Director of the Bureau of Community Health Services, the services presently offered by some centers that are not reimbursable, such as lead-paint screening and safe-water-supply programs, as well as political activities sponsored by the center, are being phased out.[21] The repercussions of this policy are also evident in the Watts NHC, where the community health-education program, health-manpower-training program, and children's breakfast program have been discontinued owing to lack of funds.[22] Further extension of this policy may hasten the demise of the NHC program, or at least radically alter the unique character of its service-delivery system, as these examples suggest.

SECONDARY EFFECTS

Like many of the "Great Society" programs, the promises created by neighborhood health centers were, to a large extent, only promises. Consumer-controlled accountability and accessible sources of care were primarily illusions. The cycle of inflation of expectations, followed by an inability to realize goals, undoubtedly contributed to the social unrest of the 1960s.

The conflicts surrounding the establishment (or nonreaction) and operation of these centers were a part of this generalized syndrome.

OVERALL IMPACT ON ACCESS TO PRIMARY CARE

As demonstrated in the evaluation of the 21 NHCs surveyed by Geomet between 1970 and 1971, NHC has been quite effective in meeting the objectives of delivering comprehensive health and social services to low-income populations. Target-area size and location, type of population served, personnel resources, arrangements for continuity and coordination of care, and available finances varied considerably from center to center. Despite these differing circumstances, most centers reached sizable proportions of their eligible populations. Families that used services tended to be those with greater perceived need for health and social services. The centers had enhanced the supply of available services in their target areas, and in many areas were providing more nearly continuous care at higher levels of patient satisfaction than that available to nonusers or control groups in comparable populations. Active outreach and community involvement in provision of care and in administration had been developed in most centers. Such characteristics tended to be associated with those centers most successful in meeting guidelines.

Centers ranking highest on continuity and patient satisfaction tended, however, to rank lower in comprehensiveness of care and appropriate use patterns. Commenting on this dichotomy, the Geomet investigators noted it may be impossible to achieve high ratings in all performance areas within a single NHC. They surmised that centers serving smaller target populations may be better able to promote continuity of care and patient satisfaction, but with fewer resources they are ill equipped to provide a comprehensive range of services and encourage appropriate use. Nevertheless, larger centers, well endowed with resources, may efficiently organize a network of comprehensive services and achieve appropriate use patterns. At the same time, these larger settings may tend to reduce continuity of care and increase patient dissatisfaction.

If their hypothesis is correct, the flexible and multifaceted NHC model, which in practice increased the supply of services and decreased or eliminated financial barriers to access for many low-income populations, has not in all instances eliminated organizational barriers. In the final analysis, it appears that the more successful centers were able, at least partly, to minimize organization barriers by serving smaller populations with greater personnel resources and larger budget allowances per registrant, being thus able to tailor the NHC model more closely to the health and social services needs and demands of their registrants.

SUMMARY

Neighborhood Health Centers were created for a variety of reasons—social, political, economic, and medical. Designed to circumvent the problems of "The System" by creating alternate sources of care, they were effective but not cost-effective. They achieved considerable impact on access to care for the limited populations they served by dealing with all barriers simultaneously. They also have had an impact on "The System" that they confronted, and these effects (consumer participation, use of community outreach workers, etc.) are still being felt after the "quest for community" of the Great Society seems on the verge of becoming part of the American dream.

FOURTEEN

Children and Youth Programs:

COMPREHENSIVE HEALTH CARE FOR CHILDREN OF LOW-INCOME FAMILIES

REASONS FOR DEVELOPMENT OF PROGRAMS

When social and political concerns in the early 1960s focused on the disad-vantageous position of low-income inner-city residents with respect to health status and availability of health resources, the need for facilities offering comprehensive health care to children in these families became apparent. These children were often afflicted with debilitating conditions such as malnutrition—vitamin and protein deficiencies—iron-deficiency anemia, and a variety of chronic problems infrequently found among children in higher income families. Although children of low-income families as a group had poorer health than children under 18 in other income groups, nonwhite children were at a particular disadvantage. The nonwhite child was far more likely to belong to a low-income family; 59 percent of the nonwhite population under 18, as com-pared to 15 percent of the white population, were in families with incomes below the poverty level.[1] In addition to nutritional deficiencies, low-income nonwhite children experienced a greater incidence of infectious diseases, such as influenza and pneumonia, than did white children from similar income families.[2]

Despite their poor health, low-income children did not use health services to the same extent as children in higher income families. The findings of a survey of the use of personal health services by a sample of the United States population in 1963, reported by Andersen and Anderson in 1967, documented the continuing relation of use of health services to income. Whereas young children from middle- and upper income families were more likely to have made physician visits than any other age group, those aged 1–17 in the low-income group were the least likely to have seen a physician during the year (see Table 32). Access to comprehensive care for these low-income children was inhibited in part because their usual sources of care (if indeed they had one) tended to be hospital emergency rooms and outpatient clinics.[3]

There was precedent for federal funding of health care for this particular group in the categorical health-services projects established during the late 1950s and early 1960s, particularly those included in the Maternal and Child Health Services program. The Special Projects Grants for Health of School and Preschool Children authorized in 1965 established the Children and Youth Program and markedly increased federal involvement in the funding and provision of health care to children of low-income families.

Table 32   Percent of Persons Visiting a Physician During 1963, by Age and Family Income[a]

	Income		
Age	$0–$3999	$4000–$6999	$7000 and over
1–5	52	76	87
6–17	41	53	70
18–34	57	67	70
35–54	54	64	69
55–64	69	70	66
65 and over	68	66	71
	—	—	—
Total	56	64	71

SOURCE.   Ronald Anderson and Odin W. Anderson, *A Decade of Health Services: Social Survey Trends in Use and Expenditures,* The University of Chicago Press, Chicago, 1967, Table II, p. 29.
[a] Based on a multistage area probability sample of the total noninstitutionalized population of United States in 1963; percentages calculated only on those in the sample for the entire 12-month period.

NATURE OF INTERVENTION

In 1965 Congress authorized a program of Special Projects Grants for Health of School and Preschool Children under Title V of the Social Security Act amendments (P.L. 89–97). These grants provided funding to public and nonprofit agencies to cover 75 percent of the costs of supplying comprehensive health care to low-income children. Services were provided through Children and Youth projects established by the grantee agencies. Unlike the benefits available to children under Medicaid, which only subsidized their demand for health services, the Children and Youth projects provided those services directly, at little or no charge to the patient. Like the neighborhood health center, the Children and Youth projects were multifaceted interventions in the health-services delivery system, including efforts to reduce financial, geographic, supply, fragmentation, and psychosocial barriers to access to primary care. The characteristic differentiating Children and Youth projects from neighborhood health centers was their focus on a specific age group within the low-income population, whose health status required a specific and comprehensive response.

SOURCES

The Systems Development Project at Minnesota Systems Research, Inc., under the direction of Vernon Weckwerth, Ph.D., is conducting an ongoing analysis and evaluation of the performance of Children and Youth projects under a research grant from the Maternal and Child Health Service. Selected issues of the study report series, made available by Weckwerth and a colleague, Willy de Geyndt, Ph.D., provided most of the data used in this case study. Few other studies of the Children and Youth program have been undertaken, and those that were available have been included where relevant to the issues addressed.

DESCRIPTION OF PROGRAMS

Program Guidelines

Guidelines for development of Children and Youth (C & Y) projects did not specify any one organizational format for the delivery of comprehensive health services to low-income children, since a primary concern was that each project should respond to local community needs. A wide-ranging definition of health care was used, including but not limited to screening, diagnosis, treatment, preventive and corrective services, inpatient hospital care, and aftercare. Projects were encouraged to develop the ancillary health and social services necessary to promote use of the full range of available services, and to coordinate C & Y services with those of local health, welfare, and educational institutions. Definitions of the target areas and eligible children were to be developed by each project.

Extent of Effort

The special project grants supporting C & Y projects are administered through the Maternal and Child Health Service, a division of the Bureau of Community Health Services, in the Health Services Administration, Department of Health, Education, and Welfare. By 1972 (April–June), the Service had awarded grants to 76 C & Y projects in the United States, the Virgin Islands, and Puerto Rico.[4] Most went to state health agencies, medical schools, and teaching hospitals who had actively solicited funding for establishment of C & Y projects.

EVIDENCE OF EFFECTIVENESS

Penetration of Target Population[5]

Some 15.4 million children of low-income families were potentially eligible to receive health care under C & Y legislation. At the end of FY 1972, the estimated total number of children (under 21 years) in the 76 target areas was 3,276,847, or 21.3 percent of those potentially eligible. As would be expected, most projects used financial-means tests to identify low-income children eligible for registration and care; however, virtually all projects also set upper age limits to determine eligibility further. In a sample of 57 projects reporting in 1971, 51 percent of the responding projects used 17–19 years as the cutoff age; 10 percent registered only those 8 and under; others restricted registration rolls to certain categories, such as high-risk children. Therefore, the estimated number of children eligible by reason of age and location was 2,945,262, approximately 89 percent of the target-area children and about 19 percent of all potentially eligible low-income children in the United States. Actual registration in mid-1972 numbered 487,263, only 16.5 percent of those eligible according to criteria for age and location. However, 63.9 percent of the 59 projects surveyed in 1971 reported delivering care to nonregistered children, and it was a common practice to refer ineligible children to other sources of care. (See Table 33 for age distribution of registrants as of mid-1972.)

Among the 57 projects reporting numbers of children registered in 1971,

Table 33   Age Distribution of Registrants in
C&Y Projects, April–June 1972

Age	Number	Percent
Under 1	22,587	4.6
1–4	128,282	26.3
5–9	142,420	29.2
10–14	115,804	23.8
15–17	50,069	10.3
18–20	28,101	5.8

SOURCE. Vernon E. Weckwerth, project director, *Quarterly Summary Report, April–June 1972.*
Systems Development Project, Report Series
No. 18 (Minneapolis, Minnesota: Systems Development Project, 1972).

registrations ranged from 1007 to 38,528. Projects operating under the auspices
of a medical school C & Y grant tended to be larger than the health-department
projects and were more likely to register all children in a family when the first
child filed an application for care.

Scope of Services Available

Although a child's first contact with a C & Y project may be precipitated by an
acute illness or an injury requiring immediate care, the primary goal of C & Y
projects is delivery of continuing and comprehensive care. As soon as possible
after enrollment, a child receives a complete health assessment, and thereafter
preventive and diagnostic services as needed, along with regular periodic
checkups. Supplementing the basic core of medical services, most C & Y
projects make available a variety of special programs and services in conjunction with local health and welfare agencies, to provide "comprehensive" health
care.

Screening Programs.   Projects conducting screening programs generally make
them available to children through community schools and day-care centers,
regardless of their eligibility for registration. Screening programs for vision and
hearing problems are common, and most projects screen for speech and language problems, learning disabilities, and emotional disturbances as well.
Screening for sickle-cell trait is a communitywide service offered by projects
with large numbers of black children in their target areas. In 1971, 44 projects
screened routinely for this trait.[6] Lead poisoning, an acute problem in inner-
city urban areas where dwellings are deteriorating, is the target of publicity

campaigns and screening programs in many projects. In Chicago, more than 100,000 children were screened for lead-paint poisoning over a three-year period by the C & Y project, working in conjunction with other state agencies and Office of Economic Opportunity programs. In New York City and Baltimore, project volunteers have canvassed neighborhoods in screening programs for lead poisoning and have acted as representatives for the community in dealing with landlords and other involved parties to prevent its occurrence. The Brooklyn C & Y was instrumental in relocating 60 families over a two-year period as part of its lead-paint-poisoning control effort.[7]

Dental Care.   Dental care is viewed as an important component in the total health care of children, but poor dental-health status resulting from the lack of prior dental care in most poverty areas presents difficulties for the limited capabilities of the projects. Backlogs in dental checkups mounted, and many projects have reacted to the magnitude of unmet need by allocating dental resources to specific age groups, usually the youngest, and by emphasizing proper preventive dental care through fluoride treatment and health education.

Nutrition Programs.   Common nutritional problems found in target areas are iron-deficiency anemia, stunted growth, and obesity resulting from high-carbohydrate diets. Cooperation with local public agencies enables C & Y projects to guide registrants to supplemental food programs, such as food stamp and community school-breakfast programs. Nutritionists in these projects plan diets, instruct mothers in principles of nutrition, and work closely with children requiring special diets.

Social services.   The approach to comprehensive health care adopted by C & Y projects emphasizes treating children within an awareness of their social and physical environment to understand better and cope with the factors affecting their health status. Social service workers counsel parents on how best to deal with a wide spectrum of problems related to low-income and inner-city residence and direct them to available services beyond the range provided by the C & Y project.

Adolescent programs.   Within the last decade, many adolescents have rejected traditional health-care providers and turned to "crisis" centers and free clinics, which they perceive to be more responsive to their health and social needs. According to a sample of physicians specializing in the care of adolescents, it is the responsibility of federally sponsored health programs to provide services in a fashion that recognizes the adolescent as a "complex and unique entity, no longer a child and not yet an adult, with special needs and requiring care provided by those knowledgeable and responsive to that unique entity." Whereas less than half of all C & Y registrants were between 10 and 20 years of age (39 percent in mid-1972), about 20 projects have placed a special emphasis on the problems of the adolescent. The development of programs based on the psychological, emotional, and physiological processes associated with adolescence is viewed as a means of increasing the accessibility of primary care for this age group.[8]

The program for pregnant girls initiated by Mt. Zion Hospital Comprehensive Care C & Y program in San Francisco is an example of the intensive work required and the benefits resulting from these special programs for adolescents. Over a period of two academic years, the program enabled 122 girls to continue their education in a project school while concurrently receiving comprehensive medical and obstetrical care, health education, and psychological support. The project provided the girls with an alternative to dropping out of school, and with the provision of infant care and psychological counseling after delivery, they were more likely to return to school. A follow-up study of a group of 35 pregnant girls revealed that 76 percent of the babies were registered in the project's well-baby clinic after delivery and that 75 percent of the girls had returned or intended to return to school.[9]

Impact of C & Y Projects on Geographic Barriers

C & Y projects are located predominantly in urban areas. Two-thirds of 57 projects reporting in 1971 were classified as urban, and approximately 90 percent of their registrants resided in the inner-city. Target-area sites ranged from a minimum of 0.1 square mile to 6300 square miles, with a median of 6 square miles. In all, 171 sites were operated by the 57 projects. C & Y projects sponsored by health departments provided services at a larger number of sites, 4.5, than hospital projects (2.3) and those under the auspices of medical schools (2.5) did. Approximately 75 percent of the registrants lived within a mile of the locations of services, and a majority of projects facilitated access through the provision of transportation or reimbursement of the cost of private or public transportation. In rural areas greater geographic accessibility is fostered through the use of mobile clinics equipped with medical and dental supplies.[10]

In both urban and rural areas, the C & Y projects have attempted to minimize the geographic barrier for the target-area population. Working within the fixed limits of geographic boundaries, however, most have had to restrict services to residents of those areas and thereby, unavoidably, have erected geographic barriers for nontarget-area low-income children. In mid-1972, 46 percent of the 7027 children designated as ineligible were removed from registration rolls because they lived outside the target area. Furthermore, projects have reacted to constantly rising registration rates and limitations of funding by narrowing the scope of the target areas to maintain an adequate level of care for registered children. In 1971, 24 projects took this action, which was, in effect, a reimposition of the geographic barrier for those affected.[11]

Impact on Continuity of Care and Barriers of Fragmentation

One aspect of continuity of care, the referral system, was examined by Willy De Geyndt.[12] This system is the process through which a child is directed to C & Y project services, is cared for by a variety of providers within the project, and, if necessary, is guided to other specialized services outside the project. Self-referral and referral by a relative were most frequently cited as sources: one-third of all *new* registrants during the one-year study period of 1968–1969 were referred in these ways. De Geyndt speculated that the prominence of these two modes of referral suggested that many children or their families were selecting the C & Y projects as alternatives to emergency rooms or outpatient departments. The second most common referral source, for about one of six new registrants, was found to be the C & Y projects themselves, which either registered all family members of the child seeking care or recruited eligible children from the target area through outreach efforts. Throughout the study year, there was a marked increase in self-referrals and a decline in C & Y referrals. The latter phenomenon was due, in part, to a conscious effort on the part of some projects to control the number of newly entering children because of growing budgetary limitations.

High rates of self-referral to the C & Y project correlated with the large number of black children in the target-area population, with the large target-area size, with the large number of acute medical episodes before complete health assessment was accomplished, and with increased community involvement in the project. Projects with a lower rate of self-referrals tended to have high rates of well children among the registrant population.

Most C & Y projects attempt to maintain continuity of care within the project by use of liaison or continuity personnel and a team approach to care. Thirty of 57 projects reporting in 1971 employed a staff member, usually a nurse or community health worker, and in some instances a team of staff members, to function in liaison or coordinator roles for each registrant and family members and the project.[13] Liaison personnel also explain forms and project operation to registrants and interpret when language difficulties exist.

Since 1969, when only 52 percent of the projects used a team approach to care, C & Y projects have increasingly adopted this format for delivery of services. Fifty-one (89 percent) of the projects filing reports in 1971 promoted continuity of care through staff teams, composed of physicians (most often pediatricians), social workers, and nurses, and occasionally including a psychologist, dentist, speech and hearing therapist, or clerk. The functions of these teams include the assessment of the health status of new registrants, and, in 80 percent of the projects with teams, follow-up during care for all registrants. In some projects, teams have been developed to care for special groups, such as high-risk children, infants, adolescents, abused children, and those with behavioral and learning disorders.[14]

Coordination of services and use of available community resources did not, according to De Geyndt, meet the federal standards for interagency cooperation and exchange. This study suggests that referral for interagency continuity of care was not functioning smoothly in introducing children into the C & Y system and moving them to other resources in the community. Within the C & Y projects, however, high levels of continuity had been achieved.[15]

Supply of Providers[16]

The widespread use of new professionals and allied health personnel by the C & Y projects augments the supply of health-related workers, which, in turn, enhances the possibility of providing a broader range of services. In 1971, 46 of 57 projects' professional staff were assisted by such workers. These projects employed 443 allied health personnel for an average of 9.6 per project who functioned as nurses' aides or community health workers. Acting also as mediators between the project's professional staff and the community, the aides were considered a means of reducing barriers related to psychosocial factors and supply of services.

The supply of providers has been further expanded in at least 20 projects by the use of pediatric nurse practitioners (PNP)—4 of these projects were in central cities, 1 in a rural area, and 3 in semiurban areas. The PNP performed functions such as total health assessment, well-child care, and the treatment of minor illnesses.

Another source of assistance has been students and volunteers. According to a 1970 survey, 4600 students and volunteers were involved in 43 projects. Included were 2000 nursing students; 1700 students, interns, and residents in medicine; and 512 in dentistry. Most medical and nursing students were associated with the projects for intervals of less than two months, but medical residents (216) averaged 8 months, dental residents (16) 11 months, and psychology students (62) 10 months of affiliation. Whether involvement in a project was a determining factor in choice of a medical specialty is questionable, but at the New York University–Bellevue Hospital, the number of students applying for pediatric internships has recently increased, and it has been suggested that student contact with the affiliated C & Y project might have been influential in their specialty choices.

Community influence on project policy has most often affected the scope of services. In the year ending September 30, 1971, 28 projects (of 57 reporting) cited the impact of community input in this area. Specific results of community intervention were the lengthening of the hours of daily service, addition of a new service site or a better appointment system, and formation of Mothers Advisory Groups. However, 80 percent of the projects responding pointed out that community representatives on advisory or policy boards had little or no influence on decision-making.

Impact on Availability of Care[17]

In mid-1971, all projects but one offered complete on-site services at least five days a week. Thirty-two projects were open for longer hours, and 10 provided partial service or emergency care, or both, 24 hours a day. Services to patients who walked in were provided without appointments in 44 projects and constituted 50 percent or less of the patient load in 40 projects.

A problem for most projects has been growing backlogs in appointments for registrants, as well as longer intervals between routine assessments. There has been an almost constant increase in the estimated length of time required to eliminate the backlogs for medical and dental appointments. The estimated length of time before the backlogs in the medical services would be eliminated was 8.5 quarters in June 1972, as opposed to almost 2 quarters in early 1968. Dental backlogs in June 1972 averaged almost 25 quarters (6.25 years) before catching up, as opposed to only 5 in 1968. The estimated interval between initial dental and medical assessments and reassessment had also increased since 1968, although not as markedly.

These backlogs, and in many projects closed registrations rolls, have resulted from the pressure of growing numbers of registered children coupled with relatively constant supplies of resources, despite efficiency measures adopted by many C & Y projects to extend organizational capabilities. These organizational barriers to access to primary care are likely to persist in the future unless additional resources are made available, productivity increases, or quality of care is sacrificed.

Impact on Quality of Care[18]

The impact and the quality of care of the comprehensive health services received by the C & Y registrants were evaluated by De Geyndt. The measures used in defining quality of care were as follows: (1) a change in the distribution of visits for episodic care before and after a complete assessment of the child's health status and the provision of needed health care services; (2) a comparison of the distribution of disease conditions found during an initial health assessment of the child to those diagnosed during a recall assessment; and (3) the utilization rate of inpatient hospital services.

The preventive and curative features of C & Y dental programs were credited for the relative decrease in dental caries. Vision screening and treatment programs resulted in a decline of refractive disorders. No explanation was offered for the decline in the remaining diagnostic categories.

A relative increase occurred between preassessment and posttreatment visits in eight conditions, none of which can be totally prevented in any population. This increase was interpreted as further evidence of greater acceptance of the

C & Y projects by the target-area populations, which became more inclined to seek prompt medical care for these illnesses rather than to defer care until the problems reached serious proportions. Many of these gains resulting from C & Y service continued to be seen as patients made follow-up visits and had their health status reassessed.

The final measure, inpatient hospital admission rates, was used as a proxy measure of quality of care, the assumption being that a rise in ambulatory-care services would be paralleled by a decrease in days of hospital care required by these populations. Over the two-year period, although quarterly variations did occur in the rate of inpatient hospitalization, there was an overall decline of 47.5 percent in the proportion of all registrants hospitalized. In general, the data on all three outcome measures documented a high level of quality of care (as defined by the investigator).

The quality of care was also investigated in a comparative study of health-care delivery systems conducted by Morehead. Included in the analysis of differences in the level of quality care were medical-school-affiliated hospital outpatient clinics, neighborhood health centers, group practices, health-department well-baby clinics, and C & Y projects. Baseline medical audit scores rating three specialty areas (internal medicine, pediatrics, and obstetrics) were developed as indicators of the level of quality of care. The average score for the hospital outpatient department was arbitrarily designated as a standard to establish relative values. In pediatric care (the only service on which C & Y projects were evaluated), the four projects surveyed achieved an average total score higher than the other institutional providers and 60 percent higher than the standard of the hospital outpatient department. The baseline medical audit scores in the pediatric areas are shown below:

Medical-school-affiliated hospital outpatient departments	83
OEO neighborhood health centers	40
Group practices	84
Health-department well-baby clinics	93
C & Y projects	133

PROGRAM COSTS[19]

The amounts of federal funds obligated annually to C & Y projects from FY 1966 through FY 1973 (estimated) are shown in Table 34. Whereas direct obligations to this program represented the major source of funds, some operating expenses were met by monies from outside sources. Approximately 10 percent of C & Y budgets in 1971 were derived from outside sources, slightly more than two-thirds contributed through Medicaid.

Table 34   Amount of Federal Funds Obligated Annually to C&Y Projects, FY 1966–FY 1973

FY	Amount of Federal Funding (millions)
1966	15
1967	35
1968	37
1969	39
1970	39
1971	44
1972	47
1973	53 (estimated)

SOURCE.   Emily Sano, *Children and Youth Projects: Comprehensive Health Care in Low-Income Areas.* DHEW Publication No. (HSM) 72-5006 (Washington, D.C.: Government Printing Office, 1972), p. 27.

When adjusted for inflation, the level of funding has remained relatively stable since FY 1968, although the number of children registered had increased from 250,000 at the end of FY 1968 to about 490,000 by the end of FY 1972. As a result, the average project expenditures per child decreased. In 1968, those expenditures averaged $200 per child for operating projects. By 1971, the average cost of care per child was $126 for medical-school C & Y projects, $142 for those sponsored by teaching hospitals, and $151 for C & Y projects run under the auspices of health departments. The lower costs per child were related in part to the substitution of preventive or follow-up health services for the more expensive acute-illness care often required at initial contact with the C & Y.

SECONDARY EFFECTS

Perhaps some of the problems discussed with reference to Neighborhood Health Centers are relevant to Children and Youth programs, that is, unfulfilled promises with consequent frustration and anger. There was also the suggestion that these programs may have drawn a sizable number of practicing pediatricians (serving middle-class families) into nonpracticing administrative roles. There are no data to substantiate this suggestion.

OVERALL IMPACT ON ACCESS TO PRIMARY CARE

Although they serve a very small number of all the children of low-income families, C & Y projects have had considerable success in reducing many of the barriers to access to care for those children they do serve. Financial barriers have been virtually eliminated. Using a broad definition of "health care" and a variety of providers, the projects generally offer a wide range of high-quality medical, dental, and health-related services. The availability of these services, as indicated by daily hours of service and frequency of walk-in visits, is adequate. However, the backlogs of appointments for both medical and dental care represent barriers, erected in response to pressures of fast-growing registration rolls on supply of services.

Although coordination of C & Y services with those of existing local health and welfare services has not been optimal, continuity of services within the C & Y projects appears adequate. Definite inroads against geographic barriers have been made by locating C & Y centers and their satellites near patients and by providing transportation when necessary. These successes have been offset by subsequent redrawing of target-area boundaries, again, to curtail registration in the face of heavy demands on limited resources. Inflation in medical-care costs, the demonstration status of the projects, and reduced funding have prevented projects from adding many of the resources necessary to keep pace with these growing demands.

Thus, the philosophy underlying the organization and delivery of care by C & Y projects reflects a flexible and responsive approach in tailoring services to fit the health problems of specific populations. That approach, although limited in scope, has had considerable impact on increasing access to primary care.

SUMMARY

Children and Youth projects are yet another of the fragmented and categorical attempts to provide services to an age-specific, income-specific subsegment of society. They achieved their missions at considerable cost for less than 5 percent of those for whom such programs were designed. Increasing costs of care and decreasing political emphasis on community-based services make it seem unlikely that they will ever represent more than a token effort to increase access to primary care—even for the specific target group in question.

FIFTEEN

Health-Maintenance Organizations:

GUARANTORS OF ACCESS TO MEDICAL CARE?

REASONS FOR DEVELOPMENT OF PROGRAM

Lack of Access Related to Supply and Cost Barriers

Over the past decade, public concern with the performance of health-services delivery systems has focused on their inability to make available and accessible a full range of medical-care services at a reasonable cost. Contrary to expectations, massive infusions of federal funds through Medicare and Medicaid did not ensure access to care for beneficiaries in specified age and income groups. Instead, experience indicates that reduction or elimination of financial barriers might take unlimited funds, a requirement that cannot realistically be met. The need for cost containment has overshadowed the commitment to reduce all financial barriers to care, and rapidly rising costs have been followed by limitations in benefits and increases in copayment levels.[1] This trend has affected not only federal programs; private health insurers have also countered rising reimbursement claims costs with premium rate increases and more stringent utilization reviews.

Attempts to reduce or eliminate financial barriers to care, for even a portion of the population, have exposed major deficiencies in the delivery system. Supply problems have become paramount: there are not enough health providers and services available when and where needed. Moreover, after an entry point to the system is found, lack of continuity and coordination in the provision of services by physicians and hospitals makes existence of an organized delivery system questionable. Concerns for the appropriateness and quality of services actually provided have also been raised. Analysis of problems exacerbated by unavailability and maldistribution of providers and services, and by fragmentation of available services, suggests to some that these barriers are intimately related to, and perhaps caused by, the prevailing mode of service delivery—fee-for-service medical care by solo practitioners.

HMO: Organization of Services plus Cost Control

For many years, prepaid group practice (PGP) has been advocated by some as the logical answer to the problems of fragmentation of services, reduction of financial barriers to access, and control of costs. After an effective "repackaging" effort, coupled with some substantive changes, the underlying concepts of the PGP emerged in the form of "Health Maintenance Organizations," advocated in the Nixon Administration's 1971 "Message . . . Relative to Building a Health Strategy." The core principles of this strategy were (1) ensuring equal access, (2) balancing supply and demand, (3) organizing for efficiency, and (4) building on strengths. Development and support of health-maintenance organizations (HMOs) nationwide was the proposed guarantee of those principles and was expected to achieve the major policy features of the strategy, noted as follows: (1) emphasis on health maintenance, (2) preservation of cost consciousness, (3) reorganization of the delivery of services, (4) meeting the special needs of scarcity areas, (5) meeting the personnel needs of a growing medical system, and (6) prevention of illness and accidents.[2]

Although the Nixon Administration subsequently backed away from full endorsement of HMOs, advocating instead an "experimental" approach, Congressional impetus to achieve the "promise" of the HMO remained. The 1972 Social Security amendments to the Medicare program (P.L. 92–603) offered to beneficiaries, as of July 1973, the option of choosing to receive covered health services through an HMO.[3] Finally, after three years of discussion, debate, and negotiation on a variety of House- and Senate-sponsored bills, Congress passed the Health Maintenance Organization Act of 1973 (P.L. 93–222), requiring that enrollment in a qualified HMO be offered as a health-insurance option to all personnel in businesses employing at least 25 persons.[4]

NATURE OF INTERVENTION

The HMO organizes the supply and delivery of health care to serve an enrolled population and finances that organization and delivery with premiums prepaid by enrollees. In so doing, it intervenes in the existing system of health-services delivery at virtually all points, in effect *replacing* that system as a source of care for its enrolled population. This total intervention, or substitution, is considered by many to be particularly desirable, since certain features of the HMO are believed to solve, or at least minimize, problems of access and cost inherent in the existing system. (HMO features are described more extensively in a following section.)

Since delivery of the services is unrelated, in time or volume, to payment, there should be no financial barrier to inhibit the HMO enrollee from seeking or receiving needed medical services. Furthermore, since the monthly capitation payment is fixed for the contract period, the enrollee is not faced with unexpected medical bills.

Identification of the source and location of services establishes for the enrollee a known point of entry to a range of medical-care services, specified in his contract, reducing barriers of fragmentation and lack of coordination in the provision and use of services. These barriers are further reduced by the coverage of all types of physicians' services, wherever rendered, as well as hospital and ancillary services.

The HMO must contain costs since it operates on a fixed prospective budget and involves all providers and administrative personnel in the effort to remain within that budget while providing services. Furthermore, since ambulatory services are available and covered, the physician is encouraged to promote health maintenance and early detection of disease and thereby avoid the far higher costs of hospitalization.

SOURCES

The pros and cons of the concept of health maintenance organizations and the theoretical bases for the HMO's performance have been debated extensively in recent years, and the literature on these subjects is voluminous. Documentation of actual performance, particularly in controlled studies, is less extensive, but considerable amounts of data are available. Such studies have been reviewed and analyzed periodically for across-plan consistency of performance on many variables, and these reviews provided an invaluable introduction to the literature and to major findings on access-related variables. Particularly helpful in this regard were the review–evaluations by Weinerman in 1964, by Donabedian in 1965 and updated in 1969, by Klarman in 1971 and 1973, and by Roemer and Shonick in 1973. These sources were supplemented by information from studies by individual plans on topics related to access to care in HMOs where available.

Information on the extent and funding of the federal HMO effort was obtained from reports issued periodically by the Health Maintenance Organization Service, Health Services Administration, Department of Health, Education, and Welfare. Information on the cost performance of the California prepaid health plans had been newly released when this case study was being prepared. Steven Lipton, consultant to the California Assembly Health Committee, was instrumental in obtaining copies of that information for use in the study.

DESCRIPTION OF PROGRAMS

Distinguishing Features of the HMO Model

An HMO is identified as an organization that accepts contractual responsibility for making available and providing to all enrollees a specified range of medical-care services at an identified location (or locations) in return for their prepaid capitation payments. The contract between the individual, family, or employee-group enrollee and the HMO usually covers at least ambulatory and in-hospital physicians' services and related ancillary services. It may also include supplemental benefits in return for an additional premium.

A cardinal feature of the HMO premium is that it is paid by each enrollee before services are used and regardless of the volume or type of covered services actually provided. In addition to this basic capitation payment, some HMOs use deductible and copayment mechanisms. Except for occasional fee-for-service payments by nonenrollee users, the HMO's operating budget derives entirely from prepaid capitation payments, supplemented by additional premiums and cost-sharing fees. The organization thus assumes prospective financial risk for producing all services demanded by enrollees during the contract period and usually for reimbursement of payments made by the enrollee for services provided outside the HMO area in emergency situations.

Services are provided in central outpatient facilities or satellite clinics, or both, and in hospitals owned by the HMO or in those in which arrangements are made for hospitalization of enrollees. Unless the organization is physician sponsored, the HMO must directly employ or contract with a group of physicians to provide requisite services, and occasionally contracts with outside agencies for ancillary services.

Variations of the Model

Two forms of the HMO model have been identified in health-services research literature and by the recent HMO bill: the prepaid group practice and the foundation for medical care. (The bill distinguished these forms as "medical group practice" and "independent practice association.") The distinction between these two forms is chiefly one of professional organization, since the prepayment and HMO–enrollee contract features apply to both.

In the prepaid group practice (PGP), as suggested by its name, services are provided by physicians practicing together in an organized group, sharing facilities and ancillary personnel, and usually remunerated with a predetermined salary related to specialty and seniority, rather than to volume of services provided. In contrast, subscriber services in the medical society-sponsored foundation for medical care (FMC) are provided by participating member physicians in independent practice, out of private offices and in local hospitals. Each physician is remunerated on the basis of a fixed-fee schedule in relation to the number and type of services provided. To retain the fee-for-service feature and still operate within a fixed budget, the FMC characteristically reviews the services provided for appropriateness as well as quality and reserves the right to refuse payment or to make partial fee payment if the services do not meet established criteria.

Extent of Effort

Health-services systems representing prepaid group practice have operated in the United States for as long as 40 years. The foundation for medical care had its origins in the United States some 20 years ago. Among the PGP prototypes were the Ross–Loos Medical Clinic (Los Angeles, 1929), The Group Health Association (Washington, D.C., 1937), the Kaiser–Permanente Medical Care Program (Oakland, 1942), the Group Health Cooperative of Puget Sound (Seattle, 1947), and the Health Insurance Plan of Greater New York (1947). Sponsors of these original PGPs were physician groups or business interests, or both. The San Joaquin Foundation for Medical Care (Stockton, California, 1954), founded by that county's medical society, was the first FMC established in the United States.[5]

Before the federal government's involvement in promoting HMOs began in 1971, approximately 30 HMO-type health-services delivery plans were in operation across the country. After President Nixon's health message, the Health Maintenance Organization Service (HMOS) was established in the Health Services Administration, Department of Health, Education, and Welfare (HEW), to encourage HMO development through financial and technical assistance.

Stimulated in part by the promise and then the existence of federal support, HMO planning and development have proceeded rapidly. In early 1974, the HMOS identified some 120 HMO-type plans in operation nationwide, serving more than 5 million enrollees. Included in the count, which is not all-inclusive, are prototype PGPs and more recent models, many medical-society-sponsored FMCs, and prepaid health plans established for California Medi-Cal beneficiaries. (Another 1 to 2 million persons are enrolled in prepayment plans considered to be less than comprehensive or more restrictive than the HMO model.)

Federal grants for preoperational planning and development have gone to 84 different groups (including 5 funded through the Social and Rehabilitation Service, HEW). Although no grants and contracts have been awarded for initial operating expenses, 31 plans that received federal financial, technical, or resource-development assistance are now operational, serving 189,000 enrollees.

Thirteen states have implemented prepaid Title XIX contracts that cover some 900,000 Medicaid eligibles. The 68 existing contracts, 49 of which are with prepaid health plans (PHPs) in California, provide coverage for more than 344,500 enrollees. In addition, HEW and the Social Security Administration are working to implement participation of HMOs in coverage of Medicare beneficiaries. Currently, there are 67 contracts with PGPs for this coverage, with total enrollments of some 350,000 Medicare beneficiaries.

Financial and developmental assistance for these plans has come from the private sector as well, including national Blue Cross and Blue Shield plan organizations, insurance companies, banks, and other private interests. Through their Alternative Delivery System activities, 56 Blue Cross plans are involved in planning, marketing, and making contractual arrangements for hospital services for developing and operating HMOs. As of October 1973, at least 55 insurance companies had become involved or interested in the development of some 70 HMO-type plans.[6]

EXTENT OF EFFECTIVENESS

HMO Performance: Rhetoric versus Reality

The political promise of the HMO as a guarantor of access to medical care while containing costs was not founded entirely on experience. Confusion persists between the organizational and performance features that HMOs are believed or expected to achieve and the results that have been demonstrated or documented by established programs.

Evaluations of HMOs have emphasized the need to eliminate this confusion and have made considerable progress in that direction. They have concentrated on updating what is known about the performance of HMOs on a number of criteria and on determining the comparative advantages and disadvantages of this form of organization with respect to other forms of service delivery, particularly fee-for-service practice.

The purpose of this effort is to determine the impact of the HMO model of financing and organizing medical services on access to primary care, but not all of these evaluative studies are relevant. This discussion concentrates on the evidence that HMOs have altered or increased access to care for enrolled populations.

The HMO model is flexible. Organizational characteristics, as well as the nature of enrolled populations, vary considerably among operating plans, and this variation can lead to differences in performance. Consequently, the following analysis focuses on the aspects of performance relating to access that seem to be demonstrated fairly consistently. Furthermore, since the HMO "movement" was based primarily on knowledge and supposition about the performance of PGPs, most examples of HMO performance on access variables have been drawn from PGP experience.[7]

Impact on Enrollee Access

Financial Barriers.   Most studies of effects on financial barriers by PGPs compare the costs incurred by enrollees to those of persons covered by other types of health insurance and receiving care through the fee-for-service system. Such measures demonstrate that, although initial premiums are higher under the PGP, out-of-pocket expenses and thus total costs for all services are consistently lower than those for subscribers to commercial health-insurance programs or Blue Cross/Blue Shield plans. Moreover, since PGPs often cover a somewhat more nearly comprehensive range of medical services than that offered by health-insurance plans, particularly ambulatory-care services, the proportion of total enrollee expenditures for all medical-care services met by the PGP premium can be somewhat greater than under other plans (see Table 35).

There are signs that the assurance of accessibility to care for a fixed price, as measured by such data, plays a significant role in choice of PGP-type plans and enrollee satisfaction with those plans. When members of a United Automobile Workers union in Detroit were asked to name the reasons for their choice of a PGP in a dual-choice situation, 51 percent mentioned financial reasons, such as lower expenses and more coverage, first. The same considerations were ranked second by another 23 percent.[8] Roemer et al., comparing the PGP model with two other types of health-insurance plans in southern California in 1968, requested information on enrollee satisfaction with their plan's financial protection. Overwhelming satisfaction with the PGP as compared to commercial

Table 35 Comparison of Premiums, Out-of-Pocket Payments, and Total Costs of All Health Services Used by Enrollees in Several Prepaid Group Practice Plans to Those Incurred by Subscribers to Commercial and Provider-Sponsored Health-Insurance Plans, as Reported in Four Studies between 1961 and 1972[a]

Expenditures	Study A[b]		Study B[c]			Study C[d]			Study D[e]		
	K-P	B	K-P	MM	B	K-P	CWO	B	PGP	CI	B
Premium	109	99	122	110–120	110	284	227	285	271	208	257
Out-of-pocket	147	213	102	137	149	89	189	200	52	156	190
Total costs	256	312	224	247–257	259	373	416	485	323	364	447
Percent of total costs paid by premium	43	32	54	45–47	42	76	55	59	84	56	57

SOURCE. Adapted from Avedis Donabedian, "An Evaluation of Prepaid Group Practice," *Inquiry* **6**:3–27 (1969), Table 5, p. 14; and M. I. Roemer et al. *Health Insurance Effects: Services, Expenditures, and Attitudes under Three Types of Plan.* Bureau of Public Health Economics, Research Series No. 16 (Ann Arbor: School of Public Health, University of Michigan, 1972), text table, p. 46.

[a] Individual studies are identified in the following footnotes. Populations used in studies and costs incurred are not directly comparable across studies, and are used only to indicate possible range of differences in financial experience of PGP and non-PGP enrollees.

[b] B. Wolfman, "Medical Expenses and Choice of Plan: A Case Study," *Monthly Labor Review* **84**:116–119 (1961); data based on families in one union who chose either Kaiser–Permanente or Blue Cross–Blue Shield in a dual choice option.

[c] *Family Medical Care under Three Types of Health Insurance,* School of Public Health and Administrative Medicine, Columbia University (New York: Foundation for Employee Health, Medical Care, and Welfare, Inc., 1962); data from families of blue-collar workers enrolled in three plans in three geographic areas: Kaiser–Permanente in the West, a commercial major medical-insurance plan in the Midwest, and Blue Cross–Blue Shield in the East.

[d] D. Dozier, M. Krupp, S. Melinkoff, C. Schwarburg, and M. Watts, *Report of the Medical and Hospital Advisory Council of the Board of Administration of the California State Employees' Retirement System,* Sacramento (1964). Data are estimated expenditures on hospital and physicians' services and prescribed drugs for a "typical" family of four from the California State Employees' Association, enrolled in their choice of Kaiser–Permanente, a commercial cash-indemnity plan, and Blue Cross–Blue Shield.

[e] M. I. Roemer, R. W. Hetherington, C. E. Hopkins, A. E. Gerst, E. Parsons, and D. M. Long, *Health Insurance Effects: Services, Expenditures, and Attitudes under Three Types of Plan.* Bureau of Public Health Economics, Research Series No. 16 (Ann Arbor: School of Public Health, University of Michigan, 1972). Data are for families of all sizes, enrolled in two prepaid group practices, two commercial health-insurance plans, and Blue Cross–Blue Shield plans in southern California in 1968.

227

insurance and the "Blues" was found for all family sizes, all religious categories, all social classes, in families of high and low geographic mobility, and in
families with and without histories of chronic illness.[9] Greenlick reported in
1972 that respondents to a survey of enrollees in the Kaiser–Permanente
Health Plan in Portland, Oregon, indicated substantial overall satisfaction,
attributing it most often to the plan's financial advantages, as well as to the
actual care received.[10]

Mechanic and Tessler recently reported the preliminary results of a study of
three employee groups made soon after they had enrolled in a Milwaukee PGP
and in a Blue Cross/Blue Shield plan under a dual-choice option offered by
their employers. Respondents were first asked an open-ended question about
why they had chosen their particular plan. Following this question, various
reasons for making the choice were suggested. Respondents indicated the
importance of each to their family as well as their single most important reason
for making the choice. In response to the open-ended question, 14 percent of
those choosing the PGP mentioned that the plan was a "good deal for the
money." In addition, 45 percent of the PGP enrollees responded that knowing
in advance what their annual medical-care costs would be had been very
important in their choice of plan; 19 percent noted it was their most important
reason. Both proportions were significantly larger than those mentioning these
reasons for enrolling in Blue Cross/Blue Shield. Two of the employers paid the
entire PGP premium for employees choosing that plan, and employees in the
other group had to pay part of the monthly premium themselves upon selecting
the PGP. For respondents choosing the Blues, 15 percent mentioned that the
additional cost required for PGP coverage had influenced their choices. (Precise
dollar figures were not included in the report, but rough estimates of out-of-
pocket expenses for health care over and above health-insurance premiums
indicated that PGP subscribers reported far smaller out-of-pocket costs, statistically significant for all comparisons examined.)[11]

Such data support the conclusion that, once an enrollee meets the higher premium required by the PGP, annual expenditures for a similar or sometimes
broader range of medical-care benefits will be less than those incurred under
major commercial and provider insurance plans and that these considerations
play a major role in enrollees' choice of PGPs. The increasing frequency with
which employers pay all or a significant part of health-insurance premiums for
their employees should further ease the initial financial hurdle for these
subscribers.

A cautionary note must be interjected into this thus far positive assessment of
the PGP's ability to reduce financial barriers for its enrollees. Some plans use
deductible and copayment provisions, as do most other types of health
insurance. Under a deductible arrangement, the enrollee is responsible for the
first X dollars incurred in the delivery of covered services. Copayment provi-

sions are of three types. The enrollee pays (1) a fixed price per unit of service, (2) a fixed percentage of all insured costs, or (3) all costs over and above a fixed price per unit of service.[12] These costs are reflected in the enrollee's out-of-pocket expenditures for medical care.

In general, these cost-sharing mechanisms operate as financial disincentives, or barriers, against the enrollee's inappropriate demand for or use of medically unnecessary services. Without entering the controversial areas of what these "inappropriate" demands or uses are, it can still be suggested that any inhibitory influence very likely will selectively affect those who can least afford care and the consumption of those services over which the patient exercises the most control, that is, those provided upon initial entry to the system in a new illness episode.

In their recent article on utilization control mechanisms, Stuart and Stockton reviewed the results of several investigations on the impact of coinsurance that tend to support the latter allegation. Coinsurance appeared to have no effect on hospital use in one study. Another suggested that, although coinsurance deterred overutilization in nonserious illness or for medical conditions with minimal "psychological disturbance," use of intensive care was not altered by imposition of coinsurance.[13] Demand for and use of hospital and intensive-care services are controlled by the physician rather than the patient. Further support for this point is found in two studies reporting the effect of imposition of a 25 percent coinsurance provision in a comprehensive prepaid group-practice plan. The greatest change was a 24.1 percent decline in the use of physicians' services; little impact was seen on demand for ancillary services, which are obtained on physician referral.[14]

As Axelrod recently noted, however, there are few unequivocal data reflecting the precise impact of coinsurance or deductibles on access and use.[15] In another study reviewed by Stuart and Stockton, those with full coverage under a Blue Cross plan tended to be admitted to the hospital more frequently and to remain longer than those who were responsible for some part of these expensive services.[16]

There is at least one indication that the cost-sharing mechanisms used in two PGP models may be somewhat less financially severe than those used by indemnity health-insurance plans in the same region.[17] Nevertheless, the indications that access to care in these plans, as measured by use of services, can be adversely affected by the imposition of coinsurance points to a possible financial barrier. Its precise strength and effect cannot be measured presently, but intimations of its impact detract from the comparatively "open" financial access suggested earlier. This point is important, in view of utilization and cost-control measures imposed during recent years by government-sponsored health-insurance programs and the inclusion of cost-sharing provisions in the HMO legislation.

Availability of Services.   The PGP contract specifies the range and type of medical services to be provided by the PGP in return for the enrollee's prepaid capitation payment. Since the contract often covers a broader range of services than other health insurance plans—outpatient physicians' services in particular—the PGP enrollee apparently has more service benefits available than those covered by other forms of health insurance do. Comparisons of benefit packages provided by three types of plans in southern California showed that the PGPs provided somewhat more hospitalization coverage, in terms of benefit days, and covered far more ambulatory-care services than the commercial health insurers or provider-sponsored plans (the Blues) did.[18] Hospital benefits available to the Milwaukee PGP enrollees and Blues subscribers as reported in the Mechanic–Tessler study were comparable. Employer-sponsored benefit packages available through Blue Cross/Blue Shield were fairly liberal in outpatient benefits as well. The major difference in coverage of ambulatory care was that the Blues generally covered only emergency and accident care along with outpatient surgery and limited diagnostic services, whereas the PGP covered all ambulatory-care services, as well as physical and vision examinations and immunizations.[19]

In contrast to health-insurance plans, which offer financial protection against the costs of certain medical-care services that subscribers obtain from whomever they choose, the PGP establishes the location(s) where services are available and organizes the supply of those services through physician and allied health providers employed by the PGP. Such a feature is an important component in reducing access problems related to lack of an identified source of care or of entry into the system.

The contractual features of comprehensive service benefits, identified point of entry, and organized supply of physicians and ancillary services promise access to care. The services actually provided and the extent of their availability can be indicated by information on the following parameters:

- average number of hours per day and per week the PGP facility is open;
- provision of emergency after-hours services;
- range of covered services available at central facility versus range available on referral outside;
- ease of referral to outside consultants;
- average time elapsed between perception of medical care and encounter;
- average waiting time before appointment;
- average waiting time at appointment for encounter;
- length of encounter;
- average travel time to facility;
- percent of enrollees with no encounters per year;

- out-of-plan utilization;
- resignation from plan.

Such parameters have been identified as necessary for evaluating the availability and accessibility of PGP health-care services, as well as those of other delivery modes.[20] The extent to which operating plans regularly collect data on these variables for program analysis is unknown, and few investigators have included these measures in published studies of PGP performance to date. A recent exception to this statement is a comparative study of consumer satisfaction with prepaid group practice and an alternative Blue Cross/Blue Shield plan in Milwaukee reported by Mechanic and Tessler. To compare accessibility of services, the investigators collected information about respondents' convenience in getting to a doctor, reported time to get to a doctor, waiting time to obtain an appointment, perceived difficulty in obtaining an appointment, reported waiting time at the doctor's office, perceived waiting time, and reported amount of time the physician usually spent with the patient during the consultation.

Although not statistically significant, larger proportions of PGP patients reported waiting longer to obtain appointments, and perceived greater difficulty in obtaining appointments, then Blue Cross subscribers did. PGP enrollees waited about 10 days on the average, whereas the usual wait for Blue Cross subscribers was about 8 days. On the other hand, waiting time at the office appeared to be somewhat less for PGP subscribers, although the difference was not statistically significantly. Slightly more than 80 percent of PGP enrollees in the two employee groups reported waits of less than 30 minutes; close to 70 percent of the subscribers to Blue Cross in comparable employee groups reported waits of less than 30 minutes. PGP enrollees were also significantly less likely to perceive waiting time in the doctor's office as "somewhat" or "much too long." The time spent with the doctor was approximately the same under each plan; the majority in each spent 15 minutes or less with the physician during an appointment.

Significant differences were found between the plans in reported convenience of reaching the physician and in the actual time spent in getting to the doctor. The number of Blue Cross subscribers traveling 15 minutes or less to the physician was twice that of the PGP enrollees; most PGP enrollees spent between 15 and 30 minutes in reaching the facility. The investigators pointed out that this measure reflects the problems in physician access stemming from a single location of ambulatory care for PGP enrollees, a problem also documented by Weiss and Greenlick.[21]

Further information on this facet of access comes from investigations of enrollee satisfaction with PGP plans that have measured only enrollee perception on these "availability" indicators without including the companion temporal statistics, and a reverse or negative measure of satisfaction and availability—out-of-plan use of services. Most of these studies have found substantial enrollee satisfaction with the plans surveyed.[22] Specific areas of dissatisfaction frequently reflect, however, the enrollee's perception of actual availability of service. Weinerman noted this in his 1964 summary of prior studies on prepaid group practices:

In general, the various investigations of attitudes of group health members suggest much appreciation for the technical standards of group health care, but less satisfaction with the doctor-patient relationship itself. In one way or another patients report disappointment with the degree of personal interest shown by the doctor and with the availability of his services when requested.[23]

In 1971, Leyhe and Procter, comparing Medicaid Old Age Security (OAS) and Aid to Families with Dependent Children (AFDC) beneficiaries enrolled in a southern California PGP to a similar group of beneficiaries obtaining care through the fee-for-service market, found few differences between the two groups in their appraisals of services received. Four questions of the 51 asked did prompt significantly different responses from the two groups, all relating to perceptions of availability of service. On three counts, the PGP enrollees perceived *less* availability of services than those obtaining care from individual fee-for-service practitioners did. The differences were:

- the PGP/OAS enrollees responded more frequently that they felt they could *not* see the same doctor if they wanted to;
- a large number of PGP/OAS enrollees felt they could *not* talk to the doctor by telephone;
- more PGP/OAS enrollees did not ask for house-call service;
- the non-PGP/AFDC group felt there were more reasons that would keep them from seeing a doctor when they should.

The first three differences were interpreted by the researchers as indicating for the PGP/OAS enrollees, as compared to PGP/AFDC and all non-PGP enrollees, a feeling of lack of continuity or accessibility of PGP physician contacts for the aged. Many of the barriers cited by the non-PGP/AFDC population, such as lack of transportation, money, and baby-sitters, and refusal of service by physicians, were averted for the PGP population, who were provided with transportation and baby-sitters and whose welfare status was accepted by the plan.[24]

Respondents to a 1972 survey at the Kaiser–Permanente Health Plan in Portland, Oregon, exhibited satisfaction with the care received once they saw the physician, but more than 50 percent expressed dissatisfaction with the length of time required to get the appointment.[25]

Enrollee dissatisfaction with the availability of PGP services, and the sometimes greater convenience in obtaining them elsewhere (including emergency services), are two factors explaining the use of services outside the plan. Other factors are, of course, operating. Prominent among these is the existence of a previous physician–patient relationship. The earliest studies of PGPs revealed a significant amount of out-of-plan use, ranging from 15 to 40 percent of the total use of specified services.[26] More recent studies reviewed by Roemer and Shonick point to a somewhat lower out-of-plan use, about 10 to 12 percent for all services.[27] The authors speculate that this may relate to greater experience with the PGP model, and thus to greater willingness to "stay with it," or perhaps to improved efficiency in PGP operations.

Data reported by Mechanic and Tessler tend to support the argument that greater experience with the plan may lead to decreased out-of-plan use of services. Approximately one-third of the PGP enrollees in their study reported out-of-plan use of services, giving as a primary reason confidence in a prior family doctor. Convenience of access, in terms of shorter waiting time for appointments and shorter travel distance, was also important. This proportion, which mirrors the earlier study results rather than those compiled more recently, may relate to the fact that the enrollees had had only one or two years' experience in the PGP at the time of the study, depending on the employee group to which they belonged.[28] However, the lower use of out-of-plan services by more "experienced" patients may merely reflect the effects of early disenrollment of unsatisfied patients and initial choice of other plans by those who perceive problems in service availability related to the PGP-type plans.

The evidence on the accessibility of PGP services to enrollees suggests that enrollees encounter or perceive certain problems that limit access and may prompt use of outside services. Lengthy waits for appointments, difficulties in making appointments, and problems in reaching the physician appear to be the most common for the PGP enrollee groups surveyed. Whereas this generalization is supported in great part by enrollee perceptions, which as subjective measures may well overstate the unavailability of services or reflect unrealistic expectations, these perceptions are borne out by actual measures on these variables, at least in the Mechanic–Tessler study. Until other studies confirm enrollee perceptions by measuring access more precisely on the parameters indicated earlier, the current evidence suggests that the accessibility of services to PGP enrollees may not be all that proponents or contracts promise.

Lack of Fragmentation, Promotion of Continuity.   The ability of a PGP to provide complete and continuous health-care services, rather than respond only to acute-illness episodes, is thought to stem in part from its organization of the providers of care for enrollees. The broad range of services covered by the contract, the presence of different medical specialties, and a unit medical record are considered to be significant features underlying that organization, absent for the patient who must obtain care through fee-for-service systems.

Clearly, to the degree that they are available and taken advantage of, covered ambulatory services can enhance nonfragmented delivery of care. Although information from several PGPs and studies on others point out a broad range of providers available through the plan (usually physicians and allied health personnel practicing internal medicine, obstetrics and gynecology, pediatrics, and general surgery), the actual continuity of this type of practice, the ease of access to outside specialists, and the possibility of ancillary medical and social services on referral have not been measured. Moreover, whereas distinct theoretical and logistical advantages for continuity are offered by a single medical record on each enrollee, shared by cooperating physicians, its actual effects on PGP remain to be determined when the overall continuity of PGP performance is investigated.

Another factor given extreme importance is the apparent focus of the PGP on preventive or "health maintenance" services, hence the label "HMO." Broad coverage of ambulatory care, as well as hospitalization, was believed to encourage preventive services and early detection of illness, since patients could seek care early in an episode with few financial or supply restraints, and physicians could act to avert later and far more costly hospitalization. To confound the discrepancy between these beliefs and actual performance, one of the earliest documented facts about PGP performance was a strikingly lower rate of hospital use for PGP enrollees as compared to fee-for-service patients with third-party health insurance. More recent research continues to confirm the low hospital use under PGPs. The literature on this topic is extensive, and a recent summary of the overall experience has estimated "that prepaid group practices show an average of about 20 percent less hospitalization per capita adjusted for age and sex."[29]

Decreased hospitalization seems, however, to be related primarily to the decreased availability of hospital beds to admitting physicians. Many plans operating their own hospitals have far lower ratios of hospital beds per thousand persons than nonplan hospitals across the country have. Another contributory factor, at least in the early experience of the Hospital Insurance Plan of Greater New York, was the difficulty for HIP physicians in obtaining admitting privileges to local hospitals, since the plan did not operate its own inpatient facility.[30] Many thought that greater access to ambulatory and preventive health care would lead to greater use of these services than among other populations and that this factor would contribute to reduced hospitalization. No conclusive research has established that the PGP encourages greater ambulatory-care use. Perterson found that enrollees in the Columbia (Maryland) Medical Plan made more office visits than the national average, and Roemer et al. reported somewhat greater use of ambulatory and preventive health services for a PGP population in southern California when compared to similar populations covered by other types of health insurance.[31] Mechanic and Tessler reported, however, essentially similar use of ambulatory and preventive services for the PGP and non-PGP populations they compared.[32] Other well-established plans, among them Group Health Association, HIP, Kaiser California, and Ross–Loos, report annual physician visit rates ranging from four to six per person, virtually the same as national rates for annual physician visits in most age, sex, and income groups.[33] Furthermore, no causal relations between increased access to and/or use of ambulatory care and decreased hospitalization have been demonstrated; there is *no* proof of health maintenance on this score.

Cost Containment

Cost containment is not itself a direct indicator of accessibility. Efforts in that direction may well, however, create organizational barriers to restrict the use of services that the PGP is at financial risk to provide. Instances of such barriers have already appeared in the discussion, such as imposition of coinsurance and deductibles, length of time required to get an appointment, and difficulty in obtaining appointments. Another is seen in the example of a recently founded PGP, which originally planned to expand its in-house service capabilities upon reaching 20,000 enrollees by adding a plan-owned hospital, X-ray and laboratory services, and other specialists to the basic core in pediatrics, internal medicine, obstetrics and gynecology, and surgery. The decision not to do so, even though enrollment numbers 44,000, was attributed in part to the belief that outside referral arrangements for these services were adequate and that physician control over requests for such services prevented "excessive costs."[34]

Many of those opposed to the PGP model of organizing and financing the delivery of health-care services point to a possible incentive not to provide services stemming from the provider-payment mechanism. Since there is no financial "reward" for each service rendered, they fear the plan might provide as few services as possible, sharing the unexpended operating funds in year-end bonuses. Although this allegation is rarely supported by any hard evidence, it must be taken into consideration, since very little *is* known about how the PGP does contain costs (except for the obvious reduction in hospital costs). PGP cost containment has been attributed in theoretical analyses to organizational size and efficiency, and to increased physician productivity through the use of allied health personnel, but on reviewing the evidence recently, Yordy concluded: ". . . [it] reveals no savings for [PGPs] because of economies of scale, organizational efficiencies, or other factors providing higher productivity."[35] Attempts to regulate or police the possibility of underservicing may, moreover, very likely involve sizable administrative costs not related to delivery of services.

The promise of cost containment is not always borne out. A case in point is the experience of prepaid health plans (PHPs) providing services to Medi-Cal beneficiaries in California. PHP is a designation encompassing many provider-insurer categories, other than PGPs or FMCs, all of which provide or subcontract provision of a stipulated range of physician, hospital, and ancillary services in return for enrollee capitation payments paid directly by the state. PHP development was encouraged by the California Assembly in its 1971 Medi-Cal Reform Program (Chapter 577, Statutes of 1971, California State Assembly) on the assumptions that PHP services could be provided at 90 percent of the fee-for-service Medi-Cal rates and that PHPs would minimize direct government involvement in the health-care industry.[36]

PHP experience, though inadequately documented, has not yet substantiated the belief that PHPs can provide the same services at 90 percent of the fee-for-service cost. In fact, for two of the largest PHP contractors, Foundation Community Health Plan, covering Sacramento, Nevada, Yolo, Placer, and El Dorado counties, and Consolidated Medical Systems, in Los Angeles County, capitation rates charged the state were as high or higher than the *100 percent* fee-for-service rates in Sacramento and Los Angeles counties.[37]

Calling this experience the result of administrative and regulatory inadequacies in the Medi-Cal PHP program, various analysts have recommended more involvement in the regulation of these plans by the state Department of Health. Although this still does not involve the government in direct provision of health-care services, it clearly would *not* reduce their regulatory or administrative involvement in the industry.[38] The apparent need for such regulation also suggests that the incentive to contain costs may not be a "natural" feature of these plans.

A recent report by the State Auditor General on a sample of 15 plans revealed that an average of 52 percent of the state-funded capitation payments was spent on administrative costs or returned to the plan as profits. On the average, 48 percent was spent for health services delivered to Medi-Cal beneficiaries. The proportions spent on administrative costs ranged from 24 to 93 percent, whereas profits represented from 1 to 26 percent of capitation revenues. Owing to limitations on financial reporting and problems in making estimates, the report notes that these proportions very likely *underestimate* the administrative costs and profits for these plans.[39] In comparison, a recent estimate of HMO administrative expenses based on the experience of several existing plans placed them at 9.5 percent of the premium dollar.[40]

The Director of the California State Department of Health, which administers the PHP program, made the following comment on the distribution of costs:

Since the PHP contractors have been in operation for at most two years, and are now operating substantially below their maximum authorized enrollment, it is possible that start-up costs, including initial development and enrollment costs, have caused administrative costs to be higher than normal. Therefore, it is possible that as enrollment of Medi-Cal increases, administrative costs, as a percentage of total costs, will decrease.[41]

Although it does not specify a "normal" range for administrative costs, this comment does have some basis in fact. The 15 programs had enrolled about 60 percent of all PHP Medi-Cal enrollees statewide and had received about 72 percent of total state payments to PHPs for services to those enrollees. Their total enrollment of 122,000 (as of December 31, 1973) represented only 34.4 percent of their maximum enrollment capability. The Director overlooked, however, data reported by the Auditor General comparing the cost performance of established and newly operating plans. The four oldest and largest PHP contractors among the 15 had received about $48 million of the $56.5 million expended in capitation payments to the plans (87.5 percent) but together spent only 44 percent on delivery of health-care services. In contrast, the two newest plans had spent 66 percent of their combined $1.8 million capitation revenues for services to enrollees.[42]

Eight of the plans had established several subsidiary for-profit companies, linked through interlocking directorships, with whom they contracted for services to enrollees. Little financial information was available on the operations of these for-profit subcontractors, and although the report does not make the direct allegation, the suggestion that high administrative costs may be incurred in the provision of services through for-profit subsidiaries is apparent. It may be that the complexities of organization in such arrangements may produce high administrative costs, but the profit incentive could well result in administrative "control" of the use of services.

PROGRAM COST

Slightly more than $31.4 million was obligated for the federal HMO development effort between its inception in 1971 and early 1974. Original funding activity concentrated on planning and development grants to assist HMOs in their preoperational stages and on contracts to agencies for development and testing of Experimental Health Services Delivery Systems and HMO-type plans. Since 1972 the program has continued to disburse a large part of the funds toward new and ongoing planning and development grants, and technical-assistance and resource-development projects have received major emphasis. Over the four-year period, planning and development grants represented almost 55 percent of total obligations, followed by technical-assistance and resource-development projects at 32.0 percent. Contracts to generate HMOs and evaluation and analysis projects received 7.6 and 5.5 percent of the funding, respectively.

During these four years, there was no specific legislative authority for federal support of HMO activities, and therefore no funds were directly allocated to HMOS. To support the program, funds were diverted from other programs authorized under the Public Health Service Act with provision for experimentation in health-services delivery systems. Major sources for the HMOS effort were the Comprehensive Health Services program (41.5 percent), the Regional Medical Programs (29.3 percent), and the National Center for Health Services Research and Development (23.2 percent).

Passage of the 1973 HMO bill represented legislative approval of the federal HMO experiment and authorized direct funding for the HMOS program. An aggregate appropriation for feasibility surveys and for planning and initial development grants and contracts to HMO-type plans authorized $250 million for FY 1974 through FY 1977. Another $75 million was authorized for FY 1974 and FY 1975 to capitalize a revolving loan fund for initial operations.

A total of $40 million was authorized for research and program development in quality assurance over the period FY 1974 through FY 1978. This was in addition to the special $10 million authorized for the overall study of quality-of-care methodology to be carried out over the next two years.[43]

SECONDARY EFFECTS

It has been suggested that the funding of health-maintenance organizations has created interest primarily among those more concerned with cash than care. This is certainly not unique, however, to this particular piece of legislation (if, in fact, it has occurred).

OVERALL IMPACT ON ACCESS TO PRIMARY CARE

On the basis of the experience reviewed here, HMO-type delivery systems perform unevenly in guaranteeing access to comprehensive care for enrolled populations. Financial barriers appear to have been significantly reduced, yet not eliminated, and inclusion of cost-sharing provisions, as allowed under the recent HMO bill, threatens to reerect this barrier. Although there is often a broader range of services available to the enrollee than under third-party-reimbursement health-insurance plans, and the provider and location are identifiable, enrollees do not always find services easy to reach and to use. Performance on increasing continuity and reducing fragmentation is little researched and inconclusive. Contrary to popular opinion, no causal relation has been demonstrated among increased access to primary-care services, their use, and decreased rates of hospitalization for enrollees. Attempts to contain costs appear to have been made—*in some cases*—at the expense of use of services, suggesting that cost containment may not be a general attribute of the HMO's organization and delivery of services.

This performance record, based on the experience of those few PGPs that have been adequately researched and of the PHP Medi-Cal contractors in California as revealed in audits and legislative analyses, cannot be generalized to represent the performance of all HMO-type delivery systems now in operation. Nor should it be taken as predicting what access to care might be under a nationwide system of such delivery organizations. As noted at the outset, there is no single HMO formula: characteristics of enrolled populations vary widely. Despite common factors of voluntary enrollment, prepayment, comprehensive coverage, and contractual responsibility for delivering services, the organization of services and the administration of the plan do not fit a single pattern. These differences, indicative of the flexibility of the HMO model, or looseness of the HMO rubric, will certainly increase as development of new HMOs continues under impetus of recent legislation and funding.

To the pragmatist, demonstrated performance must be given more weight than generalizations based on expected performance. There are clear indications that the HMO model can and does make positive contributions to the partial solution of problems of health-services delivery. From the available evidence, there is no suggestion that problems of accessibility, cost containment, and lack of comprehensive services will be completely solved by widespread adoption of HMO-type delivery systems. Public and private efforts to foster development of HMOs must replace rhetoric with demonstrated performance, as revealed by a standardized mechanism of evaluation that will monitor parameters of access and cost.

SUMMARY

The legislation promoting health-maintenance organizations is the newest of the interventions examined. As such, it is too early to determine the effectiveness of this effort to improve access to care. The concepts underlying this approach are sound, and certain prepaid group-practice programs have achieved the dual goals of cost containment and improved access to services of acceptable quality. These programs represent, however, physiologic systems, and it is apparent that, to realize their objectives, all the elements of (1) pre-payment by (2) a defined population cared for by (3) a group of physicians who are (4) at financial risk must be present. It remains to be seen whether this program generates health-maintenance organizations that are functionally competent in achieving this goal or disease-oriented, unstable disorganizations.

SIXTEEN

Summary and Conclusions

There is no reason to believe that the programs described were planned to occur in the sequence observed as part of some grand strategy. All the evidence points to the contrary—that there is no overall health-care policy in the United States and that most of these programs represented separate, noncoordinated efforts. Viewed from a certain perspective, however, their sequence, as well as their impacts, might seem to be predictable.

THE PRINCIPAL DETERMINANTS OF ACCESS TO CARE

In a cost-effective system designed to provide complete access to care, at least three conditions must exist:

1. Physicians or other primary-care providers are available so that individuals can obtain services within time intervals considered to be reasonable and from a source that involves traveling a reasonable time/distance. In addition, providers at the point of first contact must have access to any secondary backup services required (laboratories, consultants, and hospitals).
2. There are no financial obstacles to care.
3. Patients and physicians must utilize these health services appropriately.

In fact, physicians are maldistributed both geographically and by specialty. Financial barriers do exist, and the behaviors of consumers and providers are not always appropriate.

The definitions of "reasonable" and "appropriate" involve value judgments on the part of both providers and consumers. The reasonableness of travel and waiting times are related to the nature of the problem—a heart attack versus a headache of two years' duration. They are also defined by social expectations of the consumer.

The appropriateness of providers' decisions about the use of laboratory tests, procedures, drugs, and hospital beds is a measure of the quality of their care. These behaviors are the concerns of the recently mandated Professional Standards Review Organizations. Physicians as a group believe, however, that only they are capable of evaluating the appropriateness of medical decision-making.

The behaviors of consumers are more difficult to label as appropriate/inappropriate. Some individuals delay in seeking care in the face of symptoms suggesting serious illness or fail to comply with medical recommendations for treatment. Such behaviors are inconsistent with the achievement of optimal outcomes of care. In a variety of health-care programs serving defined populations, from 10 to 15 percent of those eligible for services use 40 to 50 percent of all resources. Most of these high users do not have underlying biological problems susceptible to medical treatment. The definition and alteration of inappropriate overutilization of services presents a most difficult problem with economic, ethical, and social implications.

In the final analysis, the effects of unreasonable delays and inappropriate behaviors on health status must be weighed against the costs of resources necessary to decrease waiting or travel times and alter patients' and physicians' use of resources.

THE NATURE OF THE SYSTEM

There has been considerable criticism of the lack of a health-care system in the United States. In a true system, a change in one element or subsystem produces secondary effects on other subsystems. The impacts of the interventions for improving access to care suggest that a health-care system does, in fact, exist. It may not be rational or efficient or achieve the results desired by either providers or consumers, but there is a system. The sequence of events that occurred during the past decade is illustrative.

During the middle 1960s, federal legislation was enacted to increase the access of the aged and the poor to care. Titles 18 and 19 of the Social Security Act reduced the financial barriers to care for these segments of the population. The increased effective demand for care that followed the improvement in the purchasing power of these groups revealed the extent of the shortage of primary-care manpower. As part of the response to demand's exceeding supply, prices for services increased rapidly. There was also an unintended effect on the distribution of consumption of services. The aged poor and the aged black received fewer benefits from these programs than their more affluent or white counterparts.

In a system that lacked effective mechanisms for controlling utilization, prices, or behaviors, the total costs of services increased at an alarming rate as a result of this improvement in access. Policymakers were faced with a variety of alternatives. One means of dealing with these costs was to reerect financial barriers—and thus diminish access—by requiring copayments, coinsurance, or larger deductibles. A second alternative was to change the method of financing care in these programs from fee for service to one that permitted some prediction of costs during a specific time period by promoting health-maintenance organizations, or, as they were known before repackaging, prepaid health-care plans. A third approach involved altering the balance of supply and demand by increasing the number of physicians, particularly those providing primary-care services, or the number of individuals who would serve as physician substitutes, or both. Other options included encouraging the application of technology as a means of decreasing the need for professional manpower, and altering the health and illness behaviors of consumers.

An analysis of governmental activities following the enactment of Medicare and Medicaid reveals that almost all of these alternatives have been pursued. Amendments requiring copayment and deductibles have been enacted; attempts to increase the supply of physicians, particularly those in primary care, have been initiated. The development of health-maintenance organizations has been supported; Professional Standards Review Organizations have been legislated to make the costs of care and utilization of services under these programs more appropriate and predictable.

Programs to improve access to primary care can be viewed in terms of their impact on certain barriers. They may also be examined from the perspective of their effects on the health-care systems, the perturbations they produce, and why these occur. In reviewing each of these case studies, it is important to ask not only how much a certain barrier was reduced but also what other barriers were affected as a result.

OBJECTIVE: ELIMINATION—RESULT: TRANSLOCATION

The principal effect of most efforts to improve access to care in the past has been to translocate barriers from one area of the system to the other. When economic barriers become politically unacceptable, legislation is passed. When such legislation becomes financially unacceptable, financial barriers are partly reerected and others increased or created.

The administration of Medicaid in California (Medi-Cal) illustrates the translocation phenomenon. The Medi-Cal program began with a very liberal benefit structure. The costs of this program soon became unacceptable, and there was no effective means of controlling these costs. A move was made to control costs by developing an administrative structure with elaborate paperwork barriers. These reduced claims by increasing the amount of effort required for each benefit dollar paid out. Despite the relative success of this approach, costs continued to escalate.

One way of predicting and controlling costs was to provide services to as many Medi-Cal recipients as possible through prepaid health plans under contract to the state. The burden of providing and regulating services was thus transferred from the state to the contractees—prepaid health plans. Although some of these have operated in an accountable fashion, a recent report suggests that, in general, administrative overhead in these plans has far exceeded the costs of benefits provided. There is also evidence that some Medi-Cal recipients have been enrolled without knowing it and that others have had considerable problems with access to care once enrolled. Thus, a financial barrier first became an administrative barrier and subsequently was translocated into an intraorganizational barrier.

If most interventions seem to translocate barriers rather than to eliminate them, it is important to consider what kinds of barriers to access can be most effectively assessed or monitored. Translocation of a fiscal barrier into an organizational barrier creates a new and more complex problem. In the first instance there are means of assessing the changes in volume and distribution of services as a result of altering the level of the financial barrier. In the latter instance, there is no method now available for assessing organizational barriers, which may be subtle, elusive, and impossible to monitor. From a management standpoint, it is important to know why and where problems exist; politically, ignorance may mean reelection.

FINAL SUMMARY

The primary determinants of access to care are the behaviors of consumers and providers, the numbers and locations of primary-care providers and their access to necessary backup resources, and the presence of financial barriers to care. Interventions to date have attempted to deal with only one of these, or else have created artificial microsystems that have dealt with most or all of them at once.

Most of the programs focused on one barrier have either failed to demonstrate the desired impact or else have created secondary, and almost intolerable, side effects. The multibarrier approaches have demonstrated impact but have proved politically and economically unfeasible. As is evident, all of these have been somewhat tangential attempts to deal with primary determinants of access to care.

The natural history of these interventions, as well as their outcome, may be somewhat predictable by an examination of the political forces involved. Three vested-interest groups must be dealt with by anyone who would change the health-care system: consumers, providers, and the organizations producing providers. Consumers cannot tolerate the unavailability of care and also find the costs of care unacceptable. Providers have strongly resisted any attempts to alter the fee-for-service method of payment, as well as attempts to eliminate solo practice in favor of health-care organizations. Providers and the institutions producing providers are opposed to any undemocratic processes that would regulate the numbers of physicians in certain areas and specialties.

The interventions described in the case studies represent a series of attempts to deal with the primary concerns of consumers, within the political constraints created by providers and their organizations. The only intervention to date that has attempted to deal with the process of producing physicians in the United States has been the legislation creating departments of family practice in medical schools and residency programs for postgraduate training of primary-care specialists. These legislated additions to medical-school curricula provide a means to the end desired, but they will require considerable assistance and reinforcement through funding mechanisms if they are to achieve the results promised.

Given the political process prevailing in the United States, it is not surprising that there has been a trial-and-error approach to reformation of the health-care system through marginal rather than radical changes. The evidence to date suggests that the United States is staggering pluralistically and phlegmatically, as befits the democratic process, toward the creation of a system with almost equal access for all.

PART THREE

OPTIONS

RASHI FEIN

SEVENTEEN

Learning from the Past

In Part I of this book, David Mechanic presents our broad conception of the meaning of primary care and of access. He discusses the barriers that the public faces in achieving greater access to care and considers their significance.

In Part II, Dr. Lewis examines and assesses 11 health-care and financing programs whose objective, or hoped-for by-product, has been to increase access to the medical-care system and to primary care.

In this third and final part, I build on the conceptual model and program experience and ask how policy might be developed to move toward the goal of increased access to primary care. I consider the implications of expansion of the individual programs already examined, the need to develop a coherent and interrelated set of policies, and a possible strategy for the future.

The 11 specific interventions, their costs, secondary effects, and overall impact on access are summarized in Tables 36 and 37. In considering these summaries and in assessing the impact that each program had relative to its costs, we must remember that the various efforts were phased in at different points in time and often operated almost alone in what might be termed "a hostile world." Negative assessments of some of the programs may lead the reader to classify them as failures, and yet, their shortcomings, their "failures,"

Table 36 Programs Designed to Affect Barriers Related to Production of Services

	Practice Commitment/ Loan Forgiveness	Rural Preceptorships	Family Practice	Increased Numbers of Physicians	New Health Practitioners	National Health Service Corps
Intervention	Loans for tuition; forgiven for practice in areas of physician shortage	Exposure to rural practice (real world)	Boards in Family Practice Residency training Undergraduate departments of Family Practice	Increase size of classes Add more schools Shorten curricula	Increase supply and scope of services available	Match physicians to shortage areas
Costs	Most loans: $3000–6000 per borrower over 4–5 years Administrative expense: $300–400 per borrower over 4–5 years (est.)	Per full-time equivalent student: $12,000–15,000 annually	Residency: $25,000–35,000/position per year $20 × 10^6 in federal funds since 1971	Construction funds: $186,000 for each new place added Education costs (unknown)	FY 1969–1974: $39 × 10^6 federal funds Costs/unit of time similar to medical education	$12/visit
Secondary effects	—	Political pressures to change type of preceptor?	—	—	Increased attention to quality education costs, etc. Increasing conflict among professional organizations	—
Impact on access to primary care	*Marginal:* Most effective in reinforcing motivations of those with prior decisions to locate in these areas	*Marginal:* Most effective in reinforcing motivations of those with prior decisions to locate in these areas	Recent efforts *probably effective* (too early to tell degree of effect) Prior efforts not effective	*Minimal, if any:* No effects on trends toward specialization and location of practice	*Some:* Dependent upon location of practice Generally increased access and productivity	*None to minimal*

Table 37 Programs Designed to Affect Barriers to Consumption of Services

	Medicare	Medicaid	Neighborhood Health Centers	Children and Youth Projects	Health Maintenance Organizations
Intervention	Reduced financial barriers for aged	Reduced financial barriers for welfare recipients and medically needy	Reduce financial, geographic, organizational, psychosocial barriers Increase availability of services	Reduce financial, geographic, organizational, psychosocial barriers Increase availability of services	Predictable costs (prepaid) for organized services at fixed locations
Costs	FY 1967 = 3.4×10^9; FY 1973 (est.) = 9.5×10^9 Out-of-pocket expenses of those 65 and over: 1966 $238 1968 $165 1972 $276	Pre Title XIX costs for assistance = 1.2×10^9 FY 1973 (49 programs) = 8.9×10^9	$1.08–7.33 \times 10^6$ per center $72–$400/ Registrant (Data incomplete)	FY 1968: $200/child FY 1972: $135/child	FY 1971–FY 1974: 31.4×10^6 in federal funds for technical assistance and start-up funds; no support for operating expenses No good data on average start-up and operating costs
Secondary effects	Exposed limits of supply Inflated costs Benefits not equitably distributed among those covered	Exposed limits of supply Inflated costs Benefits not equitably distributed among those covered	—	—	Potential development of intraorganizational barriers
Impact on access to primary care	*Yes, positive* but decreasing with additional barriers of 1970s	*Yes, positive* but very wide variations in value of benefits and unequitable distribution	*Very effective* but costs are very high	*Very effective* on small proportion of target population Moderate costs	*?* Too early to determine

may be due to the environment and social conditions in which they were launched, prevailing attitudes, particular aspects of timing, and special characteristics. They may also be due to the fact that the programs were, in large measure, "free standing." They did not build one upon the other, and potentially desirable interaction effects were minimized. Thus, the assessments must be weighed carefully. They do not in and of themselves describe the possible outcomes of similar programs, implemented or regulated in a different fashion, undertaken and expanded at different times and in conjunction with other programs.

The discussion of the programs that follows and their assessments considers the degree to which the various individual programs can be expanded and the limits inherent in a piecemeal approach. Later we examine the benefits that could accrue if various efforts were linked together as part and parcel of a national health strategy.

ASSESSMENT OF INDIVIDUAL PROGRAMS

Supply Barriers

Practice-agreement/loan-forgiveness programs have been predicated on an assumption that economic inducements can affect behavior. We see little reason to question that assumption. Nevertheless, the assessment of practice-agreement/loan-forgiveness programs shows that, in largest measure, these have reinforced the decisions of students who have already chosen (or were very seriously considering choosing) to enter primary-care practice in underserved, rural areas. Apparently, at existing levels of tuition (and thus of potential loan forgiveness) and with existing opportunities in the general health-care market, the level of economic inducement offered in the past has been insufficient to redistribute many practitioners and, thus, to solve the major problems of access.

Higher levels of economic inducement would be possible, but they would likely prove very costly. The income elasticity of supply is low, and the economic inducement must, therefore, be considerable—at least at current physician-income levels and marginal tax rates. Furthermore, the rewards must be offered not only to physicians who would otherwise not have gone to the rural area but also to the physicians who would have done so with no (or lesser) inducements. If, for example, loan forgiveness had to be set at $40,000 per physician to be effective in "relocating" 800 physicians, and if an additional 200 physicians who would have moved to rural areas in any case also receive program benefits, the increment of 800 physicians would involve a program cost of $40 million. With a requirement for two years of practice, a program to bring an additional 1600 physicians to rural areas would cost $40 million annually. A national program that measured up to the needs of inner cities and other underserved areas would require more than this limited number of physicians and, thus, an even larger budget. If, for example, 10 percent of American physicians (30,000 in total) were to be "relocated," the costs would approach a billion dollars per annum. Since the evidence suggests that a high proportion of physicians relocate after fulfilling their practice agreements, these costs continue year after year. The limits of a loan-forgiveness program are apparent. These limits are set, in part, because the program does not deal with the basic causes of the maldistribution.

In addition, it is evident that, at higher levels of tuition (and of loan forgiveness), severe problems of equity arise such as those between members of different income groups who would like—and are qualified—to attend medical school. Low-income students may be averse to large indebtedness. Nor is this the only discriminatory selection feature: a disproportionate number of lower income students may opt for rural practice and loan forgiveness since the monetary rewards are more important to them than to students with higher income.

The evidence we have examined thus suggests that loan-forgiveness programs have limited effectiveness. At current levels they affect few decisions. At higher levels they are likely to be costly, to yield a relatively low return per dollar expended, and to have unfavorable side effects on equity, on the characteristics of medical students, and on the distribution of practicing physicians by income group.

Rural preceptorship programs have been predicated on an assumption that exposure to rural practice would have a significant positive impact on students' decisions, that is, that behavior would change as a result of additional information. There is little evidence, however, that these programs have had any significant impact on the decisions that medical students make as they consider various career goals and practice locations. Nor is it clear that the impact of additional information would necessarily be positive: although the probability may be low that a student will "go to the farm if all he's seen is Paree," it may be the case that if he has seen the farm, the probability of his practicing there is decreased. It may be that tastes will change. Recent census data do suggest that large cities and their suburbs are becoming less appealing. Such changes in attitude need to be monitored carefully since they will affect decision probabilities.

At present, however, rural preceptorship programs are not likely to be more than marginally beneficial. Careful selection of entrants tends to limit the number of students affected. It does increase the probability that reinforcement is provided to those who enter the program, but it does not yield a solution to a general problem. Casting a wide net is also likely to prove costly per decision affected. The approach may be useful in special circumstances (e.g., in certain states and for certain students). Nevertheless, the past record, the characteristics of medical education, and the structure of the health-care delivery system suggest that it is not lack of information that is the most severe inhibiting factor in the decision-making process. Unless the more basic phenomena that lead students away from rural (and inner-city) practice are addressed (such matters as the loneliness and difficulty of practice, the frustration that comes in trying to improve health in the face of poverty, and the conditions of living), rural preceptorship programs will prove insufficient.

The programs to increase the number of family practitioners in the United States are extremely difficult to assess at present. Student attitudes and medical-school curricula are in flux, and there is a significant dynamic quality to many of the family-practitioner programs. The enthusiasm that many persons exhibit at present for expansion of family practice does represent a force whose strength should not be minimized. Though, by itself, this enthusiasm will prove insufficient unto the task, it may—if joined with other efforts—provide grounds for optimism. It is, therefore, possible that the observation that efforts to increase the number of family practitioners were not especially effective in the past tells us relatively little about the future.

If the apparent increased interest in a family-practice specialty among medical students is not transient, if there are adequate inducements (or enforcements) for medical schools to support family-practice training programs at the undergraduate level, and if the prestige and other reward systems in medicine undergo change, the various forms of intervention may have considerable impact.

We should not, however, minimize the need to alter a number of variables almost simultaneously and the difficulty inherent in accomplishing this. Changes in medical education alone will not be sufficient. The "culture" of the medical school is only part of the culture of medicine. To a significant degree, the former reflects the latter even as it helps mold it. Thus, changes in both the organization and financing of medical care will also be necessary. Such changes will alter the "demand" for the products of the medical schools. It is only if there is a demand pull to accompany the supply push, that family-practitioner programs will prove successful and will flourish in a sustainable manner.

Although the costs of large-scale expansion of family-practice programs would be considerable, if successful, the long-term impacts of such investments would be great. Continuing rather than single-year or short-term benefits (as may be the case, for example, with temporarily altered location decisions) would substantially increase the cost-effectiveness of the efforts. For some time to come, individual programs will exhibit significant differences in organization, approach, and achievement of goals. Continuous assessment and monitoring of the various programs to increase family practice and their relative accomplishments will be required.

Attempts to increase the number of physicians in the United States have been successful. Medical-school student bodies have grown, and the number of graduating physicians has increased. Nevertheless, the programs have had little impact on trends toward specialization and subspecialization or on the selection of practice location in areas already well endowed with physicians. Our assessment demonstrates that growth in the number of physicians is itself not sufficient to provide increased access to primary-care services. Available evidence suggests that the present organization and financing of the health-care system makes it possible to absorb increased numbers of physicians of almost any type, in almost any area, before market forces and their economic impact might begin to have a substantial effect on distribution of physicians. Extremely large increases in the total number of physicians would be required before the primary-care and maldistribution problems would be "solved." Pursuit of this approach would, therefore, prove expensive—medical education is costly. Furthermore, such expansion would have unfavorable side effects, since a substantial increase in the number of physicians would lead to increased utilization (and risks) and inflated expenditures for medical care in those parts of the nation that would have an excess of physicians.

There are arguments for expansion of medical education, arguments that relate to educational opportunity and to the role of foreign medical graduates in the American health-care system. The case for such expansion cannot, however, rest on the needs of the primary-care sector, for expansion of M.D.s does not per se increase access to care for those who are underserved. A program to yield an increase sufficiently large to have an impact on maldistribution (is a doubling of supply sufficient?) would be irresponsible. It would be costly in resources for education and in dollars to underwrite overutilization. Unless the existing organization of medicine were changed, such a policy would not be cost-effective. If the organization were changed, such a policy would be unnecessary.

Efforts to increase the supply and the scope of activities of new health practitioners have had some favorable impact, though primarily in terms of demonstration effects. Existing programs have shown the feasibility of preparing individuals to provide a large proportion of primary care with less than 8 to 10 years of post-secondary-school education. To some degree they have also shown the employment possibilities that exist in organized settings such as hospitals and that might exist in a more rationally organized medical-care system. Yet the efforts have also pointed up the important constraints inherent in the existing organization and financing of medical care. Progress in achieving greater access by fully using new health practitioners is inhibited by the way medical care is financed, its payment mechanisms, the dependence of the new personnel on physicians, and, perhaps, by patient attitudes. These constraints influence which services are provided, as well as where, to whom, and by whom they are offered. It is clear that producing new personnel is a very different issue (and one that is easier of solution) than that of using such personnel in ways that would substantially increase access. Without attention to organization and finance, the kind of personnel that might be created would not be employed in ways that would appreciably affect access to care. The consequences of failure would be continued inefficiency as well as an underemployed and frustrated group of new health workers. If special conditions exist in particular locations, programs to train new kinds of personnel whose employment is ensured merit support. It is only prudent, however, to adjust any national program expansion to the willingness of the labor market to absorb new personnel, to a willingness expressed in "new hires" rather than in rhetoric about "useful division of labor."

The National Health Service Corps, a program to match physicians to shortage areas, has been small and seriously short of resources. Given its scope, it has had very little impact on national maldistribution. Its former effectiveness in recruitment seems to have been associated with the existence of the doctor draft. It is not clear, therefore, that the Corps can be significantly expanded in the future in the absence of other manpower policy changes. Any such efforts would face severe limits given the program's essentially voluntary nature and the existing alternative opportunities for medical-school graduates. In many respects the evaluation of the Corps' potential is similar to that of loan-forgiveness programs.

The program's usefulness to individual communities and physicians cannot be denied. It does provide information to physicians and communities and serves as "marriage broker." Nevertheless, the limited scope of the effort and the need for careful matching of needs and resources suggest that a voluntary National Health Service Corps will continue to represent a marginal effort providing some limited temporary relief to a limited number of areas rather than a solution to the nation's primary-care access problems.

Demand Barriers

Medicare and Medicaid were enacted in the context of and as a response to the accumulating evidence on the inadequacy of programs designed to assist certain parts of the population in obtaining health care. Both programs have succeeded in reducing financial barriers to care and in increasing access to care for those covered or eligible. Yet, with inflation, the effectiveness of both programs has been partly eroded, and financial barriers, once reduced, have been increasing. This has been especially true with Medicaid as both the federal and state governments have tightened eligibility criteria and narrowed benefit structures. Fiscal pressures are likely to reinforce these trends. It is necessary—and the passage of time will make it ever more necessary—to address the very same problems that Medicare and Medicaid were to have solved.

While reducing barriers, in the absence of organization changes in medical-care delivery, both programs have contributed to unfavorable secondary effects: to rising prices and rapidly escalating costs of care, affecting all consumers of care. An important lesson of Medicare and Medicaid is that it is difficult and expensive to operate on the demand side alone. This lesson and the secondary effects have provided the major stimuli for efforts to change the organization of, and to develop a planning structure for, health care. This task has, however, hardly begun. Thus, while there is significant need and room for improvement in Medicare and Medicaid, major expansion of financing programs without organizational change (and the required structure and political and economic leverage) is likely to exacerbate the unfavorable side effects. Nor would the removal of economic barriers to care, by itself, appreciably increase access for those who cannot find or reach the care. This is especially true of primary care. The particular resources necessary to increase and enhance primary-care delivery are in short supply, and specific policies to stimulate increases in supply are required. Important as it is to remove economic barriers, programs to do so should not simply underwrite existing inefficiencies or assume that the new dollars will solve maldistributions. The larger the programs, the greater the potential monetary and other benefits that would accrue from a rationalized delivery system.

Neighborhood Health Centers and Children and Youth programs, part of the "great society" movement, were designed to increase both the supply of and demand for services. There is little doubt that they were effective in increasing access to care for specific and limited target populations. This effectiveness was, however, accompanied by substantial costs associated with the provision of wide-ranging services (often extending beyond health care) and with the establishment of reformed miniature health-care systems in the context of a total system that remained substantially unchanged. Expansion of Neighborhood Health Centers and Children and Youth programs can be justified, since organized delivery systems are necessary if target populations are to have increased access to health care. This is particularly the case if we are to achieve progress in the short run, for, even if new financing mechanisms are deliberately constructed to stimulate change in the delivery system, the supply of services available to target populations can hardly be expected to change rapidly.

It should also be clear, however, that Neighborhood Health Centers and Children and Youth programs cannot in and of themselves be viewed as solutions to the access problem for all Americans. Their costs are high, and they carry the risk of the potential development of a dual system of medical care. Furthermore, large-scale expansion may face severe resource constraints, since the programs are voluntary and must, therefore, compete with the rest of American medicine for scarce resources. In the past, these centers and programs have been able to recruit a sufficient number of physicians. It is not clear, however, what the recruitment potential would be if these programs were to be multiplied substantially in size or number. Indeed, it is even possible that the pioneering character of, and the enthusiasm and dedication found in, a number of these efforts (and their consequent effectiveness) could be jeopardized if programs designed to solve particular problems for target populations were generalized and forced to attempt to solve the national problem of access to medical care. There is a difference between a belief that further support for and expansion of such delivery systems is justified and the view that they can be the source of a national solution to a problem that derives in part from the organization of the rest of the health-care system.

It is still far too early to comment on the potential impact of legislation promoting the development of health-maintenance organizations. The program is young, and as with many federal efforts, it is difficult to project the level of funding that will be made available in future years. Thus, the degree of commitment associated with program development and the degree of expansion of the program itself are unknown. Even more than this is involved as we look to the future of health-maintenance organizations. Although previously reported results from prepaid group-practice medical-care programs do provide encouragement, these past achievements involved organizations that dealt with the interdependency of capitation, prepayment, elimination of fee-for-service payment of physicians, and controls on the utilization of resources (particularly hospital facilities). It is not clear that the formation of health-maintenance organizations that possess less than all of these elements will prove as beneficial in the future as prepaid group medical care has proved in the past. "Health-maintenance organization" is a generic term that includes organizational forms other than prepaid group practices. Our experience with these alternative organizational entities is much too recent and far too limited to permit us to evaluate their full potential at this time.

In general, as true of Part II, this discussion and the material in Tables 36 and 37 show that programs for affecting supply of services and thus for increasing access (in particular to primary care) had very little large-scale or long-run success. In large measure, this was owing to the complexity of the health-care field and the failure (or unwillingness) to recognize and take account of this complexity in developing public policy. Whereas programs that operated on the demand side were more successful—in part perhaps because they were more significant interventions, with much larger budgets and much more control and authority—they, too, revealed the difficulty and expense of attempting to increase access by funding of services alone. Even though these programs involved many more dollars, given the size and scope of the health sector, they, too, were limited interventions. Nor were they generally pinpointed at the problem of access to primary care. Just as increasing the number of physicians did not increase the supply of resources available and ready to offer primary care, so, too, the dollars spent in programs that purchased services went largely for services outside the primary-care arena.

The nation, it appears, was not ready to restructure delivery systems, to intervene with authority on the supply side. Such action involved a high political price. Neither was it willing to pay the very considerable costs that might be required to achieve greater access under conditions where actions were limited to payment for services. Such a route involved a high monetary price. Thus, we have witnessed a retreat, a pulling back. Yet the goals remain, and a newly acquired understanding—that limited intervention into an industry whose annual funding exceeds $100 billion can bring only limited success and that simultaneous actions to remove the various barriers are required—cannot help but lead to a more coherent policy.

THE NEED FOR A COMPREHENSIVE POLICY

Throughout this book and in the previous discussion, we have stressed the interrelationships of the various parts of the health-care system, its economic arrangements and organizational, sociological, and psychological dimensions. These interrelationships create a situation in which the attainment of objectives can often be frustrated by interactions with programs and variables believed to be extraneous to the issue being considered or acted upon. Without an understanding of the general characteristics and interrelationships of the health-care system, particular actions may be advocated whose indirect consequences may negate many of their benefits. Conversely, that kind of understanding makes possible the adoption of policies and incentives that are mutually reinforcing and that significantly multiply the leverage that might otherwise be expected. The interaction effects are potentially very powerful. If policies are selected wisely—as a consequence of a broad understanding of, and with reference to, the various components of the health-care system—these interaction effects will add to the positive contribution of various programs rather than cancel them out.

We have pointed to the need for a broad, concerted, and simultaneous attack on a number of elements of the health-care system and its financing if access to care is to be maximized without wasting valuable personnel and dollar resources. Limited and modest intervention—sometimes termed "incrementalism"—along one axis at a time is neither responsible nor sufficient.

The call for an incremental approach to the solution of America's health-care problems most probably derives from general experiences with social programs in the mid- and latter 1960s and from particular experiences with large-scale health programs, for example, Medicare and Medicaid. There are those who argue that we should have learned that large programs lead to large frustrations, that we can be overwhelmed by administrative problems, that we must learn as we go along, and that we must, therefore, take small steps toward the ultimate objective. It is additionally suggested that the incremental approach is consonant with the American tradition. We believe that this represents a significant misreading of the experience of and the knowledge gained in the 1960s as well as of the American tradition.

It can be argued that the programs of the 1960s, instead of pointing to the need for incrementalism, represented elements of incrementalism at their weakest: large—but, nonetheless, inadequate—funding; unwillingness to follow through; shifting commitments; single, variable, or uncoordinated attacks on complex problems; and a short time span. Furthermore, in the health field the efforts often represented beginnings of individual ad hoc programs, many of which bore little relation to other programs and were eroded with the passage of time. The limited experience of the mid-1960s can hardly be used to assess the strengths of an incremental approach.

Nor is the call for incrementalism as in keeping with American tradition entirely accurate. The nation has mounted programs that, from their very beginning, were conceived of as massive in scope, funding, dedication, and commitment. Although such efforts have, perhaps, most often been undertaken in the defense or space sectors of the economy, they have also been pursued in domestic areas and have not been found wanting. The Social Security System is one example. This program has been amended and strengthened over time, but that does not imply that it began as a modest venture, in a hesitating fashion. The 200 years of American history, instead of providing evidence that large-scale change cannot be accomplished, suggests that it cannot occur if there is only a partial commitment to such change. The attainment of extensive goals is inconsistent with incremental funding of either the programs or of its administrative infrastructure.

Some who argue for incrementalism do so to avoid making the commitments necessary to solve problems and bring change. Perhaps they hope that by postponing action they may be spared the need to make that commitment, that the "system" will come to do its job, that the problems will solve themselves or be solved with a minimum of effort. This argument has little merit in the health sector. The problems are too massive and too interrelated to permit of solution by small interventions. Furthermore, the interrelationships involved necessarily mean that attempts at solution, even by large-scale intervention and funding but only along a single axis, are apt to prove very costly.

In contradistinction to a definition of incrementalism that calls for interventions of modest and limited scope is a definition that emphasizes the importance of phasing in programs designed to bring change. That type of incrementalism calls for the enactment of programs that can be effectively administered, monitored, and guided and, on the basis of which, we can then move to the next logical stage of development and legislation. Such a policy, that of taking things a "step at a time," may be advantageous. If that course is to be effective, however, a series of requirements must be met. It is necessary (1) that the step be in the correct direction and lead logically to further steps—that it not lock the system or program into a pattern itself difficult to change without major dislocation; (2) that public policy not be limited to attempts to alter only one of a large number of critical variables—that a "step at a time" not mean a "variable at a time"; (3) that the incremental effort not be underfunded relative to its requirement—that the step-by-step approach not be viewed as an inexpensive solution to a set of complex problems.

We must be aware, however, that small steps, however well designed and however well joined they may be with other actions, may create their own problems: progress is necessarily limited, and the failure to move in a rapid and highly visible fashion, particularly when the legislative process has led to rising expectations, may cause social frictions. It is difficult, at one and the same time, to articulate the massive and interrelated nature of the health-care problems the nation faces and then to advocate a limited approach toward their solution. Moving slowly and deliberately has its place—"walk before you run." For certain problems, however, it may not be the preferred approach—"one does not leap over a chasm in two steps."

EIGHTEEN

Policy Toward Primary Care

WILL THE MARKET WORK?

In considering questions of public policy on access, we must first be responsive to this potential question: "Why, if primary care is as important as those who advocate its development believe, will it not evolve through the pressure of market forces, aided and abetted by changing tastes on the part of consumers and/or of providers—why are policy changes needed?" To consider this question and the strategies necessary to deal with access to health care, we first examine some of the special characteristics of the health-care sector. The need for and the nature of the policy interventions required are derived from these characteristics.

An extended discussion of the economic structure of medical education and of the medical-care system, and a careful examination of government funding patterns and of insurance coverage and other third-party payments, are beyond the scope of this book. Nor are these the only matters that would bear discussion in a complete answer to the question asked. A number of elements appear, however, to be of special significance. In considering them we will move closer to a diagnosis of the factors that have created the inadequacies, to a better understanding of the problems that need solution and of the possible actions we could pursue.

The health-care-delivery and financing system is extremely complex: it deals with life-and-death matters and routine matters; it contains for-profit and not-for-profit institutions; it is funded through private and through public sources. This system exists, in largest part, to provide personal services to a population that numbers more than 200 million, a population with widely differing characteristics: age, sex, residential location, occupation, income, education, health status and habits, cultural traditions and attitudes. Services, by definition, are not mass-produced in central locations and shipped out to wholesale distributors and retail outlets. They cannot be stocked in inventory or sit on shelves waiting for purchasers. Their very nature requires that those who produce the services be accessible (a requirement that does not apply to those who manufacture products or who grow nonperishable agricultural products). Nor can purchasers easily sample or evaluate the different available offerings, balancing their tastes against costs. Medical services (as contrasted with other services such as haircuts or TV repair) have, at least in the past, precluded easy "shopping around" or assessment of the professional aspects of the service.

These considerations affect the strength and nature of the competitive forces present in the market for health care. If the economics of the health-care sector is different from that of other sectors—and it is—the differences relate to such things as economic arrangements, institutions, financing mechanisms, and licensing arrangements. These, in turn, reflect the special characteristics of health and of medical-care services and the economic consequences of these characteristics.

The first and perhaps the most important matter to consider is the strength of the competitive market forces in medicine and of consumer information and sovereignty, important preconditions for effective competition. A number of observers question the strength and impact of consumer sovereignty, even in other sectors of the American economy, given large budgets for advertising, techniques for molding public opinion, and the presence of oligopolies and monopolies. Whatever its strength in other areas, in medicine the impact of consumer sovereignty appears to be particularly weak. A number of studies have indicated that, to a significant extent, physicians control and determine demand for their services and that patterns of third-party coverage have insulated the consumer and his utilization decisions from the economic considerations that impel him in other economic activity.

If it were the patient who determined the demand for care, there would be much less room in the analysis for the phenomenon described as "overdoctoring." If "overdoctoring" could not occur, the forces of competition, pressing upon an increased supply of physicians, would reduce prices of medical services and relative incomes in specialty and geographic areas of relative oversupply. Thus, over time, and in response to economic pressures and signals, physician resources would redistribute themselves. If a competitive model were descriptive of reality, programs to expand the number of physicians in the aggregate and reliance on market forces to yield appropriate distribution patterns could be justified. Such programs have, however, proved ineffective, and that is not a reflection of their relative newness and their lack of sufficient time to lead to market adjustments. Rather, the problems are that "overdoctoring" can occur, consumer sovereignty is lacking, and competition is weak.

If, to these considerations about services and consumer information, we add the special sociologic and psychologic dimensions of medical care, the significant emotional concern about health matters, and the desire of many consumers to rely on expert opinion, we begin to understand some of the factors that permit the delivery system to function in an essentially unaltered manner, even in the presence of gnawing and vague consumer feelings that some (undefined) component of care is missing. Consumers (patients and potential patients) are not the key factors or decision-makers. Presumably, the health-care system exists to serve their needs and wants; yet, their needs and wants are, in large measure, defined for them. The fact that consumers may need primary care does not mean that they can adequately articulate that need or that, even if that were done, professionals would face economic considerations that would make it advantageous for them to meet the need.

Some might, however, argue that, even though consumers cannot specifically define what they want and, if a definition did exist, could not translate it into a market force, an increasing number of physicians will come to recognize the primary-care problem and, operating on the supply side, will attempt to build a strong primary-care sector and create the demand for this new product. We find this argument wanting. The economic incentives and pressures that might impel such behavior are lacking. Medical care is different from other industries in which a new technology or organization could be developed and consequent economic rewards could be reaped. The competitive structure and organization of the market does not suggest that there will be high rewards to those "who build a better mousetrap," the more so since we are dealing with a nonstandardized, personal service in a system heavily imbued with ethical constraints and not-for-profit orientation and subject to complex patterns of financing. The range of covered services under third-party payment, for example, has emphasized hospital care over ambulatory care. Coinsurance and deductibles have further tended to deemphasize preventive care and early treatment. Given these funding patterns and given the institutional emphases of American medicine, the economic and psychological rewards for the development and utilization of primary care have been relatively small both for providers and patients.

Even more than economic impediments are involved. Primary care is not simply one more subspecialty in medicine. It calls for breadth, not for narrowness, when the pressures have been (and appear to continue to be) to define fields of competence in increasingly circumscribed ways: an inch wide and a mile deep, rather than a mile wide and an inch deep (or even more optimal combinations). The development of specialization (and subspecialization) is not unique to medicine. It exists even in the presence of eloquent statements about the need for generalists. The forces that have brought prestige and power to the subspecialties in medicine are part of a general development and are strong indeed (and among those forces we should recognize the *benefits* of subspecialization). American medical education, in part influenced by federal-funding patterns and priorities, has provided a culture and an atmosphere that reinforced subspecialization trends and socialized the student in a manner that impeded the development of primary-care physicians. As a result, many observers have commented that the goals and objectives that a number of students articulate and hold when they enter medical school are altered during their education. Others would also comment that, even if these objectives were not altered, the existing organization and funding of medical care would make it difficult for these new entrants into practice to attain their objectives.

It is impossible to estimate the degree to which each of the impediments affects the development of a primary-care sector and, further, the degree to which each interacts with others to reinforce the existing situation. We deal, after all, with an admissions process, with an educational experience (including house-staff training), with prestige, with funding relationships, with organizational structures, and, on the consumer side, perhaps with biases in favor of technology and institutions. To change any factor is difficult; nor is changing any single one sufficient. Efforts must be made on a number of fronts; in particular, on matters involving organization, finance, and manpower distribution. None of these is likely to be changed significantly solely through private actions. Constructive change will require purposeful public intervention.

It is sometimes, of course, argued that the public sector is already heavily involved both in medical care and medical education, that it is already intervening. That is true. The public funds now available for the purchase of medical care and insurance and for the support of medical institutions and the legislation now being implemented in the health sector do not operate neutrally. The high degree of intervention that accompanies such funds and legislation does affect existing relationships. The critical issue is whether the intervention will be purposeful—designed to reach certain specific objectives, including the development of a primary-care sector—or whether, as has largely been true in the past, we shall intervene in a manner that appears to be neutral because it does not stimulate change but in reality is not neutral since it often reinforces existing relationships.

Macro and aggregative "solutions" that rely on the market are often preferred because they avoid the difficult and controversial micro and distributional issues, require little knowledge of the special characteristics of particular sectors or of the motivation and behavior patterns of critical actors, and involve fewer specific decisions, regulation, and administration. But such approaches are likely to fail in achieving increased access to primary care. This goal can be achieved only if specific policies are developed to deal with three interrelated elements: manpower, financing, and organization.

MEDICAL EDUCATION

Student Selection

We begin by commenting briefly on medical-school student-selection processes and on the gains that might be expected by the primary-care sector if medical schools were to adopt different criteria for the admission of all or part of their entering classes. The argument has been made that the bias in the medical school's admission policy in favor of a certain type of student—those most likely to become researchers or subspecialists—has made an important contribution toward the difficulties of the primary-care sector. It is suggested that there is little reason to believe that past funding patterns and present faculty preferences necessarily coincide with current or future social needs. The call is heard, therefore, for criteria that would place greater relative weight than is now the case on a set of different personality characteristics, backgrounds, goals, and objectives: selecting on the basis of factors that would increase the probability of entering primary care.

The problem in adopting new and altered criteria is that we know less than we should about the interrelationships and influences of various personality and background characteristics on future decisions and performance. Furthermore, since the organization and funding of medical care are likely to change radically within the lifetime of practice of those now being admitted to medical school, we cannot be entirely confident that the criteria we believe to be important today will produce the appropriate practitioners for tomorrow. Careful consideration of the potential benefits and costs deriving from altered admission criteria is required; although it is true that one may do "better" than is now the case, it is also possible to do "worse." Much depends on the probabilities of students selecting primary care but also on the abilities that students might have in alternative types of practice. Consider two extreme alternative hypothetical conditions. In one, 99 percent of students with given characteristic X select subspecialties and only 1 percent opt for primary care— all perform well in their chosen fields. In the other, admission criteria emphasize characteristic Y, since it is found that "only" 80 percent of students with that characteristic select subspecialties and a full 20 percent enter primary care (and perform well). Yet this maximization of the number entering primary care may carry a significant price. If the remaining 80 percent do well in the specialty fields they enter, one may indeed emphasize characteristic Y in developing admission criteria. If, however, they do badly, the health system may face costs that exceed the benefits accruing from the increase in primary-care practice.

This example is not presented because it is accurate but because it is relevant. It reminds us that there may be subtle costs (unrelated to primary care) as well as benefits associated with different admission criteria. As long as present organizational patterns permit physicians to choose location and specialty under conditions of minimum constraint, these potential costs cannot be ignored.

Not knowing the various present or potential costs does not mean that they do not or would not exist. We dare not assume that the present selection processes are costless or neutral vis à vis the primary-care sector or that they serve us well. The need to know more than we now do and to study admission processes and outcomes should not, therefore, imply that we do nothing until— if ever—we have concluded the experiments and completed the studies. Times and conditions change, and even when we know more, there will be more yet to know.

On the basis of insights gained from past experience and on the basis of judgments about the needs of the future and the roles that various kinds of students might play in meeting those needs, medical schools are already moving to change the mix of student bodies. We believe this is appropriate, both for the desirability of improving primary care and for a variety of other reasons (e.g., relating to race, sex, and socioeconomic characteristics). Admission processes should consciously consider various applicant characteristics that may influence the choices and decisions that graduating students make, that affect distributional considerations, and that may be related to quality-of-care considerations (in terms of both curing and caring functions). This is not, of course, a plea for "dumb" students. Nor does it imply that only less able students would elect primary care. Rather, it derives from the observation that medical-care services are extremely complex and involve not only medical science but understanding of, and empathy with, the patient—matters that are important and may not bear a one-to-one relationship to mental ability as measured by grades and Medical College Admission Test scores.

If, as we suggest, faculties concern themselves with the question, "Education for what?" they will, perforce, have to consider the kinds of physicians society needs and the different kinds of students they will, as a consequence, want to admit. Without such concerns, either student bodies will not change or new kinds of students, admitted by decision of admissions committees but without faculty backing, will find an inhospitable environment awaiting them.

Educational Experiences

Student input is, however, only a part of the picture. Admission is followed by formal instruction and education but also by socialization and acculturation. It is, therefore, necessary that we direct our attention to medical education and its impact on the future physician.

Medical education differs substantially from other higher education. The medical school has a service responsibility and activity generally not found in other parts of the university. Furthermore, a good deal of teaching/learning is done by observation and participation in the delivery of service rather than by a didactic or other classroom experience. Thus, the service the medical school is involved in helps determine the educational experience, and the faculty's service priorities often become the models for the medical student. In addition, the services the medical student provides while being trained or educated tend to color his or her approach to medicine and confidence in regard to the tasks that might be undertaken. Although analogies are never wholly convincing, it is helpful to speculate on the problems that might exist in law if law students and faculty believed it is only through apprenticeship that one "really" learns a field, if law schools had developed a service component but primarily in relation to the practice of corporation law, and if, consequently, law-school students were trained, in large part, by serving an apprenticeship in the law office of a large corporation. In such a world, students might feel somewhat at sea in other important areas of law. Perhaps, equally important, they might read into law-school behavior a message that corporate law is the most exciting, important, prestigious, and satisfying area of law.

Implicitly, this is what medical schools have been saying about hospital practice and subspecialization. Important historical factors (as well as biological reasons related to disease processes) help explain why the hospital has become the focal point of medical education (including the internship and residency period). Nevertheless, this focus has helped lead to the relative neglect of primary-care exposure and teaching, and it has exacted substantial costs.

Medical educators may feel the criticisms they face are unwarranted or unfair. They can argue that medicine is, after all, only similar to other sectors. Other departments in the university also emphasize research and "subspecialties." The difference lies, however, in other departments and schools not having a service component. No department of economics is responsible for the economic condition of the nation or of the community geographically proximate to the department. Thus, neither the community nor the student body have or should have any illusions about the department's role. In contrast, because so much care delivery is under the aegis of the medical school, it is often assumed that the care offered is consonant with the medical needs of the community. If hospital care assumes primacy in teaching, those who would deliver care out-side a hospital setting, those who would practice primary care, may wonder whether they are providing care of lesser importance. Furthermore, they may feel inadequate to do so. The components of primary care referred to in the opening part of this volume are such as to suggest that the contents and delivery of primary care are complex. If clinical experience is desirable for one's becoming an able practitioner, it is true for primary care as well as for other areas of medicine. Learning how to relate to paients, how to sense signals, how to respond, how to offer support, in addition to the purely technical medical knowledge required, are not simple matters of intuition. These, too, require practice and supervision if expertise is to be gained.

The medical school is not likely to redress the balance between primary care and hospital care if it teaches the importance of primary care by offering lec-tures about its value and its organization and continues to offer clinical experience almost exclusively in the hospital setting or if its "prestigious" faculty is the faculty that practices in the hospital.

Existing medical schools differ substantially in tradition, student and faculty mix, primary care and other clinical opportunities, and the characteristics of the populations served. These and other factors contribute to differences in the comparative advantages possessed by the individual schools. Thus, it can be anticipated that a variety of curricula and approaches will be appropriate if primary-care education is to be strengthened. Developing these new approaches will not be easy. It is difficult to teach and to organize teaching activities in the ambulatory setting. It is also difficult to fund such teaching. Nevertheless, medical schools that are serious about the need for relatively greater attention to primary care will find it insufficient to continue the patterns of the recent past while adding a minimal exposure to ambulatory care, sometimes in a grudging fashion almost as if it were offered under duress, and on occasion guided by persons not intellectually or professionally committed to primary care. Many leaders in U.S. medical education have delivered eloquent addresses on the need for primary care. These are not, however, a substitute for action, and the actions of the future will have to measure up to the eloquence of the addresses of the past if we are to avoid reaping a harvest of cynicism. Bright students and others can distinguish between the language that places primary care at the central core of medicine and the actions that often place responsi-bility for primary-care education on weak and "stepchild" departments.

We have discussed medical education because we believe it provides an arena in which actions that ultimately would help increase access to primary care are both necessary and possible. Nevertheless, even if admission policies of medical schools alter, and even if the four years of medical education change, primary care will still face severe problems that relate to the present organization of the health-care system. If the existing system fails to change, the barriers to access will remain, even in spite of changes in the educational sector. Producing an increased number of physicians acquainted with, interested in, and motivated to enter primary care is surely not sufficient if the system is organized and financed in ways that negate the value of primary care. The benefits of changes in education can, however, be significant if these changes are accompanied by change in the organization and financing of care, by change in the external variables that help determine what and where physicians practice. Furthermore, educational changes can be helpful in creating a larger number of physicians who would support system changes. Educational change need not, therefore, wait for system change. It can be undertaken even as critical components of the delivery system itself are reconstructed.

MANPOWER POLICY AND THE
SIMULATED LABOR MARKET

We turn to the components of the medical-care system that impinge directly on the difficulties in developing a strong primary-care network. These variables lie at the heart of the access problem, and change would yield more than marginal benefits.

Today's medical-care market abounds with restrictions of all kinds and yet, at the same time, with a high degree of freedom. On the one hand, for example, the number of available spaces in medical schools is an order of magnitude below the number of qualified applicants, and individuals have great difficulty in gaining admission. On the other hand, once they are admitted, their probability of graduation is very high, and there is a great deal of freedom in choice of specialization and of a place in which to practice.

Physicians are not, however, a homogeneous product. It makes a substantial difference whether they turn out to be surgeons or dermatologists, internists or pediatricians, opthalmologists or family practitioners; whether they choose to practice in rural areas, inner cities, or wealthy suburbs. These are the distributional considerations that ultimately determine access. What, then, is the basis for a "hands-off" policy on such important matters?

There appear to be two potential rationales for this behavior. The first is that those who make policy feel that they do not know how to determine the numbers of physicians needed in the various specialties and locations or how to control their allocation and distribution. The second is the belief that those determinations and allocations can and should be left to the free interplay of market forces that (presumably) will signal oversupply and undersupply by relative changes in income and that these, in turn, will influence future practitioners' decisions (albeit with a lag). We examine both these arguments.

As already indicated, the market has its shortcomings. These derive from a number of considerations, some of them fiscal but also more fundamentally from the fact that, to a significant extent, physicians can influence the demand for their services. As a result, physicians are not subject to the same market pressures found in other areas of economic activity. It is no trivial matter that observers of medicine in the United States believe that there can be "overdoctoring" and, further, that such a situation can be stable over time. One seldom hears a description of other sectors that involves the use of the term *over*, for example, "overretail marketing." If there were "too many" grocery stores, gas stations, or movie theaters, this situation would be temporary and would not represent a stable equilibrium. In other areas of economic activity, the term *too many* means "more than the market will support." As a consequence and over a period of time, market pressures would change the number and alter resource allocations. That is not, however, true in medicine.

"Overdoctoring" means more than that some areas have more physicians per capita than other areas do. Such differences in physician–population ratios may result from population differences in age distribution, in medical needs and tastes, and in incomes, from provider differences in productivity, and from appropriate regionalization of specialty services. The problem we refer to results from physicians' ability to increase the demand for their services even beyond the medically "necessary" or desirable and, thus, to insulate themselves from the market pressures that would change fees and relative incomes and that would provide income signals impacting on decisions about specialization or location. It is difficult to measure the physician's power to influence demand. Relatively little is known about what physicians do in their practices and about the efficacy of various medical procedures. Furthermore, there is little consensus on concepts and measurements of medical needs.

The problem is made even more complex by the fact that the resources required to meet these needs vary with the way medical care is organized, the linkages between parts of the system, and the kinds of personnel that stand ready or can be created to offer different levels of care. Medical services can be produced in many ways, with many different combinations of inputs. Nevertheless, though not quantified, "overdoctoring" does exist. Physicians are insulated from normal market pressures by their ability to influence demand. Furthermore, the combination of a restrictive entry to medical schools and of importation of physicians from abroad—helping, in part, through the use of a dual labor market to meet various pressing public needs—provides further insulation from market pressures.

Perhaps, however, the "hands-off" policy on distributional issues is advocated, not because the advocators believe in the market as allocator but because it is not clear what a proper "hands-on" policy would entail. Thus, the relative paucity of public policy in regard to maldistribution by specialty and by location may not derive from a feeling that problems will solve themselves but rather from a feeling that, though they won't, it is not known how to solve them (at least within American traditions). This would help explain the curious combination of well-articulated descriptions of the maldistribution problem and rather poorly developed articulation of policy measures designed to solve it. A relevant question is, therefore: "Are solutions really as difficult as may be imagined?"

The answer depends, in large measure, on the constraints that we set and that are set for us. One constraint, for example, relates to the facts that at present a large proportion of medical care in the United States is delivered in a hospital setting and that much of this care is delivered by house staff. If the locus of delivery of care does not change, large numbers of house staff are required. A limit is thereby set on how rapidly distributional problems can be solved.

The problem can be illustrated by putting it extremely. Given that the stock of physicians is large relative to the flow of new entrants into medicine, the characteristics of practicing physicians will change only over a long period of time unless the flow exhibits characteristics substantially different from those held by physicians already in practice. The problem is similar to that found in other areas of social endeavor, for example, in attempts to alter racial income and employment distributions that reflect the legacy of past discrimination. Suppose that to cope with the laws of arithmetic it were decided that all newly graduating physicians should enter primary-care-practice residencies (largely in ambulatory-care-delivery settings) in an effort to increase the stock of physicians in primary-care practice as quickly as possible. The impact of such a policy on hospitals would be considerable. It is apparent that one constraint that limits the speed of change is the need of hospitals for house staff who deliver services. Nevertheless, progress is possible even within the constraint if we act judiciously, deliberately, on the basis of planning, and over a period of time.

Over a period of time, the number of residencies available in various specialties will have to be reduced (even as the patterns of medical-care delivery are changed). Such actions will not come easily. It is not clear that hospitals and medical schools can or will organize themselves for voluntary action. At some earlier time, such voluntary action was possible, and institutions might have cooperated in allocating the fruits of growth and expansion. Today, however, an allocation of cutbacks is needed. Inevitably, it is much more difficult to reach voluntary agreement about the sharing of a smaller pie. The need and role for an external force are clear. Government is one such force. Since it funds much of medical education, its power (and responsibility) is apparent.

A system that plans for and allocates the number of residencies available in the various specialties will require a high degree of flexibility, that is, an ability to change course. Changes in social and demographic variables (e.g., in birth rates) will necessitate changes in the number of various specialties. Advances in medical knowledge will call for more of one kind of physician and less of some other. How the appropriate signals that call for change will be generated to government and how government will react to these signals remain important and unanswered questions. Thus, the call for the development of a planning mechanism and of a public policy is not based on a belief that everything will work smoothly and perfectly in some bright future. The valid comparison is not, however, between the mechanisms of the future and an imaginary ideal state but, rather, between these mechanisms and the system as it exists today—a system in which signals are also conspicuously absent and misallocations take place. The future will not be perfect, but it can be made better than the present.

The special characteristics of medical care and its organization and financing provide physicians with a considerable latitude in their selection of both an area of specialization and a geographic location. The profession considers measures that would diminish this latitude a restriction of freedom. Yet in other sectors of the economy these "freedoms" are in fact affected by market forces (including the market for labor) that lead to price and income changes. These changes, in turn, affect decisions and result in resource-allocation adjustments. Only in medicine is freedom defined as the absence of such market forces or equivalent substitutes.

Most Americans who enter an occupation or profession recognize in advance that the economic system does not guarantee a free choice of *both* a particular job and a particular location. A violinist may aspire to perform in Boston with the Boston Symphony Orchestra. He is aware, however, that if the Boston Symphony Orchestra has no openings, he may have to choose between living in Boston but entering a different profession or being a violinist but residing in, say, Indianapolis. The Boston Symphony does not guarantee employment to as many violinists as might like to join its ranks or even to as many qualified violinists as might wish to do so. Similarly, if one grew up in Nashville and wanted to live in Nashville but also wanted to be a marine geologist, one would recognize the need for choice: will it be marine geology but without Nashville, or Nashville but without marine geology?

These choices are imposed by the economic system, by the employment and labor market. The need to choose is not typically viewed as a restriction of freedom.

Essentially the same mechanism operates for those who are self-employed, who enter business. The market imposes its discipline, and as a consequence, a large number of business enterprises (including service establishments) annually close their doors because they "can't make a go of it" in that particular location. Society does not underwrite the existence of as many cheese and wine shops as are opened by individuals who desire to be cheese and wine shop operators. The market exerts its influence.

It is not our purpose to glorify the market, the impersonal and sometimes brutal market. We do not imply that individuals who are hurt by market forces should accept them or their results with equanimity. As this is written, unemployment rates are rising as are small-business bankruptcies, and those affected feel powerless in the face of (and seek protection from) events over which they have no individual control. The point is not that all is well with the market nor that individuals can do without protection from its impacts. Rather, the point is that the generation of price and income signals by market forces provides useful information. Without an effectively operating market and the signals and choices it produces, other allocation criteria become necessary. Allocative devices are required. Either medicine must face a discipline similar to the kind that the labor market imposes on most other Americans or it must face a discipline imposed by planning and regulation.

A variety of mechanisms might be developed to create or simulate the operation of a physician labor market and, thus, help generate labor-market signals for physicians. Many other nations have, of course, restructured their medical-care systems so that all, or a large proportion, of physicians (or of specialists) are employed. Such systems create a labor market for many physicians (e.g., for hospital physicians who are employed in a limited number of positions). The employment of hospital-based specialists in a restricted number of hospital posts (and the feedback on the decision-making processes of physicians) represents a major step toward the effective control of specialty distribution. It is not likely, however, that this type of employment market (which often involves a wall of separation between hospital and nonhospital physicians) would soon take hold in the United States.

Prepaid group practice also creates an employment and labor market. Prepaid groups do not simply add physicians who would like to join in delivering care. They employ physicians as their need and as their total income permits. Although prepaid group practice is not likely to become the dominant model for the delivery of American medical care in the near future, elements of the prepaid approach in which decisions on hiring are made in relation to need and total premium income may be incorporated in other settings. The critical element is not the group association but the prepayment mechanism. It is the latter that makes possible control of premium income and thus creates a total budget constraint, the ingredient necessary to force a recognition of the scarcity of resources, of the allocation problem, and of the need for choice.

Public policy can strengthen the development of this awareness by more actively supporting the development of health-maintenance organizations and of regional and local budgeting devices that include a "bottom-line" figure for the delivery of medical care. These budget constraints are similar to the kinds of constraints that impinge on decision-making in other sectors of the economy. They would help provide the discipline that the health sector lacks at the present time.

The critical need is for an *ex ante* determination of the total bill for physicians' services. Whereas capitation payments to or salaries for physicians help in structuring labor markets (they force *ex ante* budget decisions), other methods of paying physicians are also possible. The important consideration is whether budgets are defined and fixed in advance and whether their constraints are used to force social allocative decisions or whether expenditures are determined afterward and simply ratify the private decisions of physicians. It is much more difficult to control a health-care system in which the total expenditure is determined by adding up what was spent (as in the United States) instead of deciding what shall be spent (as in Great Britain). Indeed, control may be achieved with much less trauma (for practitioners as well as for society) via a system of budget allocations that permit individual and local decision-making within the budget constraint than via systems of regulation designed to compensate for absence of budget control.

FINANCING MEDICAL CARE, NATIONAL HEALTH INSURANCE

Linked closely to the *ex ante* budget process and its potential impact on maldistribution problems are the changes required in the financing of medical care. The allocation of resources reflects (determines and is determined by) the dollar flows in the health sector. If the former are to change, the latter must be altered. Thus, if increased access is to be achieved, removal of supply barriers will not prove sufficient. Financial barriers must also be eliminated. The need for a national health-insurance program to enhance financial access and to help stimulate system change has, therefore, become increasingly apparent. What remain at issue are the design characteristics of such a program.

These design characteristics are vital. They can speed change or retard it; they can stimulate progress or "freeze the system"; they can solve inequities or increase them. The details of the legislation are not neutral. They cannot be so since they affect dollar flows. National health insurance is, therefore, more than the provision of financial protection. It is important to develop that protection, to translate "need" into "effective demand," to increase access to care. It is also necessary that the goals one holds for American medicine enter into the debate on, and are reflected in the characteristics of, a universal health-insurance program.

The issues in the national health-insurance debate are many. Although all are important, our discussion must be selective. To explore all appropriate criteria is beyond our scope. Our focus is not, therefore, on the general access questions involved in an insurance program—often subsumed under the term *equity*—but on those specific matters that most directly affect system interrelationships and the primary-care sector.

We have already emphasized the system advantages that could accrue from *ex ante* budgeting mechanisms. These could be developed most effectively within a program of universal insurance that, while permitting and encouraging diversity in medical-care delivery, centralizes the sources and uses of funds. Indeed, without the central control of funds, it is difficult to conceive of effective *ex ante* budgeting devices without the substantial regulation that, in turn, would inhibit the development of diversity. Under national health insurance new budgeting devices would be required (and possible) not only to enhance effective control over total costs but also to provide incentives for the effective redistribution of resources.

More, however, is involved in the relationship of national health insurance to the development of primary care than budgeting mechanisms. National health-insurance legislation has many goals and objectives and cannot be viewed solely as a measure promoting primary care. Neither, however, should it (overtly or by freezing the present system) retard such a development. In the context of a concern about primary care, it is necessary to recognize the very substantial negative impact on primary care that arises if various primary- and preventive-care services are excluded from the package of covered services or if the program includes coinsurance and deductibles whose impact would be inequitable and would most directly be felt by the primary-care sector. The maintenance of economic barriers to access for services at the central core of medical care cannot help but affect dollar flows and the consequent allocation of resources. It is necessary to enact a national health-insurance program to increase financial access. It is also necessary that the program be designed in a manner that does not favor high-cost specialists and hospital care and discriminate against primary-care services. A policy that negates the importance of reallocation of resources to primary care will leave the system as it is. If, therefore, there is agreement that the primary-care sector needs strengthening, that agreement needs to be reflected in the manner in which national health-insurance legislation is written, in the "nitty-gritty" of the fiscal and financial arrangements.

ORGANIZATIONAL APPROACHES: A NEW PERSPECTIVE

The advancement of primary-care networks able to undertake the tasks outlined in the first part of this volume requires even more than the creation of fiscal devices that enable us to solve maldistribution problems and of insurance devices that remove financial barriers to access. It also requires that medicine adopt a community orientation and population perspective, that it extend its concern not only to those who seek care (who come through the door) but also to those who fail to enter the system. Such a perspective would be enhanced by developing approaches in which enrolled or specified populations are related to specific providers or groups of providers. This involves more than simply enrolling individuals or groups into a health-insurance mechanism that offers financial protection. The crux of the "enrollment" concept, as here used, means defining a relationship with a provider or with groups of providers and, thus, linking the population to elements of the system that are themselves linked together. Such a defined population serves as a foundation for *ex ante* budgets and the planning process necessary for their development. In the absence of a defined population, it is difficult to develop meaningful defined budgets.

Defined populations make possible monitoring and assessments and evaluation of the performance and efficacy of the health-care system and elements thereof. They also make it possible to examine the referral network of its operation. It has, for example, been suggested that there would be system improvement—on both the health and cost fronts—if specialized services were not available except by referral through primary-care physicians. It may, however, be too early to prescribe this as a general constraint. What may be desirable for one set of services, for example, surgery, may be undesirable for another, for example, ophthalmology. Furthermore, the history of the Medicare requirement that one service be utilized before another service becomes available (e.g., hospital services before nursing homes) suggests that such general requirements may have substantial costs even when they involve benefits. It is clear, however, that primary care can flourish effectively only so far as it is linked to other elements of the delivery system. Enrolled and defined populations will permit the development of protocols for referral and the monitoring of the implications of such protocols. They will also generate epidemiologic and other data that can be incorporated into planning.

A prerequisite for the implementation of an enrolled-population concept is the development of a new social perspective: that someone assume the responsibility for making certain that required medical-care resources are available and medical-care services accessible. This responsibility and accountability are lacking at the present time. Nor will the assumption of financial responsibility by a health-insurance program for the costs of using health services automatically put into place the resources required to increase the availability of medical care. The market will not be fully effective in solving supply problems. It is, therefore, necessary that consumers (patients and potential patients) know where to turn to complain about a lack of resources and know whom to hold accountable for failure to develop and allocate the resources required to make care accessible. In general, school boards make certain that there are enough classrooms and enough teachers to provide needed educational services. The schools do open every year. Parents do know who is responsible if inadequacies occur. In general, the market pressure for profits makes certain that there are enough gas stations and food stores to meet consumer demands. Without market pressures in medicine, is it not required that someone assume the kind of responsibility that school boards have assumed for their sector? Will an effective health-care system (of which the primary-care component is a subsystem) be developed until that is done, until someone is accountable?

ANALYTICAL CAPABILITIES AND ADMINISTRATIVE PROCESSES

The implementation of the various measures and concepts discussed may be preconditions for a full solution to the national access problems. They are by no means sufficient. Passing a law is only the beginning of a process. Laws can be implemented well or badly, with conviction or with passivity. The measures discussed are complex and difficult. There will be errors of commission and omission.

The minimization of error will require improvement in our knowledge and understanding of the complexity of the health-care system and in the processes that help determine public policy. Today we are deficient in both.

It is difficult to determine the influence that each of a large number of independent variables has on the dependent variables and to measure the interaction effects. Analysis is made more complex by our dealing with dynamic relationships that alter over time. To separate the fundamental from the trivial, the stable from the transient, is a task requiring high analytic skills, deep insights, and a strong appreciation of institutional constraints and their evolution and of the multiple influences affecting human behavior. No single individual or discipline is likely to make more than a modest contribution to the understanding of the dynamic health system.

It is quite likely, however, that our knowledge of the interrelationships among organizational, economic, sociologic, and psychologic factors will improve over time and enable us to anticipate better the benefits and costs of alternative actions. The knowledge we possess will be significantly broadened and deepened. In part, improvement will come as a result of an increased willingness to design, develop, and fund social experiments designed specifically as experiments and organized to be evaluated. So designed, we will be able to gather the very kinds of data that were, in large measure, unavailable to us in our own examinations.

Though our understanding will be enriched, there will always remain a large area reserved for judgment. We are, and always will be, dealing with relationships that involve human beings who themselves are part of the learning experience, who are subject to many varied and changing influences, whose needs and desires alter, and whose behavior is not fully predictable. Additionally, medical care, and especially primary care, involves multiple outputs that are, and will remain, difficult to measure and whose interrelationships are complex.

If the analysis and judgment needed to understand a dynamic and complex system are lacking, it is also true that the formulation of public policy is structured in a manner that places little premium on, indeed that inhibits, the development of multiple and mutually reinforcing programs and approaches. The structure of programmatic responsibilities is, and to some extent will remain, divided between the public and private sector, among the various levels of government, departments, agencies, and bureaus. Each has its own programs, responsibilities, specific goals, and objectives, though all may be interrelated in promoting better health care, greater equity, and access. This situation, useful as it may be in promoting diversity and multiplicity, has its costs. Bureaus, concerned that their achievements in attaining their objectives are to be assessed and that their programs are to be evaluated, may exhibit a lack of interest in considering the impact that they have on other programs "housed" in other bureaus. Competition has its price, especially in arenas where cooperation is required.

This problem is made even more severe by the fact that legislative initiatives and responsibilities in the health field are shared by a number of legislative committees. At the federal level, for example, taxation and finance committees have had responsibility for the Medicare and Medicaid programs. Conversely, health subcommittees have had responsibility for manpower, education, and facility-development programs. This division of labor on intertwined matters has made it difficult to develop a coherent policy. Given the different routes that health legislation may follow and the different loci of legislative jurisdictions and administrative responsibilities, the need for and usefulness of general conceptual models have not been readily apparent. Public policy is not formulated in relation to, or in terms of, a "grand design" or national policy, not only because we lack the requisite state of knowledge but also because such "grand designs" appear irrelevant to the legislative, budgeting, regulatory, and administrative processes.

These observations are not, however, grounds for despair. The conditions described are likely to improve. Significant changes in the organization of the legislative and budgeting process have recently been instituted at the federal level. Efforts at improving knowledge about and understanding of components of the health-care system on the part of legislators and their staffs have been organized. There is a greater interest in public-policy research in the universities and perhaps even a growing interest in attempting to seek answers to important questions rather than in exhibiting technical and methodologic expertise. Most importantly, the enactment of a national health-insurance program that calls for central budgeting and accountability would necessarily provide a major impetus to the pressure for rationalization of legislative and administrative processes. It would be damaging to fantasize about a perfect world, but it is reasonable to exhibit some (bridled) optimism about improvement.

NINETEEN

Some Options for the Short Run

There is a danger that our focus on broad issues (simulated labor markets, budgeting mechanisms, national health insurance, enrolled populations) may lead to an inference that *nothing* can be done to improve access and to develop primary care until and unless society implements measures designed to bring comprehensive change. Such an inference would be in error. Fundamental solutions to the national access problems do require the enactment of fundamental changes in financing and in system priorities, but this does not imply that the public and private sectors can do nothing to improve access even in the absence of major restructuring. Medical care is delivered at the micro level, and it is possible for those working at that level to effectuate change—within the limits set by the overall system and its financing—in their delivery program, in their medical school, in their community.

It is an error to retreat from the battle for major changes by pleading the need for small and limited steps at a time. It is equally an error to retreat from the battle for limited improvements by pleading the need for system change. Both postures result in less change than is necessary or possible. Furthermore, the (limited) changes that can be made within a system whose major characteristics remain unaltered do help prepare the way for a more successful implementation of major restructuring. Access problems will not automatically disappear at the hour that national health insurance is enacted or implemented and simulated labor markets are created. Changes at the organizational level will be required to speed and maximize the effectiveness of comprehensive programs. Many of the reforms that would bring improvement even today are ones that would ultimately be required in the context of system change. It is not helpful to live with illusions: the illusion that no improvement is possible except in the context of major restructuring or the illusion that national problems can be solved by the kinds of improvements we can stimulate without major restructuring. Both illusions are in error.

What, then, can be done to help increase access even in the absence of the more nearly comprehensive health programs that are needed? What roads are worth traveling even though they bring only limited improvement in a national problem? What strategy can be adopted that will better equip us for tomorrow and at the same time improve access today?

The assessments presented by Dr. Lewis in Part II of this volume help provide answers to these questions. They suggest possible courses of action and policy strategies. Within the constraints, some programs proved more, and others less, effective. The more successful ones can be built upon.

Some of the supply programs that attempt to deal with maldistribution, medical education, and organization of delivery systems do appear to be potentially fruitful areas for increased program development and funding efforts. We are not, however, especially optimistic about efforts to develop loan-forgiveness policies. The success of such programs would depend heavily on government manpower policies, which remain in flux, and on major restructuring of tuition levels in medical schools. It hardly seems desirable to embark on major changes in the economics of medical education simply to enhance the operation of loan forgiveness. Loan forgiveness would remain as a stopgap effort with inequitable side effects. Investment of resources in attempts to expand and enlarge loan-forgiveness programs substantially do not appear warranted.

Neither is an expansion of the rural preceptorship program likely to yield significant returns. Individual schools with special characteristics that provide grounds for optimism about the role that such programs might play for their students should be supported in their efforts to expand such efforts and to assess their effectiveness. There is little reason, however, to believe that a large-scale national program is justified. The effectiveness of these programs in the past is not likely to be significantly increased in the future. Scarce resources are likely to be more appropriately utilized in other areas of endeavor.

Although we have expressed our skepticism concerning the long-run effectiveness of attempted changes within medical education (including residency training) in the absence of fundamental changes in the financing and organization of health delivery, we do believe that support of efforts by schools desirous of increasing their emphasis on family practice and primary care is warranted. The efforts that some schools are making can be expanded and an even larger number of schools can be stimulated to increase their attention to primary care. Financial support should be available to assist schools in developing a richer intellectual atmosphere and a backup for their primary-care efforts and to relate these efforts in a more effective fashion to departments of community, social, or preventive medicine and the disciplines found therein. If primary care is to flourish within the medical school and its student body, the intellectual fabric of the effort must involve medical-school faculty. Outside resources may be helpful but only if inside resources are available, committed, and carry the ultimate responsibility. The development of the required faculty merits support.

Medical schools play a large role in delivery of service. There is much, therefore, that medical schools and teaching hospitals can do in the service context both within and outside their walls in developing linkages to primary-care physicians in practice. It has been argued that primary care cannot develop to its full capabilities in rural and inner-city areas if primary-care physicians are "lonely," that is, are not linked into other parts of the system and are left without an intellectual home base. The development of the linkages and of the intellectual ties is a task that can be carried forward by the medical-education sector. It must reach out to practicing physicians and offer itself to others who might enter primary-care practice. This is a task whose undertaking need not await the enactment of national health insurance and comprehensive organizational change. Medical schools can be assisted to begin, even now, to address these issues more effectively.

Support of collective efforts at rationalizing the number of residency opportunities in the various specialties is also justified. It is not likely that voluntary efforts in the private sector will be successful, but there is a significant amount of planning that can and must be done in preparing for effective allocation programs. It is easy enough to note maldistribution in the number of physicians in the various specialties. It is quite another thing to determine with some degree of confidence how many physicians should be trained in various fields and to conceptualize programs that would attain the desired levels while maintaining the quality of training programs and the existing strengths of the medical-care-delivery system. The need for support for the requisite analysis and planning efforts is clear.

There is also a need for support of organizational change and for the development of new organizational entities. Technical assistance and administrative and financial resources are required if health-maintenance organizations are to expand. These organizations deal with defined populations and face fixed budgets. We have much to learn from continuing evaluation of their strengths and weaknesses. Furthermore, and especially in the case of prepaid group practice, Neighborhood Health Centers, and Children and Youth programs, they appear to offer significant opportunities to develop and strengthen primary-care-delivery systems in contexts that permit us to analyze the tasks performed by various kinds of health workers, and the skills required for the various tasks, and that encourage us to assess health benefits. Even with the enactment of national health insurance and the removal or minimization of financial barriers, there will remain the need for delivery mechanisms that organize resources and services so that target populations have accessible services available to them. Today's strengthening of such resources for the delivery of care builds effectively for the future.

Efforts on the demand side are different. The problems of financial access are massive, and the financial resources needed to improve financial access are available only to government. There is much less room for private action. Surely government can, and should, reverse the erosion of the Medicare and Medicaid programs. It does not, however, seem desirable to expand financial protection by a series of additional fragmented and categorical programs. These approaches of the past have not served the health needs of the nation well. A universal national health-insurance program is called for. Temporary and partial palliatives will not ultimately add up to the comprehensive coverage required.

Thus there is a need for further development of planning and administrative capabilities; the building of the infrastructure that is and will be needed; and the establishment of the "front-end" resources to create additional settings for medical-care delivery and of the capital facilities such organizations require. There is also a need for additional basic and applied research in the organization and delivery of primary-care services and the development of more effective mechanisms to disseminate and make operational the results of such research. To facilitate such research, additional resources from a wide variety of disciplines will have to be attracted into the field, into the applied area of medical care.

Underlying all the efforts is the requirement that adequate data systems and assessment possibilities be developed as part and parcel of any special programs. The issues are too important, and resources (including human energy and zeal) too scarce, to indulge in the luxury of supporting programs whose basis for support is *and remains* intuitive. Some programs will be more effective than others, and it is necessary to learn which are which. It is especially important to ascertain the marginal return, the limits to program expansion. It is regrettable that in previous program efforts there has been little analysis of the resources required to maintain earlier levels of effectiveness as programs grow in size and scope and can no longer rely on volunteers and the enthusiasm of the early founders. Nor, conversely, do we know how much costs might be reduced when initial development and "learning experiences" have been completed and can be built upon. The cost effectiveness of programs may change markedly as programs are expanded and as marginal returns diverge from average. It is required that evaluation programs recognize this phenomenon so that resources are allocated to the various endeavors in a manner that maximizes total returns. Though the dollars spent on data systems and assessment do not themselves increase access, they do make possible more effective mobilization of other resources. Underfunding of evaluation efforts wastes rather than conserves resources.

Better and more nearly comprehensive knowledge and understanding, a more highly developed infrastructure and planning capability, the development of legislative and administrative mechanisms to apply knowledge, the strengthening and expansion of organized delivery mechanisms, changes in medical education—all these are helpful. They will contribute to the solution of the national problem of access. We must recognize, however, that in addressing access to primary care, we address an issue that lies at the heart of American medicine—its organization, education, and economics. If access to primary care is to be appreciably increased, it will not be sufficient to dabble at the margin. Primary care cannot be grafted onto the health-care system without affecting the structure and the power relationships of that system. More effective delivery of primary care cannot be attained while leaving all other parts of medicine as they are today.

Change is not likely to come easily or voluntarily, since, to a significant degree, the present allocation of resources reflects the preferences of those who today control or strongly influence the allocations. If primary care cannot be developed as an "add-on" to medicine as it exists, if access to primary care cannot be achieved within reasonable budget constraints without new forms of administration, regulation, and financing, then those who find the present system comfortable are not likely to view the growth of an effective primary-care sector as entirely benign. Effective primary care is more than just another specialty, more than just a group of dedicated physicians and other health professionals, more than just another body of knowledge. An effective primary-care sector, linked into the rest of medicine, cannot coexist with the rest of medicine without having its important impact on all that it is linked to and that is linked to it.

There will be those who resist change. It is not necessary to ascribe motives to this resistance: do those in positions of power and trust resist changes because they are self-serving or because they honestly believe there is more to be lost from change than is to be gained? The point is that vigorous resistance is likely to occur and that vigorous advocacy will be required as a counterforce.

Those who would bring change will have to articulate their goals clearly and will have to spell out the benefits that they feel will accompany the change. In the absence of these statements, they will fight a lonely battle, for they will be without their potentially strongest ally: the public. Perhaps change will come even if the battles are fought only within medicine, but change will come only very slowly and in a spotty fashion. Conversely, if the battles for a better health-care system that provides increased access for all the people are understood by the public and its representatives, change may be more readily accomplished. The task of implementing a primary-care network will be most demanding. To undertake that task without public understanding of the issues and without public support would be foolish indeed.

The education and the mobilization of the public thus also remain part of the agenda that must be dealt with. It is a rich agenda. There is much to be done if the goals that have been articulated are to be achieved. The stakes are high, and the costs of delay are large. It is time to proceed.

APPENDIX A

Tables

Table A1   Major Provisions of 11 State

State	Year Initiated	Sponsorship	Eligibility	Approved Service Area
Arkansas	1949	State legislature	State resident Admitted to University of Arkansas School of Medicine Agree to practice in a rural community in Arkansas	Community of 4000 or less
Georgia	1951	State legislature	State resident Admitted to accredited medical school Agree to practice in approved area in Georgia	Community of 10,000 or less in need of physician Facilities operated by Dept. of Public Health or Dept. of Correction
Iowa	1952	State legislature	N.A.	Practice in Iowa
Kentucky	1946	State legislature and state medical society	State resident Admitted to accredited medical school Agree to practice in approved area 1 yr for each loan received Agree not to practice in certain areas Agree not to practice in another state until completion of obligation in Kentucky	Rural county Critical county (10 rural counties of greatest need) Semicritical county (10 rural counties of next greatest need)
Minnesota	1952	State medical society	State resident Admitted to a medical school in Minnesota Agree to practice in an approved rural area after internship or family practice residency	Rural community in need of physician (each community separately evaluated)

SOURCE.   Based on information in H. R. Mason. Effectiveness of student aid programs tied to a service commitment. *Journal of Medical Education* **46**:575–583, 1971, Table 3, pp. 578–580; and CONSAD Research Corporation. *An Evaluation of the Effectiveness of Loan Forgiveness as an Incentive for Health Practitioners to Locate in Medically Underserved Areas* (Report on Contract HEW-OS-73-68), Pittsburgh, Pennsylvania, 1973, Table III-3, pp. 13–14. Where descriptions were incomplete or disagreed, confirmation was obtained on 1971 provisions from state programs.

Practice-Agreement/Loan-Forgiveness Programs as of 1971

Maximum Loan	Forgiveness Provision	Repayment Provision	Special Provisions
$5000/yr up to 4 yr	1 yr of practice in rural community cancels each annual loan Minimum of 2 yr of practice before forgiveness granted	Full amount of loan must be repaid with interest	Prior approval required for residency training before practice begins No more than 2 yr of residency training permitted
$2500/yr up to 4 yr	1 yr of practice in approved area cancels ⅕ of total loan plus interest Minimum of 3 yr of practice before forgiveness granted	Full amount of loan must be repaid with 4% interest First annual payment due 1 yr after internship completed	May pay back loan balance plus interest after 3 yr of service Prior approval required for residency training before practice begins
$775/yr up to 4 yr	5 yr of practice forgives ½ of loan 10% of loan forgiven for each additional year of practice	Full amount of loan must be repaid at 7% interest	
$2500/yr up to 4 yr for commitment to practice in rural county $3000/yr up to 4 yr for commitment to practice in critical county	Available *only* for practice in critical or semicritical counties 1 yr of practice in critical county forgives each annual loan 6 mo of practice in semicritical county forgives each annual loan	Full amount of loan plus interest All borrowers other than those practicing in critical or semicritical counties must repay loan	Prior approval required for residency training *before* practice begins Loan contracts renewed annually
$1000/yr up to 4 yr	1 yr of practice forgives ⅕ of loan	Full amount of loan plus interest Must be repaid in full immediately	

Table A1   (*Continued*)

State	Year Initiated	Sponsorship	Eligibility	Approved Service Area
Mississippi	1946	State legislature	State resident Admitted to accredited medical school Agree to 5-yr practice in rural Mississippi	Community of 5000 or under Public health work State mental institution State eleemosynary hospital
North Carolina	1945	State legislature	State resident Admitted to accredited medical school as fulltime student Agree to practice in North Carolina 1 yr for each full- or partial-year loan granted	Communities under 10,000 with critical need State or local public health departments State mental, tuberculosis, and rehabilitation facilities; community mental health clinics; facilities for mentally retarded
North Dakota	1955	State legislature	State resident Completed first and second years at University of North Dakota Accepted as 3rd or 4th-yr student in qualified school of medicine Agree to practice in approved North Dakota community	Town of 5000 or less designated as in need of physician
South Carolina	1952	State legislature	State resident Admitted to Medical University of South Carolina Agree to practice as private, general practitioner 1 yr for each loan in approved community	Rural community under 5000 State medical institution

Table A1   *(Continued)*

Maximum Loan	Forgiveness Provision	Repayment Provision	Special Provision
$1250/yr up to 4 yr	1 yr of practice forgives $1/5$ of loan plus interest Minimum of 2 yr of practice *required* Forgiveness provision in effect 1946–1960	Repayment allowed *only* after 2 yr of practice; repay balance of loan Recipient considered in breach of contract if does not practice at least 2 yr *and* repay loan practice out-of-state before in-state practice in state but not in approved area if enters unapproved residency	Prior approval of advanced training required; usually granted only for family or general practice residencies
$2000/yr up to 4 yr	1 yr of approved practice cancels each annual loan	Full amount of loan plus interest payable on demand if recipient does not enter approved practice	Physicians must begin practice within 3 yr after graduation Prior approval of residency training Loans approved annually
$2500/yr up to 2 yr	1 yr of practice forgives $1/5$ of loan plus interest	Full amount of loan plus interest payable over 6 yr following internship	$2000 annual loans are available without a prior practice agreement and are similarly forgiven
$1000/yr up to 4 yr (paid as tuition plus $75/ mo for academic year)	1 yr of practice cancels each annual loan	Full amount of loan plus interest if recipient does not enter approved practice	Must begin practice after internship

Table A1   (*Continued*)

State	Year Initiated	Sponsorship	Eligibility	Approved Service Area
Virginia	1942	State legislature	State resident or nonresident admitted to Medical College of Virginia or University of Virginia Medical School Agree to practice family medicine in area of need in Virginia 1 yr for each annual loan	Area of need defined by State Health Commissioner Virginia Public Health Service State Dept. of Mental Health institutions State Dept. of Welfare institutions
West Virginia	1960	State medical society	State resident Admitted to West Virginia University School of Medicine Agree to practice in West Virginia for 4 yr	State of West Virginia

Table A1   (*Continued*)

Maximum Loan	Forgiveness Provision	Repayment Provision	Special Provision
$1500/yr up to 4 yr	1 yr of practice cancels each loan	Full amount of loan plus interest payable on demand if recipient does not enter approved practice	Must begin practice within 3 yr after graduation
$1000/yr up to 4 yr	1 yr of service in West Virginia cancels each loan	Full amount of loan plus interest if recipient does not enter approved practice	At least 2 yr practice required before any forgiveness granted

Table A2   Experience of Pilot Family-Practice and General-Practice Programs, by Affiliation, 1964–1969[a]

Year	Approved Programs	Positions Offered	Positions Filled	Percent Filled	Positions Vacant	Percent Vacant	Positions to Be Offered Two Years Later
			Affiliated				
1964–1965	5	20	11	55.0	9	45.0	24
1965–1966	7	32	15	46.9	17	53.1	32
1966–1967	10	44	21	47.7	23	52.3	42
1967–1968	9	40	24	60.0	16	40.0	b
1968–1969[b]	—	—	—	—	—	—	—
			Unaffiliated				
1964–1965	9	52	26	50.0	26	50.0	44
1965–1966	10	49	29	59.2	20	40.8	41
1966–1967	7	41	15	36.6	26	63.4	28
1967–1968	7	35	12	34.3	23	65.7	b
1968–1969[b]	—	—	—	—	—	—	—

SOURCES.   American Medical Association, "Thirty-Seventh through Forty-Third Annual Reports on Graduate Medical Education," *Journal of the American Medical Association* **194**:765 (1965); **198**:875 (1966); **202**:764 (1967); **206**:2025 (1968).
[a] All program data are as of September 1 in the academic year noted; affiliation not available, 1960–1964.
[b] Programs were being discontinued by the end of 1967–1968, or converting to the new three-year family-practice residency programs.

Table A3 Experience of Two-Year General-Practice Residencies, 1950–1973[a]

Year	Pro-grams	Positions Offered	Positions Filled		Positions Vacant		Positions Filled by U.S. or Canadian Graduates		Positions Filled by Foreign Graduates		Positions to Be Offered Two Years Later
			Number	Percent	Number	Percent	Number	Percent	Number	Percent	
1950–1951	66	224	97	43.3	127	56.7					
1951–1952	93	371	142	38.3	229	61.7					
1952–1953	112	357	182	51.0	175	49.0					
1953–1954	131	499	289	57.9	210	42.1					
1954–1955	155	614	404	65.8	210	34.2					
1955–1956	168	638	444	69.6	194	30.4					
1956–1957	169	642	461	71.8	181	28.2					
1957–1958	195	747	468	62.7	279	37.3					
1958–1959	200	857	592	69.1	265	30.9					
1959–1960	187	717	528	73.6	189	26.4					
1960–1961	184	790	549	69.5	241	30.5					
1961–1962	184	870	481	55.3	389	44.7					
1962–1963	184	857	398	46.4	459	53.6	177	47.8	193	52.2	879
1963–1964	165	783	370	47.3	413	52.7	140	37.1	237	62.9	808
1964–1965	158	767	377	49.2	390	50.8	168	34.0	326	66.0	810
1965–1966	162	833	494	59.3	339	40.7	132	33.4	263	66.6	893
1966–1967	146	824	395	47.9	429	52.1	144	35.3	263	66.6	835
1967–1968	158	856	408	47.7	448	52.3	180	44.8	264	64.7	897
1968–1969	154	902	402	44.6	500	55.4			222	55.2	980
1969–1970[b]											
1970–1971	121	662	267	40.3	395	59.7	83	31.1	184	68.9	734
1971–1972	91	537	246	45.8	291	54.2	75	30.5	171	69.5	576
1972–1973	69	437	271	62.0	166	38.0	56	20.7	215	79.3	446

SOURCES. American Medical Association, "Twenty-Fifth through Forty-Sixth Annual Reports on Graduate Medical Education, Inclusive," *Journal of the American Medical Association* **147**:387 (1951); **150**:280 (1952); **153**:280 (1953); **153**:321 (1954); **159**:258 (1955); **162**:284 (1956); **165**:459 (1957); **168**:527 (1958); **171**:670 (1959); **174**:576 (1960); **177**:625 (1961); **182**:765 (1962); **186**:677 (1963); **190**:626 (1964); **194**:771 (1965); **198**:881 (1966); **202**:770 (1967); **206**:2031 (1968); **210**:1498 (1969); **218**:1235 (1971);**222**:997 (1972); **226**:927 (1973).

[a] Program data are as of September 1 in the academic year noted.
[b] The American Medical Association did not issue an annual report on graduate medical education for the academic year 1969–1970.

Table A4 Major Reports on the Physician Shortage, 1953–1970

1953	President's Commission on the Health Needs of the Nation	*Building America's Health* (Washington, D.C.: Government Printing Office, 1953).
1958	Department of Health, Education, and Welfare, Secretary's Consultants on Medical Research and Education (Bayne–Jones Committee)	*The Advancement of Medical Research and Education through the Department of Health, Education, and Welfare* (Washington, D.C.: Government Printing Office, 1958).
1959	Surgeon General's Consultant Group on Medical Education (Bane Committee)	*Physicians for a Growing America* (Washington, D.C.: Government Printing Office, 1959).
1960	Committee of Consultants on Medical Research (to the Subcommittee on the Departments of Labor and Health, Education, and Welfare of the Senate Appropriations Committee)	*Federal Support of Medical Research*, U.S. Senate, 86th Congress, 2nd session, May 1960.
1965	President's Commission on Heart Disease, Cancer, and Stroke	*A National Program to Conquer Heart Disease, Cancer, and Stroke* (Washington, D.C.: Government Printing Office, 1964–1965).
1967	National Commission on Community Health Services, Task Force on Health Manpower	*Action to Meet Community Needs*, Public Affairs Press, 1967.
1967	Bureau of Health Manpower, Department of Health, Education, and Welfare	*Health Manpower Perspective, 1967*, PHS Publication No. 1667 (Washington, D.C.: Government Printing Office, 1967).

1967	National Advisory Commission on Health Manpower	*Report of the National Advisory Commission on Health Manpower* (Washington, D.C.: Government Printing Office, 1967).
1969	American Medical Association-Association of American Medical Colleges joint committee	March and April: untitled (reports calling for increased enrollments in medical schools to enroll all qualified applicants) September: *Financial Support of Medical Schools by the Federal Government*.
1970	Carnegie Commission on Higher Education	*Higher Education and the Nation's Health* (New York: McGraw-Hill, 1970).
1970	Association of American Medical Colleges Committee on the Expansion of Medical Education (Howard Committee)	*A Bicentennial Anniversary Program for the Expansion of Medical Education*, Association of American Medical Colleges, September 24, 1970.

Based on B. Senior and B. A. Smith, "The Number of Physicians as a Constraint on Delivery of Health Care: How Many Physicians Are Enough?" *Journal of the American Medical Association* **222:**178–183 (1972), Table 1, p. 179; and Office of the Secretary, Department of Health, Education, and Welfare, *Report to the President and the Congress: The Health Professions Educational Assistance Program* (Washington, D.C.: Department of Health, Education, and Welfare, September 1970), Chapter 1, pp. 1–15.

Table A5   Number of U.S. Medical Schools by Developmental Status, 1960–1961 and 1972–1973

| Year | Total | Schools with Students | | No Students | |
| | | Accredited | | Developmental Status | |
		4-year M.D. Program	2-year Basic Science Program	In Operation	Developmental Only
1960–1961	86	81	4	1	5
1961–1962	87	83	3	1	5
1962–1963	87	83	3	1	5
1963–1964	88	84	3	1	11
1964–1965	88	84	3	1	12
1965–1966	88	84	3	1	15
1966–1967	89	84	3	2	14
1967–1968	94	85	3	6	11
1968–1969	99	85	6	8	8
1969–1970	101	87	6	8	13
1970–1971	103	89	6	8	12
1971–1972	108	94	6	8	6
1972–1973	112	98	6	8	—

SOURCE.   American Medical Association, "Annual Reports on Medical Education, Sixty-First through Seventy-Third Inclusive," *Journal of the American Medical Association* **178:**583–584 (1961); **182:**736–739 (1962); **186:**650–651 (1963); **190:**598–601 (1964); **194:**732 (1965); **198:**851 (1966); **202:**729, 736 (1967); **206:**1993–1999 (1968); **210:**1460–1467 (1969); **214:**1483–1487 (1970); **218:**1204–1209 (1971); **222:**966–971 (1972); **226:**898–902 (1973).

Table A6 Specialty Distribution of U.S. Physicians in 1963, 1967, and 1972, with Numerical and Percentage Changes for 1963–1967 and 1967–1972

Specialty	1963	1967	Change 1963–1967	Percent Change	1972	Change 1967–1972	Percent Change
Total[a]	275,140	308,630	33,490	12.8	356,534	47,904	15.5
General practice	73,489	68,920	−4,569	−6.2	55,348	−13,572	−19.7
Medical specialties	56,593	68,927	12,334	21.8	84,153	15,226	22.1
Allergy	835	962	127	15.2	1,638	676	70.3
Cardiovascular diseases	1,732	2,263	531	30.7	5,883	3,620	160.0
Dermatology	3,277	3,796	519	15.8	4,227	431	11.4
Gastroenterology	564	749	185	32.8	1,839	1,090	145.5
Internal medicine	34,742	42,325	7,583	21.8	47,994	5,669	13.4
Pediatrics	14,024	17,348	3,324	23.7	19,610	2,253	13.0
Pediatric allergy	73	91	18	24.7	383	292	320.9
Pediatric cardiology	110	175	65	59.1	514	339	193.7
Pulmonary disease	1,236	1,218	−18	−1.5	2,065	847	69.5
Surgical specialties	70,496	82,192	11,696	16.6	91,058	8,866	10.8
General Surgery	25,493	29,687	4,194	16.5	30,989	1,302	4.4
Neurological surgery	1,822	2,315	493	27.1	2,753	438	18.9
Obstetrics and gynecology	15,720	17,964	2,244	14.3	20,202	2,238	12.5
Ophthalmology	7,849	9,083	1,234	15.7	10,443	1,360	15.0

SOURCES. 1963 and 1967 data from C. N. Theodore and J. N. Haug, *Selected Characteristics of the Physician Population, 1963 and 1967* (Chicago: American Medical Association, 1968), Table B, p. 7. 1972 data from G. A. Roback, *Distribution of Physicians in the U.S., 1972. Volume 1: Regional, State, County* (Chicago: American Medical Association, 1973), Table 1, p. 21.
[a] Columns will not add to total since not classified, inactive, and address unknown are not included.

Table A6 *(Continued)*

Specialty	1963	1967	Change 1963–1967	Percent Change	1972	Change 1967–1972	Percent Change
Orthopedic surgery	6,820	8,426	1,606	23.5	10,356	1,930	22.9
Otolaryngology	5,185	5,583	398	7.7	5,662	79	1.4
Plastic surgery	993	1,303	310	31.2	1,786	483	37.1
Colon and rectal surgery	673	644	-29	-4.3	649	5	.8
Thoracic surgery	1,300	1,725	425	32.7	1,927	202	11.7
Urology	4,641	5,462	821	17.7	6,291	829	15.2
Other specialties	56,629	74,033	17,404	30.7	90,344	16,311	22.0
Aerospace medicine	764	792	28	3.7	921	129	16.3
Anesthesiology	7,639	9,630	1,991	26.1	11,853	2,233	23.1
Child psychiatry	532	1,080	548	103.0	2,268	1,188	110.0
Diagnostic roentgenology	21	49	28	133.3	2,076	2,027	4,136.7
Forensic pathology	45	47	2	4.4	194	147	312.8
Neurology	1,802	2,466	664	36.8	3,494	1,028	41.7
Occupational medicine	1,814	1,706	-108	-6.0	2,506	800	46.9
Psychiatry	16,049	19,749	3,700	23.1	22,570	2,821	14.3
Pathology	7,302	9,471	2,169	29.7	11,024	1,553	16.4
Physical medicine and rehabilitation	932	1,208	276	29.6	1,551	343	28.4
General preventive medicine	832	1,007	175	21.0	840	-167	-16.6
Public health	1,778	1,627	-151	-8.5	2,906	1,279	78.6
Radiology	8,697	10,727	2,030	23.3	11,910	1,183	11.0
Therapeutic radiology	33	101	68	206.1	931	830	821.8
Not recognized	2,347	4,101	1,754	74.7	7,010	2,909	70.9
Unspecified	22,365	23,170	-805	-3.4	8,290	-14,880	-64.2

Table A7   Top Ten Specialties Ranked in Descending Order by Size of Numerical Increase for 1963–1967 and 1967–1972

1963–1967	1967–1972
Internal medicine	Internal medicine
General surgery	Cardiovascular diseases
Psychiatry	Psychiatry
Pediatrics	Pediatrics
Obstetrics–gynecology	Obstetrics–gynecology
Pathology	Anesthesiology
Radiology	Diagnostic radiology
Anesthesiology	Orthopedic surgery
Orthopedic surgery	Pathology

SOURCE.   Based on Appendix Table 6.

Table A8   HPEI Obligations, by Type of School and Type of Grant, FY 1966–FY 1971[a]

Type of School	Institutional Grants	Special Project Grants	Total Grants	Percent Distribution
Medicine	$109,800[c]	$115,400	$225,200	60.3
Dentistry	48,000	40,200	88,200	23.6
Pharmacy	19,800	400	20,200	5.4
Optometry	7,600	6,900	14,500	3.9
Osteopathy	5,800	5,800	11,600	3.1
Podiatry	3,500	3,800	7,300	2.0
Veterinary medicine	5,100	1,500	6,600	1.8
Total:	$199,600	$174,000	$373,600	100.1[b]

[a] Funds obligated under Comprehensive Health Manpower Training Act extension of HPEI not available.
[b] Does not add to 100.0, owing to rounding.
[c] All dollars expressed in thousands.

Table A9   HPEA Construction Program Obligations, by Type
of School, FY 1964–FY 1969[a]

Type of School	Obligation (in thousands)	Percent Distribution
Medicine	$360,317	67.1
Dentistry	118,387	22.1
Public health	19,327	3.6
Pharmacy	9,854	1.8
Nursing[b]	8,831	1.6
Osteopathy	8,463	1.6
Veterinary medicine	6,661	1.2
Optometry	5,137	1.0
Podiatric medicine	0	–
Total:	$536,977	100.0

SOURCE.   Office of the Secretary, Department of Health, Education, and Welfare, *Report to the President and the Congress: Health Professions Educational Assistance Program* (Washington, D.C.: Department of Health, Education, and Welfare, September 1970), Appendix Tables 2 and 3, pp. 142 and 143.

[a] Information not available for FY 1970 and FY 1971.

[b] Includes funds obligated for nursing schools under the HPEA program in FY 1965 and FY 1966. Authority for nursing school construction grants was provided by the Nurse Training Act, beginning in FY 1967.

Table A10   HPEA Construction Grant Program: First-Year Places Added and Federal Share per Added Place, by Type of School, FY 1965–FY 1969[a]

Type of School	Federal Share of Cost	First-Year Places Added	Federal Share per Added Place
Medicine and osteopathy[b]	$368,780	1,983	$186,000
Dentistry	118,387	896	132,000
Public health	19,327	465	42,000
Pharmacy	9,854	387	25,000
Nursing	8,831	779	11,000
Veterinary medicine	6,661	124	54,000
Optometry	5,137	157	33,000
Podiatric medicine	0	0	0
Total:	$536,977	4,791	$112,000

SOURCE.   Office of the Secretary, Department of Health, Education, and Welfare, Report to the President and the Congress: Health Professions Educational Assistance Program (Washington, D.C.: Department of Health, Education, and Welfare, September 1970), Appendix Table 33, p. 186.

[a] These figures for federal share of cost, FY 1965–FY 1969, are the same as those noted in Table 10 for obligations by type of school, FY 1964–FY 1969. No explanation for the divergence in FY designation is given in the tables or footnotes.

[b] Separate figures for medicine and osteopathy are not available.

Table A11   Distribution of Medicare HI Enrollees by Race and Sex, FY 1971

Race and Sex	Persons Enrolled in HI (in thousands)	Percent	Median Age
Total HI enrollees	20,742	100.0	73.1
Men	8,628	41.6	72.5
Women	12,114	58.4	73.6
White	18,582	89.6	73.1
Men	7,751	37.4	72.6
Women	10,830	52.2	73.5
All other races	1,672	8.1	72.5
Men	745	3.6	72.0
Women	926	4.5	73.0
Races unknown	489	2.4	76.9
Men	131	0.6	71.3
Women	358	1.7	79.1

SOURCE.   Office of Research and Statistics. *Medicare: Health Insurance for the Aged, 1971, Section 2: Persons Enrolled in the Health Insurance Program*. DHEW Publication No. (SSA) 73-11704 (Washington, D.C.: Government Printing Office, August 1973), text table, p. xii.

Table A12   Short-Stay Hospital Utilization Rates for Persons Aged 65 and Over, 1965 and 1967 (NORC Survey Data)

	Percent with Stays	No. of Stays	Days of Care	Mean Number of Days per Person	
		(Rate per 1000 Persons)		With Stays	Per Stay
1965	16.7	222	3143	18.9	14.2
1967	18.6	247	3924	21.2	15.9

SOURCE.   Regina Lowenstein, "Early Effects of Medicare on Health Care of the Aged," *Social Security Bulletin* **34**:3–20 (April 1971); based on Table 1, p. 6. Adjusted rates per 1,000 from Julian Pettengill, "Trends in Hospital Use by the Aged," *Social Security Bulletin* **35**:3–15 (July 1972); from Table 2, p. 6.

Table A13   Short-Stay Hospital Utilization Rates for Persons Aged 65 and Over, by Race, 1965 and 1967 (NORC Survey Data)

	No. of Stays	Days of Care	Mean Number of
	(Rate per 1000 Persons)[a]		Days per Stay
1965			
White	227	3200	14.1
Nonwhite	143	2370	16.6
1967			
White	255	3960	15.6
Nonwhite	130	3510	26.9

SOURCE.   Regina Lowenstein, "Early Effects of Medicare on Health Care of the Aged," *Social Security Bulletin* **34**:3–20 (April 1971); based on Table 2, p. 7.

[a] To maintain consistency for all surveys presented, the NORC data reported as rate per 100 was adjusted for rate per 1000.

Table A14 Hospital Utilization Rates for Persons Aged 65 and Over, FY 1967–FY 1971 (AHA Survey and Medicare Control Records Data)

Measures of Utilization	1967		1968		1969		1970		1971	
	AHA	MCR	AHA	MCR	AHA	MCR	AHA	MCR	AHA	MCR
Admissions per 1000	275	266	285	297	300	307	308	306[a]	311	309[a]
Days of care per 1000	3475	3232	3779	3874	3972	4101	3937	3944	3872	3829
Average length of stay (days)	12.7	12.2	13.3	13.1	13.2	13.4	12.8	12.9	12.4	12.4

Annual Percentage Change

	1967–1968		1968–1969		1969–1970		1970–1971	
	AHA	MCR	AHA	MCR	AHA	MCR	AHA	MCR
Admissions per 1000	3.6	11.7	5.3	3.4	2.7	-0.3	1.0	1.0
Days of care per 1000	8.7	19.8	5.1	5.9	-0.9	-3.8	-1.7	-2.9
Average length of stay (days)	4.7	7.4	-0.8	2.3	-3.0	-3.7	-3.1	-3.9

SOURCE.   AHA refers to American Hospital Association, Hospital Indicators, sample of community hospitals. MCR refers to Medicare Control Records, census of all claims records for hospitals certified for participation in the HI program. Total hospital utilization for all aged is slightly understated in MCR data because not all are Medicare enrollees. See: Julian Pettengill, "Trends in Hospital Use by the Aged," *Social Security Bulletin* 35:3–15 (July 1972); based on Table C, p. 13; Table E, p. 14; Table 4, p. 7.
[a] Estimates.

Table A15 Percent of Aged 65 and Over with Ambulatory-Care Visits and Mean Number of Visits by Location of Care, 1965 and 1967

Place of Visit	Percent with Visits		Mean Number of Visits	
	1965	1967	1965	1967
Total	73.2	74.3	6.6	6.1
Private physician (total)	68.5	71.9	5.9	5.7
Home	14.2	11.2	0.8	0.5
Office	64.6	69.1	5.1	5.1
Clinic, emergency room, health center	14.2	8.6	0.8	0.3
Private laboratory	0.0	2.2	0.0	0.1

SOURCE.   Regina Lowenstein, "Early Effects of Medicare on Health Care of the Aged," *Social Security Bulletin* **34**:3–20 (April 1971); text table, p. 13.

Table A16 Estimated Utilization of Ambulatory-Care Services Under SMI, by Place and Type of Service, FY 1967–FY 1970 (Current Medicare Survey, Medical Insurance Sample)

Type of Services	Persons Served per 1000 Enrolled			
	1967	1968	1969	1970
Total[a]	791	790	786	791
Physician's services (nonsurgical medical care)				
Office	701	688	675	667
Home	143	137	120	95
Outpatient	172	162	172	190
	Average Visits per Person			
Total	[b]	15.8	17.0	16.8
Physician's services (nonsurgical medical care)				
Office	6.3	6.2	6.5	6.5
Home	3.8	4.4	4.3	4.8
Outpatient	2.9	3.1	3.0	3.3

SOURCE. "Current Medicare Survey Report: Use of Medical Care Under Supplementary Medical Insurance, 1967–1970 (CMS-19)," *Health Insurance Statistics* (February 22, 1972), pp. 2–3.

[a] Other services not listed here: nursing home, hospital nonsurgical, surgical services, service of other medical persons, ambulance services, other medical services and supplies.

[b] Comparable data not available.

Table A17   Physician Visits for Elderly Persons, by Region, 1968–1969

	Percent of Elderly Persons Seeing Physician during year	Physician Visits per Elderly Person per Year	Physician Visits per Elderly Person Seeing Physician
All areas	71.3	6.1	8.6
Northeast	72.8	6.5	9.0
North Central	68.8	5.6	8.1
South	71.5	6.0	8.4
West	72.8	6.7	9.3

SOURCE.   Data from Health Interview Survey, in Karen Davis, *Financing Medical Care: Implications for Access to Primary Care.* Paper presented at the Sun Valley Forum on National Health, Sun Valley, Idaho (June 28, 1973), text table, p. 24.

Table A18 Amount and Percent of Expenditures for Personal Health Care of Those Aged 65 and Over, by Source of Payment, FY 1966–FY 1972

Fiscal Year	Total	Out-of-Pocket Payments	Third-Party Payments			
			Total	Private Health Insurance	Government	Philanthropy and Industry
Total Amount (in millions)						
1966	$ 8,242	$4,382	$ 3,860	$1,309	$ 2,460	$91
1967	9,990	3,681	6,309	589	5,644	76
1968	12,102	3,191	8,911	658	8,179	74
1969	13,838	3,533	10,304	769	9,457	78
1970	15,710	4,621	11,089	893	10,115	81
1971	17,699	5,234	12,465	1,009	11,366	90
1972	19,753	5,553	14,200	1,140	12,966	94
Amount per Capita						
1966	$440.68	$234.29	$206.38	$69.98	$131.53	$4.87
1967	528.35	194.68	333.67	31.15	298.50	4.02
1968	626.66	165.23	461.42	34.07	423.52	3.83
1969	710.22	181.33	528.89	39.47	485.42	4.00
1970	799.25	235.09	564.15	45.43	514.60	4.12
1971	891.14	263.53	627.61	50.80	572.80	4.53
1972	981.42	275.90	705.52	56.64	644.21	4.67
Percentage Distribution						
1966	100.0	53.2	46.8	15.9	29.8	1.1
1967	100.0	36.8	63.2	5.9	56.5	0.8
1968	100.0	26.4	73.6	5.4	67.6	0.6
1969	100.0	25.5	74.5	5.6	68.3	0.6
1970	100.0	29.4	70.6	5.7	64.4	0.5
1971	100.0	29.6	70.4	5.7	64.2	0.5
1972	100.0	28.1	71.9	5.8	65.6	0.5

SOURCE. Based on Table 7 in Barbara S. Cooper and Nancy L. Worthington, "Age Differences in Medical Care Spending, Fiscal Year 1972," *Social Security Bulletin* **36**:1–15 (May 1973), p. 14.

Table A19   Changes in Cost-Sharing Requirements for HI and SMI, 1966 to 1974

	Hospital Insurance				Supplementary Medical Insurance		
	Inpatient Hospital Deductible			Extended-Care Facility Coinsurance After 20 Days	Annual Deductible	Coinsurance	Monthly Premium
Beginning	First 60 Days	After 60 Days	After 90 Days				
July 1966	$40	$10	$ [a]	$ [a]	$50	20%	$ 3.00
January 1967	—	—	20	5.00	—	—	—
January 1968	—	—	—	—	—	—	—
April 1968	—	—	—	—	—	—	4.00
January 1969	44	11	22	5.50	—	—	—
January 1970	52	13	26	6.50	—	—	—
July 1970	—	—	—	—	—	—	5.30
January 1971	60	15	30	7.50	—	—	—
July 1971	—	—	—	—	—	—	5.60
January 1972	68	17	34	8.50	—	—	—
July 1972	—	—	—	—	—	—	5.80
January 1973	72	18	36	9.00	60	—	—
January 1974	84	21	42	10.50	—	—	6.30

Percentage Increases

Beginning	First 60 Days	After 60 Days	After 90 Days	Extended-Care Facility Coinsurance After 20 Days	Annual Deductible	Coinsurance	Monthly Premium
July 1966	—	—	—	—	—	—	—
January 1967	—	—	—	—	—	—	—
January 1968	—	—	—	—	—	—	—
April 1968	—	—	—	—	—	—	33.3
January 1969	10.0	10.0	10.0	10.0	—	—	—
January 1970	18.2	18.2	18.2	18.2	—	—	—
July 1970	—	—	—	—	—	—	32.5
January 1971	15.4	15.4	15.4	15.4	—	—	—
July 1971	—	—	—	—	—	—	5.7
January 1972	13.3	13.3	13.3	13.3	—	—	—
July 1972	—	—	—	—	—	—	3.6
January 1973	5.9	5.9	5.9	5.9	20.0	—	—
January 1974	16.7	16.7	16.7	16.7	—	—	8.6

SOURCE.   Howard West, "Five Years of Medicare—a Statistical Review," *Social Security Bulletin* **34**:17–27 (December 1971), Table 1, p. 18. *Your Medicare Handbook.* DHEW Publication No. (SSA) 73-10050 (Washington, D.C.: Government Printing Office, June 1973). Percentage

Table A20   Estimated Utilization and Charges for SMI Services Incurred by
Selected Categories of SMI Enrollees without Hospital Stays, 1969

	Public Medical Assistance	High Family Income	Low-to-Moderate Family Income
Number of enrollees (in thousands)	1900	1380	7670
With charges for covered services	1650	1050	5220
Percent of enrollees			
Not using covered services	13	24	32
Deductible not met	37	30	36
Deductible met	50	46	32
Average number of visits and services per user			
Users of covered services with charges	22	9	8
Users of covered services meeting deductible	34	13	13
Percent of enrollees by charge interval			
$ 1–49	46	42	57
$ 50–99	19	23	22
$100 or more	35	35	21
Average charge per user			
Users of covered service with charges	$134	$ 95	$ 73
Users of covered services meeting deductible	218	141	132

SOURCE. Evelyn Peel, and Jack Scharff, "Impact of Cost-Sharing on Use of
Ambulatory Services under Medicare, 1969," *Social Security Bulletin* **36**:3–24
(October 1973); from Table 2, p. 8.

Table A21   Average Annual Percentage Increase in the Consumer Price Index and the Medical Care Price Component during the Post-Medicare Period, 1966–1972

Year	CPI	Medical Care
1966	2.9	4.4
1967	2.9	7.1
1968	4.2	6.1
1969	5.4	6.9
1970	5.9	6.3
1971	4.3	6.5
1972	3.3	3.2

SOURCE.   Consumer Price Index, Bureau of Labor Statistics, in Office of Research and Statistics, *Medical Care Expenditures, Prices, and Costs: Background Book*. DHEW Publication No. (SSA) 74-11909 (Washington, D.C.: Government Printing Office, September 1973), text table, p. 64.

Table A22   Ratio of Medicaid Recipients to All Low-Income Persons, by Age
Group and State, 1970

	Ratio of Recipients to Low-Income Persons		
State/Region	Under 21	21–64	65 and Over
United States	.55	.61	.69
Northeast	1.24	1.31	.67
Maine	.48	.46	.32
New Hampshire	.46	.37	.52
Vermont	.80	.60	.72
Massachusetts[a]	NA	NA	NA
Rhode Island	.72	1.02	1.30
Connecticut	1.04	.53	.51
New York	1.68	1.72	1.02
New Jersey	.70	.63	.22
Pennsylvania	.97	1.28	.38
North Central	.49	.41	.40
Ohio	.40	.36	.29
Indiana	.26	.22	.21
Illinois	.70	.50	.34
Michigan	.51	.62	.47
Wisconsin	.66	.47	.62
Minnesota	.72	.40	.55
Iowa	.43	.32	.32
Missouri	.33	.33	.55
North Dakota	.20	.22	.40
South Dakota	.14	.31	.28
Nebraska	.31	.14	.39
Kansas	.51	.55	.36
South	.20	.23	.53
Delaware	.81	.48	.28
Maryland	.73	.83	.68
District of Columbia	1.10	.72	.67

SOURCE.   Based on tabular data presented in: Karen Davis, *National Health Insurance* (Washington, D.C.: The Brookings Institution, April 15, 1974, unpublished).

[a] Data not reported for Massachusetts and North Carolina. Regional and national totals do not include these states.

[b] Arizona and Alaska did not have Medicaid programs in 1970. Regional and national totals do not include these states.

Table A22   (*Continued*)

State/Region	Ratio of Recipients to Low-Income Persons		
	Under 21	21–64	65 and Over
Virginia	.20	.18	.28
West Virginia	.38	.39	.19
North Carolina[a]	NA	NA	NA
South Carolina	.09	.19	.38
Georgia	.26	.31	.71
Florida	.20	.25	.43
Kentucky	.38	.37	.68
Tennessee	.16	.17	.32
Alabama	.10	.11	.49
Mississippi	.11	.07	.49
Arkansas	.06	.10	.19
Louisiana	.08	.18	.94
Oklahoma	.37	.43	.64
Texas	.08	.09	.66
West	.96	1.29	1.97
Montana	.28	.26	.31
Idaho	.26	.29	.26
Wyoming	.18	.18	.24
Colorado	.40	.55	1.34
New Mexico	.26	.29	.37
Arizona[b]	—	—	—
Utah	.27	.73	.50
Nevada	.47	.34	.55
Washington	.70	1.13	.67
Oregon	.35	.47	.31
California	1.33	1.73	3.17
Hawaii	.92	1.01	.96
Alaska[b]	—	—	—

Table A23   Medicaid Coverage of Required and Optional Services by Recipient Category and State, 1972

State	Required Services[a,b]	Optional Services[c] 1	2	3	4	5	6	7	8	9	10	11	12	13	14	15	16	17
Alabama	C		C								C							C	C[d]
Arkansas	C	C		C		C					C		C		C	C	C	C
California	M	M	M	M	C	M	M	M		M	M	M	M	M	M	C	M	M
Colorado	C	C	C	M	C	M	M				C		C	C	M	C		C
Connecticut	M	M	M	M	M	M	M	M	M		M				M	M	M	
Delaware	C	C			C			C	C		C					C		M
District of Columbia	M	M	M	M	M	M		M		M	C		M	M		M		
Florida	C	C									C					C		M
Georgia	C	C							M	C	C			C				C
Hawaii	M	M	C	M	M	M	M	M	M	M	M	M	M	M	C	C	M	M[d]
Idaho	C	C				C	C	C	C	C	C	C	C	M	C	M		M
Illinois	M	M	M	M	M	M	M	M	M	M	M	M	M	M	M	M	M	M
Indiana	C	C	C	C	C	C	C	C	C	C	C	C	C	C	C	C	C	C[d]
Iowa	C	C	C	C	M	M	M	M	M	M	M	C	M	M	M	C	C	M
Kansas	M	M	M	M	M	M	M	M	M	M	M	M	M	M	M	M	M	C[d]
Kentucky	M	C	C	C	C	C	C	C	C	C	C	C	C	C	C	M	M	C[d]
Louisiana	C	C	C	M	M	C	C	M	C	C	C	C	C	C	C	C	C	M[d]
Maine	C	C					C	C	C	C		C		C		M	M	C[d]
Maryland	M	M	M	M	C	M	M	M	M	M	M	M	M	M	M	M	M	M[d]
Massachusetts	M	M	M	M	M	M	M	M	M	M	M	M	M	M	M	M	M	M[d]
Michigan	M	M	M	M	M	M	M	M	M	M	M	M	M	M	M	M	M	M
Minnesota	C	M				M	M	M	C	C	C		M	M	C	M	C	
Mississippi	C	C	C	C	C	C	C	C	C	C	C	C	C			C	C	
Missouri	C	C	C	C	C	C	C	C	C	C	C	C	C	M		C		
Montana	C	C	C	C	C	C	C	C	C	C		C	M			C		C
Nebraska	M	M	M	M	M	M	M	C	C	M	M	M	C	M	M	M	M	M[d]
Nevada	C	C	C	C	C	C	C	C	C	C	C	C	C		C	C	C	C[d]
New Hampshire	M	M	M											M	M			
New Jersey	C	C		C		C	C	C	C	C	C	C	C	C	C	C	C	C

State																								
New Mexico	C	C	C	C	C	C	C	C	C	C	C	C	C	C	C	C	C	C	C	C	C	C	C	C
New York	M	M	M	M	M	M	M	M	M	M	M	M	M	M	M	M	M	M	M	M	M	M	M	M
North Carolina	M	M	M	M	M	M	M	M	M	M	M	C	M	C	C	M	M	M	C	M	M	M	M	
North Dakota	C	C	C	C	C	C	C	C	C	C	C	C	C	C	C	C	C	C	C	C	C	C	C	C
Ohio	M	C	M	C	C	M	M	M	C	M	M	M	M	M	C	C	M	C	C	M	M	C		M
Oklahoma	C	C	C	C	C	C	C	C	C	C	C	C	C	C	C	C	C	C	C	C	C	C	C	
Oregon	M	C	C	C	C	C	C	C	C	C	C	M	C	M	C	C	M	C	C	C	M	C	C	C
Pennsylvania	M	M	M	M	M	M	M	M	M	M	M	M	M	M	M	M	M	M	M	M	M	M	M	C
Rhode Island	C	C	C	C	C	C	C	C	C	C	C	C	C	C	C	C	C	C	C	C	C	C	C	C
South Carolina	C	C	C	C	C	C	C	C	C	C	C	C	C	C	C	C	C	C	C	C	C	C	C	C
South Dakota	C	C	C	C	C	C	C	C	C	C	C	C	C	C	C	C	C	C	C	C	C	C	C	C[d]
Tennessee	C	C	C	C	C	C	C	C	C	C	C	C	C	C	C	C	C	C	C	C	C	C	C	C
Texas	M	M	M	M	M	M	M	M	M	M	M	M	M	M	M	M	M	M	M	M	M	M	M	M[d]
Utah	M	M	M	M	M	M	M	M	M	M	M	M	M	M	M	M	M	M	M	M	M	M	M	M[d]
Vermont	M	M	M	M	M	M	M	M	M	M	M	M	M	M	M	M	M	M	M	M	M	M	M	M
Virginia	M	M	M	M	M	M	M	M	M	M	M	M	M	M	M	M	M	M	M	M	M	M	M	M
Washington	C	M	C	C	C	C	C	C	C	C	C	C	C	C	C	C	C	C	C	C	C	C	C	M
West Virginia	M	M	M	M	M	M	M	M	M	M	M	M	M	M	M	M	M	M	M	M	M	M	M	
Wisconsin	C	C	C	C	C	C	C	C	C	C	C	C	C	C	C	C	C	C	C	C	C	C	C	M
Wyoming	C	C	C	C	C	C	C	C	C	C	C	C	C	C	C	C	C	C	C	C	C	C	C	C[d]

SOURCES. Based on Table 4 in John Holahan, *Financing Health Care for the Poor: The Medicaid Experience*. Working Paper No. 976-01 (Washington, D.C.).

[a] Required Services: inpatient hospital services; outpatient hospital services; other laboratory and X-ray services; skilled nursing-home services for individuals aged 21 or older; physician services; early and periodic screening, diagnosis, and treatment of individuals under the age of 21; and home health-care services for any individual entitled to skilled nursing-home services.

[b] C: offered for money-payment recipients. M: offered for medically needy.

[c] Optional services, for which federal financial participation is available, including: (1) clinic services; (2) prescribed drugs; (3) dental services; (4) prosthetic devices; (5) eyeglasses; (6) private-duty nursing; (7) physical therapy and related services; (8) other diagnostic, screening, preventive and rehabilitative services; (9) emergency hospital services; (10) family-planning services; (11) skilled nursing-home services; (12) optometrists' services; (13) podiatrists' services; (14) chiropractors' services; (15) care of patients 65 and over in institutions for mental diseases; (16) care of patients 65 or older in institutions for tuberculosis; (17) institutional services in intermediate-care facilities.

[d] Does not include extended-care facility services in institutions for mentally retarded.

Table A24   Physician Visits per Person by Income, FY 1964, FY 1967, and CY 1969

Income Groups[a]	FY 1964	FY 1967	CY 1969[b]
Low income	4.3	4.3	4.9
Middle income	4.5	4.2	4.2
High income	5.1	4.6	4.4

SOURCE.   Karen Davis and Roger Reynolds, *Impact of Medicare and Medicaid on Access to Medical Care* (Washington, D.C.: The Brookings Institute, 1974, unpublished); from Table 1, pp. 3 and 3a.

[a] Low income is defined as under $4000 in 1964 and under $5000 in 1967 and 1969. Middle income is defined as $4000–9999 in 1964 and $5000–9999 in 1967 and 1969. High income is defined as $10,000 and over in all three years.

[b] Physician visits per capita differ from published data of National Center for Health Statistics. Prior to 1971, NCHS did not count physician visits for persons who could not recall the days on which they made visits; thereafter, NCHS counted physician visits for such persons. Counts here for 1969 reflect that change retroactively.

Table A25 Medical-Vendor Payments[a] on the Basis of Eligibility FY 1968–FY 1972[b]

	1968		1969		1970		1971		1972	
	Dollars	Per-cent	Dollars	Per-cent	Dollars	Per-cent	Dollars	Per-cent	Dollars	Per-cent
Total (in thousands)	3,484,100	100.0	4,273,439	100.0	4,807,535	100.0	5,939,236	100.0	6,299,050	100.0
Age 65 and over	1,581,800	45.0	1,803,391	42.2	1,884,554	39.2	2,227,214	37.5	1,925,178	30.6
Blind	27,900	1.0	34,188	0.8	33,653	0.7	47,514	0.8	44,511	0.7
Permanently and totally disabled	533,100	15.0	760,672	17.8	999,967	20.8	1,235,361	20.8	1,353,916	21.5
Children under 21 (AFDC and non-AFDC)	b		867,508	20.3	807,666	16.8	1,092,819	18.4	1,174,695	18.6
Adults in families with dependent children	b		376,063	8.8	831,704	17.3	1,116,577	18.8	961,919	15.3
Other adults	480,800	14.0	431,617	10.1	249,992	5.2	219,752	3.7	838,831	13.3

[a] Expenditures from federal, state, and local funds under federally aided assistance programs. Excludes per capita payments into agency pooled fund, and into Social Security Administration.
[b] The 1968 data did not include non-AFDC children. Expenditures for members in families with dependent children under 21 is $860,600.

Table A26 Average Annual Number of Ambulatory-Care Visits per Person in Nine OEO Baseline Survey Sites, 1968–1969

Area	Average Number of Visits
Roxbury	5.4
Bedford–Stuyvesant	5.5
Red Hook	5.5
Philadelphia	5.7
Cardoza	4.0
Atlanta	3.0
Charleston	3.2
Mission	5.0
East Palo Alto	5.0

SOURCE. Unpublished OEO baseline survey data in Gail R. Wilensky, *Utilization of Ambulatory Care*. Working Paper 963-3 (Washington, D.C.: The Urban Institute, 1973, unpublished), p. 16.

Table A27 Percent of OEO Baseline Survey Populations Using Hospital Clinics as Usual Source of Care, by Health Status, 1968–1969

		Health Status	
Area	Total	With Chronic Illness	Without Chronic Illness
Roxbury	89.9	86.1	90.6
Bedford–Stuyvesant	68.9	72.8	67.6
Red Hook	39.5	45.6	37.7
Philadelphia	50.0	52.1	49.4
Cardoza	71.9	70.7	72.2
Atlanta	82.6	79.7	85.8
Charleston	72.2	67.6	73.0
Mission	29.4	25.4	32.9
East Palo Alto	13.2	15.8	12.6

SOURCE. Unpublished OEO baseline survey data in Gail R. Wilensy, *Utilization of Ambulatory Care*. Working Paper 963-3 (Washington, D.C.: The Urban Institute, 1973, unpublished), p. 37.

Table A28   Percent of OEO Baseline Survey Populations Traveling Less Than 20 Minutes to Usual Source of Care, by Source of Care, 1968–1969

	Usual Source of Care		
Area	All Sources	Private Physician	Hospital Clinic
Roxbury	32	52	35
Bedford–Stuyvesant	40	49	35
Red Hook	52	64	17
Philadelphia	56	69	40
Cardoza	24	45	28
Atlanta	16	38	17
Charleston	42	68	41
Mission	34	36	33
East Palo Alto	65	75	27

SOURCE.   Unpublished OEO baseline survey data in Gail R. Wilensky, *Utilization of Ambulatory Care*. Working Paper 963-3 (Washington, D.C.: The Urban Institute, 1973, unpublished), p. 25.

Table A29 Federal HMO Grant and Contract Activity and Obligations for New and Continued Projects, by Funding Category, FY 1971–FY 1974[a]

	Funding Categories			
	New		Continuations	
Fiscal Year	Number	Dollars	Number	Dollars
Planning and Development Grants				
1971	41	3,416,653	0	—
1972	43	3,142,927	30	4,418,163
1973	0	—	36	4,783,426
1974	0	—	12	1,476,720
Total:	84	6,559,580	78	10,678,309
Generator Contracts				
1971	10	1,838,000	0	—
1972	0	—	3	548,401
1973	0	—	0	—
1974	0	—	0	—
Total:	10	1,838,000	3	548,401
Evaluation and Analysis Projects				
1971	8	694,742	0	—
1972	5	460,038	1	252,000
1973	3	186,239	1	134,587
1974	0	—	0	—
Total:	16	1,341,019	2	386,587
Technical Assistance and Resource Development Projects				
1971	7	744,988	0	—
1972	40	5,839,912	4	696,121
1973	16	944,126	22	1,313,758
1974	0	—	10	521,905
Total:	63	7,529,026	36	2,531,784
Grand total:	173	17,267,625	119	14,145,081

SOURCE. Based on information in: Office of the Associate Bureau Director (HMO), *Health Maintenance Organization: Program Status Report, February 1, 1974* (Rockville, Maryland: Bureau of Community Health Services, Health Services Administration, Department of Health, Education, and Welfare, March 1974), Appendix 5, p. 34.

[a] Does not include funds authorized for FY 1974 by recent HMO bill.

Table A30 Total Federal HMO Grant and Contract Obligations, FY 1971–FY 1974[a]

Fiscal Year	Obligations
1971	$ 6,694,383
1972	15,349,552
1973	7,369,146
1974	1,999,625
Total:	$31,412,706

SOURCE. Based on information in Office of the Associate Bureau Director (HMO), *Health Maintenance Organization: Program Status Report, February 1, 1974* (Rockville, Maryland: Bureau of Community Health Services, Health Services Administration, Department of Health, Education, and Welfare, March 1974), Appendix 5, p. 34.

[a] None of these funds supported operating expenses.

Table A31 Sources of Federal HMO Grant and Contract Obligations, FY 1971–FY 1974, Prior to Program Authorizations in 1974 HMO Bill

Program	Authorizing Section of Public Health Service Act	Obligation	Percent
Comprehensive Health Services	314(e)	$13,042,184	41.5
Regional Medical Programs	910(c)	9,190,445	29.3
National Center for Health Services Research and Development	304	7,276,385	23.2
Social and Rehabilitation Service	1100[a]	1,405,818	4.5
National Institutes of Mental Health	513	297,087	1.0
Miscellaneous	10,600, Title 5, and P.L. 91–596	200,787	0.6
Total:		$31,412,706	100.1[b]

SOURCE. Based on information in Office of the Associate Bureau Director (HMO), *Health Maintenance Organization: Program Status Report, February 1, 1974* (Rockville, Maryland: Bureau of Community Health Services, Health Services Administration, Department of Health, Education, and Welfare, March 1974), Appendix 5, p. 34.

[a] Section of Social Security Act.

[b] Exceeds 100.0, owing to rounding.

Summary of Main Features of 1973 HMO Bill (P. L. 93–222)

PAYMENT MECHANISM

- periodic prepayment, fixed on community rating basis, supplemented by copayments (so long as they do not act as a barrier to delivery of services) to cover provision of basic range of health-care services regardless of amount used
- supplemental payments as contracted for supplemental health services provided

PROVISION OF SERVICES

Services Requirements

- availability,
- accessibility,
- continuity

Basic Range of Necessary Services

- physician services, including consultation and referral
- inpatient and outpatient hospital services
- medically necessary emergency services, both in and outside service area
- short-term outpatient mental-health services (20-visit maximum)
- drug and alcohol abuse treatment and referral services
- diagnostic laboratory, and diagnostic and therapeutic radiology services
- home health services
- preventive health services, including voluntary family planning, infertility studies, preventive dental care for children, corrective eye examinations for children

Supplemental Health Services (Optional Inclusion in Enrollee Contract)

- intermediate and long-term facilities services
- vision, dental, and mental-health services not included in basic range
- long-term physical medicine and rehabilitative services
- provision of prescription drugs required in conjunction with services provided under contract

ORGANIZATION AND OPERATION OF SERVICES

- must be fiscally sound
- assume full financial risk on a prospective basis for provision of basic health services to enrollee population (can insure against unusually large expenses)
- must enroll broadly representative population groups (unless in medically underserved areas, where no more than 75 percent of enrollees can come from medically underserved population; this percent does not pertain in a rural medically underserved area)
- provision of physician services through physicians organized in 'medical group' (traditional group practice arrangement) or in 'individual practice association' (medical care foundation arrangement), supported by necessary allied health professionals
- required open enrollment periods annually

- no refusal to enroll or disenrollment related to health services utilization allowed
- at least 30 percent of organization's policymaking board must represent membership; that part of enrollee population from medically underserved population must be proportionately represented
- grievance mechanism
- quality assurance mechanism
- provide medical social services and health education for enrollees
- develop procedures for collecting program management data, including costs, utilization patterns, parameters of availability, accessibility, and acceptability, drug use patterns, and member health status

FINANCING

Feasibility Surveys

- up to $50,000 for each project
- funded for one year, with possibility of a one-year extension
- at least 20 percent of amount obligated annually under feasibility grants and contracts section to go to projects expected to draw at least two-thirds of their membership from nonmetropolitan areas
- no more than 90 percent of these costs to be met by federal monies, unless rural area, where up to 100 percent may be financed

Planning and Initial Development Costs

- contracts/grants to be let for significant expansion of existing HMOs or initial development of new HMOs
- will also guarantee to non-federal lenders payment of principal and interest on loans taken out for such purposes
- up to $125,000 available for each grant/contract for expansion
- up to $1 million available for each grant/contract for initial development
- particular attention to such projects in medically underserved areas
- no more than 90 percent of these costs to be met by federal monies, unless rural area, where up to 100 percent may be financed

Loans and Loan Guarantees for Initial Operation

- loans for losses incurred in first three years of operation
- loans for losses incurred in first three years after significant expansion
- loan guarantees for above if HMO in medically underserved area
- up to $1 million available annually for each project; aggregates not to exceed $2.5 million

Notes and References

Chapter 1

1. Stephen Strickland, *U.S. Health Care: What's Wrong and What's Right* (New York: Universe Books, 1972), p. 33; Ronald Andersen, Joanna Kravitz, and Odin Anderson, "The Public's View of the Crisis in Medical Care: An Impetus for Changing Delivery Systems?" *Economic and Business Bulletin* (Temple University), 24(1):44–52 (Fall 1971).

2. Herbert Klarman, *The Economics of Health* (New York: Columbia University Press, 1965), p. 11.

3. Talcott Parsons, *The Social System* (New York: Free Press, 1951), Chapter 10.

4. *President's Health Message of 1971* (Washington, D.C.: The White House, February 18, 1971).

5. K. J. Arrow, "Uncertainty and the Welfare Economics of Medical Care," *American Economic Review* 53:967 (1963).

6. Victor Fuchs and Marcia Kramer, *Determinants of Expenditures for Physicians' Services in the United States, 1948–68* [Washington, D.C.: DHEW Publication No. (HSM) 73-3013]; Herbert Klarman, *The Economics of Health* (New York: Columbia University Press, 1965), pp. 139–141; Martin Feldstein, *The Rising Cost of Hospital Care* (Washington, D.C.: Information Resources Press, 1971), pp. 30–32; and Kong-Kyun Ro, "Patient Characteristics, Hospital Characteristics, and Hospital Use," in Victor Fuchs (Ed.), *Essays in the Economics of Health and Medical Care* (New York: National Bureau of Economic Research, 1972); J. P. Bunker, "Surgical Manpower: A Comparison of Operations and Surgeons in the United States and England and Wales," *New England Journal of Medicine* 282:135–144 (1970); Charles Lewis, "Variations in the Incidence of Surgery," *New England Journal of Medicine* 281:880–884 (1969).

7. Lewis, *op. cit.,* p. 950; also see Victor Fuchs, "The Growing Demand for Medical Care," *New England Journal of Medicine* **279:**190–195 (1968).

8. See note 1.

9. Robert Merton, *Social Theory and Social Structure* (rev. ed.; New York: Free Press, 1957), pp. 121–160.

10. Harold Wolff, *Stress and Disease* (rev. ed.; Springfield, Illinois: Thomas, 1968).

11. David Mechanic, *Public Expectations and Health Care* (New York: Wiley-Interscience, 1972), pp. 80–101.

12. Rashi Fein, *The Doctor Shortage: An Economic Diagnosis* (Washington, D.C.: The Brookings Institution, 1967), pp. 62–89.

13. A. L. Cochrane, *Effectiveness and Efficiency* (London: The Nuffield Provincial Hospitals Trust, 1972).

14. David Mechanic, *Medical Sociology: A Selective View* (New York: Free Press, 1968), pp. 115–157.

15. Kerr White, "Organization and Delivery of Personal Health Services: Public Policy Issues," *Milbank Memorial Fund Quarterly* **46:**225–258 (1968).

Chapter 2

1. Kerr White, Franklin Williams, and Bernard Greenberg, "The Ecology of Medical Care," *New England Journal of Medicine* **265:**885–892 (1961).

2. Robert Huntley, "Epidemiology of Family Practice," *Journal of the American Medical Association* **185:**175–178 (1963); John Fry, *Profiles of Disease: A Study in the Natural History of Common Diseases* (Edinburgh, Scotland: E and S Livingstone, Ltd., 1966).

3. David Mechanic, "Social Psychologic Factors Affecting the Presentation of Bodily Complaints," *New England Journal of Medicine* **286:**1132–1139 (1972).

4. Kerr White, "Evaluation of Medical Education and Health Care," in Willoughby Lathem and Anne Newberry (Eds.), *Community Medicine: Teaching, Research and Health Care* (New York: Appleton-Century-Crofts, 1970), p. 247.

5. Mechanic, *Medical Sociology.*

6. Charles Kadushin, *Why People Go to Psychiatrists* (New York: Atherton, 1969).

7. See, for example, Thomas McKeown et al., *Screening in Medical Care: Reviewing the Evidence* (Fair Lawn, New Jersey: Oxford University Press, 1968); and R. Thorner, "Whither Multiphasic Screening," *New England Journal of Medicine* **280:**1037–1042 (1969).

8. Committee on the Costs of Medical Care, *Medical Care for the American People* (Washington, D.C.: Public Health Service, 1970 reprint).

9. Walter McNerney, "Why Does Medical Care Cost So Much?" *New England Journal of Medicine* **282:**1458–1465 (1970).

10. *Ibid.*

11. National Center for Health Statistics, *Physician Visits—Volume and Interval Since Last Visit, United States—1969,* Series 10, No. 75, [Washington, D.C.: DHEW Publication No. (HSM) 72-1064, July 1972, Table 20, p. 34].

12. W. Follette and N. A. Cummings, "Psychiatric Services and Medical Utilization in a Prepaid

Health Plan Setting," *Medical Care* **5**:25–35 (1967); I. D. Goldberg et al., "Effect of a Short-Term Outpatient Psychiatric Therapy Benefit on the Utilization of Medical Services in a Prepaid Group Practice Medical Program," *Medical Care* **8**:419–428 (1970).

13. National Center for Health Statistics, *Physician Visits.*

14. Mechanic, "Social Psychologic Factors . . . ," pp. 155–157.

15. National Center for Health Statistics, *Physician Visits,* p. 10.

16. Mechanic, "Social Psychologic Factors . . . ," p. 148.

17. *Ibid.,* p. 168.

18. Alberta Parker, "The Dimensions of Primary Care: Blueprints for Change," in Spyros Andreopoulos (Ed.), *Primary Care: Where Medicine Fails* (New York: John Wiley, 1974), p. 60.

19. P. Ley and M. S. Spelman, *Communicating with the Patient* (London: Trinity Press, 1967).

20. Vida Francis et al., "Gaps in Doctor–Patient Communication: Patients' Response to Medical Advice," *New England Journal of Medicine* **280**:535–540 (1969).

21. Barbara Dohrenwend and Bruce Dohrenwend (Eds.), *Stressful Life Events: Their Nature and Effects* (New York: Wiley-Interscience, 1974).

22. Lawrence Hinkle, "The Effect of Exposure to Culture Change, Social Change, and Changes in Interpersonal Relationships on Health," in Dohrenwend and Dohrenwend (Eds.), *Ibid.,* pp. 9–44.

23. Harrison Gough, "The Recruitment and Selection of Medical Students," in Robert Coombs and Clark Vincent (Eds.), *Psychosocial Aspects of Medical Training* (Springfield, Illinois: Thomas, 1971), pp. 5–43.

24. *Ibid.,* p. 25.

25. Samuel Bloom, "The Process of Becoming a Physician," *The Annals of the American Academy* **346**:77–87 (1963).

26. Robert Merton et al. (Eds.), *The Student-Physician: Introductory Studies of the Sociology of Medical Education* (Cambridge, Massachusetts: Harvard University Press, 1957).

27. Stephen Miller, *Prescription for Leadership: Training for the Medical Elite* (Chicago: Aldine, 1970).

28. Julius Richmond, *Currents in American Medicine* (Cambridge, Massachusetts: Harvard University Press, 1969).

29. American Medical Association, *1972 Reference Data on the Profile of Medical Practice* (Chicago: Center for Health Services Research and Development), p. 1.

30. National Center for Health Statistics, *Physician Visits,* p. 9.

31. American Medical Association, *1972 Reference Data . . . ,* p. 59.

32. Parker, "The Dimensions of Primary Care," Department of Health and Social Security, *Annual Report, 1971* (London: Her Majesty's Stationery Office), Cmnd. 5019, p. 170.

Chapter 3

1. Rosemary Stevens, *American Medicine and the Public Interest* (New Haven: Yale University Press, 1971).

2. Milton Roemer, "On Paying the Doctor and the Implications of Different Methods," *Journal of Health and Human Behavior* 3:4–14 (1962).

3. Eliot Freidson, *Patients' View of Medical Practice* (New York: Russell Sage Foundation, 1961).

Chapter 5

1. "Soaring Medical School Costs," *Medical World News* (January 4, 1974), p. 27.

2. See Charles C. Edwards, "A Candid Look at Health Manpower Problems," *Journal of Medical Education* 49:19–26 (1974); and "Soaring Medical School Costs," *Medical World News* (January 4, 1974), pp. 27–35.

3. August G. Swanson, M.D., Director, Department of Academic Affairs, Association of American Medical Colleges, as quoted in "Soaring Medical School Costs," *Medical World News* (January 4, 1974), pp. 33–34.

4. "Can Washington Tell Doctors Where To Go?" *American Medical News* (September 13, 1974), pp. 45–54, especially commentary re Kennedy and Roy bills.

5. Congressman Fogarty, as quoted in U.S. Congress, House of Representatives, *Health Professions Educational Assistance Amendments of 1965.* Serial No. 89-13, June 8 & 9, 1965 (Washington, D.C.: Government Printing Office, 1965), p. 36.

6. Description based on information in CONSAD Research Corporation, *An Evaluation of the Effectiveness of Loan Forgiveness as an Incentive for Health Practitioners to Locate in Medically Underserved Areas.* Report on Contract HEW-OS-73-68, for the Office of the Secretary, Department of Health, Education, and Welfare (Pittsburgh, Pennsylvania: January 1973), Table III-3, pp. 13–14; William C. Christoffel, *Option Paper on the Geographic Maldistribution of Health Professionals* (Washington, D.C.: September 5, 1973), Appendix A, pp. 3–4; U.S. Congress, *Emergency Health Personnel Act Amendments of 1972,* October 27, 1972; and "Scholarships Offered: U.S. Will Assist Future Rural MDs," *American Medical News* (June 3, 1974), p. 16.

7. H. R. Mason, "Effectiveness of Student Aid Programs Tied to A Service Commitment." *Journal of Medical Education* 46:575–583 (1971), p. 576.

8. CONSAD, *An Evaluation of the Effectiveness of Loan* Forgiveness . . . (1973), p. 26.

9. Only the response from the North Carolina practice-agreement/loan-forgiveness program included demographic data on borrowers. These figures show that, whereas one-quarter of all borrowers between 1946 and 1969 had been blacks, 48 percent of those borrowers in school in 1969 were nonwhites. In the 1960 census, 25.4 percent of the state's total population was nonwhite. The possible effect of discrimination against the most needy students is reflected in the fact that, of the 20 nonwhite physicians practicing in North Carolina in 1969, 11 percent had received state loans to finance their medical education; the proportion of white physicians so assisted was far lower. Based on information from North Carolina Medical Care Commission. *The Expansion of Medical Facilities and Services in North Carolina, 1946–1969* (Raleigh, North Carolina: 1969).

10. Mason, "Effectiveness of Student Aid Programs . . ." (1971), Table 2, p. 577; and American Medical Association, "Medical Education in the United States," *Journal of the American Medical Association* 226:915 (1973), Table 28.

11. Christoffel, *Option Paper* . . . (1973), Appendix A, p. 6.

12. CONSAD, *An Evaluation of the Effectiveness of Loan Forgiveness* . . . (1973), pp. 30–35.

13.   Information from Harry W. Bruce, Jr., D.D.S., Acting Associate Director for Operations, Bureau of Health Resources Development, Health Resources Administration, Department of Health, Education, and Welfare (March 27, 1974).

14.   Christoffel, *Option Paper . . .* (1973), Appendix A, p. 6.

15.   Office of the Secretary, Department of Health, Education, and Welfare, *Report to the President and the Congress: Health Professions Educational Assistance Program* (Washington, D.C.: Department of Health, Education, and Welfare, September 1970), Appendix Table 42, p. 195.

Chapter 6

1.   Bruce Steinwald and Carolynn Steinwald, *The Effect of Preceptorship and Rural Training Programs on Physicians' Location Decisions* (Chicago: Center for Health Services Research and Development, American Medical Association, draft, 1973), Table 1, p. 5. This description is further supported by information obtained from files at the Manpower Distribution Project, National Health Council, during a January 30–February 1, 1974, visit.

2.   Steinwald and Steinwald, *The Effect of Preceptorship and Rural Training Programs . . .* (1973), p. 7.

3.   Information in the Manpower Distribution Project files indicates that many of the medical schools currently supporting preceptorship projects, and most developing them, do so to influence students to select rural and/or primary-care practice. Responses to the Project's survey from other health-professions schools suggest that preceptorship programs are a fairly common device where a commitment has been made to influence geographic distribution.

4.   Steinwald and Steinwald, *The Effect of Preceptorship and Rural Training Programs . . .* (1973), pp. 4–5 and Table 1.

5.   From review of files at Manpower Distribution Project.

6.   U.S. Comptroller General, *Report to Congress: Program to Increase Graduates from Health Professions Schools and Improve the Quality of their Education.* B-16403 (2) (Washington, D.C.: General Accounting Office, 1972), p. 10.

7.   Information from Shirley Johnson, Program Officer, Division of Medicine, Bureau of Health Resources Development, Health Resources Administration, HEW (June 11, 1974).

8.   Theodore J. Phillips, *Community Clerkships for Educating Family Medicine Students: Process of Development.* A WAMI Progress Report (Seattle: Department of Family Medicine, University of Washington School of Medicine, draft, 1973).

9.   Theodore J. Phillips and August G. Swanson, "Teaching Family Medicine in Rural Clinical Clerkships: A WAMI Progress Report," *Journal of the American Medical Association* 228:1408–1410 (1974).

10.   Sam A. Banks, Alice H. Murphee, and Richard C. Reynolds, "The Community Health Clerkship: Evaluation of a Program," *Journal of Medical Education* 48:560–564 (1973).

11.   J. Z. Bowers and H. A. Page, "Study of a Preceptorship Program," *Journal of the American Medical Association* 173:1923–1927 (1960).

12.   J. Z. Bowers and R. C. Parkin, "The Wisconsin Preceptor Program: A Thirty-Year Experiment in Medical Education," *Journal of Medical Education* 32:610–612 (1957).

13.   L. G. Kindschi, "Role of the Preceptors in the University of Wisconsin Preceptor Program," *Journal of Medical Education* 34:649–653 (1959).

14.   H. A. Page and P. P. Anast. "An Alumni Evaluation of the Wisconsin Preceptorial Program," *Journal of Medical Education* **32:**613–617 (1957).

15.   J. D. Rising, "The Rural Preceptorship: A Ten-Year Report on the K.U. Program," *Journal of Medical Education* **63:**81–84 (1962).

16.   S. E. Silvertson and T. C. Meyer. "Student Evaluation at Wisconsin Medical School," *Wisconsin Medical Journal* **70:**39–41 (1971).

17.   Phillips and Swanson, "Teaching Family Medicine . . ." (1974), p. 1410.

18.   Jack Hadley, *Physicians' Specialty and Location Decisions: A Literature Review.* Discussion Paper Series No. 10, Economic Analysis Branch, Bureau of Health Services Research (Rockville, Maryland: Health Resources Administration, May 1973).

19.   Center for Health Services Research and Development, American Medical Association, *Contributions to a Comprehensive Health Manpower Strategy* (Chicago: American Medical Association, January 1973, revised July 1973); see especially discussions by John McFarland, "Toward an Explanation of the Geographic Location of Physicians in the U.S.," pp. 26–67; and by Norbert Budde, "Distribution of Physicians by Specialty and Practice Patterns," pp. 68–102, and their respective bibliographies.

20.   Bond L. Bible, "Physicians' Views of Medical Practice in Nonmetropolitan Communities," *Public Health Reports* **85:**11–17 (1970).

21.   Donald Yett and Frank Sloan, *Analysis of Migration Patterns of Recent Medical School Graduates.* Paper presented at Health Services Research Conference on Factors in Health Manpower Performance and the Delivery of Health Care, Chicago (December 1971); to be published.

22.   W. F. Breisch, "Impact of Medical School Characteristics on Location of Physicians Practice," *Journal of Medical Education* **45:**1068–1070 (1970).

23.   Student American Medical Association, *SAMA–MECO Project: Final Report, 1971.* Available from Student American Medical Association, 1400 Hicks Road, Rolling Meadows, Ill., 60008.

24.   SAMA (1971).

25.   Student American Medical Association, *SAMA–MECO Project: Final Report, 1972.* Available from Student American Medical Association, 1400 Hicks Road, Rolling Meadows, Ill., 60008.

26.   SAMA (1971), p. 11.

27.   SAMA (1972), p. 12.

28.   K. A. Heald, J. K. Cooper, and S. Coleman, *An Analysis of Two Surveys of Recent Medical School Graduates.* Final Report on Contract HEW-OS-71-125, Department of Health, Education, and Welfare (Washington, D.C.: Rand Corporation, draft, January 1974); see appendices for reproductions of questionnaires used in surveys.

29.   A note on the numbers and percents presented in the following discussion on this subgroup is in order. There are slight differences between the Steinwald analysis and Rand's final report in the number of respondents who had chosen a practice location *and* who had answered the question about participation in rural training programs, and on the number of participants in rural training programs. From the Steinwald paper, these groups number 3729 and 482, respectively; in the Rand report, they are 3728 and 485, respectively. The Rand analysis focused on comparing the subgroup of respondents who had chosen primary-care practice to the entire group of respondents that had chosen practice locations. Thus, although it is the final report, the Rand paper does not include tabulations on all characteristics of rural training program participants. For this reason,

the Steinwald numbers are used as base figures for calculation of most percentages in this discussion.

30.   Heald et al., *An Analysis of Two Surveys* . . . (1974). The work done under the contract had three purposes: to identify factors underlying the unequal distribution of physicians; to determine policy-relevant factors in physicians' location decisions; and to suggest methods for correcting their relative deficiency in rural areas. An annotated bibliography of the relevant literature was presented in K. A. Heald and J. K. Cooper, *An Annotated Bibliography on Rural Medical Care.* Rand Report R-966-HEW (Washington, D.C.: Rand Corporation, April 1972).

31.   Steinwald and Steinwald, *The Effect of Preceptorship and Rural Training Programs* . . . (1973), Table 3, p. 12.

32.   *Ibid.,* Table 7, p. 17.

33.   *Ibid.,* Table 3, p. 12.

34.   *Ibid.,* p. 11.

35.   Heald et al., *An Analysis of Two Surveys* . . . (1974), Table 29, pp. 42–43. Regression analysis results are presented in Table 28, pp. 39–40, and specific characteristics considered in each of the seven regressions are noted therein.

36.   *Ibid.,* Table 14, p. 20.

37.   *Ibid.,* Table 15, p. 21.

38.   Steinwald and Steinwald, *The Effect of Preceptorship and Rural Training Programs* . . . (1973), Table 4, p. 13.

39.   Heald et al., *An Analysis of Two Surveys* . . . (1974), Table 22, p. 27; also in Steinwald and Steinwald, *The Effect of Preceptorship and Rural Training Programs* . . . (1973), Table 7, p. 17.

40.   Heald et al., *An Analysis of Two Surveys* . . . (1974), Table 23, pp. 29–30.

41.   Steinwald and Steinwald, *The Effect of Preceptorship and Rural Training Programs* . . . (1973), p. 14.

42.   *Ibid.,* Table 5, p. 14.

43.   *Ibid.,* Table 7, p. 17.

44.   *Ibid.,* Table 6, p. 16.

45.   Information provided by Shirley Johnson, Bureau of Health Resources Development, Health Resources Administration, HEW (July 11, 1974).

46.   Estimates provided by Theodore J. Phillips, M.D., Professor and Chairman, Department of Family Medicine, School of Medicine, University of Washington (July 10, 1974).

47.   Heald et al., *An Analysis of Two Surveys* . . . (1974), Table 29, pp. 42–43.

48.   Steinwald and Steinwald, The *Effect of Preceptorship and Rural Training Programs* . . . (1973), p. 17.

Chapter 7

1.   See, for example, Rosemary Stevens, *American Medicine and the Public Interest,* (New Haven: Yale University Press, 1971); Kerr L. White, "General Practice in the United States," *Journal of Medical Education* 39:333–345 (1964).

2.   "First FP Priority: Filling the Primary Care Gap," *Medical World News* (September 21, 1973), pp. 72–73.

3. Stevens, *American Medicine and the Public Interest* (1971), pp. 312–314.

4. Robert R. Huntly, "Epidemiology of Family Practice," *Journal of the American Medical Association* **185:**175–178 (1963), p. 175.

5. Committee on Preparation for General Practice, American Medical Association, "Final Report on Preparation for Family Practice," in American Medical Association, "Annual Report on Graduate Medical Education, 1960–1961," *Journal of the American Medical Association* **177:**636–639 (1961).

6. American Medical Association, "Annual Report . . . , 1960–1961," *Journal of the American Medical Association* **177:**634–635 (1961).

7. American Medical Association, "Annual Report on Graduate Medical Education, 1963–1964," *Journal of the American Medical Association* **190:**622 (1964).

8. Robert J. Haggerty, "Etiology of the Decline in General Practice," *Journal of the American Medical Association* **185:**179–182 (1963).

9. Robert Graham, M.D., Assistant Director, Division of Education, American Academy of Family Physicians, personal communication (July 16, 1974).

10. George A. Silver, "Family Practice: Resuscitation or Reform?" *Journal of the American Medical Association* **195:**188–191 (1963).

11. J. Willard, Chairman, *Meeting the Challenge of Family Practice*. Report of the Ad Hoc Committee on Education for Family Practice of the Council on Medical Education, American Medical Association (Chicago: American Medical Education, September 1966).

12. J. S. Millis, Chairman, *The Graduate Education of Physicians*. Report of the Citizens' Commission on Graduate Medical Education (Chicago: American Medical Association, 1966).

13. American Medical Association, *Essentials of Approved Residencies, 1973–1974* (Chicago: American Medical Association, 1973), p. 370.

14. American Medical Association, *Essentials . . . , 1973–1974,* pp. 370–378.

15. Anne E. Crowley and Glen R. Leymaster, *Family Medicine Programs in Medical Schools*. Special Study, AMA Council on Medical Education (Chicago: American Medical Association, October 15, 1973), p. 7.

16. Based on information from American Academy of Family Physicians, *Medical School Family Practice Programs*. AAFP Reprint No. 164 (May 2, 1974).

17. Based on information from American Academy of Family Physicians, *Approved Graduate Training Programs in Family Practice*. AAFP Reprint No. 135B (revised April 26, 1974).

18. American Academy of Family Physicians, *Final Results: Survey of Family Practice Residency Programs, July 1973*. AAFP Reprint No. 614A (August 23, 1974).

19. See Crowley and Leymaster, *Family Medicine Programs in Medical Schools* (1973), p. 7; and B. J. Stanford, "Portraits of Family Practice Residencies," *American Family Physician/General Practice* **1:**149–158 (1970), p. 149.

20. See descriptions of varying curricula in American Medical Association, *Essentials . . . , 1973–1974,* p. 372; Stanford University Medical School, 1970; and John P. Geyman, "Conversion of the General Practice Residency to Family Practice," *Journal of the American Medical Association* **215:**1802–1807 (1971).

21. Crowley and Leymaster, *Family Medicine Programs in Medical Schools* (1973), p. 7.

22. Newsletter, *American Family Physician/General Practice* **6:**119 (1972).

23. "Education Emphasized as AAFP Convenes," *American Medical News* (October 15, 1973), p. 21.

24. Information on Board requirements and recertification from Thomas L. Stern, M.D., formerly Director, Residency in Family Practice, Santa Monica Hospital, Santa Monica, California, during conversation on October 22, 1973. Dr. Stern is presently Director, Division of Education, American Academy of Family Physicians.

25. Thomas L. Stern, "Funding the Family Practice Residency Program." Paper presented at Workshop in Family Practice, American Academy of Family Physicians, Kansas City, Kansas (July 31, 1973).

26. Stern, Communication (1973).

27. "Fifty-One Family Practice Programs to Benefit from 1973 Grants," *American Family Physician/General Practice* 8:133–134 (1973).

Chapter 8

1. Office of the Secretary, Department of Health, Education, and Welfare, *Report to the President and the Congress: The Health Professions Educational Assistance Program* (Washington, D.C.: Department of Health, Education, and Welfare, September 1970), p. 5.

2. Editorial, "New Medical Schools for the Future," *Journal of the American Medical Association* 178:653 (1961).

3. American Medical Association, "Sixty-eighth Annual Report on Medical Education," *Journal of the American Medical Association* 206:1990 (1968).

4. *Ibid.* "Sixty-Ninth Annual Report on Medical Education," *Journal of the American Medical Association* 210:1457 (1969).

5. *Ibid. A Report on Physician Manpower and Medical Education.* Adopted by the AMA House of Delegates (June 1971), (Chicago: American Medical Association, 1971).

6. Malcolm C. Todd, M.D., in November 1973 speech to the Yale Political Union, quoted in: "AMAGRAMS," *Journal of the American Medical Association* 226:833 (1973).

7. Except where specific sources are noted, the following description of programs is based on Office of the Secretary, Department of Health, Education, and Welfare (September 1970); and on U.S. Comptroller General, *Report to the Congress: Program to Increase Graduates from Health Professions Schools and Improve the Quality of their Education.* B-16403(2) (Washington, D.C.: General Accounting Office, 1972).

8. American Medical Association, *Journal of the American Medical Association* 210:1456 (1969).

9. Office of the Secretary, Department of Health, Education, and Welfare, *Report to the President . . .* (September 1970), p. 124.

10. American Medical Association, "Seventy-Third Annual Report on Medical Education," *Journal of the American Medical Association* 226:903 (1973).

11. *Ibid.* 226:898 (1973).

12. Office of the Secretary, Department of Health, Education, and Welfare, *Report to the President . . .* (September 1970), pp. 110–118 and Appendix Table 37, p. 190.

13. *Ibid.*, p. 114 and Table 34, p. 187.

14.   *Ibid.,* pp. 110–118 and Appendix Table 37, p. 190.

15.   American Medical Association, *Journal of the American Medical Association* **226:**907 (1973).

16.   U.S. Comptroller General, *Report to the Congress* (1972), p. 30.

17.   D. E. Mattson, D. E. Stehr, and R. E. Will, "Evaluation of a Program Designed to Produce Rural Physicians," *Journal of Medical Education* **48:**323–330 (1973), pp. 323–324.

18.   See C. N. Theodore, J. N. Haug, B. E. Balfe, G. A. Roback, and E. J. Franz. *Reclassification of Physicians, 1968: New Base for Health Manpower Studies.* Special Statistical Series (Chicago: American Medical Association, 1971), pp. 1–29, especially Tables C and D, pp. 18 and 20.

19.   Tables are presented in this section only for HPEI and HPEA construction program categories of the entire HPEA program. See Appendix tables in Office of the Secretary, Department of Health, Education, and Welfare (September 1970), for breakdowns of authorizations, appropriations, and obligations in other program categories.

20.   Office of the Secretary, Department of Health, Education, and Welfare, *Report to the President . . .* (September 1970), p. 111.

21.   *Ibid.,* p. 112.

22.   An estimated 11,500 students graduated from schools of medicine in 1974 (see Table 9); approximately 500 students graduated from schools of osteopathy in 1971, the latest year for which figures were available (see National Center for Health Statistics, *Health Resources Statistics, 1972–1973.* DHEW Publication No. (HSM) 73-1509 (Washington, D.C.: Government Printing Office, 1973), Table 96, p. 200.

23.   William O. Roy, *Post-Graduate Physician Training Act of 1974.* Draft (December 12, 1973).

24.   "Administration Offers Medical School Bill with Emphasis on Primary Care, Distribution," *American Medical News* (June 3, 1974), p. 8.

Chapter 9

1.   J. P. Connelly, J. D. Stoeckle, E. S. Lepper, and R. M. Farrisey, "Physician and Nurse: Their Interprofessional Work in Office and Hospital Settings," *New England Journal of Medicine* **275:**765–769 (1966).

2.   H. K. Silver, L. C. Ford, and S. C. Stearly, "Program to Increase Health Care for Children: Pediatric Nurse Practitioner Program," *Pediatrics* **39:**756–760 (1967).

3.   P. A. Ford, M. S. Seacat, and G. G. Silver, "Broadening Roles of Public Health Nurse and Physician in Pre-natal and Infant Supervision," *American Journal of Public Health* **56:**1097–1103 (1966).

4.   C. E. Lewis and B. A. Resnick, "Nurse Clinics and Progressive Ambulatory Care," *New England Journal of Medicine* **277:**1236–1241 (1967).

5.   Personal communication with H. C. Ford, J. D. Stoeckle, and M. S. Seacat.

6.   Minutes of the meetings of the American Medical Association's Council on Health Manpower during the early 1970s reflect this orientation, which is also noted in the current *Guidelines* (see Reference 11).

7.   The Uniform Manpower Evaluation Protocol proposed by the National Center for Health Services Research and Development contained such a task inventory.

8.   C. E. Lewis, B. A. Resnick, G. Schmidt, and D. Waxman, "Activities, Events, and Outcomes in Ambulatory Care," *New England Journal of Medicine* **280**:645–649 (1969).

9.   W. O. Spitzer et al., "The Burlington Randomized Trial of the Nurse Practitioner," *New England Journal of Medicine* **290**:604–611 (1974).

10.   L. L. Fine and H. K. Silver, "Comparative Diagnostic Abilities of Child Health Associate Interns and Practicing Physicians," *Journal of Pediatrics* **83**:332–335 (1973).

11.   Department of Allied Medical Professions and Services, Division of Medical Education, American Medical Association, *Educational Programs for the Physicians' Assistant* (Chicago: American Medical Association, 1974), pp. 12–13.

12.   *Extending the Scope of Nursing Practice,* A Report of Secretary's Committee to Study Extended Roles for Nurses (No publication information, November 1971), pp. 9–12.

13.   This contract is being monitored by Dr. Margaret Sheehan of the Division of Nursing, Bureau of Health Resources Development, Department of Health, Education, and Welfare.

14.   Richard Smith, "Towards Solving the 'Great Training Robbery,'" *Pharos* **37**:47–52 (1974).

15.   Several graduates of the Cornell Primex Program are providing care in housing units and storefront clinics in New York City; North Carolina Primex graduates figure prominently in the Governor's plan for rural health by providing services, as part of a system, in underserved rural areas.

16.   M. S. Davis, "Variations in Patients' Compliance with Doctors' Orders: Analysis of Congruence Between Survey Responses and Results of Empirical Investigations," *Journal of Medical Education* **41**:1037–1048 (1968).

17.   Although the cost analysis of these training programs has not been as vigorous as might be desired, a variety of estimates from Medex and Primex training programs would suggest that the cost of preparing a trainee is in the range of $8000–$12,000 annually per full-time equivalent.

Chapter 10

1.   This discussion draws from commentary about the National Health Service Corps in Eric Redman, *The Dance of Legislation* (New York: Simon and Schuster, 1973); and in U.S. Senate, Committee on Labor and Public Welfare, *Amending the Public Health Service Act for the Establishment of a National Health Service Corps.* Senate Report No. 91-1194 (September 17, 1970).

2.   U.S. Congress, *Emergency Health Personnel Act of 1970* (December 31, 1970), p. 1.

3.   U.S. Congress, *Emergency Health Personnel Act Amendments of 1972* (October 27, 1972), p. 1.

4.   For a full history of program development, process of scarcity-area identification, and data-collection forms used in that process, see Office of Monitoring and Analysis, Bureau of Community Health Services, *Background Paper: Health Services Scarcity Area Identification Program* (Rockville, Maryland: Department of Health, Education, and Welfare, August 1973).

5.   U.S. Senate, Committee on Labor and Public Welfare (September 17, 1970), p. 6.

6.   Charles H. Avery, "Educational Implications of a National Health Service Corps," *Journal of the American Medical Association* **218**:1194–1197 (1971).

7.   Based on data from *ibid.,* p. 1196; "Washington's Week," *American Medical News* (December 3, 1973), p. 12; and those provided by Gloria Price, Public Health Advisor, National Health Service Corps, during telephone conversation on April 15, 1974.

8.   U.S. Senate, Committee of Labor and Public Welfare (September 17, 1970), p. 6.

9.   The decrease has received much publicity and was confirmed by the Personnel Office at the Corps. The precise extent of the decline in numbers of Commissioned Corps applicants, as compared to those before abolition of the "doctor draft," and the numbers subsequently chosen by the Corps for assignment, were requested from that office. Although the information is apparently available, repeated requests failed to secure it for use in the case study.

10.   Martin P. Wasserman, M.D., former Acting Director of Professional Services, National Health Service Corps, as quoted in "How Effective is the Health Corps?" *The House Physician Reporter* (Feature Supplement: NHSC Evaluated), (September–October 1973), p. 1; and information from Gloria Price (April 15, 1974).

11.   Martin P. Wasserman, "New Directions for the National Health Service Corps," *Journal of the American Medical Association* **228**:1422–1423 (1974).

12.   "Medicine's Week," *American Medical News* (May 6, 1974), p. 2.

13.   Wasserman, 1974, p. 1422; this information was first provided by POMI staff Douglas Stafford and James Norris, personal conversation, Washington, D.C. (February 27, 1974).

14.   H. McDonald Rimple, M.D., former Director, National Health Service Corps, as quoted in Pat Perry Gray, "National Health Service Corps Teams Filling Health Manpower Void," *Health Services Reports* **87**:479–490 (1972), p. 480.

15.   Information provided by Gloria Price (April 15, 1974).

16.   Numbers of approved and staffed areas, as of April 15, 1974, from Gloria Price. Year-by-year figures for these categories were requested and apparently are available, but repeated requests failed to secure them for use in the case study. Some figures have been published, but they vary considerably, depending on the time of year the information was obtained. Anecdotal evidence from David Kindig, M.D., former Director of Professional Services, National Health Services Corps, suggests that some 16 to 20 physicians were sent to some 10 to 16 sites in January 1971 in a trial match. No figures are available for the first formal match, which took place July 1971. Some 140 to 150 physicians were sent out in the second match, and at least another hundred were matched in July 1973.

17.   Alabama Regional Medical Program's commentary on state efforts to reduce manpower shortages, from materials in files at National Health Council, Manpower Distribution Project (1974).

18.   Information provided by David Kindig, M.D., during telephone conversation (January 11, 1974).

19.   Description of site review procedure and its development drawn from unpublished in-house memoranda provided by William Christoffel, formerly Director, Office of Program Planning, Evaluation, and Legislation, National Health Service Corps, during personal interview in Rockville, Md. (February 26, 1974).

20.   Based on information in Avery, "Educational Implications . . ." (1970), p. 1196; and from

Howard Hilton, Ph.D., Deputy Director, National Health Service Corps, during personal interview in Rockville, Md. (February 26, 1974).

21. Will Health Corps regain its health? *Medical World News* (August 10, 1973), pp. 59–60, p. 59.

22. Information provided by Howard Hilton (February 26, 1974).

Chapter 11

1. Based on Eugene Feingold, *Medicare: Policy and Politics. A Case Study and Policy Analysis* (San Francisco: Chandler Publishing Co., 1966), Chapter 2: "The Special Problems of the Aged," pp. 24–27.

2. Based on *ibid.*; Dorothy McCamman, "Income of the Aged and the Numbers Game," in Feingold, *Medicare* (1966), pp. 42–44.

3. Based on Herman M. Somers and Anne R. Somers. *Medicare and the Hospitals: Issues and Prospects* (Wasington, D.C.: The Brookings Institution, 1967), Chapter 1: "Medicare: Evolution of a Law," pp. 1–16.

4. Feingold, *Medicare* (1966).

5. Somers and Somers, *Medicare and the Hospitals* (1967).

6. Richard Harris, *A Sacred Trust* (New York: New American Library, 1966).

7. U.S. Congress, *U.S. Statutes at Large, Volume 79,* 89th Congress, 1st session (Washington, D.C.: Government Printing Office, 1966), p. 291.

8. Material for the description of Medicare legislation was compiled from the following sources: Commerce Clearing House, Inc., *Medicare and Social Security Explained* (Chicago: Commerce Clearing House, Inc., 1968); *Social Security Bulletin* 36:5–23 (March 1973); Rosemary Stevens, *American Medicine and the Public Interest* (New Haven: Yale University Press, 1971), pp. 444–472; Somers and Somers, *Medicare and the Hospitals* (1967), Chapter 1.

9. The periods considered in the following discussion were contingent on the availability of current data from SSA. The interval required to receive and process bills and disburse payments precedes statistical operations, and for this reason the data usually extend to 1971 or 1972 only. The data for utilization rates after the introduction of Medicare from each source are consistent over time, but comparability between sources is limited by definitional differences and varying time periods used in data collection. The problem of comparability is greatest for comparison of utilization rates before and after Medicare. Although the rate of change may vary in each of the several sources used, the general trend and direction of change can still be evaluated. The precise degree of change in use of services resulting from the Medicare program cannot be estimated.

10. Based on information provided by Paula A. Piro, Research Analyst, Office of Research and Statistics (March 27, 1974).

11. Office of Research and Statistics, *Medicare: Health Insurance for the Aged, 1971, Section 2: Persons Enrolled in the Health Insurance Program.* DHEW Publication No. (SSA) 73-11704 (Washington, D.C.: Government Printing Office, August 1973), p. xiii.

12. *Ibid.*

13. U.S. Comptroller General, *Improvement Needed in the Administration of the Program to Provide Medicare Benefits to Welfare Recipients.* DHEW B-164031 (3) (August 14, 1973).

14. Office of Research and Statistics (August 1973), p. xiii.

15.   Karen Davis, *Financing Medical Care: Implications for Access to Primary Care.* Paper presented at the Sun Valley Forum on National Health, Sun Valley, Idaho (June 18, 1973), p. 10.

16.   Regina Lowenstein, "Early Effects of Medicare on Health Care of the Aged," *Social Security Bulletin* **34**:3–20 (April 1971), p. 7.

17.   Karen Davis and Roger Reynolds, "Impact of Medicare and Medicaid on Access to Medical Care." Paper presented at the Conference on the Role of Health Insurance in the Health Services Sector (May 31 and June 1, 1974). Sponsored by Universities–National Bureau Committee for Economic Research (New York: unpublished), pp. 31–33.

18.   Lowenstein, Early Effects of Medicare . . ." (1971), p. 13.

19.   Office of Research and Statistics, *Medicare* (1973), p. xiii.

20.   Karen Davis and Roger Reynolds, *Medicare and the Utilization of Health Care Services by the Elderly* (Washington, D.C.: The Brookings Institution, December 1973 unpublished), p. 15.

21.   Davis and Reynolds, *Impact of Medicare and Medicaid* . . . (1973), p. 4.

22.   Davis, *Financing Medical Care* (1973), p. 25.

23.   Barbara S. Cooper and Nancy L. Worthington, "Age Differences in Medical Care Spending, Fiscal Year 1972," *Social Security Bulletin* **36**:15 (May 1973), p. 10.

24.   Dorothy P. Rice and Barbara S. Cooper, "National Health Expenditures, 1929–1971," *Social Security Bulletin* **35**:18 (January 1972), pie chart, p. 8.

25.   Davis and Reynolds, "Impact of Medicare and Medicaid . . ." (1973), p. 4.

26.   Cooper and Worthington, "Age Differences . . ." (1973), Table 5, p. 11.

27.   *Ibid.,* pp. 10–11.

28.   Marjorie Smith Mueller, "Private Health Insurance in 1972: Health Care Services, Enrollment, and Finance," *Social Security Bulletin* **37**:20–40 (February 1974), p. 30.

29.   Evelyn Peel and Jack Scharff, "Impact of Cost-Sharing on Use of Ambulatory Services under Medicare, 1969," *Social Security Bulletin* **36**:3–24 (October 1973), p. 5.

30.   *Ibid.,* pp. 6–7.

31.   *Ibid.,* p. 7.

32.   *Ibid.,* p. 16.

33.   *Ibid.,* pp. 16–17.

34.   *Ibid.,* p. 18.

35.   Percentages calculated from Table 20.

36.   Figures for 1969 through 1972 can be found in "Current Operating Statistics," *Social Security Bulletin* **37**:39–68 (April 1974), Tables M-20 and M-22, pp. 56 and 58.

37.   Barbara S. Cooper and Nancy L. Worthington, *Personal Health Care Expenditures by State.* Volume 1: *Public Funds, 1966 and 1969.* DHEW Publication No. (SSA) 73-11906 (Washington, D.C.: Government Printing Office, 1973), p. 8.

38.   Cooper and Worthington, "Personal Health . . ." (1973), p. 13.

39.   Factors influencing the trend in Medicare expenditures are discussed in Howard West, "Five Years of Medicare: A Statistical Review," *Social Security Bulletin* **34**:17–27 (December 1971), p. 20; and in Office Research and Statistics, *Medicare* (1973).

40. Several studies have analyzed the factors accounting for the rise in medical care prices. See Office of Research and Statistics, *Medical Care Expenditures, Prices, and Costs: Background Book*. DHEW Publication No. (SSA) 74-11909 (Washington, D.C.: Government Printing Office, September 1973); Dorothy P. Rice and Loucele A. Horowitz, "Early Effects of Medicare on Health Care of the Aged," *Social Security Bulletin* **31**:3–11 (November 1968); Karen Davis, "Hospital Costs and the Medicaid Program," *Social Security Bulletin* **36**:18–36 (August 1973).

41. U.S. Congress, Senate, *Medicare and Medicaid: Problems, Issues, and Alternatives*. Report of the Staff to the Committee on Finance, 91st Congress, 1st session (Washington, D.C.: Government Printing Office, February 9, 1970), p. 3; part of the unexpected rise in costs in the early years of the program has been attributed to the influx of nursing homes wanting to participate in the program. See Bruce Stuart and Ronald Stockton, "Control over the Utilization of Medical Services," *Health and Society/Milbank Memorial Fund Quarterly* **51**:341–394 (1973).

42. Herman G. Brotman, "The Fastest Growing Minority: The Aging," *American Journal of Public Health* **64**:249–252 (March 1974), p. 251.

43. Barbara S. Cooper, Nancy L. Worthington, and Paula A. Piro, "National Health Expenditures, 1929–1973," *Social Security Bulletin* **37**:2–19 (1974), p. 9.

44. Max H. Seigel, "A Medicare Shortfall of up to $70 million Is Reported Here," *The New York Times* (March 24, 1974), p. 43.

45. Comptroller General, *Sizeable Amounts Due the Government by Institutions That Terminated Their Participation in the Medicare Program*. Report to the Congress, B-164301 (Washington, D.C.: Government Printing Office, August 4, 1972), pp. 2–3.

46. Davis, *Financing Medical Care* (1973), p. 12; and Julian Pettengill, "Trends in Hospital Use by the Aged," *Social Security Bulletin* **35**:3–15 (July 1972), pp. 9–10.

47. Davis and Reynolds, *Impact of Medicare and Medicaid . . .* (1974), pp. 31–33.

Chapter 12

1. John Holahan, *Financing Health Care for the Poor: The Medicaid Experience* (Former title: *An Economic Analysis of Medicaid*). Working Paper No. 976-01 (Washington, D.C.: The Urban Institute, February 7, 1974).

2. National Center for Social Statistics, *Medicaid and Other Medical Care Financed from Public Assistance Funds, Selected Statistics 1951–1969*. NCSS Report B-6 (Washington: D.C., Government Printing Office, 1970), p. 55; Alonzo S. Yerby, "The Problems of Medical Care for Indigent Populations," *American Journal of Public Health* **55**:1212–1216 (1965), p. 1213.

3. Ronald Andersen and Odin W. Anderson, *A Decade of Health Services: Social Survey Trends in Use and Expenditure* (Chicago: The University of Chicago Press, 1967), Chapter 2, pp. 10–30.

4. Yerby, "The problems of Medical Care . . ." (1965), p. 1214.

5. See U.S. Congress, Senate, Special Committee on Aging, *Medical Assistance for the Aged: The Kerr-Mills Program, 1960-1963* (Washington, D.C.: Government Printing Office, 1963).

6. U.S. Congress, *U.S. Statutes at Large,* Volume 79, 89th Congress, 1st Session (Washington, D.C.: Government Printing Office, 1966), p. 343.

7. Program description based on Holahan, 1974; Commerce Clearing House, Inc., *Medicare and Social Security Explained* (Chicago: Commerce Clearing House, Inc., 1968); *Social Security Bulletin* **36**:5–23 (March 1973); Rosemary Stevens and Robert Stevens, "Medicaid: Anatomy of a Dilemma," *Law and Contemporary Problems* **35**:348–425 (1970).

8.   Tax Foundation, Inc., *Medicaid: State Programs after Two Years*. Research Publication No. 15 (New York: Tax Foundation, Inc., 1968), p. 19.

9.   National Center for Social Statistics, *Numbers of Recipients and Amounts of Payments under Medicaid, 1972*. Advance Copy (Washington, D.C.: Government Printing Office, April 25, 1974), Table 2.

10.   *Ibid.,* Table 7.

11.   National Center for Social Statistics, *Numbers of Recipients and Amounts of Payments under Medicaid and other Medical Programs Financed from Public Assistance Funds, 1970*. NCSS Report B-4 (Washington, D.C.: Government Printing Office, October 16, 1972), p. 2.

12.   Estimates are not actuarial values but indicators of variance among states in payments per eligible person. Holahan, *Financing Health Care . . .* (1974), pp. 24–26.

13.   Ronald Andersen et al., *Health Service Use: National Trends and Variations, 1953–1971*. DHEW Publication No. (HSM) 13-3004 (Washington, D.C.: Government Printing Office, 1973), Tables 5 and 25; Karen Davis and Roger Reynolds, *Impact of Medicare and Medicaid on Access to Medical Care*. Paper prepared for the Conference on the Role of Health Insurance in the Health Services Sector, New York (May 31 and June 1, 1974), p. 2.

14.   Klaus J. Roghmann, Robert J. Haggerty, and Rodney Lorenz, "Anticipated and Actual Effects of Medicaid on the Medical Care Pattern of Children, *New England Journal of Medicine* **285:**1053–1057 (1971).

15.   Nora Piore, Deborah Lewis, and Jeannie Seeliger, *A Statistical Profile of Hospital Outpatient Services in the U.S.: Present Scope and Potential Role* (New York: Association for Aid of Crippled Children, August 1971).

16.   The Blue Cross children also experienced a similar shift but not in the same degree. A decline in the use of a private physician (from 87 percent in 1967 to 76 percent in 1969) occurred with a concomitant rise in "no regular source of care" (from 22 percent in 1967 to 39 percent in 1969). Roghmann et al., Anticipated and Actual Effects of Medicaid . . ." (1971).

17.   Margaret C. Olendzki, Richard P. Grann, and Charles H. Goodrich, "The Impact of Medicaid on Private Care for the Urban Poor," *Medical Care* **10:**201–206 (1972), Table 1, p. 202.

18.   The public-assistance categories included in the analysis were the disabled, AFDC adults, and AFDC children money-payment recipients. Medicaid services were restricted to physician and outpatient care, both required services. The utilization variable was defined as the proportion of the total eligible population (i.e., all recipients in the above categories who received public assistance at any time during the years 1969 and 1970) who used one or more ambulatory-care services. For a complete description of the model and findings, see: Holahan, *Financing Health Care . . .* (1974), pp. 60–75 and 89–109.

19.   The sample included only public-assistance recipients and physicians' services—the mandatory recipient categories and required services—to minimize variation resulting from state program features. The model of utilization of physician services is estimated from data from the 1969 Health Interview Survey of the National Center for Health Statistics. For an account of the model used and findings, see Karen Davis and Roger Reynolds, *Impact of Medicare and Medicaid on Access to Medical Care*. Paper presented at the Conference on the Role of Health Insurance in the Health Services Sector (May 31 and June 1, 1974), pp. 12–23.

20.   Sarah A. Butts, *Public Assistance Social Services Related to Medicaid*. DHEW Publication No. (SRS) 72-23011 (Washington, D.C.: Government Printing Office, 1972), pp. 7–11.

21.   National Center for Social Statistics. NCSS Report B-4 (1972).

22.   *Ibid., Numbers . . . and Amounts . . . (1974),* Table 7.

23.   Medicaid expenditures include premiums paid for low-income Medicare beneficiaries under the "buy-in" arrangement. Barbara S. Cooper, Nancy L. Worthington, and Paula A. Piro, "National Health Expenditures, 1929–1973," *Social Security Bulletin* **37**:2–19 (1974), p. 7.

24.   Barbara S. Cooper, and Nancy L. Worthington. *Personal Health Care Expenditures by State.* DHEW Publication No. (SSA) 73-11906 (Washington, D.C.: Government Printing Office, 1973), p. 8.

25.   *Ibid.,* pp. 6–8.

26.   National Center for Social Statistics. NCSS Report B-6 (1970), p. 55.

27.   Stevens and Stevens, "Medicaid . . ." (1970), p. 381

28.   Conversation with Jack Ebeler, Program Analyst for Medical Services Administration (March 26, 1974).

29.   Barbara S. Cooper, and Nancy L. Worthington. *Cost and Benefit Incidence of Government Medical Care Programs.* Paper presented at the 101st Annual Meeting of the American Public Health Association, San Francisco (November 7, 1973).

30.   Stephen M. Davidson, "Community Hospitals and Medicaid," *Medical Care* **12**:115–120 (1974).

31.   Martin Tolchin, "Tri-State Area Is Found Lagging on U.S. Health Aid for Children," *The New York Times* (December 9, 1973).

32.   Cooper, Worthington, and Piro, "National Health Expenditures . . ." (1974), p. 7.

Chapter 13

1.   *Report of the National Advisory Commission on Civil Disorders* (New York: Bantam Books, Inc., 1968).

2.   Data from the OEO baseline survey and from the 1969 Health Interview Survey made by the National Center for Health Statistics were used with permission from: Gail R. Wilensky, *Utilization of Ambulatory Care.* Working Paper 963-3 (Washington, D.C.: The Urban Institute, unpublished).

3.   Harold B. Wise, "Montefiore Hospital Neighborhood Medical Care Demonstration," *Milbank Memorial Fund Quarterly* **46**:297–306 (1968), p. 298.

4.   Foline Gartside, Carl E. Hopkins, and Milton I. Roemer, *Medicaid Services in California under Different Organizational Modes* (Los Angeles: School of Public Health, University of California, December 1973), p. 166.

5.   Gerald Sparer, and Joyce Johnson, "Evaluation of OEO Neighborhood Health Centers," *American Journal of Public Health* **61**:931–942 (1971), p. 931.

6.   Lisbeth Bamberger Schorr and Joseph T. English, "Background, Context and Significant Issues in Neighborhood Health Center Programs," *Milbank Memorial Fund Quarterly* **46**:289–296 (1968), p. 290.

7.   Joann H. Langston, James H. Herd, Robert F. Liffring, G. Edward McEvoy, Raimiro A. Montalvo, George M. Spilseth, and John R. Ward, *Study to Evaluate the OEO Neighborhood Health Center Program at Selected Centers,* Volume 1. PB-207-084 (Springfield, Virginia:

National Technical Information Service, January 1972), p. 129; and Sparer and Johnson, "Evaluation . . ." (1971), p. 931.

8. Based on Schorr and English, Background Context . . . (1968); and information from Nick Campagnoli, Program Analyst, Bureau of Community Health Services, Health Services Administration, Department of Health, Education, and Welfare.

9. Based on information from Louise Okada, now in the Division of Health Services Evaluation, Health Services Administration, Department of Health, Education, and Welfare. (Together with Gerald Sparer, former Director, Program Planning and Evaluation Division, Office of Health Affairs, OEO, Ms. Okada reported the results of the OEO baseline surveys.)

10. Except where specifically noted, all data in the section on "Extent of Effectiveness" are taken from Langston et al., *Study to Evaluate the OEO* . . . (1972).

11. See Gordon T. Moore, Roberta Bernstein, and Rosemary A. Bonanno, "Effect of a Neighborhood Health Center on Hospital Emergency Room Use," *Medical Care* 10:240–247 (1967); and Louis T. Hochheiser, Kenneth Woodward, and Evan Charney, "Effect of the Neighborhood Health Center on the Use of Pediatric Emergency Departments in Rochester, New York," *New England Journal of Medicine* 285:148–152 (1971).

12. Gartside et al., *Medicaid Services in California* . . . (1973), p. 202.

13. Mark A. Strauss and Gerald Sparer, "Basic Utilization Experience of OEO Comprehensive Health Services Projects," *Inquiry* 8:36–48 (1971).

14. Seymour S. Bellin and H. Jack Geiger, "The Impact of a Neighborhood Health Center on Patients' Behavior and Attitudes Relating to Health Care: A Study of a Low Income Housing Project," *Medical Care* 10:224–239 (1972).

15. Hugh H. Tilson, "Characteristics of Physicians in OEO Neighborhood Health Centers," *Inquiry* 10:27–38 (1973); and Hugh H. Tilson, Stability of Physician Employment in Neighborhood Health Centers," *Medical Care* 11:384–399 (1973).

16. Schorr and English, "Background Context . . ." (1968), p. 292.

17. Information from Mr. Campagnoli, Program Analyst, Bureau of Community Health Services.

18. Langston et al., *Study to Evaluate* . . . (1972), pp. 10–11.

19. *Ibid.*, p. 132.

20. Information from Mr. Campagnoli, Program Analyst, Bureau of Community Health Services.

21. Information from William White, Deputy Associate Director, Bureau of Community Health Services, Health Services Administration, Department of Health, Education, and Welfare (March 8, 1974).

22. Information from Clifton Cole, Director, South Central Multipurpose Health Services Center, Watts, Los Angeles, California (March 5, 1974).

Chapter 14

1. Robert A. Aldrich and Ralph J. Wedgewood, "Examination of the Changes in the U.S. Which Affect the Health of Children and Youth," *American Journal of Public Health* 60:7 (1970).

2. For the period 1959–1961, influenza and pneumonia were rated as the second highest cause of death for nonwhite children aged 1 to 4, or 36.2 percent of the deaths of nonwhite children compared to 11.2 percent of deaths among white children. Julius B. Richmond and Howard L. Weinberger, "Program Implications of New Knowledge Regarding the Physical, Intellectual, and Emotional Growth and Development and the Unmet Needs of Children," *American Journal of Public Health* **60**:31 (1970).

3. Ronald Andersen and Odin W. Anderson, *A Decade of Health Services: Social Survey Trends in Use and Expenditure* (Chicago: The University of Chicago Press, 1967), Chapter 2, pp. 10–30.

4. Systems Development Project, *Quarterly Summary Report, April–June 1972.* Report Series No. 18 (Minneapolis, Minnesota: Minnesota Systems Research, Inc., 1972), p. 1.

5. *Ibid.,* pp. 3–6; Nancy A. Ouradnik and Systems Development Project staff, *Project Profile III: Descriptive Profile of Children & Youth Projects as of September 30, 1971.* Report Series No. 2-5 (17) (Minneapolis, Minnesota: Minnesota Systems Research, Inc., 1971), pp. 2–8.

6. *Ibid.,* p. 15.

7. Emily Sano, *Children and Youth Projects: Comprehensive Health Care in Low-Income Areas.* DHEW Publication No. (HSM) 72-5006 (Washington, D.C.: Government Printing Office, 1972), p. 9.

8. Betty J. Hallstrom and Joachim M. Banda, *The Provision of Health Care Services to Adolescents in the 1970s* (Minneapolis, Minnesota: Minnesota Systems Research, Inc., 1972), pp. 115–128.

9. Multiservice Program Helps Pregnant Teenagers," *Public Health Reports* **85**:321–322 (1970). Abstract of paper presented at 97th annual meeting of the American Public Health Association, Philadelphia, Pennsylvania (November 1969); author not reported.

10. Sano, *Children and Youth Projects* (1972), pp. 6, 27–28; Ouradnik et al., *Project Profile III* (1971), pp. 7–8.

11. Systems Development Project, *Quarterly Summary Report . . .* (1972), p. 3.

12. Willy De Geyndt, *Referrals to, within, and from the Comprehensive Health Services Program for Children and Youth.* Comment Series No. 0-10 (35) (Minneapolis, Minnesota: Minnesota Systems Research, Inc. 1970).

13. Ouradnik et al., *Project Profile III* (1971), p. 3.

14. *Ibid.,* pp. 3–4.

15. De Geyndt, *Referrals . . .* (1970).

16. Ouradnik et al., *Project Profile III* (1971), pp. 4–7, 12.

17. *Ibid.,* p. 9; Systems Development Project, *Quarterly Summary Report . . .* (1972), p. 15; Sano, *Children and Youth Projects* (1972), p. 27.

18. Willy De Geyndt, *Quality of Care: End Results Based on a Performance Reporting System.* Comment Series No. 1-11 (39) (Minneapolis, Minnesota: Minnesota Systems Research, Inc., 1971); Mildred A. Morehead, Rose S. Donaldson, and Mary R. Seravalli, "Comparisons between OEO Neighborhood Health Centers and Other Health Care Providers of Ratings of the Quality of Care," *American Journal of Public Health* 61:1294–1306 (1971).

19. Ouradnik, *Project Profile III,* [1971], p. 10; Sano, *Children and Youth Projects,* 1972, p. 27; Systems Development Project, *Quarterly Summary Report . . .* (1972), p. 6.

Chapter 15

1. See case studies on Medicare and Medicaid.

2. Richard M. Nixon, *Message from the President of the United States Relative to Building a National Health Strategy,* House of Representatives. Document No. 92-49 (Washington, D.C.: Government Printing Office, February 1971).

3. See commentary on Medicare HMO option in Robert M. Ball, "Social Security Amendments of 1972: Summary and Legislative History," *Social Security Bulletin* **36:**3–25 (1973), p. 19.

4. U.S. Congress, Senate, *Conference Report: Health Maintenance Organization Act of 1973.* Report No. 93-621 (Washington, D.C.: Government Printing Office, December 1973), Sec. 1310(a), p. 19.

5. For a more extensive discussion of the developmental history of the PGPs, see especially Ira G. Greenberg and Michael L. Rodburg, "The Role of Prepaid Group Practice in Relieving the Medical Crisis," *Harvard Law Review* **84:**887–1101 (1971). Valuable discussions of the history of individual plans can be found in Anne R. Somers (Ed.), *The Kaiser–Permanente Medical Care Program: A Symposium* (New York: The Commonwealth Fund, 1971); Helen H. Avnet, *Physician Service Patterns and Illness Rates: A Research Report on Medical Data Retrieved from Insurance Records* (New York: Group Health Insurance, Inc., 1967).

   For discussions of the development of FMCs, see Carolynn Steinwald, *Foundations for Medical Care* (Chicago: Blue Cross Association, 1971); Richard Sasuly and Carl E. Hopkins, "A Medical Society-Sponsored Comprehensive Medical Care Plan," *Medical Care* **5:**234–245 (1967); and Richard Egdahl, "Foundations for Medical Care," *New England Journal of Medicine* **288:**491–498 (1973).

6. Discussion on extent of federal HMO program based on Office of the Associate Bureau Director (HMO), *Program Status Report: Health Maintenance Organizations, February 1, 1974* (Rockville, Maryland: Bureau of Community Health Services, Health Services Administration, Department of Health, Education, and Welfare, March 1974); for listing of operating HMOs, those supported by health insurers, and those aided by HMOS, see Appendixes 1–3 and 5; HMOs with Title XIX contracts are listed in Appendix 7.

7. See discussion on this point in Herbert E. Klarman, *Analysis of the HMO Proposal: Its Assumptions, Implications, and Prospects,* in *Health Maintenance Organizations: A Reconfiguration of the Health Services System.* Proceedings of the Thirteenth Annual Symposium on Hospital Affairs, May 1971 (Chicago: Center for Health Administration Studies, 1971), pp. 24–38. Much of the research on FMC performance relating to access and other performance variables is included in the recent review by Milton I. Roemer and William Shonick, "HMO Performance: The Recent Evidence," *Health and Society/The Milbank Memorial Fund Quarterly* **51:**271–317 (1973).

8. Avedis Donabedian, "An Evaluation of Prepaid Group Practice," *Inquiry* **6:**3–27 (1969), Table 1, p. 5.

9. Milton I. Roemer, Robert W. Hetherington, Carl E. Hopkins, Arthur E. Gerst, Eleanor Parsons, and Donald M. Long, *Health Insurance Effects: Services, Expenditures, and Attitudes under Three Types of Plans.* Bureau of Public Health Economics, Research Series No. 6 (Ann Arbor: School of Public Health, University of Michigan, 1972), pp. 5–58.

10. Merwyn Greenlick, "The Impact of Prepaid Group Practice on American Medical Care: A Critical Evaluation," *The Annals of the American Academy of Political and Social Science* **399:**100–113 (January 1972).

11.   David Mechanic and Richard Tessler, *Comparison of Consumer Response to Prepaid Group Practice and Alternative Insurance Plans in Milwaukee County: A Preliminary Report*. Research and Analytic Report Series No. 5-73, Center for Medical Sociology and Health Services Research (Madison, Wisconsin: University of Wisconsin, 1973), pp. 11 and 17.

12.   Bruce Stuart and Ronald Stockton, "Control over the Utilization of Medical Services," *Health and Society/Milbank Memorial Fund Quarterly* **51**:341–394 (1973), p. 355.

13.   *Ibid.*

14.   See Anne A. Scitovsky and Nelda M. Snyder, "Effect of Coinsurance on the Use of Physician Services," *Social Security Bulletin* **35**:3–19 (June 1972); and Charles E. Phelps and Joseph P. Newhouse, "The Effect of Coinsurance on Use: A Multivariate Analysis," *Social Security Bulletin* **35**:20–28 (June 1972). Reprinted together under same titles in DHEW Publication No. (SSA) 72-11700 (Washington, D.C.: Government Printing Office, 1972).

15.   S. J. Axelrod, *National Health Plans: Physicians' Services and the Public Health*. Speech delivered at the Symposium on National Health Plans: The Challenge of Management, sponsored by the American Public Health Association, Medical Care Section—Southern California (May 11, 1974), University of California, Los Angeles.

16.   Stuart and Stockton, "Control over the Utilization of medical services" (1973), p. 356.

17.   Roemer et al., *Health Insurance Effects* (1972), pp. 11–12.

18.   *Ibid.*

19.   Mechanic and Tessler, *Comparison of Consumer Response . . .* (1973), pp. 3–4.

20.   See Daniel M. Barr and Clifton R. Gaus, "A Population-Based Approach to Quality Assessment in Health Maintenance Organizations," *Medical Care* **11**:523–528 (November–December 1973); and Robert F. Liffring, *HMO Evaluation Schema, Phase I*. Final Report, Geomet Report No. HF-283, prepared under Contract HSM 110-72-416 for the Health Maintenance Organization Service, DHEW (Rockville, Maryland: Geomet, Inc., November 5, 1973 [processed]).

21.   Mechanic and Tessler, *Comparison of Consumer Response . . .* (1973), pp. 22–27; Richard Tessler and David Mechanic, *Consumer Satisfaction with Prepaid Group Practice: A Comparative Study*. Research and Analytic Report Series No. 11-74, Center for Medical Sociology and Health Services Research (Madison, Wisconsin: University of Wisconsin, 1974), p. 18; see also J. Weiss and M. Greenlick, "Determinants of Medical Care Utilization: The Effect of Social Class and Distance on Contacts with the Medical Care System," *Medical Care* **9**:295–315 (1970).

22.   See Roemer and Shonick, "HMO Performance" (1973); Greenlick, "The Impact of Prepaid Group Practice . . ." (1972); Donabedian, "An Evaluation of Prepaid Group Practice" (1969); E. Richard Weinerman, "Patients' Perceptions of Group Medical Care," *American Journal of Public Health* **54**:880–889 (June 1964); Dixie L. Leyhe and Donald M. Procter, *Medi-Cal Patient Satisfaction under a Prepaid Group Practice and Individual Fee-for Service Practice*. Medi-Cal Project Report No. 3 (Los Angeles: School of Public Health, University of California, Los Angeles, June 1971); and Mechanic and Tessler, *Comparison of Consumer Response . . .* (1973), and *Consumer Satisfaction . . .* (1974).

23.   Weinerman, "Patients' Perceptions . . ." (1964), p. 886.

24.   Leyhe and Procter, *Medi-Cal Patient Satisfaction . . .* (1971), pp. 33–34.

25.   Greenlick, "The Impact of Prepaid Group Practice . . ." (1972).

26.   Donabedian, "An Evaluation of Prepaid Group Practice . . ." (1969), pp. 9–10.

27.   Roemer and Shonick, "HMO Performance . . ." (1973), p. 308.

28.   Mechanic and Tessler, *Comparison of Consumer Response* . . . (1973), p. 21.

29.   Karl D. Yordy, *HMOs: Out of the Cocoon.* Paper presented at the annual meeting of the American Public Health Association, San Francisco (November 5, 1973).

30.   See discussions in Herbert E. Klarman, "Effect of Prepaid Group Practice on Hospital Use," *Public Health Reports* **78:**955–965 (November 1973); Herbert E. Klarman, "Approaches to Moderating the Increases in Medical Care Costs," *Medical Care* **7:**175–190 (May–June 1969).

31.   Malcolm L. Peterson, "The First Year in Columbia: Assessments of Low Hospitalization and High Office Use," *Johns Hopkins Medical Journal* **128:**15–23 (January 1971); Roemer et al., *Health Insurance Effects* (1972).

32.   Mechanic and Tessler, *Comparison of Consumer Response* . . . (1973), p. 33.

33.   PGP physician visit rates, as reported in Ann Bush, *Group Practice Planning and Implementation: A Community-Wise Prepayment Plan* (Albany, New York: New York State Health Planning Commission, 1971). National physician visit rates from National Center for Health Statistics, *Physician Visits: Volume and Interval Since Last Visit, United States, 1969.* DHEW Publication No. (HSM) 72-1064. Vital and Health Statistics, Series 10, No. 75 (Rockville, Maryland: Department of Health, Education, and Welfare, 1972), Table 6, p. 19.

34.   Wilbur, L. Reimers, *Experiences with per Capita Payments for Outside Medical Services,* in Michael A. Newman (Ed.), *The Medical Director in Prepaid Group Practice Health Maintenance Organizations.* Proceedings of a Conference, Denver, Colorado, April 1973 (Alexandria, Virginia: American Association of Medical Clinics, 1973), pp. 53–56.

35.   Yordy, *HMOS* (1973), p. 7.

36.   Legislative Analyst, State of California, *A Review of the Regulation of Prepaid Health Plans by the State Department of Health.* No. 73-19 (Sacramento: November 15, 1973).

37.   *Ibid.,* pp. 18, 21–22.

38.   *Ibid.,* and Auditor General, State of California, untitled report on fifteeen prepaid health plans in California, transmitted to the California Legislature by Vincent Thomas, Chairman, Joint Legislative Audit Committee, April 22, 1974.

39.   *Ibid.*

40.   Texas Instruments, Inc, *Development of an Implementation Plan for the Establishment of a Health Maintenance Organization.* Prepared for the Department of Health, Education, and Welfare (December 30, 1971), as reported in Richard T. Burke, *A Review of the Experience of Two Small HMOs* (Minneapolis, Minnesota: Interstudy, 1972), footnote, p. 4.

41.   Auditor General, untitled report . . . (1974), p. 16.

42.   *Ibid.,* p. 6.

43.   Office of the Associate Bureau Director (HMO), *Program Status Report* (1974), Appendix 4, pp. 29–33.

Index

Abused children: and C & Y programs, 214

Access to primary care, 3-13, 43; policy-making to increase, 4, 32, 258, 262; defining and measuring, 10-13, 44; barriers to, 11-12, 18, 37-38; and maldistribution, 28; and danger of overuse, 36; ways to decrease barriers to, 37, 39t, 44-45, 250t, 251t; programs to increase, 45-46; impact of family-practice programs on, 88-90; impact of increasing number of doctors, 92-110; and new health practitioners, 121-123, 126; National Health Service Corps to improve, 127, 132, 134-135, 141; and Medicare, 146, 162, 163-164, 256; Medicaid's impact on, 179, 186-187, 256; inner-city barriers to, 189, 194; impact of neighborhood health centers, 205-206, 257; and C & Y programs, 213, 216, 219, 257; translocation of barriers to, 243-244; HMOs to improve, 222; and PGPs, 232, 233, 235, 238-239; principal determinants of, 241-242, 244; and national health insurance, 275-276; assessment of ways to improve, 281-286

Activity distribution of physicians, 102-105

Acute care functions: nurse practitioner's role, 118

Addictions: and use of groups, 38; programs for, 194, 325

Administration: shifts of doctors' activity distribution toward, 102, 104t, 105

Adolescents: and family medicine, 25-26; C & Y programs for, 212-213

Aerospace medicine: number practicing and changes in percentage of, 300t

Aged: health care of, 243; Kerr-Mills Act, 166; use of medical care, 167t, 208t; and Medicaid, 168; hospital utilization by, 304t, 305t, 306t; ambulatory-care visits by, 307t; physician visits, 309t; expenditures for, 310t, 319t. *See also* Medicare

351

Date Due

DEC 1 – 1993			